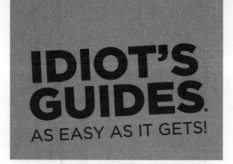

IDIOT'S GUIDES.
AS EASY AS IT GETS!

Homebrewing

by Daniel Ironside

ALPHA

A member of Penguin Random House LLC

Publisher: Mike Sanders
Associate Publisher: Billy Fields
Senior Acquisitions Editor: Brook Farling
Development Editor: Ann Barton
Cover Designer: Laura Merriman
Book Designer: William Thomas
Production Editor: Jana M. Stefanciosa
Compositor: Brian Massey
Proofreader: Cate Schwenk
Indexer: Brad Herriman

First American Edition, 2015
Published in the United States by DK Publishing
6081 E. 82nd Street, Indianapolis, Indiana 46250

Copyright © 2015 Dorling Kindersley Limited
A Penguin Random House Company
15 16 17 18   10 9 8 7 6 5 4 3 2 1
001–280452–September2015

ISBN: 978-1-61564-829-0
Library of Congress Catalog Card Number: 2015933123

idiotsguides.com

Contents

Introduction

A great homebrewer once told me, "It's easy to make good beer, but hard to make exceptional beer," and in my experience, I've found that to be true. Starting out, homebrewing is easy to do, and if you follow some basic rules, you'll be able to produce nice, good-tasting beer at home. To do so, you need not look further than the first few chapters of this book to get off and running. However, there will be a time when you will demand more of your brewing process, and strive for the next level of quality, flavor, and character. That's what the rest of the book is for, to help turn your homebrew from good to world-class through intermediate and advanced techniques as well as diagnose and prevent the undesirable qualities that may occur along the way.

You'll find that this book covers the essential topics of homebrewing, starting with basic techniques for brewing with malt extract, and building chapter by chapter to advanced brewing techniques like all-grain brewing and lager fermentation. Homebrewing is an expansive topic with simply too much brewing knowledge, experience, and practice to fit into one 400-page book. Thus, *Idiot's Guides: Homebrewing* presents the hobby in a modern light, addressing the brewing ingredients, practices, and skills used in today's homebrewing; providing clarity between brewing process at the homebrew and commercial scale; and dispelling many of the myths that continue to exist from the early days of homebrewing.

Lastly, some kind advice. Reading this book will just help you get started. The only true way to learn the science (and art) of homebrewing is by actually brewing and brewing often. Thus, you'll find this book to be more impactful if you reread it as you gain experience throughout your homebrewing career. When all is said and done, I hope you can share my passion for homebrewing, learn a thing or two, and most important, get started on the pathway toward brewing great beer at home for you to share with friends, family, and perhaps a homebrew club. Cheers!

How This Book Is Organized

Part 1, Welcome to Homebrewing, covers the very basics of the brewing process, namely making beer with malt extract. There's also a detailed step-by-step guide to help you navigate the creation for your first homebrew.

Part 2, Brewing Ingredients, provides in-depth info on malt, hops, yeast, and water and explains how these ingredients affect beer flavor and character. You'll also learn more about commonly used brewing additions such as fruit, sugars, and spices and how to add them to your beer.

Part 3, Brewing Necessities, reviews the supplies needed throughout the brewing process, from brewing equipment to cleaning and sanitization agents. You'll also learn the importance of brewing measurement and recordkeeping in your brewing process.

Part 4, The Brewing Process, extends the basics from Part 1 to the intermediate level, and fully surveys the three major steps in the brewing process: making wort with extract, standard fermentation, and packaging.

Part 5, Evaluating Your Homebrew, discusses the basic techniques behind tasting beer, from using the right glass to detecting beer flavors and off-flavors. Also, based on your brewing measurement and tasting evaluation, you'll learn how to troubleshoot common homebrew difficulties to improve your homebrewing process in future batches.

Part 6, Becoming a Brewmaster, elevates the brewing techniques from Part 4 and fully covers advanced brewing topics like making beer using all-grain methods and advanced fermentation. Mastering these topics will certainly put you on the pathway to becoming a brewmaster.

Part 7, Beer Recipes, consists of 60 great homebrewing recipes, including 16 guest recipes from pillars of the homebrewing community. You'll also learn how to read a beer recipe, modify an existing recipe to fit your brewing process, and some techniques for adding ingredients.

How to Read This Book

While there is no one way to read this book, here are just a few suggestions based on your experience level to learning practical brewing knowledge on your pathway toward becoming a brewmaster.

At the Beginner Level

Thumbing through this several-hundred page book may feel a bit overwhelming; however, starting out, homebrewing doesn't need to be difficult or highly technical. In reality, you are better off brewing every other week to gain experience rather than keeping your nose in a book. Remember: you can't learn brewing without actually brewing. To hit the ground running, read Chapters 1 and 2, which cover brewing your first extract beer.

If you'd rather acquire a bit more of the "what and whys" before brewing, give Parts 2 through 4 a look. Part 2 covers the four main brewing ingredients in Chapters 3 through 6 and the less commonly used brewing ingredients, like sugars, fruit, and spice, in Chapter 7. Part 3 covers the brewing necessities, like equipment, sanitization, and measurement in great detail. Of these chapters, I would heavily focus on Chapter 9, as you can't make great beer without stellar cleaning and sanitization practices. Finally, Part 4 details the entirety of the brewing process. Of these chapters, I would primarily focus on fermentation rather than making wort, as it has the greatest impact on the quality of beer.

At the Intermediate Level

After you've brewed a few batches, more likely than not, you'll want to improve your process. I recommend Part 5, which guides you through evaluating your homebrew, both good and off-flavors, and troubleshooting some of the problems many beginner brewers face. Also, as most problems are directly related to fermentation, I recommend reviewing Chapter 12 to better understanding fermentation, with a particular focus on temperature and pitching rates.

As an emerging intermediate brewer, you may also want to transition toward more advanced techniques, like mini-mashing and kegging. For mini mashes, I recommend reviewing Chapters 3 and 17 to learn more about malt and how to make a mash. Also, for the brewer tired of exhaustive bottling sessions, I recommend Chapter 13, which focuses on kegging equipment and forced carbonation, as well as the how-to kegging advice sections in Chapter 2.

At the Advanced Level

A master of extract and a dialed-in process, you are now looking to move onto advanced brewing. For many, advanced brewing means switching from extract and mini-mash brewing to all-grain brewing. For advanced mash/lauter techniques and all-grain equipment, check out Chapters 17 through 19. Also, as water chemistry plays a large role in an effective mash, I recommend reviewing the brewing water adjustment information in Chapter 6.

Advanced mash techniques often come with advanced fermentation, chiefly, lager and high-gravity brewing. For advanced fermentation techniques, check out Chapter 20. In addition, I recommend reviewing Chapter 12, particularly making starters and aeration, which are both critical to lager and high-gravity fermentation.

Extras

The following sidebars provide insight and guidance along the way:

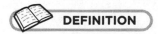

DEFINITION

Homebrewing comes with a whole new vocabulary. These sidebars will familiarize you with some of the common terms used by homebrewers.

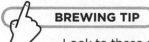

BREWING TIP

Look to these sidebars for advice, tips, and tricks to make your brewing process easier and more successful.

BREWING MYTH

Homebrewing has its share of popular lore, not all of which is accurate. These sidebars dispel popular brewing myths that continue to surround the brewing process and homebrewing hobby.

CAUTION

To make your brewing experience as safe and successful as possible, heed these warnings about what to avoid throughout the brewing process.

But Wait! There's More!

To make your brewing and record keeping easier, we've included a list of ingredient substitutions as well as the Brewer's Log from Chapter 10 in a handy printable form. You can find these at idiotsguides.com/homebrewing.

Acknowledgments

I'd like to give a big thanks to friends and family, especially my wife, Abby, who were incredibly supportive throughout the writing of this book. Also, I'd like express deep gratitude to my editors, Brook Farling and Ann Barton, for guiding me through the process of writing and developing my first book. Additionally, I'd like to raise a glass and say "Cheers!" to the guest brewers who contributed great homebrew recipes: Drew Beechum, Chris Colby, Denny Conn, Michael Dawson, Dan and Joelle Dewberry, Jay Kaffenberger, Corey Martin, Kerry Martin, Don Osborn, Chris Rauschuber, Mark Schoppe, Marshall Schott, James Spencer, Michael Tonsmeire, Chip Walton, Jamil Zainasheff. And last but not least, I'd like to give a great shout out to the members of the Austin ZEALOTS homebrew club for great brewing feedback and the always great times.

Special Thanks to the Technical Reviewer

Idiot's Guides: Homebrewing was reviewed by an expert who double-checked the accuracy of what's presented here to help us ensure learning homebrewing is as easy as it gets. Special thanks are extended to Marshall Schott.

Welcome to Homebrewing

First and foremost, welcome to homebrewing! In starting the hobby, you are joining a fast-growing movement of brewing beer at home, and more likely than not, you'll get bitten by the homebrewing bug in the pursuit of making the perfect pint. To help you dive right into the thick of it, this part covers what you need to know to get off and running with your first batch of homebrew. This part includes a handy step-by-step guide to the brewing process, establishing a strong foundation in homebrewing to build upon later in the book. Now, let's get to brewing!

Introduction to Homebrewing

The craft of homebrewing has been practiced for centuries, and there's a lot to learn about ingredients and techniques. However, it's easy to get started with just a few ingredients and very little equipment. This chapter provides a taste of what's to come with a basic overview of the brewing process and a quick guide to getting started in homebrewing.

What Is Homebrewing?

Simply stated, homebrewing is the process of making beer at home. However, homebrewing and being a homebrewer are much more than this simple answer. For many folks, homebrewing is the ability to make high-quality yet inexpensive beer to enjoy at home. For some, it's the goal of replicating beer styles from around the world and competing in beer competitions, striving for the gold. And for others, it's having the freedom to customize beer, experimenting with ingredients and techniques. Whichever type of brewer you become, at its core, homebrewing is all about making and enjoying great beer from scratch, whatever way you like it!

In This Chapter

- A brief history of homebrewing
- An overview of the brewing process
- Tips for getting started

How Is Beer Made?

So, how do you make beer? As you may already know, beer has a basic recipe: malt + hops + yeast + water = beer! While the core recipe may be simple, variations in the central ingredients and brewing techniques can produce a wide array of diverse beer styles, including the hoppy and bitter pale ales and IPAs, the dark and robust porters and stouts, the rich and malty Oktoberfest lagers, and the wildly flavorful and funky saisons. Like the range of styles, brewing beer requires a range of skills, which are collectively known as the brewing process. Simply put, the brewing process is how you make beer, and to learn it requires a bit of reading (this book, for example) and practice, both of which will put you on the pathway to become a brewmaster.

A Very Brief History of Homebrewing

Homebrewing has had an almost continuous presence in human history, and is considered a pillar of human civilization. This may come as a surprise to some, but throughout human history, beer was primarily brewed at the domestic level. It was not until the advent of the Industrial Revolution in the late eighteenth century that brewing transitioned from the home brewery to the commercial brewery, which is where most brewing happens today. However, over the past few decades, homebrewing has steadily regained popularity, chiefly due to its legalization across many Western nations during the 1970s. Homebrewing became legal in the United States in 1978, when the ban was lifted by President Jimmy Carter. It has since been legalized in all 50 states, the last of which was Alabama in 2013.

Today, homebrewing is a rapidly growing hobby, closely paralleling the craft beer movement. There are now over one million Americans brewing beer at home and participating in homebrewing culture through homebrew clubs, media platforms like the Brewing Network, and conferences like the National Homebrewers Conference.

What Makes Homebrewing a Great Hobby?

Other than the intrinsic enjoyment of the journey through the brewing process, there are a number of practical benefits and incentives for learning how to brew beer at home. Many craft beer enthusiasts turn to homebrewing as an affordable alternative to commercially brewed craft beer. A six-pack of craft beer is often $8 or more, but the same quality beer brewed at home can be made for less than half the cost, often as little as 50 cents per bottle. Homebrew is also environmentally friendly, as the packaging, like kegs and bottles, is reused rather than recycled. In addition, costs from shipping beer are eliminated, saving both money and energy.

Brewing your own beer also guarantees that your beer is the freshest you can get. Fresh beer styles like American pale ales, IPAs, and wheat beers can be brewed in less than three weeks and consumed at the peak of freshness. Last but not least, homebrewing allows you to customize and tailor beer to your preferences. This is especially important to hop, malt, and yeast aficionados looking to experiment with new ingredients, like the latest hop strain. No matter what reason, if you are a craft beer enthusiast, homebrewing is a fun and fulfilling hobby that will take your beer knowledge and appreciation to the next level.

An Overview of the Brewing Process

The brewing process is a series of techniques, methods, and procedures spanning over the course of a few weeks, the sum of which turns the four main ingredients of malt, hops, yeast, and water into beer. Of the processes involved in brewing, the majority can be collected into three major events: brew day, when the brewer makes wort; fermentation, when the malt sugars are converted into alcohol; and packaging, when the beer is carbonated in bottles and kegs. This section covers the very basics of the brewing process, from cleaning and sanitization to enjoying your first homebrew.

Make wort.   Ferment beer.   Package and enjoy!

The brewing process consists of three main steps: making wort, fermentation, and packaging.

Sanitization

The starting point for every great beer, regardless of style, is clean and well-sanitized brewing equipment. A lack of sanitization results in the dreaded contamination, the unwanted guests in the form of wild yeast and bacteria, which can sour and "funkify" a beer to the point that it becomes undrinkable. Homebrewing can begin to feel like you're cleaning for a hobby; however, this is a small and worthwhile price to pay to ensure great beer. So remember, clean and sanitized brewing is happy brewing. For more information on cleaning and sanitization in the brewing process, check out Chapter 9.

Making Wort

Before you can make beer, you must first make *wort*, the sugary liquid made from malt, hops, and water that ferments to become beer. As a brewer, the day on which wort is made is called "brew day" and is arguably the most fun part of the brewing process (other than drinking your homebrew). How you make wort depends on the beer recipe, but all wort has essentially the same basic formula: malt + hops + water = wort. The process of creating wort falls into three main steps:

1. Add malt to water, either through malt extract and/or malted grains.

2. Boil the wort with hops and other ingredients.

3. Chill.

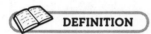 **DEFINITION**

> **Wort** is the boiled liquid that contains malt sugar and hops, which is made by the brewer before fermentation. After yeast is added, the liquid is no longer called wort and is then called beer.

The first step, adding malt, is the most divisive step in the brewing process at the homebrew scale. There are four main techniques for adding malt to wort, ranging from entry level to advanced. The most basic and straightforward technique is called *extract brewing*. In this method, condensed malt sugars in liquid or powder form, called malt extracts, are added to the wort. This method provides an easy introduction to brewing because it requires minimal equipment, and malt extracts provide accessible fermentable malt sugars.

The next level up is a form of extract brewing often called extract plus *specialty malts*. This method uses a combination of extract malts and characterful grain malts, known as specialty malts, which add body, color, sweetness, and flavor to wort. In this method, before the extract malts are added, the specialty malts, which are crushed grain, are steeped much like tea to infuse its character. For more practical how-to instruction on brewing with extract and specialty malts, look no further than Chapter 2.

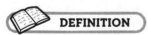 **DEFINITION**

> **Extract brewing** is a method of making wort by adding condensed malt sugars, called malt extracts, to hot water. Malt extract is available in liquid and powder forms.
>
> **Specialty malts** are characterful preconverted grain malts that contribute color, body, sweetness, and/or flavor to beer through steeping.

At the advanced level is *all-grain brewing*, where you are essentially brewing from scratch, using the *mash*, a mixture of hot water (also known as *liquor*) and crushed base malt, which converts its unfermentable starches from malted grain into fermentable sugar. All-grain brewing includes an additional step known as *lautering*, the process of separating wort from the mash, which may include *sparging*, the process of rinsing residual malt sugars with additional hot water. With practice, all-grain brewing is no more difficult than extract brewing and is considered an advanced brewing technique because it requires extra brewing equipment and additional brewing steps. For more information on the difference between all-grain and extract brewing, see Chapter 3.

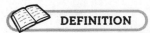 **DEFINITION**

All-grain brewing is a method of making wort by adding crushed malt to hot water to convert malt starches into fermentable sugar. This mixture is called the **mash**.

Liquor is an alternative brewing term for water in all-grain brewing.

Lautering is the process of separating wort from the mash, which may involve **sparging**, the process of rinsing residual malt sugars with additional hot water.

If you're not quite ready to tackle all-grain brewing, but want to move beyond extract brewing, there is a hybrid of the two techniques known as *mini-mash* or partial mash brewing, in which both malt extract and mash techniques are used. With this method, the mash accounts for a smaller portion of the fermentable sugars, so it can be done without serious mash equipment and malt extract does the heavy lifting. For more information on mini-mashing and all-grain brewing, check out Chapters 17 through 19.

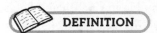 **DEFINITION**

Mini-mash brewing, or partial mash brewing, combines both extract and all-grain techniques.

Once malt is added, the remaining steps in wort production can be completed. These steps are the same regardless of the brewing method you use. After adding malt, the most important step in wort production is the addition of hops through boiling. When added early in the boil, hops lend a characteristic biting bitterness to beer. When added later on, hops infuse the spicy, fruity, and earthy flavors and aromas associated with your favorite hoppy beer styles. After hops are added, the wort is chilled down to room temperature, making way for the yeast and the next step in the brewing process: fermentation.

Steep specialty malts using a grain bag and hot water.

Remove grain bag and add malt extract to kettle.

Boil wort and add hop additions.

Chill wort.

Making wort with extract is a multistep process including steeping specialty malts, adding malt extract, boiling hops, and chilling.

Fermentation

After chilling, the wort is transferred to a fermentation vessel, called a *fermentor*, and the yeast is *pitched*, or added. This marks the end of wort production and the beginning of the fermentation process. Yeast is the true maker of beer, transforming sugary wort into alcohol and carbon dioxide through a multiphase process. The various strains of yeast are responsible for the beer styles we know as ales and lagers, with ale yeast producing ale styles and lager yeast producing lager styles.

Beyond alcohol, fermentation also produces several by-products, some good and desired and many unwanted. In balanced quantities, yeast produces chemical compounds called esters and phenols, fermentation by-products that add fruity, spicy flavors to beer, common in English and Belgian ales. However, when mishandled, yeast produces several off-flavors, like acetaldehyde and diacetyl, which are rarely desired in beer. Thus, brewers use tailored fermentation to produce a "clean," or well-tasting fermentation, known as controlled fermentation.

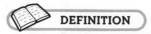 **DEFINITION**

A **fermentor** is the vessel where fermentation occurs. This is typically a brewing bucket or carboy.

Pitch is the brewing term for adding yeast to wort. The term **pitching temperature** refers to wort that is at the right temperature to add yeast, and the **pitch rate** is the number of yeast cells that the brewer adds to the wort. (A high pitch rate means more yeast cells are added.)

As the brewer, you have several tools available to create a well-fermented beer. Temperature is the primary means of control, as all yeast strains have a preferred temperature range for fermentation. Indeed, as previously mentioned, beer style is partly determined by the yeast strain (ale vs. lager yeast), and the chief dividing line in these two yeast types are fermentation temperature. In general, ale yeasts are fermented at warm temperatures, usually between 65°F and 72°F, while lager yeasts are fermented at cooler temperatures, between 48°F and 58°F. As such, ales are more fruity and complex as a result of increased ester and phenol production whereas lagers are cleaner, crisp, and more refined.

In addition to temperature, the brewer uses aeration and *pitch rate* to produce a strong and healthy fermentation. Aeration is the process of forcing oxygen into the solution, which is used by yeast in the beginning of fermentation. Pitch rate refers to the number of yeast cells added to the wort by the brewer. The pitch rate must be high enough to ensure a strong and quick start to fermentation, and is important for beating out any unwanted residual contaminants like bacteria or wild yeast.

Toward the end of fermentation, the yeast cleans up undesirable by-products during a phase known as conditioning. Then the yeast clumps up and drops out of suspension, a process known as *flocculation*. Ales typically have short conditioning durations, but for lager styles, the beer will go through an extended cold conditioning know as *lagering*. As a result, a well-conditioned beer will have good clarity and a clean, refined beer character.

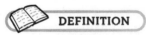

DEFINITION

Flocculation is the process by which yeast clumps together and falls out of suspension, typically occurring toward the end of fermentation.

Lagering is the process of conditioning lager-style beer under cold temperatures for an extended period of time to produce beer with an exceptionally clean, clear, and refined character.

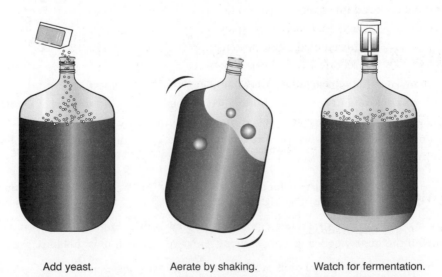

Add yeast.   Aerate by shaking.   Watch for fermentation.

Fermentation is a multistep process including pitching yeast, aerating wort, and allowing the yeast to do its magic.

Packaging

After conditioning is complete, it's time to package and carbonate your beer. Much like commercial brewing, homebrewers use bottles and kegs to package beer. To carbonate in bottles, brewers use a natural carbonation technique known as priming, where a controlled amount of sugar is reintroduced to beer to generate and dissolve a small amount of CO_2 when capped. Alternatively, kegs use forced carbonation via an external CO_2 tank, in which high pressure CO_2 is applied to the keg and controlled via a CO_2 regulator. Must beginners start out using bottling; however, many brewers transition to kegs due to its more controlled process of carbonation and ease of use.

Enjoying Your Homebrew

Once full carbonation and maturation is reached, you've reached the end of the brewing process. After patiently (or impatiently) waiting, it's time to crack open a bottle and enjoy some well-deserved homebrew. Although the brewing process may be complete, the journey is far from over. As you enjoy your beer, it's good practice to evaluate your final product. More than likely you won't be perfectly happy with your first few brews as you gain experience and dial in your process. For many, the end of one homebrew is simply the start of another, learning from what you've done through brewing measurements, log keeping, and tasting evaluation, and applying your experience to future batches.

Lastly, homebrew is to be shared with friends and family, or perhaps a local homebrew club, which is a good venue for feedback on improving a beer or simply for bragging about your awesome homebrew. Remember to enjoy your hard-won homebrew, take some notes, and share the love of your beer with others.

Building a Homebrewery

In order to make the leap into brewing beer at home, you'll need a few basic items. However, before you run out to your local homebrew store and buy everything in sight, it's worth considering the cost of various pieces of equipment and the space they take up. Whether you are brewing on a budget or living with limited storage space, give your homebrewery a bit of thought and planning before jumping in.

Basic Equipment

Starting out, you won't require much equipment to brew beer at home. In fact, you may already have many of the items needed to start brewing. However, as with most hobbies, the bare minimum of equipment isn't necessarily the best route. For this reason, I've provided two lists: a bare-bones list, essentially the minimum brewing equipment needed to produce a 5-gallon batch of beer using malt extract, and a recommended list, with suggested items that will help create better beer and make the brewing process a bit easier.

Bare-bones Equipment

Cleaning and Sanitization

- ❑ Your preferred cleaning agent
- ❑ Your preferred sanitizing agent (may be the same as the cleaning agent)

Wort Production and Fermentation

- ❑ Brew kettle (at least 4–5 gallons in volume for partial-boil extract batches)
- ❑ 6-gallon fermentor (a food-grade carboy or bucket)
- ❑ Airlock with suitable stopper

Bottling

- ❑ Racking cane
- ❑ Tubing with clamp to start and stop the flow of wort or beer
- ❑ Crown-top bottles, caps, and capper, or swing-top bottles (at least 48 12-ounce bottles and caps for a standard 5-gallon batch)

> **BREWING TIP**
>
> Consider buying a starter kit. Most homebrew shops offer these kits, which include most of the basic equipment you need and often cost less than buying the items individually. However, before purchasing a kit, make sure the items are of good quality and check that it includes everything on the "Bare-bones" list.

Recommended Equipment Additions

Cleaning and Sanitization

- ❑ Percarbonate cleaning agent, such as PBW
- ❑ Sanitizing agent, such as Star San
- ❑ Bottle and carboy brushes
- ❑ Jet washer

Measurement

- ❑ Digital thermometer
- ❑ Hydrometer with sample test tube
- ❑ Brewing log book
- ❑ Sample thief

Wort Production and Fermentation

- ❑ Big spoon
- ❑ Adhesive strip thermometer
- ❑ Blow off tubing
- ❑ Extra airlocks and stoppers
- ❑ 5-gallon secondary fermentor (for conditioning)

Bottling

- ❑ Bottling bucket with spigot
- ❑ Bottling wand

You probably won't be surprised to know that the items listed here are just the tip of the iceberg. Beyond the basics, there is a plethora of additional equipment used throughout the brewing process, particularly for intermediate and advanced brewing techniques such as all-grain brewing and kegging. In addition, there is a range of cost and quality among many brewing items such as brew kettles, fermentors, and measurement devices, which are worth taking into consideration, depending on the enthusiasm you have for homebrewing. For more detailed information on brewing equipment from the basic to advanced levels, check out Chapter 8. For more information on measurement devices used in the brewing process, see Chapter 10.

Brewing Space Considerations

When you begin brewing, it's a good idea to consider the space requirements of brewing equipment before committing to a particular kit. Fortunately, the equipment that comes in most typical starter kits doesn't take up much space. Most 5-gallon batch starter kits can easily fit inside a large plastic storage tote, or possibly even within a plastic bucket fermentor. When fermenting, you'll need an out-of-the-way spot, like a spare closet floor, to keep the active fermentor away from light and heat. Lastly, once your beer is packaged in bottles, you'll need a place to store them all, around 50 in total for a 5-gallon batch.

As you move toward more advanced brewing techniques, you'll likely require more equipment. All-grain brewing can require a *mash tun* and extra brew kettles, but alternative mashing technology, like brew in a bag, can save some space. Also, kegging is a large space consumer as kegs need storage that also requires refrigeration, such as a kegerator, to keep it at serving temperatures. Thus, keep in mind when progressing through the hobby that little by little more space may be necessary.

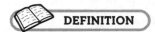 **DEFINITION**

> A **mash tun** is the traditional brewing vessel where the mash is constructed. Mash tuns are often insulated to maintain temperatures between 110°F and 170°F as well as a lautering device to separate the wort from the mash. For more information on mash equipment, see Chapter 18.

Space considerations for homebrewing are generally more pressing to those living in apartments or homes with limited spaces. I have lived in a small apartment throughout my adult life, and while it has not prevented me from brewing extract and all-grain batches on my stovetop, these space considerations did require a bit more finesse. If you are wary of brewing because of limited space, many of the space requirements can be alleviated by scaling down the batch size from the standard 5-gallon batch to a smaller batch size in the 1 to 3 gallon range.

Small batches sizes utilize more storable equipment, like smaller brew kettles and fermentors, and since you are producing less beer, fewer bottles and smaller kegs can be more easily stored. In my early days of homebrewing, I was more interested in the brewing process and becoming a better brewer than drinking the beer, so small batches allowed me to brew more often without have to store nearly 50 bottles of beer from a 5-gallon batch. Just remember, the bigger the batch size, the bigger the equipment needed to handle the beer as well as its bottles or kegs, all of which require storage.

Starter Equipment Costs

One of my least favorite topics of discussion is money; however, like space and storage, brewing costs can also be a limiting factor and worth consideration. For the beginner, homebrewing starter kits are fairly inexpensive, with prices ranging from $100 to $200, depending on the amount of equipment included. Starter kits usually contain most of the items recommended on the previously detailed lists; however, they often do not include brew kettles and some other equipment, like big spoons. Be sure to check what equipment comes in the kit and factor any additional equipment purchases into your brewing budget.

When budgeting for starter equipment, make sure to also budget for replacements. Many brewing items are not designed to last forever, and must be replaced after many uses. In particular, plastic items like racking canes, tubing, and buckets wear out over time, forming scratches and cracks that require replacement. Also, there are consumables like cleaning and sanitizing agents, bottle caps, etc., that must be replenished after a number of batches. I would recommend setting aside around half the cost of your starter kit to cover the cost of replacement equipment.

Undoubtedly, after a few extract batches, you'll want to move on toward more advanced brewing methods like all-grain brewing and kegging. These brewing techniques require additional equipment, some of which can be quite expensive. For those brewing on budget, you can take advantage of used brewing equipment. Kegging can be done on the cheap by purchasing lightly used kegs and refrigerating appliances. All of my kegs were purchased secondhand and work great after a bit of cleaning and seal replacement.

Similarly, when going all-grain, you can forgo the mash tun and associated equipment and utilize the brew-in-a-bag technique as a low-cost option. Alternatively, many brewers fabricate their own mash tuns from previously used brew kettles and/or cooler equipment. My mash tun was fabricated from my original partial-boil stainless steel brew kettle with a braided hose and weldless ball valve. No matter what direction you take, homebrewers are of the thrifty type, so give your trusted forum a search and you'll likely find a low-cost solution to your homebrewing question.

Lastly, consider homebrewing as an investment rather than a cost. I started homebrewing as a poor graduate student, and I figured I could make high-quality craft beer less expensively with a bit of practice. This ultimately became the justification for buying my first starter kit and definitely has worked well in the long run, not only as a cost saver but also becoming a passionate hobby in my life. So for those tight on cash, figure in the future cost savings by brewing your own as a budgeted way of starting the hobby.

The Least You Need to Know

- Homebrewing is a fun hobby that, with practice, allows you to produce fresh, high-quality, customized beers at home.
- The brewing process consists of three major steps: making wort, fermentation, and packaging.
- Homebrewing can be scaled to fit your space and budget.
- With a brew kettle, a fermentor, and a few extra items, all commonly found in starter kits, you can be on your way to brewing beer at home.

Brewing Your First Extract Beer

The best way to learn is by doing. Now that you know the basics of brewing process and technique, it's time to brew your first extract beer. This chapter will guide you through the process, from brew day to bottling. Now, let's brew some beer!

Before You Begin

The first step to brewing beer is selecting a recipe. If you're not sure what recipe to start with, consider purchasing a prebuilt recipe kit from your homebrew shop. These usually contain a recipe along with all the necessary ingredients to make it, so you don't have to worry about formulating one from scratch. Stick with something simple and straightforward; American-style ales like an amber, brown, or pale ale are a good place to start.

In This Chapter

- Pre-brew day preparation
- Brew day guide to wort production
- Post-brew day direction for fermentation, conditioning, and packaging

If you want to choose a recipe and buy the ingredients separately, check out the extract recipes in Chapter 22. I recommend starting out with an entry-level recipe such as one of the following:

West Coast Pale Ale, a hoppy yet balanced American-style pale ale from the Pacific Northwest featuring Cascade hops.

Texas Brown, a hoppy American brown ale with stylistic origins rooted in California and Texas.

Changing Colors Amber Ale, an American amber ale with rich malt, toasted and caramel in character.

This chapter assumes that your first batch is a 5-gallon batch, a common batch size in home-brewing. If you want to make a smaller batch, you can cut everything by a constant proportion, although some small adjustments may be necessary depending on the recipe.

Extract Pre-Brew Day Prep

Before brew day begins, it's best to get things checked and organized. This can be done minutes before, but is best done at least a day before in case any last-minute brewing items are needed. For new and advanced homebrewers alike, it is useful to look through the following brew day checklists to prevent any brew day disasters. A planned and organized brew day is a peaceful and fun brew day.

Brewing Supplies Checklist

If any ingredients are missing or unavailable, and there is not enough time to pick them up, check out the ingredient substitutions at idiotsguides.com/homebrewing to make the closest possible match in your beer recipe.

Ingredients

- ❑ Malt: malt extract, specialty malts for steeping
- ❑ Hops: bittering, flavor, aroma additions
- ❑ Yeast: healthy cells in suitable quantities, typically 100 to 200 billion cells for a 5-gallon batch of 4 to 6 percent ABV beer
- ❑ Water: clean source water, RO water, brewing mineral additions as necessary
- ❑ Other ingredients: sugars, spices, herbs, wort clarifiers, foam control, yeast nutrient, etc., depending on the recipe goals
- ❑ Recipe, including ingredients, other brewing instructions, recommended boil duration, ingredient addition timing, etc.

Supplies

- ❑ Basic equipment: appropriately sized brew kettle and fermentor, along with air lock, drilled stopper, big spoon, racking cane, and tubing.
- ❑ Basic measurement tools: hydrometer with thief and test tube, thermometer, liquid measure, paper and pen for brewing log.
- ❑ Cleaning supplies: cleaning tools, like brushes and jet washer, along with enough cleaning and sanitizing agents to clean and sanitize all necessary equipment, including spoons, racking cane, tubing, and most of all, the fermentor.
- ❑ Straining bags: appropriate sizes for steeping grains and hops as required.
- ❑ Chilling supplies: ice, wort chiller, etc.

Other Pre-Brew Day Considerations

Check the weather. If you plan to brew outdoors, check the local weather for any adverse conditions, such as high winds, rain, snow, zombie apocalypse, etc.

Check your yeast. Examine the packaging date on your liquid or dry yeast to determine if there are enough viable yeast cells for your desired fermentation. If not, consider buying more yeast or making a yeast starter.

Check propane levels (if using a burner). If you are using a propane burner, check your propane tank levels to ensure enough gas for a full 60-minute boil. In general, it's best to keep a back up tank for these purposes.

Stock up on ice (if needed). If you're using an ice bath for chilling, make sure you have sufficient ice on hand. A 5-gallon batch will likely need at least 10 pounds of ice to chill.

Review your recipe. If you've ordered a recipe kit, check to make sure your recipe doesn't have any base malts in non-extract form, like Maris Otter, Munich, and Pilsner. If so, you'll need to perform a mini mash. Don't worry; just go to Chapter 19 for step-by-step instructions. In lieu of the mini mash, you can also place the base malt aside and replace with an equivalent portion of dry or liquid malt extract.

Also make sure you have the means to crack any specialty malts called for in the recipe. If your specialty malts are not crushed and you are without a mill, you can do it at home using a rolling pin. Simply place your malt in a plastic freezer bag and roll over it using a rolling pin and slight pressure. It does not need to be pulverized, just cracked. You can also take your malt to your local brew store to be milled for a nominal fee.

Clean your brew kettle. This is especially important if this is your very first batch. Kettles straight from the manufacturer often have residual oil and metallic dust inside. Simply cleaning it with some dish soap, warm water, and a clean sponge should do the trick. Also, it wouldn't hurt to do a full boil with water as an extra precaution, especially for aluminum pots, to avoid any off-flavors. If you've already used your kettle, just make sure there isn't any stuck-on hot break or hop matter from previous brew sessions. If so, gently clean with a soft sponge and warm water.

Clean your fermentor. Even if the fermentor appears spotless by visual inspection, there still may be soil. Clean your fermentor with any appropriate cleaning agent as detailed in Chapter 9. Hold off on sanitization until the chilling stage.

Clean the kitchen. If you brew in your kitchen, it wouldn't hurt to give everything a light cleaning to help prevent contamination and to give you an uncluttered workspace. Clear the counter, wash the stovetop, etc.

Check thermometer calibration. If you are using a thermometer, now would be a good time to check its calibration. If it's off, follow the manufacturer's recommendation for recalibration.

Let's Make Wort

Now that everything is in place, it's time to start making wort. At this point, having your recipe in hand would be a good idea. If you're not sure on how to read a beer recipe, give a quick look at Chapter 21.

Initial Preparation

Just before you start making wort, there are a few steps that can be done to make the brew day process flow a bit smoother. These steps do not have to be done in any particular order. For more experienced homebrewers or those who are good at multitasking, these steps can often be interwoven throughout the brew day. For beginners, it's advisable to complete these items before turning on the stove.

Warm up your liquid malt extract. Like molasses, cold malt syrup does not flow easily. Placing a can, jug, or pouch of malt extract in a tub full of warm water should help to reduce its viscosity.

Bring yeast to pitching temperature. For dry yeast, this is as simple as removing your sachet from the refrigerator. For liquid yeast, activate the smack pack or drive yeast into suspension with vials. For the smack pack, check for signs of inflation after a few hours to ensure the yeast is healthy and metabolically active.

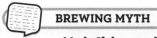 **BREWING MYTH**

Myth: If the smack pack is not fully inflated, it means the yeast is bad.

Smack packs do not need to be inflated like a balloon and bulging at the seams as a sign of healthy yeast. Yeast manufacturers designate approximately 1 inch of inflation as the confirming sign of healthy yeast.

Presanitize equipment. If you're worried about keeping things sanitized, consider presanitizing your brewing tools by keeping them in a tub full of sanitizer. That way, when the boil is finished, all of your tools will be sanitized and ready for use. When you're done using the tool, rinse clean and place back in your sanitized tub, ready and sanitized for its next use in the brewing process.

Step 1: Steep Specialty Malts

If your recipe calls for specialty malts, either roasted or crystal in variety, your first step will be to steep them using the following procedure. If none are called for, you can skip this and go straight to the next step. Also, if your specialty malt addition is small, like ¼ pound, the water level in the brew kettle may be too shallow to perform a steep. Instead, use a small saucepan or large glass liquid measure to perform the steep and then add it back to the kettle after it is complete. More information on specialty malt steeping can be found in Chapter 11.

Specialty Malt Steep Procedure

Ingredients and Equipment

Specialty malts, cracked

Clean brewing water (1 gallon per
    pound of malt)

Muslin or grain bag

Saucepan or brew kettle

Thermometer

Directions

1. Add water to brew kettle or saucepan. Approximately 1 gallon of water per pound of cracked specialty malt is considered a good steeping ratio.

2. Heat water over high heat until it reaches 160°F. Turn off heat.

3. Place cracked specialty malt in a grain bag.

4. Add bagged specialty malts to the hot water.

5. Allow bagged malts to steep for 30 minutes, adjusting the burner temperature as needed to keep the temperature between 150°F and 170°F. Make sure the grain bag isn't touching the bottom of the kettle when heating, as it may scorch.

6. After 30 minutes, remove the grain bag. Allow it to drain for a bit; malt absorbs quite a bit of water. You can squeeze the grain bag gently, but avoid aggressive squeezing as this action may extract tannins from the husk, yielding an over-steeped, tea-like off-flavor.

7. If you used a saucepan or liquid measure for steeping, pour the steeped infusion into your brew kettle.

After steeping, allow specialty malts to drain.

 BREWING TIP

If you're using a vinyl grain bag, rinse it out and save it for another use. Muslin grain bags typically cannot be reused.

Step 2: Add Source Water to the Kettle

At this point, it's time to add source water to your brew kettle. If you are performing a partial boil, add water to yield approximately 3 gallons in volume, including any infusion from specialty malt steep. In you are performing a full boil, add water to yield roughly 6 gallons in volume, including any infusion from the specialty malt steep.

Although pH and water chemistry are not vital to extract brewing, if you plan to add mineral additions to enhance beer character, now would be the time. In doing so, follow the dosing recommendations in Chapters 6 and 11. If this is your first batch, it's best to hold off on any major water modification until you've gained more brewing experience. However, if you are using tap water, consider adding a bit of sodium metabisulfite or a Campden tablet.

Step 3: Add Malt Extract

With the kettle full of brewing water and possibly an infusion from a specialty malt steep, it's time to add that malt extract. Introducing malt extract to a brew kettle is as simple as pouring it in; however, there are some best practices depending on the variety of malt extract.

For DME: Kettle water should be warm but not hot, as near boiling water can cause DME to lump up in balls that can persist throughout the boil.

DME should be added to warm, but not hot, water to prevent clumping.

For LME: Kettle water should be quite hot. LME is very dense, like molasses, and takes time to dissolve. Hot water speeds up the process; however, make sure the burner power is off before adding. Due to its high density relative to water, LME falls straight to the bottom of the kettle, and a burner on full blast will likely burn the LME, resulting in undesirable burnt wort flavors.

Once the malt extract is added to the kettle, stir until the malt extract is dissolved and then turn the burner off. Congratulations, you now have wort! If your recipe calls for a late malt addition, hold that off to the side until called for in the recipe. For more information on late malt additions and the pros and cons between partial and full boils, check out Chapter 11.

Step 4: Bring the Wort to a Boil

With malt extract added and fully dissolved, it's now time to bring the wort to a boil. At this point, you may be tempted to walk away from the brew kettle, likely to watch some TV or drink a homebrew. Wrong! It may feel like a watched pot will never boil, but trust me, it will. The unwatched pot will boil over and make a sticky mess all over your stove or propane burner. This is because wort is rich in protein, and, like pasta water, has a propensity to foam during the first few minutes of the boil. The foaming is called the hot break.

If you suspect you are near a boilover, there are a few tricks to keep the hot break from rising beyond control. First, turn off the source of the heat. If you use an electric heating element, remove the kettle from the burner, even after it's been turned off. Next, use a spray bottle of water to spritz the surface of the rising hot break, bursting its bubbles and reducing surface tension. Lastly, with a big spoon, stir vigorously to diminish the hot break volume. Once minimized, return the brew kettle to a boil. Keep in mind that a hot break can return, and it's in your best interest to keep an eye on the pot.

Step 5: Add Ingredients to the Wort

Once the hot break has subsided, it's time to start adding brewing ingredients, especially hops. Before doing so, you may want to adjust the boil rate. If the wort is boiling vigorously, practically jumping out of the pot, then the boil is too hard. However, if the boil is hardly moving, you may want to bump it up a bit. The wort boil rate is up to the brewer, but most prefer a slow rolling boil, at the level of an elevated simmer. Too soft a boil can't really hurt, but a hard boil can.

With the boil rate adjusted, it's time to begin the boil countdown and start a timer. Boil duration for most extract brews is 60 minutes unless otherwise specified by the recipe. Boil additions are added in countdown format, like on New Year's Eve or a rocket countdown. For example, a 60-minute addition comes at the very beginning of the boil and a 15-minute addition is added with 15 minutes remaining in the boil (45 minutes after beginning). The following boil procedure for extract-based wort provides a general guideline for boil additions. For specific additions, consult your beer recipe. It should specify the type, amount, and timing in the boil.

General Boil Procedure for Extract-Based Wort

1. Bring wort to a gently rolling boil. Keep an eye on the pot and watch for boilovers.

2. Set a timer for 60 minutes.

3. Add bittering hop addition with 45 to 60 minutes left in the boil.

4. Add flavor hop addition with 10 to 30 minutes left in the boil.

5. Add late malt extract sugar additions with 5 to 15 minutes left in the boil.

6. Add wort clarifiers and yeast nutrients with 5 to 15 minutes left in the boil.

7. If using an immersion wort chiller, place it in the boiling wort with 15 minutes left in the boil. This will sanitize the chiller.

8. Add other ingredient additions with 0 to 60 minutes left in the boil.

9. Add aroma hops additions with 0 to 10 minutes left in the boil.

Step 6: Chill the Wort

After the boil duration is up, the boil is over and it's time to chill. However, before moving forward with chilling, it is worth emphasizing this point: everything that touches the wort or beer must be cleaned and sanitized from this point on. Not doing so puts your wort or beer at risk of contamination. When I say everything, I mean it. This includes sanitizing obvious things like the fermentor and racking cane, but also less obvious things like thermometer probes, airlocks, and big spoons. Also, when using cleaning and sanitizing agents, make sure to use the correct dilutions and contact durations as recommended by the manufacturer. Going forward, when in doubt, clean and sanitize; it may be overkill, but at least you won't risk introducing contaminants. For more information on sanitization and cleaning agents, check out Chapter 9.

BREWING TIP

Keep a small spray bottle filled with sanitizing solution handy for sanitizing on the fly.

The most common form of chilling used by the new brewer is the ice bath. While it isn't the most efficient method, it will do the job. Setting up an ice bath is as simple as it sounds, essentially adding a large amount of ice and cold water to a tub or large vessel capable of holding your brew kettle. Some brewers use the kitchen sink, but for large brew kettles, a plastic storage tote may accommodate more ice and water, allowing for quicker chilling. Regardless of the kettle type, make sure there is a sufficient amount of ice and water to chill to pitching temperatures; usually more than 10 pounds of ice is necessary. Also make sure the ice bath level won't overflow, as the brew kettle will displace some of the water when submerged.

For the multitasker, the ice bath can be set up during the last 10 minutes of the boil, so it is cold and ready for the hot kettle once the boil is complete. Chilling durations vary greatly depending on the amount of ice and the size of the boil, but in general, a full boil will take longer to chill than a partial boil. Most of my ice baths take at least 30 minutes to chill wort to pitching temperatures; however, the only way to be sure wort is properly chilled is to measure the wort temperature with a sanitized thermometer.

After a few ice baths, many brewers move onto more advanced chilling equipment, called wort chillers. These devices essentially create a heat exchange between hot wort and cold water and can achieve very quick chilling times. New brewers usually start out using an immersion chiller, which consists of a long piece of coiled metal tubing. This coiled tubing is submerged in the hot wort, and cold water is run through it, chilling the wort.

To use an immersion chiller, you simply add it to the brew kettle during the last 15 minutes of the boil to sanitize. At the end of the boil, connect its tubing to a faucet and run cold water through the chiller until the wort is chilled to pitching temperatures. When turning on the source water, be mindful not to splash any chilling water into the wort. Also be careful not to burn yourself on the exiting water, which can be very hot. Like ice baths, chilling times depend on the batch size and quality of immersion chiller. The only way to be sure the wort is sufficiently chilled is to measure the wort temperature with a sanitized thermometer. For more information on chilling wort, check out Chapter 11.

 BREWING TIP

When switching to an immersion chiller, give it a test run before the brew day by boiling 5 gallons of water in your brew kettle and then chilling it. This will identify any leaks in the tubing, season the new metal, and give you a ballpark idea of chilling times to expect on the brew day.

Step 7: Transfer the Wort to the Fermentor

Once the wort is cool, it's ready to transfer to the fermentor. Before transferring, make sure the wort temperature is below 80°F, as higher temperatures may be harmful to the wort and yeast. Better yet, chill the wort to 65°F to 70°F for ale yeast or 52°F to 58°F for lager yeast. This will reduce the formation yeast derived off-flavors, especially when brewing without active temperature control.

When transferring wort to the fermentor, brewers use a variety of methods. Many brewers simply dump the kettle contents straight into the fermentor. This technique is a good option starting out since it makes quick work of the transferring process and also aerates the wort, a necessary step in the fermentation process.

While dumping the wort into the fermentor, you'll likely notice some sludgy gunk at the bottom of the kettle. This brewing debris is a mixture of hop matter and coagulated proteins known as *trub*. Hold back on dumping that last bit of wort to avoid transferring a great deal of trub and hop matter to the fermentor. This results in clearer wort, but does leave behind about a half-gallon of wort in the brew kettle. Alternatively, some brewers use a sanitized mesh filter to capture this content and prevent it from getting into the fermentor; however, this can be frustrating as highly hopped wort will become clogged and make the transferring process difficult.

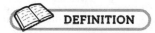 **DEFINITION**

> **Trub** is a mixture of coagulated proteins that form throughout the boil and chilling process when making wort. Trub can appear as a sludgy sediment at the bottom of a brew kettle or fermentor.

Another route for wort transfer and trub separation is using a racking process. By drawing off the top of the kettle, nearly all of the clear wort can be siphoned off while leaving the majority of the trub behind at the bottom. Also, when full boils or larger batches are made, dumping batches is nearly impossible, as they exceed 60 pounds in weight. Additionally, the dumping process can be messy even when funnels are used, and leave behind a sticky floor. For these reasons, I prefer racking the beer into the fermentor in my brewing process. It's a bit slow, and I yield a bit less wort, but it's worth it for clearer wort and less cleanup.

Finally, the transferring process is a good time to collect a small portion of wort using a *sample thief* to test for original gravity. Although not critical to the brewing process, this measurement will at least tell you the starting gravity. For more information on the measurement and calculation of ABV from original and final gravity, check out Chapter 10.

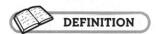 **DEFINITION**

> A **sample thief** (or just "thief") is a device that removes a sample from a vessel (usually a fermentor) for testing and evaluation.

Let's Get Fermenting

Once the wort is in the fermentor, it's time to start fermentation. At this point, the brewer is no longer in the driver's seat, and the yeast is firmly in control, converting sugar into alcohol. The brewer's role is to set up the best possible conditions, both at the time of pitching and throughout fermentation. For the new brewer, these key responsibilities are aerating the wort, pitching the yeast, and monitoring the temperature.

Step 1: Aeration

While oxygen is generally unwanted throughout the brewing process, the one time it is desired is at pitching, as it is a vital yeast nutrient important to cell wall development during the early phases of fermentation. Brewers use several techniques to force oxygen into the solution; however, most new brewers employ the shaking method, a technique that forces dissolved oxygen from the air into the wort via vigorous fermentor shaking.

Aeration via shaking can take anywhere from 45 seconds to over 5 minutes to achieve saturation. Starting out, give your fermentor a vigorous back and forth shake for at least 2 minutes to sufficiently aerate your wort. If you're using a glass carboy, be careful; one misstep can leave an awfully big mess and a hazardous situation. For more information on the importance of oxygen in beer and advanced aeration techniques, check out Chapter 12.

Step 2: Pitch the Yeast

With the wort well aerated, it's now time to pitch the yeast. More likely than not, you'll be pitching from a yeast package. Here are a few tricks to ensure smooth pitching.

If you're using liquid yeast from a smack pack, give it a firm shake to rehomogenize the yeast mixture. Next, cut open the smack pack with sanitized scissors and gently pour the yeast into the fermentor. Liquid yeast in vials often separates and needs to be shaken back into a homogeneous mixture before pitching. However, doing so is much like shaking up a can of soda, as these vials have some residual carbonation. Thus, you may want to let the vial settle for 30 minutes before cracking it open and pouring the contents into the fermentor.

If you are using dry yeast, you may consider rehydrating it before pitching. While not necessary, rehydration allows for an easier transition from the freeze-dried state into cellular form. To do so, follow the manufacturer's instructions or use the basic rehydration recipe in Chapter 12. If you're not rehydrating, use sanitized scissors to cut open the sachet and sprinkle it across the surface of the wort.

Later out in your brewing career, you may want to pitch a greater quantity of yeast. While buying more yeast can easily solve this problem, most seasoned brewers use what is known as a yeast starter to culture up greater quantities of yeast for pitching, which can significantly improve the quality of your beer. For more information on yeast starters, check out Chapter 12.

Step 3: Watch the Fermentor

After pitching, it's time to watch the fermentor to gauge the level of yeast activity. Glass carboys are best for this, but if you're using a plastic bucket, just lift the lid to see what's going on. The first major milestone you'll want to confirm is the formation of krausen, the creamy, yeasty mass that forms on the top of fermenting beer.

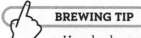

BREWING TIP

Have backup yeast on hand. In some cases, liquid or dry yeast is dead on arrival, either due to poor shipping or just bad luck. This is usually apparent when a smack pack does not swell or if initial fermentation is nonexistent or sluggish 24 to 48 hours after pitching. In either case, it's good to have a backup option. Dry yeast works best since it has a long shelf life. I keep a sachet of US-05 in my refrigerator at all times as my backup yeast.

Krausen activity is often corroborated by airlock action. Since fermentation produces carbon dioxide, its rate of production is often seen as another gauge of yeast progress. Many brewers will keep track of how many glugs per minute an airlock will make to determine whether fermentation activity is ramping up or slowing down. Also, when krausen is rising, you'll want to make sure the airlock doesn't become clogged. If you see a quickly rising krausen, it might be best to prematurely replace the airlock with a blow off tube to avoid pressure buildup in the fermentor and to keep your yeast happy and uncontaminated.

Throughout fermentation, it's good practice to monitor the temperature, especially when active temperature control is not being used. This means making sure the fermentor is within the desired fermentation temperature range and is not experiencing large temperature swings, which are not good for healthy fermentation. Temperature monitoring and control is especially important during the first few days, as yeast generates heat throughout fermentation, causing the beer temperature to rise independently of the room temperature, sometimes enough to push the fermentation outside the recommended ranges. During this period, you can simply move your fermentor to a warmer or cooler room as necessary to help keep it within the desired temperature range. For information on other means of temperature control, check out Chapter 20.

Step 4: Conditioning

From the time you pitch the yeast, the duration of fermentation should be 5 to 10 days for an ale and 7 to 14 days for a lager, depending on the temperature, original gravity, and yeast strain used. Toward the end of fermentation, the conditioning phase begins. Here, the airlock activity will noticeably slow and the once-high krausen will fall. At this point, take a gravity reading in order to judge whether fermentation is complete. If the final gravity remains unchanged over consecutive days, this means you've hit terminal gravity, and any time past here is good to go for packaging. Also, if you recorded an original gravity, you can use the final gravity and a bit of calculation (usually done online these days), to figure out the ABV for your new brew.

Even if you've hit terminal gravity, you may decide to wait a few days before packaging to benefit your fermented brew. An extra week in the primary fermentor will allow for full reabsorption of fermentation by-products and allow for the yeast to flocculate, reducing the amount of sediment in your bottles or keg come packaging time. Many brewers utilize a secondary fermentor for the conditioning process, although with your first homebrew, it's best to skip this step and keep it all in the primary.

Lastly, if your recipe calls for dry hops, now would be the time to add them. Depending on your recipe, dry hops usually remain in contact with the beer for 3 to 7 days.

Time to Package

With fermentation complete and all conditioning stages observed, it's now time to package. Two main packaging types are used in homebrewing: bottles and kegs. While the packaging process is easy, it has quite a bit of detail and nuance that are discussed in full in Chapter 13. If it's your first time, I encourage you to check out Chapter 13 for more information on both processes, especially the finer points of priming and carbonation. However, the following is a quick guide for those homebrewers using the "learning to swim by jumping in the water" method.

Bottling Your Homebrew

If you are just starting out, more likely than not, your first batch of homebrew will be bottled rather than kegged. On bottling day, you have three main tasks in addition to bottling the beer: keeping things clean and sanitized, making a priming solution, and limiting oxygen incorporation in your fermented beer. For cleaning and sanitization, use the previously mentioned agents and make sure everything that touches your beer is sanitized to avoid contamination. Also, while racking, avoid splashy siphoning to limit oxygen incorporation, which will reduce shelf life and produce oxidative off-flavor with age.

 BREWING TIP

Make sure the spigot on your bottling bucket is closed! Racking beer into the bottling bucket with the spigot open is a common brew day disaster that results in a sticky mess on the floor and the loss of some delicious homebrew. Before racking, double check (perhaps even triple check) that your spigot is in the closed position.

Finally, in order to achieve carbonation in the bottles, you need to add back a measured amount of fermentables into the beer. This process is known as making a priming solution. Starting out, a simple solution of 4 ounces of corn sugar and 16 ounces of water should do the trick, making sure the sugar water solution is sanitized via boiling before adding to the beer. Also, if you are bottling an aged, high gravity, and/or lager beer, you may want to add active, fresh yeast at bottling time in order to achieve full carbonation. For more information on achieving a specific carbonation levels in beer, check out the priming section in Chapter 13.

Bottling Summary

Ingredients and Equipment

Fermented beer

Priming sugar (corn sugar, DME, etc.)

2 cups water

2 (16-oz.) microwave-safe glass
liquid measures

Saucepan

Bottling bucket (with spigot
assembly)

Racking cane (with tubing)

Bottling wand (with tubing)

50 (12-oz.) bottles (plus some extras)

50 bottle caps (plus some extras)

Bottle capper

Directions

1. Thoroughly clean and sanitize your bottling equipment, including the bottles and bottle caps. While some items are easy to clean, give special attention to bottles, making sure any caked-on yeast sediment is removed, and the spigot, which has many nooks and crannies, and can easily harbor contaminants. Let your sanitized bottles and equipment drip dry as best as possible.

2. While your equipment is drying, make your priming solution. Add your desired priming sugar addition (usually 4 ounces corn sugar) along with 2 cups water to a saucepan and stir to combine.

3. Bring the solution to a boil to sanitize and boil for 1 minute.

4. After the boil, chill priming solution to room temperature. Once cool to the touch, add priming solution to bottling bucket. (Make sure the spigot is closed.)

5. With a sanitized racking cane, transfer the beer from the fermentor to bottling bucket. You may want to place a sanitized lid or aluminum foil across the top of the bottling bucket to prevent any airborne contaminants from entering your beer.

6. Once the bottling bucket is filled, attach the sanitized bottling wand to the spigot and open it, allowing the beer to flow freely into the bottling wand.

7. Insert the bottling wand into a bottle and depress its tip on the bottom, allowing beer to flow into the bottle. Be careful to avoid foaming and oxygen incorporation. Also, make sure to leave at least an inch of headspace in the neck of the bottle. Most bottling wands will displace enough liquid to leave adequate headspace when removed.

8. Place a bottle cap over the crown of the bottle, use the bottle capper to crimp the bottle cap. Give the crimped cap a little twist with your hand to ensure a good seal.

9. Repeat until all the beer is bottled. It may be more efficient to fill all the bottles first before capping them.

10. Once complete, clean bottling equipment and store bottled beer in a cool, dark place to achieve full carbonation. Keep your newly bottled beer away from light, especially UV light, to avoid skunking.

Kegging Your Homebrew

After a few lengthy bottling sessions, many homebrewers transition to kegs for ease of packaging and tailored carbonation profiles. Unlike bottling, which relies on priming sugar to achieve carbonation, kegs typically rely on high-pressure carbon dioxide, or forced carbonation. Nonetheless, kegging and bottling require many of the same tasks. Chiefly, you'll have to clean and sanitize your kegging equipment before use. This includes cleaning and sanitizing the keg and its parts, such as the fittings, lid, seals, etc. Also, like bottling, you'll want to avoid a splashy siphon to limit oxygen incorporation in your beer. For more information on kegging equipment and forced carbonation, check out Chapter 13.

Kegging Summary

Ingredients and Equipment

Fermented beer

Racking cane (with tubing)

Cornelius keg (with corresponding fittings and disconnects)

CO_2 tank with regulator attachment

Directions

1. Thoroughly clean and sanitize your keg. This requires disassembling its parts, including the lid, its seal, the fittings, and the dip tube.

2. Once clean, reassemble the keg and pressurize to check that it is well sealed before racking beer. Leaky seals may require further tightening, seal lubrication, and/or seal replacement.

3. Vent keg and rack homebrew, taking special care not to incorporate oxygen from air by maintaining a smooth siphon.

4. Re-seal the keg with the lid and blow out the air in the remaining headspace with carbon dioxide to avoid oxidation. Three successive purge and venting cycles should be sufficient to remove the majority of oxygen in the head space.

5. Place the keg in a refrigerating unit such as a kegerator or keezer and slowly chill to serving temperatures.

6. While cooling, add the carbon dioxide "In" disconnect and set the regulator to a pressure corresponding to the desire carbonation level, depending on its temperature. For keg temperature around 40°F, 10 to 12 psi results in 2.4 volumes of carbonation, which is suitable for most ale and lager styles.

7. (Optional) For a quicker turn around, consider using high-pressure carbon dioxide to increase the dissolving rate of carbon dioxide into the beer. As a best practice, limit the use of high pressure gas to a couple of days to avoid over carbonation.

Maturation and Conditioning

Under both packaging methods, it is best to allow for full conditioning to take place before digging in. During this final packaging step, your keg and/or bottles will reach full carbonation, either through priming or forced carbonation. Also, this conditioning period will allow for any brewing debris and yeast kicked up during racking to settle out of suspension and provide the time for flavor development, melding, and mellowing. Give your bottles and kegs at least one week post-packaging for conditioning; however, some styles may require a long aging and maturation phase to hit peak flavor. Lastly, for bottle-conditioned beer, chill at serving temperatures to allow all carbonation generated from the priming to fully dissolve into the beer before serving. Now you'll be ready to have a drink!

Enjoying Your Homebrew

Congratulations on the completion of your first homebrew! Now it's time to sit back, relax, and enjoy a homebrew. Before serving, make sure to grab a clean glass to show off the unique character of your beer. When serving from a bottle, pour steadily, being careful not to disturb the yeast sedimentation at the bottom. Once poured, take a picture and be sure to record your tasting notes. It will be worth the memories, as this beer represents the beginning your journey into homebrewing. For many homebrewers, the hobby, experience, and the people surrounding it can be life changing.

The Least You Need to Know

- Check your brewing ingredients and supplies a day or two before brew day to make sure everything is ready.
- Don't forget to clean and sanitize any equipment that will come in contact with the wort or beer.
- On brew day, boil the wort and pitch the yeast.
- Fermentation takes about two weeks. After fermentation, your homebrew will be ready for packaging in bottles or kegs.

Brewing Ingredients

Beer is made with only four ingredients: malt, hops, yeast, and water. However, within those few ingredients there are many malt and hop varieties, numerous yeast strains, and a range of water compounds, all of which can be combined in innumerable ways to create the flavors and aromas in your favorite beer styles. This part provides in-depth information on the four main ingredients of beer and also explores common additions to beer like sugars, fruit, and spices.

Malt

In the brewing process, malt is the primary source of fermentable sugars. There are over 140 kinds of malts and grains used for brewing, each with a unique set of characteristics that can greatly impact the color, mouthfeel, flavor, and sweetness of the beer. In this chapter, you'll learn the basics of malt, its role in the brewing process, and the types of malts that are used to make your favorite beer styles.

What Is Malt?

Malt is the sprouted and kilned seed of a cereal grass or plant. In brewing, the term *malt* typically refers to malted barley; however, as the malting process is not limited to barley itself, several other grains can be malted, most commonly wheat, but also rye, oats, and even sunflower seeds.

Why use malt instead of raw grains? Good question. Malt looks very similar to a raw grain, and like a raw grain, it contains very few fermentable sugars. However, through the malting process, raw grain is transformed into malt by preparing the kernels with active enzymes, which convert the starch into fermentable sugars when mashed. Raw grain without malting cannot do this on its own.

In This Chapter

- What malt is and how it's made
- The role of malt in the brewing process
- Types and varieties malt

There are other differences as well. Malt is kilned, or dried using heat. *Kilning* lends a variety of flavor characteristics, such as biscuit-y, toasty, and even roasted qualities. Kilning also produces rich colors from straw-yellow to inky-black that raw grains do not possess. Lastly, malted grains are softer than raw grains. If you pop a handful of malted grains in your mouth, you'll be able to chew them without a problem. However, try this with raw grains, and you'll almost certainly chip a tooth.

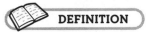 **DEFINITION**

Kilning is the process of drying using heat.

The Parts of Malt

Malted grains, in particular barley, are typically composed of five parts: hull, aleurone, endosperm, acrospire, and rootlets. The outermost layer is the hull or husk. Like skin on animals, it is intended to protect the malt contents from the environment. The next layer is the aleurone, and although quite thin, it's the location of the stored enzymes that are released during the malting process, which are critical to *saccrification*, the starch-to-sugar conversion process. At its center is the endosperm, which is a complex matrix of proteins and carbohydrates. In brewing these are loosely called "starch," and they comprise the majority of the kernel volume. The last parts are the acrospire and rootlets, which are the germinated parts of the malt. If allowed to grow freely, the rootlets and acrospire would form the beginnings of a rooted barley stalk. However, the malting process arrests this stage through kilning to preserve the starches and enzymes.

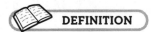 **DEFINITION**

Saccrification is the process by which enzymes break down complex starches into simple sugars. In brewing, this is accomplished in the mash.

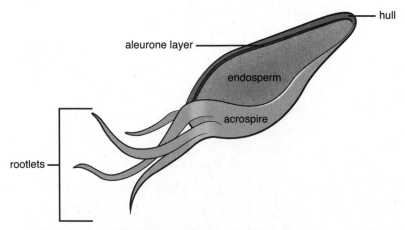

The malt kernel is composed of five parts: hull, aleurone, endosperm, acrospire, and rootlets.

The Malting Process

The malting process is quite a complicated endeavor. Although it's not necessary to understand the process in order to make great beer at home, we'll go over the basic steps of how the malt used for beer is created. *Malting* is the process of converting raw grains, such as barley and wheat, into malt. First, harvested grains are saturated with water until they germinate. This step is called steeping. Thinking it's ready to grow, the barley grain starts producing enzymes to convert its starch reserves into sugar for energy to make the roots and stalk. Small roots, or rootlets, begin to form and the acrospire, essentially a baby stalk, begins to grow.

However, before the sprouted seed can grow too much and deplete its starch reserves, the *maltster*, or person who malts grain, stops the process by kilning the grain. This preserves the stored enzymes and starches, stabilizing the grain for use at a later time, while also introducing additional flavors and color through *Maillard reactions*. Finally, the malt is cleaned and the rootlets are removed. It's now ready to be used in a great batch of beer.

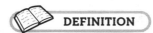 **DEFINITION**

Malting is the process of converting raw grain, such as wheat or barely, into the malt used to brew beer. A **maltster** is the person or manufacturer responsible for malting the grain.

A **Maillard reaction** is a chemical reaction between sugars and amino acids that results in browning in foods, such as bread crust, seared meats, and, of course, malted barley. This provides a wide range color and flavor to malt. The Maillard reaction should not be confused with caramelization, which also produces a browning effect but occurs through a thermochemical reaction with sugar instead.

The Perfect Brewing Grain

The primary brewing grain used in nearly all craft and homebrewed beer is barley. Indeed, if you had to make the perfect brewing grain from the ground up, you would end up with barley. Why barley? Several reasons. Barley has lots of diastatic power, essentially meaning it easily converts starches into sugar through enzymes. It's so good, in fact, that it can convert starches from other unmalted grains like corn and rice. Barley also has hulls that serve two purposes: they are natural filters, making it easy to separate wort from grain matter in mashes; and they protect enzymes and starches from the environment, allowing for long-term shelf stability. For these reasons, barley is the supreme brewing grain.

There are two types of barley used in brewing, two-row and six-row barley, each of which performs differently in the brewing process. Two-row barley is shaped like a bow tie and is the most commonly used barley in craft and homebrewing because it contributes a wide range of brewing characteristics and desirable flavors. There are several dozen varieties of two-row barley, each with its own unique set of characteristics, including protein content, malt flavors, and mouthfeel. Two-row malt can also vary based on malting conditions and growing region, both of which play a significant role in malt character differences.

Six-row barley, which is star-shaped, is less often used by craft and homebrewers. However, it is the mainstay of macrobreweries due to its high enzymatic power, which makes it easy to convert the starches of unmalted *adjuncts*, such as corn and rice, especially when used in large amounts. Six-row barley has more protein and less starch than two-row barley, and lacks the diversity in malt characteristics.

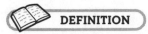 **DEFINITION**

Adjuncts are fermentable brewing ingredients that are unmalted, usually grains such as rice, corn, and oats, but also other fermentables like sugar and syrups.

Brewing Malt: The Foundation of Beer

Beer can be made in a wide range of styles, and while some may be hoppy and others yeasty, all beers have malt and some degree of malt character. Malt plays many roles in beer beyond providing the source of fermentability. It is the main source of color and structure and also adds a great deal of flavor and aroma.

The Fermentables: Malt Types

The primary purpose of malt is to provide the sugars for the yeast to ferment into alcohol. As simple as that sounds, the method for getting malt into wort to make beer is the main dividing line in homebrewing. The process for introducing malt is largely split between two methods: the all-grain brewing method, which requires mashing the base malts, and extract brewing, which uses a preprocessed, concentrated form of malt sugars.

Base malts provide the source of fermentability for all beers and contribute to flavor, mouthfeel, and color. In all-grain brewing, the brewer begins with malted grain, which is then mashed and lautered to extract the fermentable sugars. In extract brewing, the process of extracting the fermentable sugars from malted grain has already been done by a manufacturer. The brewer simply purchases the base malt in a preprocessed extract form, which is either a viscous liquid or a powder.

Specialty malts are intensely flavored malts designed for a range of applications in beer and brewing, and are responsible for the characteristic malt flavors of many beer styles, like amber ales, stouts, and porters. Specialty malts are processed differently than other malted grains, and use a wide variety of additional or alternative malting steps in order to produce rich colors and a wide spectrum of malt characteristics, such as flavor, mouthfeel, and residual sweetness. Importantly, most specialty malts are preconverted, meaning they contain sugars as opposed to unfermentable starches. As such, the extract brewer doesn't need to make a mash to utilize their wonderful qualities in beer.

Malt in all forms contributes varying amounts of sugar to beer, which brewers call "yield." To estimate yield, brewers use the metric *"specific gravity points* per pound per gallon," or ppg for short. When listed, the yield refers to the maximum possible sugars extracted. In malt extracts, since the sugars have been extracted by a manufacturer, you can expect all of these sugars in the beer; however, when using base and specialty malts, yield is variable, depending on the efficiency of the extract. High-yielding malts have maximum extractions in the 37 to 40 ppg range, while low-yielding malts are in the 25 to 30 ppg range. In general, the more highly kilned a malt, the lower the yield. For more information on efficiency, check out Chapters 18 and 21.

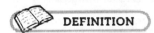 **DEFINITION**

> **Specific gravity** (SG) is the ratio of density of a liquid, in this case, wort or beer, to the density of a reference substance, typically water. The specific gravity of wort is called original gravity (OG), while the specific gravity of beer after fermentation is complete is called final gravity (FG).
>
> **Points** refers to gravity points in the specific gravity scale. For more information on specific gravity, see Chapter 10.

Color

Another characteristic that is nearly exclusive to malt is color, bringing the wide range of beer appearance from straw gold to inky blackness. Malt color is primarily derived from kilning during the malting process and secondarily with further processing, such as stewing or roasting. In general, base malts and malt extract have the lowest color contribution and specialty malts have the highest.

To gauge colors, beer and malt color is often reported in either the Standard Reference Method (SRM) or degrees Lovibond (°L) scale. Although there are slight differences, both scales increase with darkness, meaning the higher the number, the darker the malt or beer color. To give an idea of the scale, a straw-colored German pilsner is likely between 1 and 2 SRM (1–2°L), while an inky-black imperial stout is likely to exceed 40 SRM (30°L). Why the two different scales? While closely related, SRM is more frequently used to describe the overall beer color whereas Lovibond is more often expressed as a specific malt color contribution. Overall, these color scales help the brewer hit the desired color to the beer style brewed.

Malt Character: Flavor and Aroma

Often referred to as "malt character," malt has a wide spectrum of flavors ranging from bready and doughy to caramel, coffee, and chocolate. These flavors are determined by the malt varietal and the malting process, especially the kilning. Lightly kilned malts are analogous to fresh bread, with flavors that are doughy, bready, and grainy. Darkly kilned malts are more analogous to baked bread, with flavors that are toasty, biscuit-y, and nutty. Specialty malts have an even wider range of flavors and complexity due to their high-temperature kilning. They lend flavors from caramel and dried fruit to chocolate and coffee. For more detailed information regarding the spectrum of malt flavors and how to obtain them, check out Chapter 15.

Body, Mouthfeel, and Residual Sweetness

Lastly, malt is a significant contributor to the body, mouthfeel, and residual sweetness in beer. These three beer attributes from malt are often lumped together because they are interdependent. In general, malt proteins, dextrin, and unfermentable sugars contribute to body—how heavy a beer is on the palate—and mouthfeel—how the beer feels on your palate. Sweetness in beer is partially a function of fermentation, but unfermentable malt sugars, especially those found in specialty malts, also lend residual sweetness in the final beer. As a final note, malt protein and dextrin are also partly responsible for head formation and foam stability in a poured beer. For more information on the impact of malt on body, mouthfeel, and sweetness, check out Chapter 16.

Brewing with Malt Extract

If you spend time browsing at your local homebrew shop, you will notice that malt extract comes in a few different forms. Liquid malt extract, or LME, is a thick syrup formed via condensation and typically is sold in cans or drums. If your homebrew shop sells it in sealed bags or plastic jugs, it has likely been repackaged from a large drum. Dried malt extract, or DME, has been further condensed into a dry powdered form, which removes the rest of the moisture left behind in liquid malt extract. In essence, DME is only color, protein, and malt sugars.

Liquid malt extract comes in two varieties: hopped and unhopped. Hopped extract is primarily intended for no-boil quick kits, and contains hop bitterness and sometimes hop flavor. When you use hopped extract, you skip any wort production. A hopped malt extract kit is ideal for brewers looking to turn out a batch quickly.

However, for those looking to make fresh, hoppy beer styles, starting from unhopped extract is best, as it allows you to control the amount of bitterness and intensity of hop flavor and aroma. Brewing with hopped extract takes much of the know-how and fun out of the homebrewing craft, so from this point forward, we'll focus on brewing with unhopped malt extract.

LME is a thick, viscous syrup.

DME is a dry powder.

Liquid Malt Extract vs. Dry Malt Extract

Like most things in brewing, both liquid and dried malt extracts have their advantages and disadvantages. LME is often desirable because it comes in a wide variety of malt types and blends, while DME has a more limited selection. However, because it is more concentrated than LME, DME is has a higher yield and can contribute more sugars than LME. When fresh, LME lends a better malt character to the finished beer, but DME will remain shelf-stable longer than LME, and it is easier to add in small quantities. If your homebrew shop has low turnover of LME, or if you don't anticipate brewing very often, DME is a safer bet.

Malt Extract Varieties

While the fermentability and color of base and specialty malts are usually well-documented, this is not the case with malt extracts. This is largely because malt extracts can be custom made for homebrew shops, with ingredients that are sometimes kept proprietary. In general, liquid malt extracts have maximum fermentability yields near 37 ppg and dry malt extracts near 44 ppg. Colors also vary widely, even among the same style of extract, so it's best to obtain the most accurate documentation of both fermentability and color profile from your homebrew shop.

Ultra-light malt extract (1–3°L) Often the lightest color extract available, ultra-light extracts are made from lightly kilned two-row pale ale or lager malts. Some blends add small percentages of light crystal or dextrin malts to improve mouthfeel or head retention. With its light color, ultra-light extract is best used for beer styles utilizing large percentages of specialty malts like brown ales and porters. Its neutral malt flavor is also perfect for hop-forward beers, like

American-style pale ales and IPAs. It can be found in both liquid and dry forms. The DME version is useful for making yeast starters.

Pilsner malt extract (1–3°L) A subset of the ultra-light extract variety, pilsner malt extract is made entirely from German pilsner malts. Although similar in color, pilsner malt has more malt character than two-row lager malts, lending a more grainy sweetness. Great in German and Belgian-style ales and lagers, it can also make interesting blonde ales or IPAs. It is available in both liquid and dry forms.

Wheat malt extract (1–4°L) Known for its bready, doughy, flour-like character, wheat malt is the heart of wheat beer styles, which are popular among new craft beer drinkers. Wheat malt extracts are a blend of malted wheat and malted barley, because malted wheat is huskless and cannot be mashed on a commercial scale without natural barley hulls for filtration. Wheat malt extract is sold in a variety of blended ratios, such as 50/50, 60/40, and 70/30 wheat/barley blends. Make sure to check your homebrew shop's blend before brewing. Wheat malt extract is great for making American-, German-, and Belgian-style wheat beers. In small amounts, it can also be used to add body or head retention in other beer styles. It is available in both liquid and dry forms.

Munich malt extract (8–11°L) Munich malt is a darkly kilned malt famous for its rich malt and toasted bread character. Munich malt extract is often blended with pilsner malts, since it has lower enzymatic power from its darker kilning. It's sold in a variety of blended ratios, such as a 50/50 Munich/Pilsner blend. Check your homebrew shop's blend before brewing. Munich malt extract is good for making amber and dark German- and Belgian-style ales and lagers. In small amounts, Munich malt extracts are a great way to add color and malt character to beer, especially porters or amber ales. If you must have an all-Munich extract, the maltster Weyermann makes one, although it may be hard to obtain from your local homebrew shop. Munich malt extract is available in liquid form only.

Maris Otter malt extract (4–6°L) A malt extract more recently available to the homebrewer is Maris Otter, an heirloom variety of British malt used in traditional British-style ales. Maris Otter malt extracts feature a richer malt character than two-row pale ale malts, and are known for their toasted biscuit qualities and slightly darker color as a result of higher kilning temperatures. It's a must-have for British-style ales, especially bitters and ESBs. It's also great in American-style brown ales and porters. Available in liquid form only.

Rye malt extract (6–9°L) More recently available to the homebrew market, rye malt extracts have emerged due to the rising popularity of craft rye beers known for their interesting spicy, sometimes pumpernickel-like character, and complimentary pairing with American hops. Like wheat malt extracts, rye malt extracts are made from a blend of rye and barley malts. Rye malt extracts typically contain less than 25 percent of rye due to its intense spicy quality and heavy mouthfeel. Also, blends often contain medium crystal malts to add color and a caramel-like sweetness. Rye malt extract is great for making rye pale ales and rye IPAs without having to add any additional specialty malts. Available in liquid form only.

Amber malt extract (9–12°L) Generic in name, amber malt extracts are barley malt blends intended to deliver more malt character and sweetness than two-row pale malt extracts. Amber malt extracts widely vary, but typically feature a small percentage of crystal or Munich malts for enhanced malt character and sweetness. As a result, these malt extracts are darker in color, typically in the amber to light copper range. Depending on the variety, amber malt extracts are good in American-style amber and brown ales, and are a good foundation for stouts and porters. Due to the variability of blending, be sure to check the specifics from your local homebrew shop. Amber malt extract is available in both liquid and dry forms.

Dark malt extract (13–30°L) Dark malt extracts are barley malt blends intended to deliver complex malt character and sweetness. These blends vary widely in composition, but generally feature small percentages of crystal and roasted malts. As a result, dark malt extracts achieve the darkest color available in malt extracts. More recently, some dark malt extracts have begun to include unmalted grains, such as oats, opening the availability of unmalted flaked grains to the extract brewer without having to make a mash. Dark malt extract is great for stouts and porters, and also good in American and English brown ales. Due to the variability in blending, be sure to check the specifics from your local homebrew shop. It is available in both liquid and dry forms.

Brewing with Base Malts

Dozens of varieties of base malt are available to the homebrewer, each with a wide range of malt characteristics. For simplicity, I've divided base malts into lightly kilned and darkly kilned varieties. Lightly kilned base malts are known for their pale color, high enzymatic power, and relatively neutral flavor. As such, lightly kilned varieties usually comprise the largest percentage of the *grist*—up to 100 percent, unless otherwise noted. Typical usage for lightly kilned varieties falls around the 80 to 90 percent range when other darkly kilned base malts and specialty malts are used.

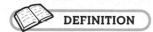 **DEFINITION**

Grist is the brewer's term for the combination of milled grains used in a recipe. Also referred to as the **grain bill**.

Darkly kilned base malts contribute darker colors than lightly kilned varieties and are more intensely flavored. Darkly kilned base malts have some enzymatic power, usually enough to self convert, but are often used in conjugation with lightly kilned malts. Usage of darkly kilned varieties varies widely, with some recipes using as little as 3 to 5 percent while others use up to 100 percent, with typical usage in the 10 to 20 percent range.

To the all-grain or partial-mash brewer, not all base malts are created equal, even among the same varietal type. Depending on a number of factors, especially the maltster and growing region, a malt varietal or style can vary significantly in character, yield, and quality. When sourcing a particular base malt, be sure to record the maltster producing the malt, as you'll find some may be more suited to your recipes than others. Also, as a reminder, base malts must be mashed or mini-mashed (when used with extract). More detailed information on the mash can be found in Part 6.

Lightly Kilned Base Malt Varieties

Two-row pale ale and lager malts (1–2°L) The foundation for most American-style ales and lagers, two-row pale malts are popular among craft brewers and homebrewers alike due to their neutral malt flavor, high enzyme levels, and light color. Lager malts tend to be less kilned than pale ale malts, resulting in less color and malt character. Two-row pale ale malts are perfect for hop-forward beers like pale ales and IPAs and work well with added specialty malts. Also, two-row pale malts are typically the least expensive base malts on the market, so consider picking up a sack or two to last through several batches of homebrew and save some money as well. Maximum yield: 37 ppg.

Six-row malt (1–2°L) Not often used by the homebrewer, six-row malt is the mainstay of macrobreweries due to its high enzymatic power, able to covert large amounts of unmalted adjuncts such as corn and rice. Comparatively, six-row barley has more protein and less starch than its two-row cousin. Homebrewers having difficulty converting malt starches into sugar can try adding a pound of six-row in the mash to help the conversion process. Try in American-style lagers and in historical Americans beers such as preprohibition lager. Maximum yield: 35 ppg.

Maris Otter (1–4°L) An heirloom variety of British malt, Maris Otter features a richer malt character than two-row pale ale malts, and is known for its toasted biscuit qualities and slightly dark color, which are the result of higher kilning temperatures. Maris Otter is a must-have in traditional British-style ales, especially bitters and ESBs, but is also great in American-style brown ales and porters. Maximum yield: 37–38 ppg.

German and Bohemian pilsner malt (1–2°L) Although similar in color to two-row pale lager malts, German and Bohemian (also known as continental) pilsner malts have a surprisingly forward malt character which, lends a grainy, sometimes graham crackerlike malt character and honeylike sweetness. These malts are great in traditional German- and Belgian-style ales and lagers, especially Munich Helles, pilsner styles, and Belgian tripel. They can also add character to blonde ales or IPAs. Use for up to 100 percent of grist. Maximum yield: 38 ppg.

Stout malt (1–3°L) An alternative to six-row malt, stout malts are a high extract, high enzymatic, and low protein two-row malt designed for mashes with high levels of unmalted grains, such as those typically found in stout style. Relatively new to the United States, stout malt is growing in popularity with craft brewers and homebrewers alike for its high-extract, plump kernels and neutral flavor. Try it in a clone for your favorite stout style or in bigger beers where more extract is required. Maximum yield: 38 ppg.

Wheat malt (2–3°L) Known for its bready, doughy, flour-like character, wheat malt is the heart of wheat beer styles, which are popular among new craft beer drinkers. There are white and red wheat malt varieties on the market, and unlike their name suggests, both are pale in color and have subtle differences in malt character. Wheat malt has enough enzymatic power to self-convert, and can be used for up to 100 percent of the grist, although typical usage for wheat beers is in the 30 to 70 percent range, mashed with either two-row pale or pilsner malts. Great for making American-, German-, and Belgian-style wheat beers, especially Hefeweizen and Witbier. In small amounts, wheat malts are also great for adding body or head retention in other beer styles. Maximum yield: 37–40 ppg.

Rye malt (2–4°L) Rye malts are becoming more popular in the homebrewing and craft brewing communities due to the rising popularity of rye beers, which are known for their interesting spicy, sometimes pumpernickel-like character and complimentary pairing with American hops. Rye malts are usually kept below 50 percent of the grist, with typical usage in the 10 to 25 percent range. In large quantities, the intense spicy character and heavy body can lend a cough syrup character. Rye malts are great for making rye pale ales and rye IPAs. Maximum yield: 37 ppg.

Smoked malts (2–5°L) Smoked malts range widely in character, and can lend bonfire or barbecue characters to beer depending on the wood used in the smoking process. The most commonly available type of smoked malt is Rauch malt, which is smoked over beech wood. Rauch malt is used for *Rauchbiers*, German for "smoked beer," from Bamberg, Germany. Usage can range from 5 to 10 percent for subtle smoked flavor up to 100 percent for intensely smoked beers. Maximum yield: 36–37 ppg.

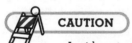 **CAUTION**

Avoid peat-smoked malts! Although great in your favorite Scotch whisky, peak-smoked malts in beer lend a harsh phenolic character instead of a smooth smoked character. Some world-class breweries, such as Stone Brewing, use peat-smoked malt; however, if you're new to smoked malts, it's best to start out with a more common variety, such as Rauch malt, to gain some experience.

Darkly Kilned Base Malt Varieties

Munich malt (6–10°L light, 8–16°L dark) Munich malt is a darkly kilned base malt famous for its rich maltiness and toasted bread character as a result of its darker kilning. Munich malts vary widely among maltsters, and are often sold as different grades based on color, with darker grades having more intense malt character than the lighter grades. Munich malt is great for making amber and dark German- and Belgian-style beers. In small amounts, Munich malt is also a great way to add color and malt character to a variety of other beer styles, especially porter and amber ales. It can be used for up to 100 percent of the grist, with typical usage below 50 percent and small additions in the 5 to 20 percent range. Maximum yield: 34–37 ppg.

Vienna malt (3–6°L) Often considered a lighter version of Munich malt, Vienna malt is known for its a malty, slightly toasted, warm bread character. Also, Vienna malt is not common in extract form, so the extract brewer looking to use this malt should perform a mini mash to yield its character in a beer. It's great in German amber lagers, such as Vienna Lager, and also makes for an interesting replacement for Munich malt in a recipe. It can be used for up to 100 percent of grist. Maximum yield: 35–37 ppg.

Melanoidin/aromatic malts (20–35°L) Often considered an intense Munich, these malts have an intensely rich flavor and very dark kilning. They can be used as a small addition to German- and Belgian-style ales and lagers. Also, these malts can be used for up to 20 percent of grist, with typical usage below 10 percent. Maximum yield: 34–37 ppg.

Victory/biscuit malts (15–25°L) With a toasted biscuit, nutty character, these malt varieties have intense malt flavors and deep amber color. They work well in American- and British-style ales, especially pale, amber, and brown ales. These malts can be used for up to 10 percent of grist; typical usage is below 5 percent. Maximum yield: 34–36 ppg.

Brewing with Specialty Malts

Simply speaking, specialty malts fall between two main categories: either caramel/crystal or roasted. Crystal malts, also known as caramel malts, are made like base malts, but after going through the malting process, they receive further processing. After steeping, crystal malts are stewed and heated, converting the starches into sugars within the husk. They are then kilned at high temperatures, darkening the hull and caramelizing the sugars. It's important to note that, caramelized sugars are unfermentable by yeast, so they add residual sweetness to beer. Also, this process creates wide range of color, body, and flavors from honeylike sweetness to heavy caramel and dark dried fruits. Crystal malts widely vary in color, ranging from the pale 6°L to the very dark 150°L.

Alternatively, roasted malts are highly kilned malts that contribute dark color and lend a host of roasted and dark fruit flavors to beer, most notably coffee and chocolate. Made from either malted or unmalted grains, roasted malts go through a high temperature kilning process much like coffee beans and have many similar qualities. Different levels of roast are available, ranging from lightly roasted just above 150°L to nearly burnt at 600°L. Like color, fermentability and yield also vary widely.

Crystal/Caramel Specialty Malts and Varieties

The use of crystal/caramel malts varies greatly in recipes, depending on the desired outcome. A small amount of crystal malt, about 1 to 3 percent of the grist, can be used for color adjustment, particularly when using the darker versions. In larger quantities, rich colors in the light amber to deep ruby range are added, along with considerable body and caramel-like sweetness.

Overall, typical usage should not exceed 15 percent of the grist to avoid cloying sweetness, although some exceptions can be made for beers with intense bitterness or roastiness, like barleywine, robust porters, and imperial stouts.

Dextrin malt (1–2°L) Processed similarly to crystal malt, dextrin malts achieve long-chained sugars known as *dextrin*, which are unfermentable by brewer's yeast. When added, dextrin malts increase mouthfeel or improve head retention without adding much color or sweetness. They can be used in any style that will benefit, especially where a lasting head is desired. There are many different brands of dextrin malt, such as CaraPils or CaraFoam, but all are effectively the same. Maximum yield: 33–34 ppg.

Light crystal malts (10–30°L) The palest variety available, light crystal malts add residual sweetness with light caramel or honey notes, along with minor color contribution. One pound in a 5-gallon batch will yield a beer color in the pale to medium gold range (4 to 6 SRM). Among the maltsters, British versions tend have toffee and butterscotch notes, while German varieties have lightly toasted character. Great in pale ales and IPAs. Maximum yield: 33–36 ppg.

Medium crystal malts (40–60°L) Medium crystal malts really are the middle of the road. They add residual sweetness with medium caramel character. One pound in a 5-gallon batch will yield a beer color in the deep gold to pale amber range (7 to 9 SRM). Among the maltsters, British versions tend to have toffee notes, while German varieties have toasted, dried fruit character. Great in amber and brown ales. Maximum yield: 33–34 ppg.

Dark crystal malts (70–90°L) The next step up, dark crystal malts add some residual sweetness with strong flavors, typically heavy caramel and dark dried fruit character. One pound in a 5-gallon batch will yield a beer color in the medium amber range (10 to 11 SRM). Among the maltsters, British versions tend to have roasted notes. Great in amber and brown ales as well as stout and porter styles. Maximum yield: 33–34 ppg.

Extra-dark crystal malts (100–150+°L) The darkest of the variety, extra-dark crystal malts add some sweetness with heavy to burnt caramel character, along with intense dark dried fruits. In small percentages, they're useful for color adjustment. However, in larger percentages, one pound in a 5-gallon batch will yield a beer color in the deep amber to light brown range (11–15 SRM). Among the maltsters, British versions tend to have burnt toffee notes, while the Special B variety is in a class of its own with rich toffee and plum/fig notes. Great in dark Belgian strong ales and German-style bocks. Maximum yield: 30–34 ppg.

Roasted Specialty Malts and Varieties

The amount of roasted malt used in a recipe can vary greatly depending on its purpose. In small amounts, 1 to 3 percent of the grist, roasted malt can be used for color adjustment without adding much flavor. For example, just 2 ounces of 525°L roasted malt will add 5.5 SRM of color in a 5-gallon batch of beer, enough to change an amber ale into a brown ale. When used in larger percentages, roasted malts contribute a great deal of color, pushing the beer into inky blackness with strong, intense flavors. Overall, typical usage should not exceed 10 percent of the grist to avoid harsh astringency and acidity, although some exceptions can be made for bigger beers, like imperial stouts.

Roasted barley/black barley (300–600°L) Made somewhat differently than other roasted malts, roasted barley is kilned from unmalted barley grain. Famous for its sharp, coffeelike flavors, this is the characteristic grain in stout styles, especially dry Irish stout. Maximum yield: 29–32 ppg.

Chocolate malt (350–500°L) A very flavorful roasted malt, chocolate malt adds dark chocolate and medium roasted coffee flavors. A must-have in porter styles and great in brown ales. Maximum yield: 28–32 ppg.

Pale chocolate malt (180–250°L) Although similar in name to chocolate malt, pale chocolate is significantly different in flavor. In addition to contributing less color, pale chocolate malt lends a heavily toasted bread character and soft roasted character. Great for small additions in amber ales and Altbier, as well as stouts and porters in larger percentages. Maximum yield: 30-33 ppg.

Black patent malt (500–600°L) Among the darkest of the roasted varieties, black patent malt is quite aggressive in character, with highly roasted, charcoal-like flavors that often compliment other roasted malts. Great in robust porter and stout styles. Maximum yield: 25–30 ppg.

De-bittered black malts (300–570°L) These roasted malts are "de-bittered" by removing the majority of the husks, the source of the bitter edge to other roasted varieties. In small amounts, they're great for color adjustment, adding virtually no flavor. In larger amounts, they lend a smooth chocolate character, great in Schwarzbier and American dark lager. Varieties are branded differently (Blackprinz, de-husked Carafa), but all have the same effect. Maximum yield: 29–33 ppg.

Unmalted Grain and Varieties

In many beer styles, unmalted grains, also referred to as adjuncts, are used and often compose large percentages of the grist. For modern craft brewing and homebrewing, unmalted grains are a great way to replicate historical styles or create greater levels of body and mouthfeel not found in malted grain varieties. Unlike base malts, unmalted grains do not have the enzymes to convert their starches into sugars. Thus, in order to be used for brewing, unmalted grains must be mashed with base malts, preferably high-enzymatic versions, such as six-row barley.

Unmalted grains can impart many desirable qualities to beer. Some are protein rich, adding body, mouthfeel, and head retention, while others provide fermentable sugars without much flavor or body. To avoid having to perform a cereal mash, you can purchase gelatinized versions of unmalted grain that can be thrown straight into the mash. However, if raw cereal grain without any flaked or gelatinization process are desired, then these grain will require a multistep mashing process called *cereal mash* to complete the conversion.

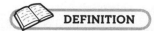 **DEFINITION**

Cereal mash is a multistep mashing process of preparing and gelatinizing starches in unmalted grains to make them accessible to the enzymes in the mash to be later broken down into sugar. See more on cereal mashing in Chapter 17.

How much to use? Amounts and percentages of unmalted grains in beer vary greatly, but typically compose a significant portion of the grist, anywhere from 10 to 30 percent. Unmalted grains typically do not exceed 40 percent of the grist due to enzymatic conversion concerns.

Flaked barley (1–2°L) Fairly neutral in flavor, flaked barley lends a slight grainy note and creamy mouthfeel. It is famously used in dry Irish stout, and also useful for adding body to low-alcohol, session-style beers. Maximum yield: 32 ppg.

Flakes oats (1–3°L) Much like their breakfast siblings, flaked oats are essentially quick oats. Oats are fairly bland and are mostly used to add silky body and mouthfeel to beer. In large proportions, an oily mouthfeel may develop, depending on mash and brewing conditions. For a toasted oatmeal cookie character, you can lightly bake flaked oats in the oven at 350°F for 30 minutes. Flaked oats are essential for oatmeal stouts, but also interesting in English mild ales and porters. Maximum yield: 32 ppg.

Flaked wheat/torrified wheat (1–3°L) Similar to malted wheat in flavor, flaked and torrified wheat adds body and produces starches, which contribute the hazy or cloudy wheat beer appearance. Great in traditional Belgian-style Witbiers or other wheat beer styles. Maximum yield: 36 ppg.

Flaked rice (0–1°L) Rice gets a bad rap from tasteless macrobrew lagers, but it can be a useful addition to increase fermentability without adding flavor or body. Try adding some to enhance digestibility and dryness to an IPA, or replicate your favorite American-style light lager for your noncraft beer friends. Maximum yield: 38 ppg.

Flaked corn/maize (0–1°L) Similar to flaked rice, flaked corn, also known as flaked maize, is another macrobrew adjunct designed to add fermentability without adding much else. In larger proportions, flaked corn can contribute clean, sweet, cornlike characters, which are desirable in some beer styles, such as pre-prohibition lagers and cream ales. Maximum yield: 39 ppg.

How to Store Brewing Malt

Like most ingredients in your kitchen, the overall quality and freshness of brewing malt can be greatly extended with proper storage conditions. When properly stored, malts can last for years without significant loss of quality or freshness.

In general, grain malts, both base malt and specialty malt varieties, should be kept in a sealed, airtight container at room temperature to maintain freshness. Although not required, it's also best to keep grain malts away from light, which can cause staling. If possible, keep all grain malts uncrushed. Uncrushed malts stay fresh longer than crushed malts, because the intact hull protects the starches, prevents them from staling, and maintains enzyme stability. When properly stored, uncrushed base malts can last for a year or more.

Malt extracts, both LME and DME, should both be used fresh, and are best within three months. LME should be kept sealed and refrigerated if use is not immediate. Any unused portion of LME should always be refrigerated and used as quickly as possible to avoid oxidation or spoilage. DME can be stored like grain malts, and is best stored in low humidity. Unused portions can be sealed in an airtight container and kept in a dry environment. Opened DME does not have to be used as quickly as opened LME, but sooner is better.

Malt Extract vs. Base Malt

In principle, the wort and beer made from malt extract is no different than the wort made from base malts. However, there are some finer points that make an overall difference. Using malt extracts has many potential upsides. Malt extracts are easier to use, allowing the brewer to better understand other aspects of the brewing process like fermentation and packaging before diving into all-grain brewing. Also, the extract brewer doesn't need to worry about converting starches into sugar using a mash, a more complex process, which can yield poor results when done improperly.

Alternatively, brewing with base malts has its own set of advantages. All-grain brewers have a greater control over the fermentability and color of the wort than extract brewers, because those qualities are fixed by the malt extract manufacturer. Also, when making wort from scratch, you are obtaining the freshest extraction available. Lastly, a minor point, malt extracts have difficultly achieving the lightest beer colors in the 1 to 2 SRM range due to darkening from the condensing process and partial boils. Wort darkening is not so much a problem for the pale ale, IPA, or stout brewer, but the German pilsner nut may lament these cosmetic difficulties.

The question of which technique is better, all-grain or extract brewing, is a loaded one. The truth is, when using fresh malts—either base malt or malt extract—and engaging in adequate brewing and fermentation practices, you can produce high-quality beers with either method. In fact, any brewer worth his or her salt is capable of making a great beer in any style using either base malts or malt extracts, which is why both brewing methods consistently win at the regional and national level in homebrewing competitions. That being said, some styles are more easily adapted to all-grain brewing than extract due to the customizability of mashes versus the fixed fermentability and color of extracts. In the great scheme of the brewing process, having dialed-in fermentation, clean brewing water, and sanitized brewing equipment are just as important as the source of your fermentables.

The Least You Need to Know

- Malt provides enzymes and starches, which, when mashed, are the source of fermentable sugars in beer.
- Many characteristics of beer, including flavor, body, mouthfeel, and color are derived from malt.
- Malt can be used in several forms, including malt extract, base malts, and specialty malts.
- There are many different types of malt available to the homebrewer, each contributing unique character and complexity.

Hops

Bitter, flavorful, and highly aromatic, hops are the yin to malt's yang. When playing a supporting role, hops can balance out malt sweetness, while other times provide intense bittering and aroma to give beer that characteristic punch in the face. In this chapter, you'll learn all about hops, their role in the brewing process, and the varieties that make your favorite hoppy beer styles.

In This Chapter

- The hop plant and how it's grown
- How hops are used in the brewing process
- The common varieties of brewing hops

The Hop Plant, *Humulus lupulus*

Humulus lupulus may sound like a spell from a wizarding text, but it is the scientific name for the hop plant. Botanically speaking, the hop plant is related to the *Cannabaceae* family, well known for its witch's brew of chemical complexity. More loosely referred to as "hops," the hop plant grows in vinelike structures known as bines, and can grow quite tall. When trellised, hops generally grow between 18 and 25 feet, but they can grow as high 40 feet, depending on the variety. There are also dwarf hop varieties, which only reach 10 to 15 feet in height.

Like most plants, hops have a preferred growing region. This area typically falls between the 35° and 50° latitude lines, with exceptional growing conditions between the 45° and 50° parallels. This region is particularly well-suited for growing hops due to cold winters and long summertime daylight hours. The soil and local climate conditions of various hop-growing regions lend unique flavor profiles to individual hop varieties.

Major hop growing regions include the United States, Germany, and the Czech Republic, with smaller growing nations including Britain, Slovenia, Poland, Australia, and New Zealand. It should be no surprise that the major hop growing regions are also major beer drinking nations, with deep roots in the brewing tradition.

Hop Cones

The female flower of the hop plant, known as the hop cone, or just hops, is the part of the hop plant that is used in beer. It creates a distinctive bitterness and also contributes a complex flavor and aroma. Hop cones look like miniature pinecones, with interwoven leaves called *bracteoles* that are attached to a core axis. Deep inside the cone center are *Lupulin* glands, which contain a yellow sticky powder made up of resins and essential oils, the source of the hop complexity in beer.

Hops are the pinecone-shaped flower of the hop plant.

Hop Resins and Oils

If you look more closely at the yellow powdery goodness of the *Lupulin* gland, you'll find a chemically complex cocktail of resins and essential oils. Among the plethora of compounds, a few are key and make up the core of hop character in beer: alpha acids, beta acids, and essential hop oils.

Alpha acids are the part of the hop resin that generates the bitterness in beer. Among the alpha acids are three main types: humulone, cohumulone, and adhumulone. Each of these three alpha acids are thought to provide different bittering characteristics. Some brewers experience a cleaner bitterness with high humulone hops and a more biting, aggressive hop bitterness with high cohumulone hops. Although this is somewhat up for debate, brewers will often look at the humulone-to-cohumulone ratio to determine the bitterness quality in the beer style to be brewed. Not much is known about the bittering quality of adhumulone due to its low concentration in hops. For more information on humulone in your hops, check out the hop compound analysis at hopunion.com.

The total alpha acid content varies greatly in hop varieties. Low alpha acid varieties have between 2 and 5 percent alpha acid content and are primarily used for flavor and aromas due to their low bitterness potential. At the other end of the spectrum, high alpha acid varieties can exceed 20 percent alpha acid content, making for efficient bittering in beer.

Hop Alpha Acid (AA) Ranges

Low AA	2–5%
Average AA	6–9%
High AA	10–14%
Ultra-High AA	15+%

Beta acids are also part of the hop resin, but unlike alpha acids, they do not contribute significantly toward bittering in beer because they do not easily dissolve in water. However, oxidized beta acids (beta acids that have deteriorated from age and air exposure) are very bitter, but the bitterness is generally undesirable. Some brewers report that high beta acid varieties have an increased aroma potential in beer, especially through dry hopping; however, at present, beta acids are thought to have little impact on the overall flavor of beer.

The essential hop oils are responsible for the highly desired flavors and aromatic qualities of hops. Due to their volatile nature, hop flavor and aroma are typically introduced late in the brewing process. Essential hop oils comprise less than 4 percent of hop content, but they are incredibly diverse, with hundreds of oils indentified. Among them, four types are commonly referenced in brewing: humulene, myrcene, caryophyllene, and farensene. Caryophyllene and humulene are highly volatile and thought to contribute to the spicy, earthy, and herbal hop character in German-style ales and lagers. Myrcene is thought to contribute to the citrus, fruity quality of American hop varieties, especially Cascade and Centennial. Lastly, farensene is thought to have little impact other than lending a light floral component to the hop aroma.

Brewing with Hops

Hops are used throughout the brewing process, and while they are primarily used for bittering, they also contribute flavor and aromas, and they help with preservation and stability. This section covers the basic roles of hops in brewing. If you're seeking information about adding hops to wort, check out Chapter 11.

Bringing the Bitterness to Beer

The primary role of hops in beer is to provide bitterness, which contrasts with the residual malt sweetness. The intensity of hop bitterness ranges greatly in beer styles. In malty styles, like blonde ales and Munich-style Helles, the hop bitterness is very low, just enough to prevent the malt sweetness from becoming cloying and to enhance overall drinkability. However, in hop-forward styles like American-style IPAs and German pilsners, bitterness is king and malt provides balance to avoid harshness or astringency. As previously discussed, alpha acids are the source of bitterness in beer; however, alpha acids are not bitter on their own, but need to be *isomerized* to yield the bitterness. The most common method for alpha acid isomerization used by the homebrewer is boiling hops in wort.

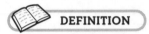 **DEFINITION**

Isomerization is a process of chemically changing one molecule into another without the loss or gain of atoms from the original molecule. In hops, alpha acids are isomerized to form iso-alpha acids, which provide the bitterness in beer.

While simple in theory, the total amount of hop bitterness through isomerization depends upon several variables, which are further discussed in Chapter 11.

Lastly, as a gauge in comparing bittering levels, brewing scientists have quantified beer bitterness through the International Bittering Units scale, or IBU. Using spectrometer methods, the isomerized alpha acid content in a beer can be measured, giving both the brewer and drinker an idea of bitterness of a beer. Homebrewers rarely measure bitterness, and instead rely on simple models to predict hop bitterness based on wort variables such as alpha acid content, boil gravity, and duration of boil.

Type	IBU Ranges	Styles
Low IBU	5–20	blonde ales, malty lagers, Scottish ales
Average IBU	25–45	pale, amber, and brown ales; stouts; bitters
High IBU	50–75	IPA styles, imperial ales
Ultrahigh IBU	80–100+	double IPAs, barleywine

Flavor and Aroma

In addition to bitterness, hops can lend a wide spectrum of flavors and aromas to beer, which vary depending on the hop variety as well as the region where the hops were grown. Overall hop flavor and aroma characters fall mainly into the following categories: citrus, floral, grassy, herbal, and piney. For specific hop varietal flavors and aromas, check out the hop variety section at the end of this chapter.

In the brewing process, flavor and aroma hops are added late in the boil to retain volatile essential hop oils. Because flavor and aroma can dissipate after a vigorous fermentation, brewers can also utilize dry hopping, a technique of adding hops back into beer after fermentation for extra character or preservation. For more on hop-derived flavor and aroma, check out Chapter 15.

Preserving Beer

While hops bring notable flavor characteristics to beer, its original purpose in brewing was preservation. Our ancestors originally made beer with other herbs and spices, and while some of those worked well, nothing worked as well as hops. More specifically, the bittering agent alpha acids and iso-alpha acids are very effective at preventing the growth of bacteria, especially *Lactobacillus*, a beer contaminant that can turn beer sour. However, hops are not effective against wild yeasts, which is why brewers must practice great cleaning and sanitization.

Head Retention

Head retention is partly a cosmetic issue, but it is often desired for appearance by the home-brewer. Malt contributes head retention and foam stability through high protein adjuncts and long-chain dextrin; however, these agents also add considerable body, which may not be desirable in hoppy beer styles. Alternatively, hop resins, specifically isomerized humulones, also have head retention properties, especially when used in large quantities. This is very useful for the brewer making lower bodied, drier beer style, like double IPAs and Belgian strong ales.

Hop Packaging

After many months of growth, toward the end of summer, the hop bines are cut down and the hop cones are removed. Historically, hop cones were harvested by hand; however, modern techniques utilize shakers and rakes for effective removal. Once harvested, hop farmers have a race against the clock to keep all of those delicate, volatile hops compounds from off-gassing and oxidation. In preservation, harvested cones are dried to remove moisture and then packed in nitrogen or sealed air-tight to increase the hop longevity. Most hops aren't kept in the whole cones form and are further processed to maximize longevity. As such, there are many hops packaging types, each with their own set of brewing advantages.

Whole Hops

The traditional form of hops, whole hops are the end result of the drying and preservation steps. Whole hops resemble either the original cone flower or leaves, and require the least amount of processing from bine to beer. Newer hop packaging forms, such as pellets, can be kept fresh for longer periods of time, but many brewers still swear by whole hops, affirming them for superior flavor and aroma and smooth bittering.

Pellet Hops

A fairly recent development in brewing ingredient technology, pellet hops are the reduced and compressed form of whole hops. After whole hops are dried, the flower is shredded and pelletized, essentially forming little pencil eraser-size bits that look like rabbit food. Craft brewers have been moving toward pelletized hops slowly but surely due to their long shelf life and hop stability. For example, some hop varieties lose only 10 to 20 percent of the alpha acid content over a year when pelletized. Also, due to the shredding process, pellet hops lend 10 to 15 percent more bitterness than whole and plug hop varieties.

Plug Hops

Developed by cask brewers, plug hops were originally made as an easy way to add dry hop casks. Plug hops are essentially whole hops that have been loosely cut and compacted into disklike tablets, typically in half-ounce weights. Less popular and increasingly harder to find on the homebrew scene, hop plugs are still a great form for all hop usages, especially dry hopping in the *cask* or keg.

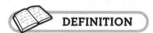

DEFINITION

A **cask** is a traditional form of beer packaging similar to a keg, but it is conditioned and carbonated using natural secondary fermentation. Also, casked beer is served unfiltered and gravity fed, without added carbon dioxide or nitrogen. Cask-conditioned beers are popular in Britain, where they are referred to as "real ale."

Hop Extract

Hop extract is a concentrated form of the compounds and essential oils of the hop cone. Hop extracts were developed for several reasons, including better hop utilization and increased wort yield due to hop matter absorption. Original formulations were harsh and unpleasant, giving hop extract a bad reputation. However, new extraction methods using liquid carbon dioxide have eliminated many of these unpleasant characteristics, and as a result, hop extracts are growing in popularity within craft and homebrewing communities.

Homebrew-scale hop extracts come in syringes, and are tarry and resinous in appearance. They can be added to the boil in place of whole or pelletized hop additions, although they are best as a bittering addition replacement. Also, hop extracts are not necessarily a one-to-one match in terms of IBU levels, so you may need to make small adjustments when using them in recipes for which you've previously used whole or pelletized hops. Overall, hop extracts are a great way to add loads of bitterness to hop-forward styles like IPAs without clogging your system with hop matter.

Wet Hops

Wet hops, as known as fresh hops, are essentially hops straight off the bine, which provide fresh and raw hop flavors when added to beer. Since they are left unpreserved, they retain their considerable moisture content. If you happen to have wet hops, either through a farmer's market or your own backyard hop garden, the rule of thumb is that you'll need six times the amount of wet hops by weight to get the equivalent intensity of dried hops. When brewing, due to the large amount of vegetation, wet hopped wort loss is increased, so plan to make a slightly larger batch if 5 gallons are desired.

Hops Storage

Hops are best stored in cold, dry places away from light, such as a freezer. Storing hops packed in nitrogen or sealed air-tight will also significantly increase longevity. Under well-packed, cold storage conditions, hops can last a few years with minimum loss to bittering potential and aromatic qualities.

It is worth mentioning that not all hop varieties store well. For example, the American hops Cluster and Galena are known for their excellent storage capacity, whereas the American hops Cascade and Columbus have a very poor storage lifetime. More recent hop breeding programs have been focused on hop longevity, so if long-term storage is something you're interested in, check out the hops supplier for more information. In general, if you source fresh hops, both you and your beer will be happy.

Whenever you brew, it's best to smell your hops before adding them to the boil or dry hopping. A cheeselike aroma is an indication that hop oils have oxidized, and the hops should be discarded. Also, some hop varieties that are aged or harvested late can produce aromas similar to onions, garlic, or cat pee. It's worth smelling before adding, as this gives you an opportunity to change hops and avoid a ruined batch. Always keep back-up hops on hand.

Hop Varieties

As enthusiasm for craft beer and homebrewing has grown, the selection of hops available to purchase has increased dramatically. There are now over 100 different hop varieties on the market, each with their own unique set of flavor and bittering characteristics. With new hop strains coming out every year, it's difficult to discuss all the currently available varieties. However, this section will cover the most well-known and popular hop varieties being used by craft brewers and homebrewers alike.

Hop varietals are sorted into three categories: bittering, flavor/aroma, and dual purpose. Bittering hop varieties are intended to be used solely to add hop bitterness to a beer, and are boiled at least an hour to drive off the flavor and aroma characteristics. Flavor/aroma hops are intended to add either flavor or aroma to a beer, and are also a good choice for dry hopping as well. Lastly, dual purpose hops have high bitterness potential as well as a pleasant flavor and aroma, and are intended to be used for both bittering and flavor/aroma. Traditionally, the distinction between bittering and flavor/aroma varieties was strictly observed; however, with the increased interest and enthusiasm for hops and the breeding of higher alpha acid varieties, most hops today are considered dual-purpose.

American Hops

The most dynamic growing region in the market, American hops have greatly expanded over the past few decades, due in large part to the U.S. craft beer movement. American hops are most notably grown in the Pacific Northwest, and host a wide range of characters, particularly intense, in-your-face flavor and bittering that ranges from fruit and citrus to pine and resin. Due to the prevalence of German-inspired macrobreweries in the United States, American hops also feature many traditional German hop varieties. Some are close copies, but should be appreciated for their own unique characteristics.

Amarillo A fairly new and popular hop, Amarillo is a very fruity, citrus-forward variety, known for its orange, grapefruit, and stone fruit qualities. Try it in American pales ales or IPAs; also great in American brown ales and black IPAs.

Alpha acids: 8 to 11 percent   Usage: dual purpose

Cascade Now one of the most ubiquitous U.S. hop varieties, Cascade was celebrated as a unique American hop during the emerging years of craft beer in the United States. Known for its citrus-grapefruit and floral qualities, Cascade is the quintessential American pale ale hop, great in any American-style ales.

Alpha acids: 5 to 8 percent   Usage: flavor/aroma

Centennial Sometimes referred to as "Super Cascade," Centennial is known for its amped-up citrus and floral qualities, but also great as a clean bittering hop. It pairs well with CTZ variety hops and is very good in American-style ales, especially IPAs.

Alpha acids: 9 to 12 percent   Usage: dual purpose

Chinook A divisive hop variety, brewers either love it or hate it due to its biting bitterness and high cohumulone levels. Originally a bittering variety, Chinook is becoming popular for flavor and aroma with a resinous, spicy, piney quality. It's great in American-style ales, especially IPAs.

Alpha acids: 12 to 15 percent   Usage: dual purpose

Citra An incredibly popular hop among brewers and hop aficionados, Citra is famous for its spectrum of fruit character, ranging from tropical fruit to strong citrus. Great in American-style ales, especially IPAs.

Alpha acids: 11 to 13 percent   Usage: flavor/aroma

Columbus/Tomahawk/Zeus Called CTZ for short, these hop varieties are grouped together due to their close similarity in character. Complex, dank, and pungent, with notes of black pepper and citrus, CTZ is great in American-style ales, especially IPAs. Be cautious though, as late-harvested versions may have an onion or garlic quality. Thus, be sure to smell CTZ before adding to wort or beer.

Alpha acids: 13 to 17 percent   Usage: dual purpose

Liberty Originality bred as a domestic version of Hallertau Mittelfrüh, Liberty has many similarities to its German cousin. It has a mild, clean, and spicy character, with notes of lemon and citrus. Try in both German- and American-style lagers.

Alpha acids: 3 to 5 percent   Usage: flavor/aroma

Northern Brewer A fairly rustic hop, Northern Brewer is known for its woody, piney, and sometimes minty quality. Actually produced throughout the international hop growing regions, Northern Brewer is included in this section because it's the quintessential hop in California common-style beers. Also, it's a very good option for bittering in German-style lagers.

Alpha acids: 6 to 10 percent   Usage: dual purpose

Palisade A relatively new variety, Palisade is an aromatic hop known for its stone fruit, floral, and grassy characteristics. Great in both American- and British-style ales, especially English bitters.

Alpha acids: 5 to 10 percent   Usage: dual purpose

Simcoe Arguably the quintessential American-style IPA hop, Simcoe is a dual-purpose hop known for its strong bittering qualities and unique aroma. With pungent characters of fresh pine and citrus, Simcoe is great in American-style ales, especially double IPAs. Depending on the harvest or storage conditions, Simcoe can sometimes have a "catty" character.

Alpha acids: 12 to 14 percent   Usage: dual purpose

Sterling A U.S.-bred hop with relations to Cascade, Saaz, and Brewer's Gold, Sterling has a wide range of characteristics including herbal, spicy, floral, and even light citrus. Sterling works well in a multitude of styles, including German-style lagers and Belgian-style ales.

Alpha acids: 6 to 9 percent   Usage: dual purpose

Willamette A hop with English Fuggle heritage, Willamette is similar in quality, with a mild spicy, floral character. Great in any American- or British-style ales.

Alpha acids: 4 to 6 percent   Usage: flavor/aroma

British Hops

Although part of the European geography, British hops have a marked difference from their continental relatives. British hops are known for their distinctively fruity, herbal, and earthy qualities and are grown primarily in southern England, where the climate is well suited to hop cultivation. When fresh, British hops are second to none, and a must-have in any British-style ale, especially bitters, ESBs, and English IPAs. Also, be sure to include a few plugs when making a cask-conditioned ale.

Challenger A great all-around British hop variety, Challenger is known for its clean bitterness as well as a pleasant spicy character, with notes of fruit and pine. Great in more hop-forward British-style ales, especially ESBs and English IPAs, and also an interesting choice for an American-style IPA.

Alpha acids: 6 to 9 percent   Usage: dual purpose

East Kent Goldings Herbal, earthy, floral, and lightly fruity, East Kent Goldings, more loosely known as Goldings, are arguably the quintessential British hop variety. Great in British-style ales, especially ESBs, English browns, and porters.

Alpha acids: 4 to 7 percent   Usage: dual purpose

Fuggle A traditional British hop variety, Fuggle was the workhorse of British brewing in the mid-twentieth century. Earthy, grassy, and spicy in quality, Fuggle is great for aroma additions and dry hopping in British-style ales, especially bitters and ESBs.

Alpha acids: 3 to 6 percent   Usage: flavor/aroma

Northdown Related to Northern Brewer, Northdown is a versatile hop with great aroma and clean bitterness. With spicy, woody, and fresh pine character, Northdown is a good choice for British-style ales, especially ESBs and English IPAs.

Alpha acids: 7 to 10 percent   Usage: dual purpose

Progress Intended as a Fuggle replacement, Progress is known for its intense fruity, herbal, and spicy character. Great in British-style ales, especially when casked.

Alpha acids: 5 to 8 percent   Usage: dual purpose

Target Related to several British hop varieties, Target emerged as a great bittering hop in the late-twentieth century. Known for its clean bitterness as well as unique aroma of sage and citrus, Target can be used for bittering in British- and Belgian-style ales, and also makes for an interesting pale ale or IPA.

Alpha acids: 8 to 13 percent   Usage: bittering

German and Czech Hops

The German and Czech Republic regions of Europe are famous for their clean, spicy, herbal hops that are collectively known as the "noble" hops. These two regions are the top two international hop growers, and the quality of their hops reflects that status. Traditional hop varieties feature low alpha acids, sometimes below 2 percent, which are used solely for flavor and aroma, while modern breeding programs look to create ultra-high alpha acid varieties pushing the 20 percent range. American hop growers have replicated many German and Czech varieties that are very good in their own right, but for the German and Czech lager connoisseur, it's best to stick with the originals.

Hallertau Hersbrucker A German noble hop known for its mild herbal, slightly spicy, and earthy character. Great in German-style lagers, especially German pilsners.

Alpha acids: 2 to 5 percent   Usage: flavor/aroma

Hallertau Mittelfrüh Like Hersbrucker, Mittelfrüh is a German noble hop with herbal and spicy character that has hints of lemony citrus. It's good in German-style lagers, especially German pilsners.

Alpha acids: 3 to 6 percent   Usage: flavor/aroma

Magnum A high alpha acid hop, Magnum is known for its clean, neutral, and slightly earthy bittering quality. It's also grown in the United States. Magnum is a personal favorite and my go-to bittering variety.

Alpha acids: 11 to 16 percent   Usage: bittering

Perle Related to Northern Brewer, Perle is similar in quality with a mild, minty, spicy character. Great in German-style lagers, also good as a bittering hop. Perle is also grown in the United States.

Alpha acids: 4 to 9 percent   Usage: dual purpose

Saaz Known for its delicate, spicy, herbal quality, Saaz is the quintessential hop in Bohemian and Czech Pilsners. It is also grown in the United States.

Alpha acids: 2 to 6 percent   Usage: dual purpose

Spalt A rustic hop that is traditionally used in Altbier, Spalt has a pleasant spicy, floral quality. Use in any German-style ale or lager.

Alpha acids: 3 to 6 percent   sage: flavor/aroma

Tettnang Related to Saaz, Tettnang is a very spicy, noble variety. Try it in German-style ales and lagers, especially Altbier.

Alpha acids: 3 to 6 percent   Usage: flavor/aroma

Australian and New Zealand Hops

Although a small growing region by total acreage, both the Australian and New Zealand hop varieties are becoming more common in the U.S. craft beer and homebrewing scene. Australian and New Zealand hops feature very unique, complexly fruity hops, and often have tropical and lime oil qualities that pair well with American hop varieties and work great in Australian-style and American-style ales, such as IPAs.

Galaxy An intense Australian variety, Galaxy hops are in-your-face fruity, with passion fruit, citrus, and stone fruit qualities. Although Galaxy has bittering potential, it is mainly used for late and dry hopping to preserve its interesting character. Try in Australian-style ales and American IPAs.

Alpha acids: 13 to 15 percent   Usage: dual purpose

Nelson Sauvin A unique hop variety with characteristics similar to the Sauvignon Blanc wine after which it's named. Fruity and white grapelike, with notes of tropical fruit, this variety makes for an interesting pale ale or IPA.

Alpha acids: 12 to 15 percent   Usage: dual purpose

Pacific Gem A hop variety from New Zealand, Pacific Gem is known for its clean bittering and neutral aroma, with subtle notes of blackberry and oak. Pacific Gem is great for general bittering purposes and mostly used in lager styles.

Alpha acids: 14 to 16 percent   Usage: bittering

Pride of Ringwood A traditional Australian hop variety used primarily for bittering, Pride of Ringwood features herbal and fruit characteristics and is berry and citruslike in quality. Use in Australian-style lagers or sparkling ales.

Alpha acids: 7 to 11 percent   Usage: bittering

Riwaka A Saaz-related hop variety from New Zealand, Riwaka has a fresh pine and tropical fruit character. Use as a Simcoe replacement in your favorite American-style IPA recipe.

Alpha acids: 4 to 7 percent   Usage: flavor/aroma

The Least You Need to Know

- Hops give beer its characteristic bitterness and also contribute fruity, herbal, spicy, and earthy flavors and aromas.
- Hop oils are the source of the hops' unique aromatic qualities, and the alpha acids in hop resins are the primary agent in bitterness formation.
- There are several dozen hop varieties, each of which contributes unique qualities to beer.
- Hop-producing countries include the United States (particularly the Pacific Northwest), England, Germany, the Czech Republic, Australia, and New Zealand.

Yeast

Brewer's yeast is the beloved critter that turns the sugar from wort into the alcoholic beverage we call beer. While fermentation is yeast's primary role, it also adds character through the production of secondary chemical compounds such as esters and phenols. In this chapter, we'll cover the basics on yeast, its impact on the brewing process, and common varieties available to the homebrewer.

What Is Brewer's Yeast?

Yeast, also known as *lees*, is a single-cell organism that is part of the fungus kingdom, home to mushrooms and mold. Although there are over 1,500 identified species of yeast, only two are responsible for beer: ale yeast, *Saccharomyces cerevisiae*, and lager yeast, *Saccharomyces pastorianus*. These two species are loosely called "brewer's yeast" because of their ability to ferment malt sugars into alcohol.

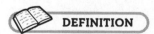

DEFINITION

Lees is an alternative name for yeast. It is most commonly used to refer to yeast sediment.

Ale Yeast: *Saccharomyces cerevisiae*

Ale yeast, known scientifically as *Saccharomyces cerevisiae*, is the species of yeast used in the fermentation of traditional ale styles. You are likely already familiar with the powers of ale yeast, as it's the same yeast species used in bread and yeast-leavened baked goods; baker's and brewer's yeast are one in the same.

In fermentation, ale yeast generally prefers warm temperatures, around 68°F, but can range widely from 55°F to 70°F or higher depending on the yeast strain. Also, because ale yeast likes to hang out at the top of beer during fermentation, it is known as a top-fermenting yeast. Stylistically, ale yeast can vary widely in character and performance. Some ale yeast yields a clean and refined, almost lagerlike beer, while others create beer that is complex, fruity, and intense. The diversity of ale yeasts has resulted in a range of ale styles, from fruity British real ales and Belgian Abbey ales to the very popular clean-fermented American craft ales.

Lager Yeast: *Saccharomyces pastorianus*

Lager yeast, known scientifically as *Saccharomyces pastorianus*, is relatively new to the brewing scene. It was first observed in the fourteenth century, but was not isolated until the nineteenth century. Lager yeast ferments at cold temperatures, doing well from 48°F to 58°F, and likes to hang out at the bottom of the fermentation vessel. For this reason, it is known as bottom-fermenting yeast. Most lager yeast has very clean fermentation with refined malt and hop character. Today, lager yeast is responsible for most macro-brewed beer. This sometimes gives lager yeast a poor reputation, but it can actually be very characterful, creating rich and refined lager styles like Munich Dunkel and the popular Oktoberfest.

Ale Yeast vs. Lager Yeast

Other than the fact that ale and lager are two different species of yeast, there are some general distinctions between them that result in key differences in the brewing process. One primary difference between ale and lager yeast is fermentation temperature. In the brewing process, ale yeasts are fermented at warmer temperatures (near room temperature), while lager yeasts are fermented at colder temperatures (48°F–58°F). Lager yeast is able to ferment at warmer temperatures, but it is generally avoided because it causes increased fruity *ester* production, which is unwanted in lager styles. On the other hand, ale yeasts have difficulty fermenting at lager temperatures; if ale yeasts become too cold they ferment poorly or fall into dormancy.

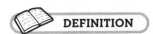 **DEFINITION**

Ester is a fermentation by-product that is often responsible for fruity flavors in beer, such as banana, pear, and cherry.

As a result of these temperature differences, ale yeast typically ferments faster than lager yeast, which means that ales mature more quickly than lagers. Many ale styles, like American-style wheat beers and IPAs, are designed to be enjoyed fresh, whereas lager styles like Bohemian pilsner and Oktoberfest benefit from a few weeks or even months of cold conditioning.

Another key difference is that ale yeast tends to ferment at the top of the wort, while lager yeast ferments at the bottom of the fermentation vessel. Although this holds true for most ale and lager yeast strains, this difference is not absolute. Lastly, given the same wort, ale yeast tends to create a fruitier, more complex beer with an aggressive malt and hop character, while lager yeast tends to produce cleaner, more refined beer with a softer malt and hop character.

Hybrid Yeast

You may see "hybrid yeast" available at your homebrew store. This is not a separate species from either ale or lager yeast, but is merely a brewing term used to refer to an ale yeast that ferments well at a lager temperature, or a lager yeast that ferments cleanly at an ale temperature. Essentially, hybrid yeasts are the exception to the rule. As such, these hybrid yeasts have a mix of ale and lager characteristics. They are typically cleaner than ale yeasts, yet fruiter than lager yeasts. Beer styles that feature these hybrid yeast strains include German Altbier and Kölsch, and California common beer.

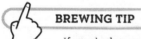

BREWING TIP

If you lack temperature control for proper lager fermentation, you can use hybrid yeast strains to ferment lagerlike beers at ale temperatures. A common homebrew example is the "ale-toberfest," an Oktoberfest-style lager recipe fermented with a clean hybrid strain, such as a Kölsch or Altbier ale strain or sometimes the California common lager strain.

Yeast Character and Performance

Although yeasts fall into more or less three main categories, each yeast has its own unique flavor and aroma characteristics and corresponding set of fermentation performance attributes that are key to the brewing process, and ultimately contribute to the creation of unique beer styles. The following is a list of the typical yeast strain metrics and how they influence fermentation.

Attenuation

Attenuation is the degree to which yeast is able to convert sugars into alcohol at the end of fermentation. Unlike wine and cider yeasts, brewer's yeast does not convert all of the fermentable sugars into alcohol. It leaves some behind, which is often the source of residual sweetness in beer. Attenuation is typically listed by the yeast manufacturer as a percentage based on a standardized wort and fermentation profile. For example, starting with an original gravity of 1.048, a yeast with 75 percent attenuation will leave a final gravity at 1.012, with the yeast converting 36 points into alcohol.

On a practical level, the attenuation percentage gives the brewer a way to estimate alcohol production, finishing gravity, body, and residual sweetness before brewing. In general, highly attenuative yeasts produce drier, less sweet beer than lower ones. For drier beer or bigger beer styles, high attenuating strains are desired, while for malty, sweeter styles, a less attenuating strain is preferred.

Attenuation percentages are not intended as an absolute number, but more as a relative figure to compare the attenuation capacity of yeast strains. The actual attenuation percentage of any given batch of beer is largely dependent on wort composition and fermentation variables. A brewer can achieve higher or lower levels of attenuation by utilizing wort production techniques in conjunction with fermentation profiles.

Attenuation Ranges

Type	Attenuation
Low	67–71%
Average	72–75%
High	76–80+%

Flocculation

Flocculation is the ability of a yeast to clump up and settle to the bottom of a fermentor at the end of the fermentation process. Yeast flocculation ranges from very low (slow to flocculate) to very high (quick to flocculate). Highly flocculent yeasts clump up readily and fall out of suspension almost immediately after fermentation is complete. These highly flocculent clumps are very large and look a little like cottage cheese.

Highly flocculent yeast is useful for creating a clear beer without the need for secondary conditioning or filtering stages to remove suspended yeast. Also, highly flocculent yeast tends to have lower attenuation, making it a good choice for maltier beer styles. However, the downside to high flocculence is that fermentation tends to have higher residual fermentation by-products, such as diacetyl or acetaldehyde, which are undesirable.

On the opposite end of the spectrum, low-flocculation yeast does not clump up and sometimes stubbornly remains in suspension for several weeks. These yeasts have a powdery or dusty appearance when in suspension and contribute to the hazy quality found in some beer styles, like Hefeweizen. Due to its prolonged suspension, low-flocculation yeast converts more sugars into alcohol, producing beer with high attenuation and low fermentation by-products. This makes it a great choice for drier styles or clean fermentation profiles. The downside to using low-flocculation yeast is that the beer will remain hazy for several weeks before the yeast falls out of suspension naturally. For rapid clearing, you can accelerate the process through cold conditioning, fining, or filtration, although very low-flocculation yeast can be still problematic.

When purchasing brewer's yeast, look for information on the packaging that indicates whether the flocculation time is fast, average, or slow.

During fermentation, flocculating yeast clumps and settles to the bottom of the fermentor.

Flocculation Ranges in Yeast

Type of Yeast	Time to Flocculation
Fast	3–5 days
Average	6–15 days
Slow	16+ days

Temperature

For the best-tasting beer, it's necessary to ferment ale and lager yeasts within specific temperature ranges. In general, ale yeast strains prefer to ferment around room temperature, 64°F to 72°F. However, some strains, such as Saison yeast, produce nice beer at 75°F to 90°F; and others, like Kölsch yeast, do well at much colder temperatures, 55°F to 60°F. At their absolute limits, most ale yeasts go into dormancy below 55°F.

Lager strains, on the other hand, prefer cooler fermentation temperatures, usually ranging from 48°F to 58°F. However, like ale, lager temperature can vary, with some lager strains fermenting near 40°F and others fermenting in the ale range, between 60°F and 68°F.

All yeast will ferment beyond 85°F; however the resulting fermented beer is rarely palatable due to harsh alcohol formation and elevated ester and phenol production. Yeast manufacturers typically recommend a temperature range in which optimal fermentation takes place. Fermenting at temperatures higher than recommended may result is strong ester and phenol production, and at lower temperatures the yeast may become too sluggish close to dormancy significantly or undesirable fermentation characteristics, such as under attenuation.

Fermentation Temperature Ranges in the Brewing Process

Style	General Range	Lower End	Upper End
Ales	64–72°F	55°F	80+°F
Lagers	48–56°F	40°F	68°F
Hybrids	58–64°F	55°F	68°F

Alcohol Tolerance

There is a limit to how much alcohol brewer's yeast can produce, and this limit is known as alcohol tolerance. When brewing beer in the standard 4 to 7 percent ABV range, alcohol limitation is not an issue, since tolerances start around 8 percent ABV. However, for the strong ale brewer, yeast strain selection is important, especially when brewing beer beyond 8 percent ABV. If yeast is pushed beyond its toxicity limit, further alcohol production is prohibited and many fermentable sugars are left behind.

Different strains of yeast have different levels of alcohol tolerance, with some having higher alcohol tolerance than others. Yeast manufacturers often report the relative alcohol tolerance of specific yeast strains based on a standardized wort and fermentation profile. Brewers looking to extend the alcohol tolerance of a particular yeast strain can do so by tailoring fermentation and wort composition. It's possible to push yeast strains with low alcohol tolerance beyond the 10 percent ABV range; however, on a practical level, it's best to select a yeast strain with higher alcohol tolerance when designing a high-alcohol beer.

Brewer's Yeast Alcohol Tolerance

Tolerance	Alcohol by Volume
Low	8–9%
Average	10–11%
High	12-15+%

Flavor Production

In addition to the fermentation character, yeast adds several flavor and aroma compounds to beer through fermentation by-products. Some yeast-derived characters are highly flavorful and pleasant, while others are harsh and undesired.

The primary flavor components produced by yeast are esters, which contribute fruit flavors and aromas to beer. All yeasts produce esters in some form; without esters, beer would taste bland. Common ester characters in beer are the banana and bubble gum flavors found in German and Belgian wheat styles, and the pear and stone fruit flavors typical in English-style ales.

Some brewer's yeast produces phenols, which can add interesting spicy characters to beer, such as clove and black pepper, which are common in German wheat ales, Belgian-style ales, and saisons. However, if phenolic character is unintentionally present, it is likely a sign of contamination by wild yeast, in which the phenol character is not pleasant, lending a plastic, medicinal character to beer.

In addition to ester and phenol production, yeast produces several other compounds in fermentation, such as diacetyl, acetaldehyde, and fusel alcohols, which may lend flavors such as buttered popcorn, cider, freshly-cut squash, and rubbing alcohol. None of these are desired, and they often make a beer harsh and undrinkable. Avoiding these flavors is one of the primary motivations of controlled fermentation, healthy yeast, and sanitization in brewing. For further discussion of off-flavors from fermentation, see Chapter 15.

Yeast Packaging

Although brewer's yeast and baker's yeast are the same species, you can't just pick up a package of baking yeast for brewing. Yeast for brewing must be brewer-grade, pure single cell cultures in a sterile environment with very low levels of bacterial or wild yeast contamination. To ensure that yeast is healthy and ready to use, yeast manufacturers use package brewing yeast in two forms: liquid and dry.

Liquid Yeast

Liquid yeast consists of yeast cells that have been suspended and concentrated in a beer solution. It is usually sold in "pitchable quantities," which, when fresh, translates to around 100 billion cells. This may sound like quite a few, but as we'll see later in Chapter 12, this may not be enough for the standard homebrewing batch size of 5 gallons.

Liquid yeast is packaged in either plastic vials or smack packs. Vials are plastic tubes filled with yeast. Smack packs are rigid plastic bags that have yeast inside as well as a wort nutrient packet. Before brewing, you whack the plastic bag to break open the nutrient packet inside (hence the name "smack pack"). When the nutrient pack breaks open, the yeast activates and releases carbon dioxide, which inflates the outer plastic bag and lets the brewer know that the yeast is healthy. Liquid yeast should be stored in the refrigerator before brewing, but do not put it in the freezer, as this will kill the yeast cells.

Dry Yeast

Dry yeast has been preserved through freeze drying, and the end product looks very similar to dried bread yeast. Dry yeast is packaged in sachets that range in size from 7 to 12 grams. That might not sound like much, but each gram of dry yeast, when fresh, contains approximately 20 billion cells per gram. However, unlike liquid yeast, most yeast strains cannot be packaged in the dry form. Only hardy yeast strains can survive the freeze-drying process, limiting dry yeast selection.

 BREWING MYTH

Myth: Dry yeast has high levels of contamination, which results in poor fermentation.

In the early days of homebrewing, dry yeast could often be contaminated and did not always ferment well. Today, however, dry yeast is produced using modern freeze-drying methods under low contamination conditions and better strain selection. As a result, dry yeast has significantly improved and is comparable in quality to liquid cultures, resulting in high-quality fermentation.

Liquid Yeast vs. Dry Yeast

When selecting yeast for brewing, there are several advantages to each packing type. The primary advantage of liquid yeast is greater varietal selection compared to dry yeast, as all yeast strains can be packaged as a liquid culture, but few yeast strains can survive the freeze-drying process. Ultimately, this limits dry yeast selection.

Alternatively, the main advantage with dry yeast is shelf stability; it can last more than a year and still maintain viability at pitchable quantities. Liquid yeast only remains viable for 4 to 6 months, with adequate pitching quantities within 1 to 2 months after packaging. Finally, dry yeast tends to be less expensive than liquid cultures, making dry yeast a very attractive option.

Which version is better? Well, it depends on your brewing process. In my brewing, I use both liquid and dry yeast. For clean American ales, a dry yeast like Safale US-05 works great. However, for beer styles with more characterful yeast, like German Kölsch and Hefeweizen, I prefer liquid cultures, as I find they yield a better fermentation character than their dry yeast equivalents. Both liquid and dry yeast, when used appropriately, will yield great results.

Yeast Varieties

Like malt and hops, there are hundreds of ale and lager yeast strains, each with its own unique fermentation properties and flavor/aroma characteristics. Many of these strains are available to the homebrewer, but beyond the capability of this chapter to list. For compactness, the following yeast strains are grouped by brewing tradition; for example, yeasts common in American ale styles, like pale ales and IPAs, are considered American ale strains. For more focused yeast-derived flavors, check out Chapter 15. Also, for direct yeast substitutions, see www.idiotsguides.com/homebrewing.

Ale Strains

American ale The mainstay of American ale styles, American ale yeast strains are a great choice for expressing both malt and hop character with low ester production, leaving an overall clean profile. In fermentation, American ale strains are alcohol tolerant and highly attenuative with low to medium flocculence, and cleanly ferment over a wide range of ale temperatures. A must-have for clean, hop-forward styles, especially American-style IPAs.

Liquid: WLP001 California Ale, 1056 Wyeast American Ale, 1272 Wyeast American Ale II
Dry: Safale US-05, Danstar West Coast

Dry English ale Characterful, yet balanced, dry English ale yeast strains are more attenuative than malty English strains, yet slightly fruitier and more balanced than hop-assertive American ale strains. In fermentation, dry English ale strains are alcohol tolerant and highly attenuative with medium flocculence, and cleanly ferment over a wide range of ale temperatures. Great for balanced British-style ales, such as porter and Northern English brown ale, or British ales requiring high attenuation, like IPAs.

Liquid: WLP017 Whitbread Ale, 1098 Wyeast British Ale, WLP007 Dry English Ale
Dry: Danstar Nottingham

Malty English ale Fruity and complex, malty English ale yeast strains are malt-forward with pronounced esters, ranging from apple and pear to orange liqueur and stone fruits. In fermentation, malty English ale strains have low to medium alcohol tolerance and low attenuation with high to very high flocculence. Fermentation is best kept between 62°F and 65°F for a cleaner profile, while fermentation above 68°F will result in an ester-forward profile. A must-have for malty or ester-forward British-style ales, such as bitters and ESBs.

Liquid: WLP002 English Ale, 1968 Wyeast London ESB, 1469 Wyeast West Yorkshire Ale
Dry: Safale S-04

Irish ale Famous in the black stout of Dublin, Irish ale yeast strains are quite versatile and especially characterful in beers with large proportions of roasted malt. In fermentation, Irish ale yeast strains are very alcohol tolerant, attenuative with medium flocculation, and ferment cleanly over the ale temperature range, although they are known to produce slightly higher concentrations of diacetyl than most ale strains. Great in stout styles, especially dry Irish stout, but also makes for interesting bitters and pale ales. Also useful in high-gravity beer, such as imperial stouts.

Liquid: WLP004 Irish Ale, 1084 Wyeast Irish Ale

Scottish ale Neutral and clean, Scottish ale yeast strains are well-suited for many American and British-style ales, but particularly great in Scottish styles. In fermentation, Scottish ale yeast strains are highly alcohol tolerant, attenuative with high flocculence, and cleanly ferment over a wide range of temperatures. Scottish ale yeast is similar to a hybrid yeast, with fermentation working well down to 55°F and slightly fruitier fermentation above 68°F. Great in Scottish Schilling beers, also fantastic in Smoked porters and Wee Heavy.

Liquid: WLP028 Edinburgh Scottish Ale, 1728 Wyeast Scottish Ale

Belgian and German wheat Fruity and phenolic, Belgian and German wheat strains produce distinctive fermentation characters, especially banana esters, along with delicate clovelike phenols. In fermentation, these wheat yeasts are alcohol tolerant, attenuative with low flocculence, and ferment characterfully over a wide range of ale temperatures, although some brewers suggest colder temperatures for more balance. A must-have for German Weizen and Belgian Witbier styles.

Liquid: WLP300 Hefeweizen Ale, 3068 Wyeast Weihenstephan Weizen, WLP410 Belgian Wit Ale, 3942 Belgian Wheat
Dry: Safbrew WB-06, Danstar Munich

Trappist ale From the Trappist monks of Belgium, Trappist ale strains are complex and characterful yeast used for Belgian strong ale styles, with intense, fruity esters and delicate phenols. In fermentation, Trappist ale strains are highly alcohol tolerant, highly attenuative with medium to low flocculence, and characterfully ferment in the upper ale temperature range, sometimes exceeding 77°F. A must-have in Trappist-style strong ales, like tripel and dubbel, but also nice in Belgian-style Witbier.

Liquid: WLP530 Abbey Ale, 3787 Wyeast Trappist High Gravity, WLP570 Belgian Golden Ale, 1214 Belgian Abbey
Dry: Danstar Abbaye, Safbrew Abbaye

Australian ale Robust yet complex, Australian ale yeast strains are fairly neutral, producing moderate esters on the woody, fruity spectrum. In fermentation, Australian strains are alcohol tolerant, attenuative with medium flocculence, and cleanly ferment over a wide range of ale temperatures, especially at warmer ale temperatures. They are known to be more heat tolerant than other ale strains. Great for a wide range of American, British, and emerging Australian craft styles, especially Australian sparkling ale and Australian pale ales.

Liquid: WLP009 Australian Ale
Dry: Coopers Pure Brewer's Yeast

Saison Complex, fruity, and spicy, saison yeast strains are just a few mutations away from being truly wild. Diverse in character, saison yeast strains vary widely in ester and phenolic character with some that are very fruity and others that are intensely peppery. Whichever strain you pick, you cannot make a saison-style beer without one. In fermentation, saison strains are alcohol tolerant, medium to highly attenuative with medium to low flocculence, and ferment over a wide range of ale temperature, some nicely above 80°F.

Liquid: WLP566 Belgian Saison II, 3724 Wyeast Belgian Saison
Dry: Danstar Belle Saison

Lager Strains

American lager The mainstay of macrobrew fare, American lager yeast strains produce easy-drinking lagers with clean fermentation and neutral character. Often, these lager strains are forgiving, and good for the new lager brewer. In fermentation, American lager yeast is alcohol tolerant, has medium-high attenuation with medium flocculation, and ferments cleanly over a wide range of lager temperatures. Try these strains in a preprohibition lager or Texas bock, especially during the summer months.

Liquid: WLP840 American Pilsner Lager, 2035 Wyeast American Lager

Dry German lager Clean and crisp, dry German lager yeast strains are neutral in character and especially good in more hop-forward lager styles. In fermentation, dry German lager yeast strains are alcohol tolerant, have medium-high attenuation with medium-low flocculence, and cleanly ferment over the lager temperature range. Great in German-style lagers, especially pilsner and Schwarzbier.

Liquid: WLP830 German Lager, 2001 Wyeast Urquell Lager
Dry: Danstar Diamond, Saflager W-34/70

Malty German lager Rich yet attenuated, malty German lager strains enhance malt character without being sweet. In fermentation, malty German lager yeast strains are alcohol tolerant, attenuative with medium flocculence, and ferment cleanly over the lager temperature range. A must-have in malty German lager styles, especially Oktoberfest, Munich Helles, and Munich Dunkel.

Liquid: WLP833 German Bock Lager, 2308 Wyeast Munich Lager.
Dry: Saflager S-23

Czech lager Malty, yet crisp and dry, Czech lager yeast strains are wonderful in Czech-style lagers. In fermentation, Czech lager yeast strains are alcohol tolerant, attenuative with medium-high flocculence, and ferment cleanly in the lager temperature range, although sulfur character may be more pronounced at lower temperatures. Great in balanced lagers, especially Bohemian pilsner.

Liquid: WLP802 Czech Budejovice Lager, 1098 Wyeast Czech Pils

Hybrid Strains

German ale Clean and neutral, German ale yeast strains produce crisp and clean lagerlike beer without the need for lager temperatures, which makes them useful to brewers without cold temperature control. In fermentation, German ale yeast strains are alcohol tolerant, medium to highly attenuative with very low flocculence, and produce a very clean ale character in the hybrid and ale temperature ranges. These yeasts are essential for German Altbier and Kölsch styles, and are also nice in American-style wheat beers and hoppy pale ales.

Liquid: 2565 Kölsch, 1007 Wyeast German Ale, WLP029 German Ale/Kölsch

California common lager Clean, yet slight fruity, California common lager yeast strains produce crisp and clean lagerlike beer in the ale temperature range, making them especially useful for the brewer without lager temperature control. In fermentation, California common lager strains are alcohol tolerant, have medium to low attenuation with high flocculence, and ferment cleanly in the hybrid and ale temperature ranges. A must-have in California common style beers, but also very nice in cream ales.

Liquid: WLP810 San Francisco Lager, 2112 Wyeast California Lager

The Least You Need to Know

- Brewer's yeast is primarily responsible for alcohol production, but also contributes to the overall beer character and flavor through the production of chemical compounds called esters and phenols.
- Yeast may be packaged in liquid or dry form.
- The type of yeast used is what differentiates an ale from a lager. Ale yeasts ferment at warmer temperatures than lager yeasts.
- There are dozens of yeast varieties available. The yeast you choose depends upon the style of beer you want to make.

Water

Water, along with malt, hops, and yeast, is a critical component of beer, but one that is often overlooked and misunderstood. Understanding your brewing water and tailoring its chemistry is a complex and tricky undertaking, and for many, the last frontier on the journey to becoming a brewmaster. In this chapter, we'll de-mystify the complex subject of water chemistry and point you down the right path toward brewing with great water.

If you've flipped ahead through this chapter, you may be thinking, *Well, this brewing thing got complicated real fast.* I don't blame you, but don't worry; the rest of brewing is much less complicated. Water chemistry and brewing water formulation is a tough business, even for veteran brewers, and takes time and effort to get right. So, if this all feels over your head, don't worry. It's okay to skip over this chapter for the moment and save it for a later time.

However, if you are up for the challenge, look through this chapter and hopefully a few things will stick. Also, if you plan to transition to an all-grain brewing method sometime in the future or are currently starting, definitely give this chapter a read through. Most mash problems stem from water chemistry at some level. Now, on to the brewing water.

In This Chapter

- The importance of water in the brewing process
- Key brewing minerals and how they affect beer
- Methods for brewing water modification

Water: The Other 90 Percent of Beer

Over 90 percent of beer is composed of water, so it's no surprise that great beer starts with great water. And while the water flowing from your kitchen faucet may appear to be clean and clear, it isn't pure H_2O. Source water is a complex cocktail comprised of small amounts of several dozen mineral *ions* and molecular compounds, which significantly impact the overall expression of flavor in your beer and the effectiveness of your brewing process.

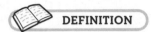 **DEFINITION**

Ions are atoms or molecules with a remaining net charge. Ions with a positive charge are called **cations,** while those with a negative charge are called **anions**. Brewers care about the ions as they are components of minerals often dissolved in brewing water that significantly impact the flavor and quality of beer.

While unpleasant-tasting tap water is never good for brewing, great-tasting tap water may not be ideal, either. Brewing water is best when it has been modified to suit a particular beer recipe. Modifying your water requires a little bit of chemistry and some calculations, but when done right, great water can turn an ordinary homebrew into a world-class example. For all brewing methods, there are two main considerations: beer flavor expression and water performance.

How Brewing Water Affects Flavor

A good way of thinking about water and its flavor impact on beer is an analogy often used by John Palmer, author of *How to Brew* and *Water*. He suggests thinking of water and brewing mineral ions like the seasoning in cooking. Underseasoned dishes are often bland on the palate, but with the addition of a little salt and pepper, the same dish can become more flavorful, with certain characters popping out. However, a little seasoning goes a long way, and once overseasoned, the dish quickly becomes unpleasant and salty.

The mineral ions that have the most impact on beer flavor are sulfates, chloride, and sodium. Brewing water high in sulfates enhances hop bitterness, crispness, and dryness, and accentuates hop character in styles like German pilsners and American IPAs. Brewing water high in chlorides or sodium softens harsh edges, accentuating malt character and sweetness, and is great for malt-forward styles like Munich-style Helles and Dunkel.

Water Performance: pH, Hardness, and Alkalinity

Water performance is primarily dependent upon how the properties of the water react with the brewing malts. To approach this, the brewer focuses on three main factors: pH, hardness, and alkalinity. While water performance is a minor concern to the extract brewer, it is of the utmost importance for the all-grain brewer, and vital in making a mash.

Since water performance is mainly a concern of the mash, we'll hold off diving into mash chemistry, and instead define its key variables. The first variable of water performance is pH, the measure of hydrogen ions in a solution, and it tells the degree to which a solution is acidic or basic. The pH scale ranges from 0 to 14, with very acidic solutions, such as car battery acids, ranging from 0 to 2, and very basic solutions, like bleach, ranging from 13 to 14. A neutral solution, such as pure water, falls in the middle at 7. For brewers, source water pH is not the sought after metric, but rather the mash pH.

The next variable in water performance is hardness, the measure of the concentration of cations in water. Brewers differentiate between two types of hardness: temporary and permanent. Temporary hardness is water hardness caused by dissolved bicarbonate minerals such as calcium bicarbonate and magnesium bicarbonate. This hardness type is called "temporary" because it can be removed by boiling. On the other hand, permanent hardness refers to the dissolved magnesium and calcium ions in water that cannot be removed via boiling. The name "permanent hardness" is a bit of a misnomer, since these minerals can be removed by other processes, but importantly cannot be removed via boiling.

Lastly, alkalinity is a metric of the buffering capacity of water, essentially the water's ability to counter changes in pH. Like hardness, there are two types of alkalinity, total and residual; however, unlike hardness, alkalinity is a comparative measure based on a preset pH range. Total alkalinity is the measure of how much strong acid is required to remove dissolved carbonates in brewing water, and thus is often quoted in units of bicarbonate. On the other hand, residual alkalinity is the amount of leftover alkalinity after a reaction takes place.

For all-grain brewers, this reaction is the mash and the amount of residual alkalinity of your mash compared to theoretical reference mash using only pure water. Based on this system, residual alkalinity can be either positive or negative and can be useful in estimating water additions to your mash. For more information on water performance within the mash, check out Chapter 17.

Reading Your Local Water Report

Before you can properly modify the water chemistry of your brewing water, you need to know its chemical profile. If you are using your local tap water for brewing, you can find this information on your local water report. Depending on your district, your local water report should be available for free online, often in multiple forms. If not, give your local water authority a call, or better yet, contact a local brewery, brew pub, or homebrew club. Those brewers should be able to point you in the right direction.

Water reports are typically released every three months, and should be checked every quarter. Your local water source may change throughout the year, which can significantly affect the water chemistry. Often these reports can be quite lengthy, but as a brewer, you're concerned about the following: calcium, magnesium, chloride, sodium, sulfate, total alkalinity, and total hardness. Generally, these ions are reported as ppm or mg/L.

On your water report, you may see carbonates reported in one of the following forms: CO_3, HCO_3, or $CaCO_3$. Depending on your brewing calculations, you can convert between these using the following: $1.22\times CaCO_3 = HCO_3$ and $0.60 \times CaCO_3 = CO_3$. The pH of your water is also likely reported, but this has very little meaning to the brewer until a mash is made. At this point, you have all of the necessary water brewing information, and are ready to engage in any water modification.

BREWING TIP

If you don't have a water report or if you want more brewing related water information, consider getting your water tested. Simple water testing kits can be picked up from your local hardware store, or for a more detail analysis, send a water sample to Ward Labs at wardlabs.com.

Key Ions and Measures in Brewing Water

The mineral ions highlighted on the water report can affect both flavor and mash efficiency. Sodium, chloride, and sulfate affect flavor; while calcium, magnesium, and carbonate affect pH, hardness, and alkalinity. The following profiles detail the specific effects of these ions in beer.

Sulfate (SO_4^{-2}) The brewing ion for hop heads, sulfate is known for its hop-expressive qualities. When present in higher quantities, sulfate aids in accentuating hop bitterness while also making the beer crisp and dry on the palate. However, when concentrations exceed 400 ppm, bitterness becomes harsh and astringent. Sulfate has negligible alkalinity and doesn't contribute to the total alkalinity of beer.

Key brewing ranges: 50–150 ppm for balanced beers, 200–350 ppm for bitter beer

BREWING MYTH

Myth: Sulfates contribute to headaches and hangovers.

Some people believe that added sulfates can exacerbate hangovers, but headaches are more likely due to high levels of fermentation by-products like acetaldehyde and/or tannins.

Sodium (Na^{+1}) While it is not an essential brewing ion, sodium can be added to soften and round flavors, helping to bring out the malt character and sweetness. However, when used at high levels along with sulfate, the combined effect can create harsh bitterness. If you are using sulfates, especially at the higher concentrations, keep sodium to a minimum.

Key brewing range: 0–150 ppm

Chloride (Cl⁻¹) Not to be confused with chlorine, chloride is a brewing ion known for its ability to accentuate malt flavors. Like most brewing ions, chloride concentration should be kept in reasonable levels; excessive chloride can cause medicinal off-flavors.

Key brewing range: 0–250 ppm

Calcium (Ca⁺²) The primary ion contributing to water hardness, calcium is a necessary brewing ion, key to mash enzyme activity, protein reactions, and fermentation. Also, calcium contributes to beer clarity and overall flavor. For the all-grain brewer, insufficient calcium concentrations in the mash may result in reduced enzyme activity, lowering saccrification efficiency.

Key brewing range: 50–150 ppm

Magnesium (Mg⁺²) Like calcium, magnesium contributes to water hardness, but has less impact overall to the water and brewing process. That being said, magnesium is a vital yeast nutrient, necessary in low concentrations. Magnesium concentration exceeding 50 ppm lends a sour-bitter flavor to beer, and above 50 ppm it may act as a laxative, so it's best to keep magnesium at low levels.

Key brewing range: 10–30 ppm

Carbonate/Bicarbonate (CO₃/HCO₃) The carbonate ions are the primary reason for brewing water modification. Carbonates take many forms (CO₃/CaCO₃/HCO₃) and all are very effective at increasing alkalinity as well as neutralizing the acidity common in dark malts. While critical in dark beer brewing, brewing water high in carbonates can wreak havoc in lighter beer styles like blonde ales and German pilsners. Doubly frustrating, carbonates are not the easiest to remove once dissolved, so later on, we'll discuss options on how to reduce these levels when desired.

Key brewing ranges: 0–50 ppm in pale, light-colored beers; 50–150 ppm amber-colored beer; 150–250 ppm dark-colored beers

Modifying Your Water Chemistry

More likely than not, as you move along in the homebrewing hobby, you'll want to change some aspect of your brewing water. Whether it's to accentuate bitterness in a double IPA or dialing-in a mash pH for a Munich Helles, there are several tools available to the homebrewer to effectively change your brewing water chemistry. Also, while reading this section, you should be aware that water chemistry modification requires some calculations that can be accomplished using a brewing water calculator, which can be found for free online.

Removing Chloramines

One modification nearly all brewers should make is the removal of chloramines, an odorless chemical added to most tap water sources to sanitize against unwanted microorganisms so you can drink straight from the faucet. While chloramines keep your tap water safe to drink, when combined by polyphenols, the compounds found in malt and hops, they generate chlorophenols. That might not sound like much, but chlorophenols have the same aroma and taste of dirty swimming pool water, which is never a desired quality in beer. Thus, when brewing with tap water, it's best to remove chloramines prior to wort production and fermentation to avoid these off-flavors. Of all the water modifications, this is the most important and should be done by both the extract and all-grain brewer when using tap water.

There are a number of ways to remove chloramines, but the two main methods used on the homebrew scale are carbon filtration and sulfite reaction. Carbon filtration works as it sounds, filtering nonwater chemicals through activated carbon micropores. For small quantities of water, a faucet filter adapter will work fine; however, if you need to filter tens of gallons of water, it's best to use a large house-scale carbon filtration system.

An alternative method for chloramine removal is using sodium or potassium metabisulfite. These can be added to the brewing water in a powder or tablet form (usually referred to as Campden tablets). A little goes a long way; ¼ teaspoon of powder or one small Campden tablet provides enough sulfite to remove chloramines in 20 gallons of water! After the sulfite is added, a short wait of 5 to 10 minutes is all that is necessary for chloramine removal. I live in an apartment, so I use powdered metabisulfite as my go-to chloramine removal option, which provides the most flexibility for smaller-scale brewing.

Adding Brewing Minerals

While many brewing ions are present in source water, you may want to add more to modify the flavor profile or alkalinity. To do so, brewers rely on common brewing minerals to accomplish this. The following is a list of the most commonly used varieties, many of which may already be present in your home kitchen.

Sodium chloride (NaCl) Also known as table salt, sodium chloride increases sodium and chloride ion concentrations. Both of these ions enhance malt character and softness without increasing water hardness through calcium or magnesium. When using table salt, stick to commercial versions without anticaking agents or added iodine (in other words, avoid iodized salt). One gram of table salt will add 104 ppm of sodium and 160 ppm of chloride in 1 gallon of water. Volumetrically, 1 teaspoon is equivalent to 6.5 grams of sodium chloride, so for 5 gallons of brewing water, ¾ teaspoon will get you close to the concentrations listed.

Sodium bicarbonate ($NaHCO_3$) Also known as baking soda, sodium bicarbonate is a useful addition when trying to increase residual alkalinity for dark mashes or low alkaline water. Also, it is a useful alternative to calcium carbonate, which can be difficult to dissolve into solution. One gram of baking soda will add 75 ppm of sodium and 191 ppm of HCO_3 in 1 gallon of water. Volumetrically, 1 teaspoon is equivalent to 4.4 grams of sodium bicarbonate, so for 5 gallons of brewing water, ⅝ teaspoon will get you close to the concentrations listed.

Calcium sulfate ($CaSO_4$) Also known as gypsum, calcium sulfate should be referred to as the "hop head" brewing mineral as it's the primary contributor of sulfates in brewing water, accentuating bitterness, crispness, and dryness. Also, the calcium ions increase water hardness, helping lower residual alkalinity often necessary for pale hoppy styles like IPA. One gram of calcium sulfate will add 62 ppm of calcium and 147 ppm of sulfate in 1 gallon of water. Volumetrically, 1 teaspoon is equivalent to 4 grams of calcium sulfate, so for 5 gallons of brewing water, ¾ teaspoon will get you to the concentrations listed. Gypsum can be purchased at your local homebrew shop.

Calcium chloride ($CaCl$) Calcium chloride helps to accentuate malt character and sweetness through chloride ions. Also, the calcium ions increase water hardness, helping lower alkalinity, which is often necessary for pale malty styles like Munich-style Helles. One gram will add 72 ppm of calcium and 127 ppm of chloride in 1 gallon of water. Volumetrically, 1 teaspoon is equivalent to 3.4 grams of calcium chloride, so for 5 gallons of brewing water, ½ teaspoon will get you close to the concentrations listed. Calcium chloride can be purchased at your local homebrew shop.

Magnesium sulfate ($MgSO_4$) Also known as Epsom salt, magnesium sulfate helps to accentuate hop-character through sulfate ions. Also, the magnesium ions increase water hardness slightly, helping lower alkalinity, a must-have when trying to replicate the famous Burton-upon-Trent brewing water. However, only small additions are recommended, as high magnesium ion concentration can lead to a sour or bitter character. Thus, if high levels of sulfates are needed, stick with calcium sulfate instead. Additionally, if your brewing water is deficient in magnesium, a vital yeast nutrient, magnesium sulfate is great to utilize for this purpose. One gram will add 26 ppm of magnesium and 103 ppm of sulfate in 1 gallon of water. Volumetrically, 1 teaspoon is equivalent to 4.5 grams of magnesium sulfate, so for 5 gallons of brewing water, ⅝ teaspoon will get you to the concentrations listed. Food-grade Epsom salt can be purchased at either your local pharmacy or homebrew shop.

Calcium carbonate ($CaCO_3$) Also known as chalk, calcium carbonate is a useful addition when trying to increase alkalinity for dark mashes. One gram will add 105 ppm of calcium and 158 ppm of CO_3 in 1 gallon of water. Volumetrically, 1 teaspoon is equivalent to 1.8 grams of calcium carbonate, so for 5 gallons of brewing water, 2 ¾ teaspoons will get you close to the concentrations listed. However, you may need up to three times the amount to yield the desired alkalinity and corresponding mash pH effects. Depending on your brewing preferences, sodium bicarbonate may be a more effective solution. Food-grade calcium carbonate can be purchased at your local homebrew shop.

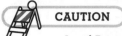

> **CAUTION**
>
> Avoid Burton water mineral salts! Often called Burtonizing, mixed packets of brewing water mineral salts are sold to the homebrewer as a quick method to replicate the water of the famous British brewing town, Burton-upon-Trent. However, you likely won't achieve the desired result when using untreated tap water, and there is no way of verifying that the blends are accurate. Instead, it's best to use individual mineral salts to replicate Burton water based on your source water mineral composition.

Decreasing Alkalinity

More likely than not, if you're brewing in the United States, the alkalinity of your brewing water is on the high side. While great for the more acidic darkly colored beers, it's not quite as great for lighter beer styles like German pilsner and American pale ale. For the all-grain brewer, high alkalinity can wreak havoc, pushing the light-colored mashes above the desired pH range and resulting in a very poor mash. For the extract brewer, this may not be a great concern; however, if your brewing water has very high alkalinity, it can cause problems in the boil. For brewing water bicarbonate concentrations greater than 250 ppm or total alkalinity greater than 200 ppm (when expressed as $CaCO_3$), pale-colored hoppy beers like those previously mentioned may extract hop polyphenols during the boil creating a harsh, astringent bitterness instead of a smooth, crisp bitterness. For these reasons, both the all-grain and extract brewer have high motivation to decrease brewing water alkalinity.

Brewing minerals For small adjustments, brewing mineral salts such as calcium chloride or gypsum can lower alkalinity though the increased water hardness of calcium and magnesium, enough to push both the alkalinity and corresponding mash pH into an appropriate range. If the alkalinity is quite a bit higher than the target desired, large mineral adjustments are best avoided, since you'll likely create very hard water and exceed the key brewing ranges, resulting in a salty or harsh character in the beer.

Acids Adding acids such as lactic or phosphoric acids in small amounts can significantly reduce carbonates in brewing water. Much like adding vinegar (an acid) to baking soda (a carbonate), these brewing acids neutralize water carbonates and thus reduce alkalinity. Acidification is most common in sparge water, where the brewer needs a lower pH sparge as the buffering capacity of mash is reduced during the runoff. To effectively introduce acids, additions depend on your source water as well as the acid type and dilution. The amount totals also must be calculated, which is most easily accomplished using a brewing water calculator. In general, a little goes a long way, with these acid additions on the order of a milliliter for 5 gallons of water. Overall, acidifying brewing water can be very effective but requires some care.

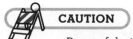

CAUTION

Be careful with acids! Some acids are quite strong, and can cause burns if they come into contact with your skin. Make sure you read up on the necessary health and safety precautions before using acids. Also, always add acids to water (rather than adding water to acids) and wear protective gear while doing so.

Boiling Boiling brewing water is another effective method for reducing alkalinity. The boiling process drives off carbonates in brewing water, and a boil as short as 30 minutes can reduce carbonate concentrations by half. The longer the boil, the greater the reduction in carbonates that can be achieved, but solubility limits the reduction to 30 ppm. Once chilled over several hours, the carbonates precipitate out of solution, and leave a chalk-like dust at the bottom of the kettle. Once racked off the bottom, your brewing water will achieve the desired reduction of alkalinity. If lower alkalinity levels are required, additional techniques can be utilized.

Diluting with distilled or reverse osmosis (RO) water By far the easiest method of reducing alkalinity is to dilute source water with a purified water source, such as distilled or RO water. Essentially, diluting brewing water by a particular proportion will reduce alkalinity by the same proportion. Brewers with highly alkaline water will often bypass the tap and build up an entire mineral profile from a distilled or RO water product. Due to its effectiveness and simplicity, dilution along with mineral adjustment is my go to strategy in my brewing. As a side note, RO water is fairly inexpensive, so dilution is also good for brewing on a budget.

Increasing Alkalinity

Since most tap water in the United States tends to have high alkalinity, the need to increase alkalinity for brewing is generally not necessary. However, if you do have low alkalinity in your brewing water or you enjoy brewing the more acidic darker styles like stouts and porters, you may wish to increase alkalinity. In general, low alkalinity is a problem for the all-grain brewer when mashing with high proportions of darkly kilned and roasted malts, which pushes the mash pH below the desire range.

Although there are a number of methods for increasing alkalinity available to the commercial brewer, many of these methods involve hydroxides and are hazardous. Instead, on the homebrewing level, it's best to stick with brewing mineral carbonates like sodium bicarbonate and calcium bicarbonate. Between the two, sodium bicarbonate is the better option, as it dissolves easily in mashes and doesn't add water hardness. However, large additions are inadvisable, as sodium concentrations beyond 100 ppm can create a harsh, metallic character to beer, especially when sulfate levels are also high.

Calcium carbonate is another option, also capable of increasing alkalinity while adding some hardness through calcium. However—and this is a big however—chalk is not very effective in alkalinity and pH adjustment for several reasons. Among them, the mash acids are too weak to neutralize chalk and empirically, not reactive enough in raising mash pH.

The Least You Need to Know

- Great beer starts with great water.
- If you wouldn't drink your tap water, don't brew with it. Unpalatable source water should, at the very least, be filtered or treated to remove undesirable compounds like chloramines.
- Brewing mineral ions in water are key to mash performance and flavor expression.
- Tailored water chemistry is achieved through a variety of water modification methods.

Other Brewing Ingredients

You only need malt, hops, water, and yeast to make beer, but many brewers add other ingredients to develop different flavor profiles. These additional ingredients may include sugars, spices, herbs, fruits, vegetables, coffee, or chocolate, depending on the brewer's preferences. In this chapter, you'll learn about the wide range of additional brewing ingredients and how to best add them to your beer.

Light-Colored Sugars

Light-colored sugars are used primarily to modify the fermentability, mouthfeel, and attenuation of a beer without adding color or flavor. They are used in all methods of brewing, but extract brewers may employ light-colored sugars more frequently due to the fixed fermentability of malt extracts. The following is a list of commonly used light-colored sugars in the brewing process.

In This Chapter

- How added sugars can improve the fermentability and flavor of your beer

- Tips for brewing with fruits, spices, coffee, and chocolate

- Important brewing aids and clarifiers

Corn sugar (0°L) Corn sugar, or dextrose, is the refined sugar of corn. Easily fermentable by brewer's yeast, corn sugar will almost always ferment out completely. This flavorless sugar is frequently used by the brewer to help attenuate big beers and drier styles without adding color or body, typically in Belgian-style strong ales, saisons, and double IPAs. Also, corn sugar is often the priming sugar of choice due to its quick fermentability and conditioning. In most beer styles, corn sugar can be added up to 20 percent of the total fermentability, but typical usage is in the 5 to 10 percent range. Yield: 45 ppg.

Cane sugar/table sugar (0°L) Cane sugar, or sucrose, is another simple sugar easily fermented by brewer's yeast. Like corn sugar, cane sugar is flavorless and does not add color or body to beer. Cane sugar is used for brewing in the same way as corn sugar and can replace corn sugar if necessary. Cane sugar can be used for priming, but will generate slightly more carbonation than corn sugar. Yield: 46 ppg.

Invert sugar (0–1°L) Invert sugar is a reduced form of cane sugar. The complex sucrose molecules are broken down into the simpler fructose and glucose molecules, both of which are more easily fermented by brewer's yeast. Invert sugar is commonly found in syrup or rock candy forms, but also can be made at home. It's traditionally used in pale Belgian strong ales, especially tripel and Golden Strong. Use up to 20 percent. Yield: 32 ppg.

 BREWING MYTH

Myth: Adding more than 10 percent sugar to the grain bill will cause a ciderlike flavor in beer.

This myth originated from the early days of homebrewing in the United States. At the time, homebrewers mistakenly diagnosed ciderlike flavors from large sugar additions in "kit-and-kilo" brewing kits, but more recent analysis suggests these flavors emerged from old malt extracts. That being said, sugar additions that exceed 20 percent of the grain bill can result in poor fermentation due to their lack of yeast nutrients.

Maltodextrin (0°L) Maltodextrin is a long-chained sugar that is unfermentable by brewer's yeast. Found in a powdered form, maltodextrin can be used by the extract brewer to reduce the fermentability of the wort and increase body without adding flavor or sweetness. Maltodextrin is also good for increasing head retention and foam stability in beer. It can be used as a replacement for dextrin malts in a recipe. Yield: 42 ppg.

Lactose (0°L) Lactose, also called milk sugar, is a colorless and flavorless sugar derived from the milk of dairy cattle. Lactose is unfermentable by brewer's yeast and used to add body and slight sweetness to beer. A must-have in milk stouts. Use up to 1 pound in a 5-gallon batch. Yield: 42 ppg.

Dark-Colored Sugars

Rich in color and flavor, dark-colored sugars add the fermentability of light-colored sugars as well as a wide range of flavors and aromas that produce interesting and complimentary character to beer. The following is a list of amber and dark-colored sugars commonly used in the brewing process.

Honey (1–8°L) Subtle in flavor, honey adds delicate floral and honeylike qualities to beer. However, not all honey is created equal, with each honey varietal adding is own unique quality and character. There are several varieties of honey ranging from the well-known buckwheat, tupelo, and orange blossom honeys, to local varietals, like wildflower.

Because it is a natural product, honey contains many unwanted guests, like wild yeast. To prevent contamination, honey must be sanitized. Adding honey to boiling wort works well; however, be sure to add it at the end of the boil to preserve its delicate flavor and aroma. Alternatively, honey can be pasteurized by heating it to 161°F and holding it there for 30 seconds. For maximum preservation of volatile compounds, pasteurized honey should be added at the end of fermentation.

You can add just about as much honey as you like to beer. Between 3 and 10 percent, honey will add subtle floral characters. Between 10 and 30 percent, honey will add strong honey flavors as well as increased varietal flavors. Past 50 percent, you'll enter into new beverage categories called *mead* and *braggot*. No matter what usage, make sure to add extra yeast nutrients when using large percentages, as honey is nutrient deficient compared to barley malt. Yield: 32–38 ppg.

> **DEFINITION**
>
> **Mead** is a honey-based fermented beverage often described as a honey wine. Like beer, there are many styles of mead. By BJCP standards, mead must have more than 66 percent honey. Mead with a significant portion of malt, a kind of beer/mead blend, is known as a **braggot**.

Agave nectar syrups (3–45°L) The fermentable source for top-shelf tequila, agave nectar is an vegan alternative to honey. Agave nectar has a wide range of colors and flavors. Lighter versions are fairly neutral in character, while darker versions will add a strong caramel-like quality. Like honey, agave nectar will mostly ferment out, so it's best to add toward the end of the boil or after fermentation through pasteurization (see honey section). Agave can be used as an alternate to corn sugar for priming, but may need adjustment for desired carbonation levels. Yield: 30–32 ppg.

Sorghum extract (2–6°L) A gluten-free option for brewing beer, sorghum extract is a maltlike sugar derived from sorghum grass. With soft, mild malt flavors, sorghum extract is a close substitute in most beer recipes. Red and white sorghum extracts are typically available to the homebrewer, and unlike their names suggest, both are pale in color. When accessible, high maltose white sorghum is a close analog to barley malt extracts in both sugar and protein composition. Also, depending on sorghum extract type, hop bittering additions may vary in strength. Yield: 37 ppg.

Unrefined cane sugars and brown sugar (1–40°L) Unrefined cane sugars are minimally processed forms of crystalline cane juice that add color and flavor character in addition to fermentability. There are several types available, each with varying color, character, and fermentability levels. Common types include demerara, turbinado, piloncillo, jaggery, and muscovado.

Brown sugar is not an unrefined cane sugar, but refined cane sugar with molasses added back. Like molasses, brown sugar comes in different grades and lends similar character to beer. Whichever you choose, unrefined cane sugars and brown sugar can add rich fruit flavors and enhance malt character in beer, especially British-style ales. Use up to 20 percent, although depending on the flavor intensity of the variety, you may want to stick with the 5 to 10 percent range. Yield: 41–46 ppg.

Amber and dark Belgian candi sugars (45–275°L) Amber and dark Belgian candi (pronounced like "candy") sugars are essentially invert sugars that have been processed to a higher temperature and caramelization. As a result, the darker candi sugars add rich colors and complex flavors, such dark fruits, rum, coffee, chocolate, and caramel. Amber and dark candi sugars are found commercially in syrup or rock candy forms, but can also be made at home. Traditionally used in dark Belgian strong ales, especially dubbels and quads. Use up to 20 percent. Yield: 32 ppg.

Maple syrup (15–40 °L) Maple syrup isn't just for pancakes and waffles; it also pairs well with beer. Like honey, real maple syrup is mostly fermentable sugar, around 95 percent sucrose, so in order to yield a noticeable maple flavor, you'll need quite a bit. In the United States, maple syrup comes in two grades, Grade A and Grade B. These sound like report card grades, but they actually refer to the color and flavor. Grade A maple syrup is light in color and more delicate in flavor. Grade B maple syrup is darker in color and has a more robust maple flavor. Of the two, Grade B will likely yield more maple-forward flavor and aroma, and is the preferable option. Do not use imitation maple syrup ("pancake" syrup). It is made with corn syrup and maple flavoring and is not suitable for brewing.

Maple syrup can be added to the boil, but character is best preserved using pasteurization and adding it at the end of fermentation. For a noticeable maple character, depending on the style, use around ½ gallon to 1 gallon for a 5-gallon batch. Yield: 30-31 ppg.

Molasses or treacle (80–100°L) Molasses, or treacle as it's known in Britain, is the by-product of the refining process of white cane sugar. Molasses is widely used in brewing, especially in traditional British-style ales, lending dark fruit, licorice, and rumlike characters to beer. Flavor quality greatly depends on molasses grade: light, dark, or blackstrap. Light versions are made from the first boiling of the refining process, and have a mild flavor and more sweetness. Darker grades, especially blackstrap, are made from the last boiling of the refining process and as a result have more intense flavors, are less sweet, and have some bitterness. Whichever type you choose, make sure to buy an unsulfured variety; nobody wants beer to taste of rotten eggs. Also, a little goes a long way with molasses, beginning with 5 percent of a light version would be a good place to start. Yield: 36 ppg.

Fruits and Vegetables

Fruit and vegetable additions are often popular in seasonal brews, with fruits showing up in refreshing summertime beers, and vegetables, notably pumpkin, a core part of many fall harvest ales. In addition to flavor, fruits and vegetables add a range of characters including color and mouthfeel, along with various degrees of fermentability. As such, brewing with fruits and vegetables requires a few extra steps in the brewing process in order to achieve good results.

Starting out, a point of clarification. While botanically speaking, common additions like pumpkin, cucumber, and chiles are strictly fruits, we align these additions according to their culinary designation as vegetables. While this may annoy the taxonomists reading this, it is solely to maintain common usage. Now, onto the brewing.

Brewing with Fruit

When brewing with fruit, there are essentially two main forms: real fruit and fruit extract. Real fruit is a broad classification that includes whole fresh fruit, canned fruit purée, and fruit juice. Regardless of the form, real fruit is best added after primary fermentation to preserve the volatile and often subtle flavor characteristics that are scrubbed by boil evaporation and carbon dioxide.

Adding real fruit after primary fermentation maximizes fruit character, but it also makes the beer susceptible to contamination. Canned fruit purée and juices are already pasteurized, but any fresh pressed, blended or frozen juice or purée must be sanitized. To do so, the brewer can utilize a few tricks, including flash pasteurization (see honey) or metabisulfite treatment, one crushed Campden tablet per thick purée of fruit works well. Lastly, make sure the fruit is fresh, devoid of defects, and free of wax and preservatives, which will kill brewer's yeast, terminating fermentation.

In addition their flavor characteristics, real fruit contains sugars that must ferment out before packaging. The degree of fermentability varies with fruit type, so if you are trying to hit a target gravity and ABV range, it is worth including fruit sugar contributions in the recipe. To ferment a fruit addition in beer, fruit can be added directly to the primary fermentor after the initial fermentation is complete; however, better yet would be to add fruit to the secondary fermentor. Why? Well, fruit often floats at the top of the beer and fruit fermentation tends to be vigorous (sometimes explosive), so racking into another fermentor gives the secondary fermentation enough headspace to accommodate fruit fermentation.

To perform a fruit-based secondary fermentation, simply add fruit to a sanitized secondary fermentor and rack the beer from the primary fermentor onto the fruit. If this is done immediately after primary fermentation is complete, pitching additional yeast is not necessary, as yeast will still be in suspension from the primary fermentation. However, in some cases it might be a good idea to add fresh yeast, especially if the primary yeast was highly flocculent or a high-gravity fermentation was performed. If sluggish yeast is suspected, pitch a neutral ale or lager yeast to achieve a quick and healthy secondary fermentation. After secondary fermentation is complete, allow any yeast and fruit debris to settle out, then rack and package as normal.

 **CAUTION**

Watch out for fruit clogs in carboys! During fermentation, fruit matter can clog the narrow neck opening of carboys, potentially pressurizing the carboy and creating an explosively hazardous situation. When fermenting fruit in a carboy, be sure to set up a blow-off tube and closely monitor the fermentation process to ensure fermentation gases are adequately escaping.

Fruit extracts are the other way of adding fruit to beer. They consist of essential fruit character without fermentability. As such, fruit extracts are a quick and convenient method for adding fruit flavor, since they do not require sanitization or secondary fermentation, and are added straight to the bottling bucket or keg after primary fermentation is complete. Fruit extracts can also be added incrementally in small amounts, allowing the brewer to gauge the desired balance of the fruit character in the beer without overshooting.

However, like many herb and spice extracts, some fruit extracts are better than others, so before taking this route, take a look at reviews to see if it's worth it. For example, many of the apricot extracts are high quality, and add a pleasant apricot essence to beer. However, I find many of the cherry extracts can lend a cough-syrup flavor to beer, which is not pleasant, making real cherry fruit worth the effort.

Brewing with Vegetables

Vegetables are one of the hardest brewing ingredients to pin down. They vary widely in flavor, form, and starch and sugar content. This variation makes it hard to give specific techniques, so instead I'll provide general advice. For starchy vegetables like squash and sweet potatoes, baking them first helps to minimize squashlike off-flavors, and they are best added to a mash, as the enzymatic action will help to convert the starches into sugars and avoid starch haze in the finished beer. Other veggies, like chile peppers and cucumber, are better treated like whole, fresh fruits. For all vegetable additions, be mindful of sanitization when adding post fermentation, and strive to create balance with the beer flavors. For more specific recommendations and techniques, look for brewers' notes on homebrewing forums, blogs, and articles.

Fruits and Vegetables Used in Beer

The fruits and vegetables used in brewing parallel their applications in the culinary world, often reflecting breads and desserts. The following are some of the more commonly used fruits and vegetables along with associated beer styles. Keep in mind that while some are more challenging than others, just about any fruit or vegetable can be added to beer, as long as appropriate balance with beer flavors is achieved.

Stone Fruit

Common Varieties: apricot, peach

Usage: For a 5-gallon batch, add 3 pounds of fruit purée or 2 ounces of extract for a light stone fruit flavor. Doubling those amounts will result in a more fruit-forward beer. Of the fruit varieties, apricot lends the most intense character, and is sometimes peachy in quality. For low-malt styles, a lower dosage is recommended when a balanced character is desired. Peach, on the other hand, can be very subtle in beer, so for a more notable character, the higher dosage rate is recommended.

Styles: Definitely try a stone fruit in a wheat beer, where it lends a peach-pie character. Apricot can also be good in pale ales and Belgian lambics.

Berry

Common Varieties: raspberry, strawberry, blueberry, cherry

Usage: Very dependent on variety. Raspberry, cherries, and blueberries lend intense flavors to beer. For a 5-gallon batch, 3 to 6 pounds of fruit purée or 2 to 4 ounces of extract are often plenty for these berries. On the other hand, strawberries are very subtle and delicate, and require 10 to 20 pounds of fresh fruit to yield a notable character to a 5-gallon batch.

Styles: All berry flavors work well in wheat beers. More intense fruits, like cherries and raspberries, pair well with the coffee and chocolate flavors of stout and porter styles, lending a berry-chocolate tart character to beer.

Melon

Common Varieties: watermelon, cucumber

Usage: Watermelon is mostly water, so large additions are often necessary to yield sufficient character, making extracts a convenient option. On the other hand, cucumber is highly aromatic, and just a few slices are sufficient to infuse its character into beer.

Styles: Unsurprisingly, neutral beers like blonde ales and wheat beers feature watermelon and cucumber flavors quite nicely. Definitely make one during the summer, as they are incredibly refreshing on a hot day.

Squash

Common Varieties: pumpkin, butternut squash

Usage: By far the most popular brewing veggie, pumpkin can be used whole or in canned form. If you plan to use a whole pumpkin, make sure you use the smaller pie pumpkin variety for the best character. If none are available, consider using butternut squash, which lends a nearly identical character in beer. For a 5-gallon batch, a 2- to 3-pound pumpkin or one 29-ounce can of pumpkin purée is sufficient. More can be used, but high usage rate risks raw, squashlike off-flavors. For more information on how to use pumpkin in beer, check out Witches Brew Pumpkin Ale in Chapter 22.

Styles: Pumpkin ales, as well as other harvest and holiday beer styles.

Chile Pepper

Common Varieties: jalapeño, habanero

Usage: You can add as much heat as your palate can handle. Removing the seeds will minimize heat and infuse more of the fruity, earthy characters associated with peppers. To maximize heat, use whole peppers or just add more de-seeded varieties. To start out, use one de-seeded pepper per 5-gallon batch for notable heat and pepper character.

Styles: Peppers pair well with hop-forward styles like pale ales and IPAs, but any style in which you think can take the heat is open to exploration.

Herbs and Spices

Brewing with herbs and spices goes far back into the brewing tradition, predating hops by several hundred years. Before hops were commonly used, herbs and spices were utilized for their bittering, preservative, and sometimes medicinal qualities in beer. While hops reign supreme today, herbs and spices are still used to add flavor and character to beer, from up-front and festive to subtle and complimentary.

Brewing with Herbs and Spices

Herbs and spices in brewing are used much like hops, which shouldn't be too surprising as hops are essentially a subset of the spice and herb category. Typically, herbs and spices are infused in wort and beer for flavor and aroma, and are treated like late hops to preserve their delicate compounds. Like late hops, herbs and spices can be added either to the boil, typically during the last few minutes, or after fermentation is complete. Herbs and spice added post fermentation are best added as an infusion for character control and sanitization concerns. Infusions of herbs and spices are accomplished using two methods: by steeping in hot water or by extraction using a neutral spirit like vodka. Once a desired infusion is reached, it can be added to either the conditioning or packaging stages for maximum preservation of herb and spice character.

The amount of herb and spice used for brewing varies based on the overall potency of a particular herb or spice. Some spices, like grains of paradise and cardamom seeds, are very intense, and only a few are needed to flavor a 5-gallon batch of beer. More subtle herbs, like heather tips, can be used by the cup without lending a strong flavor. When using herbs and spices, it's best to follow a few simple practices.

Match the spice intensity to the overall beer intensity. A light blonde ale with low malt and hop flavor doesn't need much for herb or spice character to be apparent. However, a rich imperial stout with intense roasted flavors may require quite a bit more herbs and spices for it to be notable.

When in doubt, use restraint. Like salting a dish, more can always be added, but too much can't be undone. When overshot, it may require months of aging to just mellow flavors.

Do your research. If you're interested in using a particular herb or spice, investigate how other brewers have used it. As a ballpark estimate, for any moderately intense herb or spice, 1 teaspoon is likely more than enough to flavor a 5-gallon batch.

In lieu of estimating and guesswork, a more experimental approach can be taken by tasting blended herb or spice infusions with fermented beer. First, brew the base beer without herbs or spices added. Then, after fermentation is complete, remove 12 ounces of the beer and chill to serving temperature, around 45 to 50°F. Next, add small, controlled amounts of the herb or spice infusion to the beer sample and taste. Continue to add the infusion in small amounts (about ⅛ to ¼ teaspoon) tasting after each addition until a desired balanced is reached. Then at packaging, scale this blended mixture based your batch size to achieve the desired balance in the final beer.

BREWING TIP

Use fresh herbs and whole spices! When possible, source whole spices and herbs when brewing and grind or crush them on brew day for best results. Preground spices and dried herbs can work well, but like all ingredients in brewing, the fresher, the better.

Beer Styles That Use Herbs and Spices

The herbs and spices used in brewing are also common in the culinary world. Thus, in lieu of listing several well-known herbs and spices, the following is a list of suggested and commonly used varieties associated with a brewing style. While some are more difficult than others, just about any herb or spice can be added to beer, as long as a balance between beer flavors and herb and spice character is achieved.

Belgian-style ales Many Belgian-style ales, especially Witbier, feature an array of spices, typically dried orange peel and coriander, but often others like chamomile and grains of paradise, which contribute to a floral, citrus character in the aroma and flavor.

Pumpkin-spiced ales The ever-popular pumpkin ale features traditional pumpkin pie spices, a varying blend that typically includes allspice, cinnamon, nutmeg, and ginger, and to a lesser degree, mace and clove.

BREWING TIP

Use restraint when adding clove spices to beer. Although clove is a common component to pumpkin and holiday spicing, clove is also considered an off-flavor in most beer styles, which some drinkers may find less than desirable. When adding cloves to beer, use your judgment to strike a balanced note in the overall character.

Holiday-spiced ales and mulled ales American- or British-style strong ales also known as "winter warmers" are often made with a blend of mulling spices that include allspice, cinnamon, cloves, and nutmeg, and sometimes cardamom, peppercorn, star anise, and dried orange peel.

IPAs The resin-y, floral qualities of rosemary, lavender, mint, and even spruce tips make for interesting herbal additions to American-style IPAs when used alongside Pacific Northwest hops.

Stouts and porters Stout and porter styles pair well with the herbs and spices used in chocolate and coffee desserts, such as vanilla and mint. Also, many traditional stouts and porters use licorice root as a component of the flavor profile.

Historical ales Historical ales traditionally include herbs like heather and myrtle, which were used for bittering and preservation before hops were more mainstream.

Coffee and Chocolate

Roasty, smooth, and intense, coffee and chocolate make for a fantastic pairing in beer, often complimenting the already present coffee and chocolatelike flavors in many beer styles. There are a range of methods to brew with coffee and chocolate, each resulting in a slightly different character in the final beer. While there is no best way to add coffee and chocolate, the following are some guidelines for adding their wonderful flavors to your favorite homebrew recipe.

Before getting into individual ingredients, there are some general rules of thumb to keep in mind while brewing with coffee and chocolate. Darker, maltier styles, like stouts, porters, and bocks are often the best candidates for adding coffee and chocolate because those flavors mirror and complement the already present roasty, caramel-like flavors of the beer, allowing for both the coffee/chocolate and malt flavors to intensify and pop.

It's much more difficult to strike the right balance with hoppy styles. For example, coffee/chocolate is easier to pair in a creamy milk stout than it is in a hop bomb of a double IPA. That's not to say it can't be done. On the contrary, I think a chocolate infused black IPA with late Amarillo hops would be out of this world, yielding a chocolate-orange character. However, while a chocolate stout can be nailed in one brew session, a chocolate black IPA might take a few tries to really dial it in.

Like all brewing ingredients, fresh, high-quality coffee and chocolate is key. In general, it's best to avoid coffee/chocolate infused syrups or extracts. Syrups will mostly ferment out, leaving a weak flavor behind, and extracts can often lend fake character. That's not to say that all syrups and extracts are bad; well-sourced brands that are fresh and of suitable quality are definitely worth using and can add an element of convenience. However, going forward, we'll focus on using coffee and chocolate in less-processed forms.

Brewing with Coffee

The roasted bean that gives you your morning jolt can also bring a jolt to your beer. Many of the rules that apply to brewing coffee also apply when brewing beer with coffee.

Coffee comes from many growing regions, which lend a wide range of characteristics that are expressed differently depending on the roast. While choosing specific coffee varietals is completely up to the brewer's preference, the roast quality can be given some consideration before brewing. Light to medium coffee roasts lend more of a varietal "origin flavor" along with mild toasted/roasted notes, whereas darker roasts lend a strong roasted character with little to no varietal flavor. Also, much like roasted specialty malts, roast quality may contribute color, mouthfeel, and even acidity to your beer, depending on amount used and degree of roasting.

Starting out, there are some basic rules of thumb to brewing with coffee. Like cooking with wine, if you wouldn't drink the coffee a bean makes, then don't brew with it. If you have a coffee variety that you regularly drink, that would be the best to use, since you'll have a good understanding of its overall character. Also, stick with whole beans rather than preground, and grind fresh on the day of use. Freshly roasted beans make for an even better beer, so seek out fresh roasts from coffee shops—or roast your own!

Now, here's the hard part: there is no one way to add coffee to beer. Brewers use a wide range of techniques from using ground coffee in the mash or boil to adding espresso shots post fermentation. Like hops, if you want to preserve the volatile flavors of coffee, it's best to add it late in the brewing process, after fermentation is complete. This can be done using pure coffee grounds, cold-steeped coffee, freshly brewed coffee, or espresso shots. Be sure to chill any hot brewed coffee to a yeast pitchable temperature before adding, and be mindful of any sanitation issues. Alternatively, adding ground coffee to the boil is not a bad idea, and if doing do so, add during the last 10 minutes of the boil to avoid the harsh bitterness commonly associated with burnt coffee.

How much to use? This is a question of balance and intensity, and ultimately depends on the brewer's preference. One way to figure out the right amount is by blending a small sample. First, brew the base beer without coffee added. Then, after fermentation is complete, remove 12 ounces of beer and chill to serving temperature, around 45°F to 50°F. Next, add small, controlled amounts of freshly brewed coffee (about ¼ to ½ teaspoon) to the beer sample and taste. Continue adding coffee and tasting until a desired balance is reached. When packaging, scale this blended mixture based your batch size to achieve the desired balance in the final beer.

Brewing with Chocolate

Brewing with chocolate is a bit trickier than coffee since it comes in a wider selection of processed forms. Brewers often use baker's chocolate, dark chocolate, cacao nibs, and cocoa powder. Whatever form you use, it's always best to choose a high-quality chocolate, free from waxes or additives. Also, avoid milk chocolates, as they are mostly sugar and add little flavor.

When brewing with chocolate, many of the brewing techniques used with coffee apply. Like coffee, brewers add chocolate throughout the brewing process, with specific techniques depending on the form. Dark chocolate, baker's chocolate, and cocoa powder are best added toward the end of the boil and are analogous to making hot chocolate. Alternatively, many brewers utilize a more raw form of chocolate known as cacao nibs, the cracked and roasted seed of the cacao tree. Unlike processed chocolates, cacao nibs lend a more refined chocolate character without much of the bitterness. Like dry hops, cacao nibs are best added after fermentation and left to sit anywhere from a few days to two weeks to extract the chocolate flavor. Finally, many brewers will use a spirit infusion of cacao nibs as a sanitary and more controlled method for infusing its favor in beer.

How much chocolate to add in the brewing process can be a bit difficult to gauge before giving it a go, especially when trying to achieve balance. Here are a few recommendations based on brewing experience. If you are using baker's chocolate or dark chocolate, try adding 2 to 4 ounces late in the boil for a firm chocolate flavor. If you're using cocoa powder, try adding 2 to 4 tablespoons for a 5-gallon batch. Lastly, when using cacao nibs, anywhere from 3 to 6 ounces added after fermentation lends a rich character for a 5-gallon batch. Use your best judgment when adding chocolate, and remember that it's always better to add less than more, because more can always be added later, but less cannot be taken out.

Clarifiers

Clarifiers are used in brewing for the cosmetic purpose of producing a bright, clear beer, but also for quality concerns, like flavor expression and stability. Clarifying agents, also known as finings, are added throughout the brewing process, typically before fermentation during the boil or after fermentation during the conditioning process of fermentation. There are several types available to the homebrewer, each targeting differing haze-producing compounds in beer.

Irish moss Although its name suggests otherwise, Irish moss is actually a dried form of red seaweed used as a protein clarifying agent. During wort production, Irish moss added to the boil promotes coagulation of haze-producing proteins in the wort, and during chilling, it aids in precipitation of coagulated proteins in hot break, the primary cause of chill haze and accelerated staling in beer. When brewing, add Irish moss during the last 15 minutes of the boil at a rate of 1 teaspoon per 5 gallons of wort. For better performance, rehydrate the Irish moss addition for 20 minutes in warm water before adding.

Whirlfloc tablets Whirlfloc tablets are a supercharged form of Irish moss used for the same protein-clarifying purposes. These tablets are comprised of a blend of Irish moss and its protein coagulating active ingredient, carrageenan. Many brewers, including myself, find that Whirlfloc is very effective at producing strong hot breaks and clear wort. When brewing, add 1 Whirlfloc tablet during the last 5 to 15 minutes of the boil, depending on variety.

BREWING TIP

Save a few bucks by cutting Whirlfloc tablets in half. Because they are packaged for commercial brewers, each tablet is designed to clarify 15 gallons at a time, making one half a Whirlfloc tablet more than enough to clarify a 5-gallon batch. Although adding the whole tablet to a 5-gallon batch won't do any harm, the frugal brewer can save the other half for another brew day.

Isinglass Isinglass is made from the swim bladders of tropical fish, which may not sound like something you want in your beer, but it is a collagen clarifying agent traditionally used in British real ales to accelerate yeast flocculation. Isinglass comes in dried and liquid forms for use in brewing. Dried forms must be rehydrated before using, with hydration rates depending on the manufacturer's instruction. Alternatively, prehydrated liquid isinglass solutions can be added directly; however, some brewers report that the effectiveness may be reduced due to limited shelf life. Isinglass must be added after fermentation is complete, and is best used when the beer is cold, below 60°F for optimal flocculation. When cleared after a few days, rack the beer off the sediment into bottles or kegs.

Gelatin The key ingredient in Jell-O, gelatin is a collagen-based fining used to remove yeast, protein, and even astringency-causing tannins. Like isinglass, gelatin comes in a powdered form and can be easily purchased from your local grocery store. Like Jell-O, gelatin must be rehydrated in hot water before using a mixture of ½ teaspoon in ½ cup of hot water. Once pitched, add the gelatin solution to the fermentor after fermentation is complete and rack off the sediment and into bottles or kegs after a few days or until clearing is complete. Brewers report good results when pitched into cold beer, around 50°F and racking after 24 to 48 hours.

The Least You Need to Know

- Brewing sugars are used by both extract and all-grain brewers to add ferment-ability, color, and flavor.
- Many popular beer styles are made using fruit, vegetables, herbs, spices, coffee, and chocolate for added flavor and aroma.
- Hazy beer can be cleared using clarifying agents.

PART 3

Brewing Necessities

You can't make beer without the right equipment for sanitization, brewing, and measurement. This part covers what you'll need to set up your home brewery, from the basic bare-bones equipment to the nice-to-have specialty items. You'll also find advice on best brewing practices, such as sanitizing, taking measurements, and recordkeeping.

Brewing Equipment

Before you can begin homebrewing, you'll need some basic brewing equipment. However, with hundreds of homebrewing products on the market, figuring out what you need can be a bit overwhelming. This chapter covers the range of brewing equipment, from basic to advanced, and will help you choose the right gear for your brewing process.

Note that while much of the available homebrewing equipment is covered in this chapter, discussion of some items, such as cleaning tools, kegging equipment, and all-grain equipment is left to their respective chapters.

In This Chapter

- How to select a brew kettle and fermentor to fit your brewing needs
- What you need as a beginning and intermediate brewer
- Exploring advanced brew gear for the homebrewing junkie

Essential Brewing Equipment

While many brewers use a wide array of equipment, there are only two absolutely necessary items needed to brew beer: a brew kettle and a fermentor. This section will help you select a kettle and fermentor to fit your brewing process.

Brew Kettle

There are many names for the brew kettle; it may be known as a brew pot, a boil kettle, or a copper, but its function remains the same: to boil the wort. While simply sizing a big pot to fit your wort is a major consideration, there are several factors you might further consider when selecting a brew kettle to fit your brewing needs.

What size is right for you? Well, it depends on your brewing process and whether or not you plan to perform a partial or full boil. Partial boiling does not refer to boil duration, but performing a concentrated wort boil. In a partial boil, a standard 5-gallon batch will only boil about 3 gallons of wort. The wort is then transferred to the fermentor and topped off with plain water to yield 5-gallons in the fermentor.

In contrast, a full boil starts with diluted wort and can be anywhere from 6 to 7 gallons in volume for a 5-gallon batch. The boil is concentrated through evaporation and then transferred to a fermentor, yielding 5-gallons. The advantages and disadvantages of partial and full boils are discussed in Chapter 11, but the type and size of brew pot you chose ultimately determines boil strategy.

For both partial and full boils, the rule of thumb when sizing a brew kettle is that the total kettle volume should include at least a gallon of head space before the start of the boil. Why leave head space? The main motivation is avoid a common homebrewing crisis, the boilover, where wort escapes over the side of the brew kettle, leaving a hot, sticky mess. Having at least a gallon of head room can abate this problem; however, a watchful eye is the best practice.

For the partial-boil brewer, a 4-gallon kettle is the minimum size for 3-gallon partial boils, although a 5-gallon kettle would be better. For the full-boil brewer, an 8-gallon kettle is the minimum size for 6- to 7-gallon full boils when brewing the standard homebrew 5-gallon batch size. Smaller or larger batch sizes will require different kettle sizes.

The primary material used in brew kettles and cookware in general is either aluminum or stainless steel. Both are effective at producing a world-class homebrew; however, each has its pros and cons, with the deciding factor often being your budget. Aluminum is a bit lighter than stainless steel, which may be desired when lifting is involved. It's also less expensive than most stainless steel pots, which is great for those brewing on a budget. Alternatively, stainless steel is more durable, less sensitive to wear and tear, and less prone to corrosion. Also, stainless steel kettles are more easily cleaned, whereas aluminum can be more reactive with cleaning agents.

 BREWING TIP

Season your new aluminum brew pot by boiling water in it for 15 minutes before its first use. This will help to build up a thick oxide layer, which will prevent the aluminum from leaching into your boiling wort and potentially causing metallic off-flavors.

In addition to material, kettles range in sidewall and bottom thicknesses. In general, the thicker the sidewall and bottom, the better the kettle will be for brewing. Thicker sidewalls increase durability and insulation, while thicker bottoms promote even heating and prevent scorched wort. If you're considering an aluminum pot, look for one with sidewalls and a bottom that are at least 4 millimeters thick. Stainless steel is sold in a range of sidewall and bottom thicknesses, with thicker pots commanding higher prices. Since stainless steel is less thermally conductive than aluminum, thick bottoms often integrate conductive materials like copper and aluminum to facilitate heat spreading. If you choose a budget-priced stainless steel pot with thinner walls or bottom, watch for scorching.

The total cost of a brew pot is directly related to its quality and previous considered specifications. As mention previously, aluminum will cost less than stainless steel, although thin stainless steel constructions are often comparable in price. Also, while thicker sidewalls and bottoms are better for brewing purposes, in general, the thicker the kettle, the more costly due to increased material and fabrications. Likewise, large-volume brew kettles will cost more than small volume ones. Beyond cost, make sure to consider and verify the quality of the brew kettle. Online reviews are good, but visiting your local homebrew shop would be better. Lastly, make sure to check out the handle construction. A full boil 5-gallon batch can weigh over 60 pounds; having a wimpy handle is an accident waiting to happen.

Overall, when selecting a brew kettle, find the best type for your budget. I've used both aluminum and stainless steel kettles in brewing and haven't observed any noticeable difference in the overall quality of my homebrew. I would recommend either material type for the new brewer. A stainless steel kettle will last a lifetime, and if you plan on brewing extensively, it would be worth investing in a high-quality, thick-walled stainless steel kettle. However, if you are starting out on a budget, a thick-walled aluminum kettle will deliver great results.

Fermentor

Before fermentation can begin, you'll need a place to store your freshly made wort. In brewing, the fermentor is used in multiple stages, primarily for fermentation, but also for conditioning. Like kettles, sizing a fermentor to fit your brewing needs is a major consideration, but there are several factors you might further consider when selecting a fermentor.

There are three main types of fermentors used in homebrewing: buckets, carboys, and conical fermentors. Buckets are simply large (typically 6-gallon) food-grade plastic buckets. Carboys are cylindrical jugs, similar to water cooler jugs, with a narrow opening at the neck. Lastly, conical fermentors, or conicals for short, are the fermentor of choice for pro-brewers. Like carboys, they are cylindrical in shape except they have a cone-shape bottom with several valves used to remove trub, harvest yeast, and transfer beer. It's important to note that most homebrewers do not exclusively use one type of fermentor in their brewing process, and that high-quality homebrew can be made from any type.

Fermentor materials fall into three types: plastic, glass, and stainless steel. Plastic is the most commonly used material, and all three types of fermenters can be found in plastic form. Plastic is very homebrewing-friendly due to its light weight, low cost, and durability. However, there are a few drawbacks to plastics, mainly its oxygen permeability, which makes plastic fermentors less suitable for long-duration aging due to oxidation concerns. Plastic is also susceptible to scratching, which can harbor unwanted contaminants.

BREWING TIP

Consider using PET plastic carboys as they are nearly impermeable to oxygen, making them a great alterative to the glass carboy and plastic buckets.

As an alternative to plastic, glass is impermeable to oxygen, scratch-resistant, and fairly inexpensive. Unlike other fermentor materials, only carboys are available in glass form. The drawbacks to glass are its weight, which is on the heavy side (especially once you add 5 gallons of beer), and its lack of durability. Glass carboys will shatter when dropped or mishandled, creating a big mess and a potentially hazardous situation.

Lastly, stainless steel is the main alternative to both plastic and glass in fermentors, as it yields durability, oxygen impermeability, and scratch resistance. Historically, stainless steel was only used for conicals, but due to recent homebrewing enthusiasm for stainless steel, conical-bucket hybrids are now available. The drawbacks to stainless steel are its weight, which can be heavy at times, and its cost. Like kettles, stainless steel fermentors are very expensive when compared to glass and plastic types, with many conicals costing hundreds of dollars.

When choosing a fermentor for primary fermentation, keep in mind that you'll need some additional room (headspace) above the liquid level. This is to accommodate the *krausen*, a foamy, yeasty, creamy head that forms on the surface of the beer.

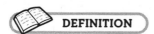

DEFINITION

Krausen is a foamy, creamy head formed by yeast at the top of beer during fermentation.

Not all krausen take the same size and shape. Some are thin, less than an inch thick, while others go berserk and exceed the volume of the fermentor. Krausen height depends on a number of factors, including yeast strain, batch size, wort composition, and fermentation temperature. As a general rule of thumb, leave at least 15 percent headspace to allow for krausen growth. For a 5-gallon batch, this means a fermentor should have at least a 6-gallon capacity, although more would be better. In many situations, krausen rise exceeds this rule and can be mitigated using a surfactant commercially sold as FermCap-S before fermentation or by installing a blow-off tube, a sanitized tube attached to the opening of the fermentor to allow for krausen to escape without clogging concerns.

When choosing a fermentor for conditioning, sizing consideration is the opposite of primary fermentation, with little to no fermentor headspace desired. This is because headspace introduces oxygen to beer, and the more headspace there is, the more rapidly the beer will oxidize. Thus, a secondary fermentor should be close to the racked batch size. A 5-gallon batch would ideally fit into a 5-gallon carboy or bucket.

Overall, when selecting a fermentor, find the one that best fits your budget and brewing process. For primary fermentation, you can't go wrong with a plastic bucket or glass carboy; both contribute to high-quality fermentation. Conicals are quite fancy, but often unnecessary at the homebrewing level. In my brewing, I prefer glass carboys simply for cleaning and sanitization effectiveness.

Building a Home Brewery

Beyond the brew kettle and fermentor, there are many other items you may find useful in your brewing process. However, before you begin building your brewery, keep in mind that a brewer with all of the equipment doesn't necessarily make the best beer; that is ultimately up to you and your brewing process.

That being said, specialized equipment can make the process easier and improve the quality of your homebrew when used appropriately. Establish your brewing techniques using basic gear, find ways to improve your process, then build and obtain equipment through which you can make these improvements, not the other way around. Finally, keep spares and backup equipment. Things break, either through wear and tear or by accident. Having a reliable backup can make or break a brew day.

Starter Equipment

The following items are recommended for beginning extract brewers. You can buy these items individually as needed, but you can also get many items together as part of a starter kit.

Airlock An airlock is a one-way valve, usually made of plastic, that's installed on the opening of a fermentor to keep the outside microbes and oxygen away from your fermenting brew. Airlocks are designed to be filled with a sanitized liquid, such as no-rinse sanitizer or distilled spirit. Carbon dioxide from fermentation is able to bubble up through this liquid and exit through the top of the airlock, but outside air is prevented from entering, keeping any unwanted guests out. Airlocks come in two types, the three-piece and the s-shape bubbler.

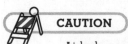 **CAUTION**

Airlocks can become clogged if too much krausen forms during fermentation. If some time has passed and the airlock is clogged, the carboy could be pressurized. This is a potentially dangerous situation as beer can eject from the fermentor into your face and all over your walls. Take care when removing a clogged airlock, and be sure to wear eye protection and have towels nearby.

Several items are recommended to improve the quality of your homebrew. Many of the items shown here are included in starter kits.

Cleaning tools A must-have for the brewer, cleaning tools such as carboy brushes and jet water sprayers help to remove brewing debris in brew kettles, bottles, kegs, and fermentors. For more information, see Chapter 9.

Basic measurement tools Quality and consistency are at the heart of brewing measurements. For the beginning brewer, there are several suggested measurement devices, such a thermometer and hydrometer with sample tube and thief. For more discussion of this equipment, its importance in the brewing process, and how to use it, see Chapter 10.

Big spoon An extra-long spoon is useful for stirring wort, particularly when adding malt extract, hops, brewing minerals, and other kettle additions. It's also a must-have for stirring mashes, although some brewers may prefer the traditional mash paddle. Available in many sizes, styles, and materials, I prefer a 21-inch stainless steel version; I've used the same one since my first brew day.

Drilled stopper Much like it sounds, drilled stoppers plug holes in fermentor openings with the drilled part holding airlocks in place, completing the airtight fermentor enclosure. As fermentors openings vary in size, so do stoppers, which are available in a whole array of sizes. For glass carboys, consider using a universal stopper, as these will fit most fermentor sizes.

Blow-off tube A blow-off tube is used as a replacement for traditional airlocks to allow rising krausen to escape without clogging or pressurization. The blow-off tube is a flexible length of clear plastic tubing, one end of which is placed at the fermentor opening and the other end sunk in a small bowl of water. This setup allows fermentation gases to escape and krausen to empty without introducing outside contamination, essentially creating a giant airlock. Blow-off tubes come in a variety of configurations depending on fermentor type, ranging from giant 1-inch diameter tubing that fits snuggly inside the neck of a carboy to small-diameter tubing that fits within a plugged drilled stopper.

In this setup, one end of the large blow-off tube is inserted into the neck of the carboy and its opposite end into a large bucket of water, allowing krausen to safely exit without contamination.

Racking cane Almost as vital as the kettle and fermentor, racking canes are the primary means for moving beer and wort from one vessel to another. Made of either plastic or stainless steel, racking canes are connected with tubing and use siphon action to get beer and wort moving. Plastic versions are fairly inexpensive and come in auto-siphon forms, which use a pumping action to get the siphon started. Stainless steel racking canes are beneficial as they can be sterilized, which is useful for top-cropping yeast cultures, and are less prone to scratching, cracking, or warping, which are common in plastic varieties.

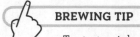

BREWING TIP

To start a siphon, the outgoing vessel must be elevated, at least above the top of the ingoing vessel. (In practice, this distance is close to the difference between the kitchen counter and kitchen floor.) Then to start the siphon action, the liquid must overcome the height difference. Auto-siphons make quick work of this through the pumping action. Alternatively, you can fill the tubing with sterilized water, then attach it to the racking cane, and drop it into the ingoing vessel. With that, wort or beer should overcome the height difference and flow feely without contamination.

Carboy carriers Carboy carriers are devices used to help lift and move carboys and come in several designs. Some devices, known as handles, attach to the neck of the carboy and are designed to lift and move only empty carboys, not full ones as many believe. Durable carboy bags, known as haulers, are an alternative to handles and are designed to lift and transport filled or empty carboys. Both are highly recommended for all carboys, especially those made of glass; a trip to the emergency room is much more expensive than any of these products.

Basic bottling equipment Most beginning brewers start out by bottling their homebrew, which requires a few special devices. In addition to a racking cane, bare minimum bottling requires bottle caps, a capper, and, of course, clean bottles. Recommended equipment for bottling includes a bottling bucket with spigot, a bottling wand, and bottle tree. For more information regarding these individual bottling items, check out Chapter 13.

Tubing All brewers need tubing, no matter what their level of brewing experience. For the beginners, tubing is necessary for racking wort and beer between kettles, fermentors, and bottles. Brewers at the intermediate and advanced levels use tubing in several parts of the brewing process, including for pumping wort and dispensing homebrew in kegging systems.

Tubing comes in all sorts of materials and sizes, each useful for different purposes. The two most common tubing materials are vinyl/PVC and silicone. Vinyl/PVC is good for all-purpose applications like racking and kegging. However, for high-temperature applications like mashing and boiling, silicone is preferable due to its heat tolerance at high temperatures.

Tubing diameter depends on whether it's intended for connecting or fitting. Tubing diameters can be a bit confusing, as both the inner and outer diameter may be given. When adding to brewing equipment, make sure the inner diameter can fit over the top of a fitting. It's best to undersize the tubing; for example, putting $\frac{3}{16}$-inch tubing onto a $\frac{1}{4}$-inch fitting, which allows for a tighter seal. Matching diameters will also work, but will require a hose clamp to keep the tubing firmly in place. Additionally, consider the thickness of the tubing for high-pressure brewing applications like kegging systems, where thicker tubes hold up better to forced carbonation and dispensing.

BREWING TIP

Make tubing setting easy by using hot water! Sliding tubing over fittings can be quite difficult, especially when fitting smaller diameter tubing. Heating the tubing end in hot water for a minute or two will make the tubing more elastic and easier to slide on during the setting. Wait a few minutes to cool, and you'll have a tight seal, ready for its brewing application.

Lastly, when shopping for tubing, remember these few tips. Make sure to buy food-grade vinyl or silicone tubes. Homebrew stores will typically sell by the foot, which is helpful when only a few are needed. However, if you need a bunch of tubing, consider buying in bulk. When building my 10-tap kegerator, I purchased two 100-foot rolls of tubing.

Intermediate Equipment

Intermediate equipment is the next step up from starter equipment, and can be used both by the extract and all-grain brewer. This equipment, although not necessary, can be utilized by the brewer looking to improve or upgrade his or her brewing process.

Wort chiller Wort chillers accelerate the cooling of wort, resulting in improved cold break, improved beer clarity, and less lag time before pitching, which lowers the risk of contamination. A wort chiller works by exchanging heat from the hot wort with a cold water source, usually your house tap water. Wort chillers come in several designs, including immersion, counterflow, and plate chillers. For more discussion on cooling wort and the pros and cons of these wort chiller designs, see Chapter 11.

Vacuum sealer Vacuum sealers are devices used by home cooks to seal perishable foods in plastic packages from which all the air has been removed. In brewing, vacuum sealers are great for storing hops, since unused hops lose bittering, flavor, and aroma when exposed to air. Vacuum sealers are especially helpful for the brewers who buy hops in bulk and repackage large unused portions, as well as backyard hop growers who want to preserve their precious hops after drying.

Stir plate Stir plates are used to create strong vortex circulation and continuous aeration in yeast starters, both of which promote improved yeast growth and strong cell walls. The vortex action is generated through a magnetically-coupled stir bar, which, when placed within a growler or Erlenmeyer flask, rotates and forces air into the solution, producing the desired effect. For more information on yeast starters, see Chapter 12.

Propane burner Propane burners are the next step up from the kitchen stove, which may not be able to generate enough heat for large batches or full boils. Propane burners are rated by BTU/hr; the greater the BTU/hr, the greater heating power achieved, and thus a faster, more robust boil. Average kitchen stovetops have an output of about 12,000 BTU/hr, so look for a burner that puts out around 30,000 BTU/hr as an entry-level model or 100,000+ BTU/hr for some serious action. If the burner is attached to a rig or tier, like a turkey fryer, make sure it's capable of holding the combined weight of your brewing gear.

Kegging system For brewers looking to move past the tedium of bottling, a draft keg system is the next step in packaging beer. Kegging has many benefits, especially quicker conditioning of fresh beer styles through forced carbonation. However, kegging can be an expensive upgrade, and requires additional gear such as kegs, CO_2 cylinders, regulators, taps, and refrigeration. For the range of options and a more detailed discussion of kegging, check out Chapter 13.

Grain mill Grain mills are used to crack specialty malts and grind base malts. Milling on brew day greatly improves beer quality, as it allows for the freshest milled malt to enter your wort. It also gives the all-grain brewer the ability to customize the grind coarseness, a key variable in the mash. At the homebrew level, grain mills come in two varieties: plate and roller mills. Plate mills, also known as corn, Corona, and Victoria mills, crush grain through rotating ribbed metal plates. Roller mills crack malt through two rotating parallel rollers. To adjust grind coarseness, you can alter the amount of space between the plates or rollers.

Overall, roller mills are more desired for base malts and all-grain brewing than plate mills, as they have a higher precision of grind coarseness, can handle several pounds of grain, and leave hulls mostly intact, key to lautering wort from the mash. Alternatively, plate mills are great for crushing specialty malts where grind precision is not necessary, and are usually less expensive. Either mill choice will work well for both extract and all-grain brewing when properly adjusted and adequate brewing practices are observed.

 BREWING TIP

Milling malt by hand can take some time and effort. Speed up your milling using a power drill. To do so, simply remove the hand crank and replace with a grain mill drill bit attachment. This way, you'll be able grind through several pounds of malt in a few minutes without too much effort, although you won't burn off as many of those homebrew calories.

Advanced Equipment

If you want to brew styles that require advanced fermentation techniques, such as lagers and high-gravity beers, or if you want to make wort from scratch by mashing malts, then you'll need some advanced brewing gear. Although the term *advanced* may sound expensive, much of this equipment can be acquired at reasonable costs, and some can be made at home. "Advanced" simply refers to the brewing technique, not the difficulty in using this gear.

Mash equipment When making wort from base malts, you'll need some extra equipment to make a mash. Traditional mash systems use a mash tun, a vessel for mashing malts and separating the spent grains from wort, along with a hot liquor tank and a brew kettle to heat sparge water. Mash tuns come in several designs, from fairly inexpensive hose-braid water coolers to fairly expensive stainless steel false bottom systems, each with their own benefits.

Alternatively, an Australian brewing method called brew-in-a-bag (BIAB) uses a brew kettle lined with a food grade strainer bag to perform the mash and lauter. Simply removing spent grain bag separates the wort, leaving it behind in the kettle, ready for the boil. The primary benefit for BIAB is that it is a very low-cost introduction to all-grain brewing. For a more in-depth discussion of all-grain brewing, mashes, and their related equipment, check out Part 6.

Brewing pumps Pumps can be useful for moving wort and hot water from one place to another. You may be thinking, why not use racking canes? Well, racking canes work well with small batches, but for large batches and all-grain brewing methods, wort and water transfer requires automation.

Brewing pumps come in several varieties depending on use; for example, whether you are transferring cold fermented beer or hot wort. Also, some pumps need to be primed, typically using gravity to start flow. Whichever make or style you chose, make sure it's designed to suit your brewing needs. I recommend food-grade stainless steel construction that can handle boil temperatures and a flow rate of 7 gallons per minute for 5-gallon batches.

Brewing sculptures A brewing sculpture isn't referring to post-modern art, but instead brewing platforms used in all-grain brewing. Quite large and sturdy, brewing sculptures are designed to hold hundreds of pounds of mash and kettle equipment while also supplying the heat for boiling wort and sparge liquor. Brewing sculptures general fall into two categories: gravity-fed systems (also called multi-tier systems) and horizontally pumped systems (also called single-tier systems).

Brewing sculptures can be purchased through your homebrew store; however, even the basic models can be quite expensive. They also take up quite a lot of space, so it's unlikely you'll be using one of these in your apartment. The overall benefit of brewing sculptures is that they make for less heavy lifting, a necessity when you are making large batch sizes and a definite upgrade from the kitchen stove.

Advanced measurement equipment With more advanced brewing processes comes more advanced measurement tools. For the advanced brewer, there are several suggested measurement devices, such a pH meter for measuring mash pH and precision scales for measuring out hops and water additions. For more discussion of this equipment, its importance in the brewing process, and how to use it, see Chapter 10.

Aeration system Aeration is necessary for yeast growth and for building strong yeast cell walls, both of which contribute to strong and clean fermentation. For small batches, you can shake and stir the wort to aerate it, but for larger batches, you may want an aeration system. There are two types available to the homebrewer: aquarium pumps and pure oxygen systems. Aquarium pumps are the same devices used to oxygenate the water in a fish tank. They deliver the same oxygen concentrations that can be achieved through shaking and stirring, but are useful for large batches sizes. A pure oxygen system is the next level up; these systems are capable of producing the higher aeration levels necessary for lager fermentation and high-gravity beers. For more information on aeration and aeration equipment, check out Chapter 12.

Temperature-controlled fermentation chamber For ale brewers, fermentation at ambient room temperatures works well without active temperature control. However, when brewing lager or hybrid styles, controlled colder temperatures—as low as 40°F—are needed. There are a variety of methods used to lower fermentation temperatures, but the most effective is through temperature-controlled fermentation chambers. This requires two items: a temperature controller (essentially a programmable microcomputer with a digital thermometer attached) and an insulated chamber, typically a temperature bypassed chest freezer or refrigerator. For more information on fermentation temperatures in brewing, check out Chapter 12. Also, for more information on temperature control and lager brewing, see Chapter 20.

Microscope For the serious yeast junkies, a microscope can be used for cell counting and pitch rate estimation. Microscopes are a must-have for those brewers looking to set up a yeast lab. They vary widely in quality and cost, but at the very least, make sure you choose one with a suitable magnification and backlight for cell observation, although an integrated camera would be even better.

BeerGun or counter-pressure filler These devices are used to fill precarbonated beer into bottles from a keg. To reduce oxygen exposure and preserve carbonation, these devices purge bottles with CO_2 and then slowly dispense beer to reduce foaming and carbonation loss. When done properly, the bottled beer will result in very low oxidation and remain nicely carbonated. Blichmann Engineering exclusively offers the BeerGun, which works slightly differently than the more traditional counter pressure fillers. I personally use the BeerGun and it works great with my process.

The Least You Need to Know

- The only two absolutely necessary pieces of brewing equipment are a brew kettle and a fermentor. These range in design, material, quality, and cost. The type you select largely depends on your brewing preference.

- There is a multitude of brewing equipment available. For basic brewing, a thermometer, racking cane, and bottling equipment is highly recommended.

- Intermediate and advanced brewing techniques often require brewing equipment such as kegs, mash tuns, and stir plates.

Cleaning and Sanitizing

Of all the steps in the brewing process, cleaning and sanitizing brewing equipment is by far the least fun. There are not many dishwashing hobbyists, right? Despite this, cleaning and sanitization are critical to producing clean, high-quality homebrew. There's excellent motivation for spotless cleaning and sanitization, as there is nothing like the great disappointment of dumping a contaminated batch of homebrew down the drain as a result of unclean brewing practices. When you follow good practices, contamination is quite rare and you will often be rewarded with good homebrew in return. This chapter covers the basics of cleaning and sanitizing as well as the consequences of not doing so properly.

Fighting Contaminants

Beware of bad bugs! Microorganism contaminants can negatively affect the fermentation process and create several defects in the finished beer, including poor fermentation and off-flavors. Wort is particularly susceptible to contamination due to its low acidity and high sugar levels. These contaminants can be one of several microorganisms, primarily bacteria and wild yeast.

Bacteria

Although they're popular in sour beers, bacteria are typically unwanted in beer fermentation for several reasons. Bacteria can grow rapidly in beer, and at high enough levels, they can overpower yeast fermentation. Also, bacteria steal much-needed nutrients and significantly lower beer acidity, further challenging yeast fermentation. In addition, bacteria can continue to grow in anaerobic (low oxygen) environments after the yeast fermentation is complete. These combined effects result in fermentation problems such as over-attenuation (lacking sweetness and body) or stuck fermentation (too much sweetness and body) and are responsible for several off-flavors. Depending on the bacteria type, common off-flavors include a sour tartness from lactic acid (similar to the zing in yogurt) bacteria or a vinegary acidity produced by acetic acid bacteria.

Wild Yeast

While brewer's yeast ultimately turns wort into delicious beer, *wild yeast* turns wort into something you wouldn't want to put in your mouth. Similar to bacteria, wild yeasts are unwanted in controlled beer fermentation. Also like bacteria, wild yeast contamination results in poor fermentation and off-flavors. A common wild yeast is *Brettanomyces*, or just Brett for short. Popular in Belgian sours, Brett can contribute funky beer flavors such as horse blanket and shower drain. Although nice in wild brews, wild yeast contamination is not desired in most beer styles.

 **DEFINITION**

> **Wild yeast** is a broad name for any yeast that is unintentionally added to the beer or uncontrolled by the brewer. The origin of wild yeast contamination can be from an exotic location like your kitchen or backyard; however, wild yeast could also originate from a previously brewed batch. Although sometimes unavoidable, most wild yeasts can be managed through proper cleaning and sanitization.

The Cleaning and Sanitization Process

In brewing, the removal of debris and contaminates on equipment is broken into two separate steps. First, a brewing object or vessel is cleaned, the process of removing the debris from all surfaces. Once cleaned, a brewing object is then sanitized, the process of significantly reducing unwanted contaminates from all surfaces. The key difference is that cleaning only removes the soil on the surface, often leaving a layer of some contaminates behind such as bacteria or wild yeast. Sanitizing significantly reduces this contamination layer.

You'll quickly find the cleaning and sanitization process to be the least fun part in homebrewing; however, it is also one of the most important parts of the brewing process. A simple way of thinking about the cleaning and sanitizing process is to imagine your beer as the yeast's new home. To make your yeast live and grow happily, it will want a home all to itself without the threat of strangers such as wild yeast and bacteria. The fewer contaminants there are, the easier it is for the brewer's yeast to move into the fresh wort. Given a sufficiently high level of contaminants, the brewer's yeast will be overwhelmed, causing very bad things to happen to your beer, such as off-flavor production or stuck fermentation. Thus, the best strategy is to keep a nice, clean home for your yeast. This will keep it very happy throughout the fermentation process and also make you happy as you'll have, in the end, clean-tasting beer. Just remember, clean first and then sanitize. It is always a two-step process.

Lastly, although the terms are sometimes used interchangeably by brewers, there is a big difference between sterilization and sanitization. Sterilization is a process resulting in the complete removal of all living microorganisms. Sanitization, however, is the process of reducing, but not eliminating, microorganisms. In brewing, sanitization significantly reduces the number of unwanted contaminates entering the finished beer.

Why is sanitization effective? The short answer is that sterilization is difficult and unnecessary in the brewing process. On the homebrew scale, fermentors are typically made of plastic or glass, and are very large, both of which makes them difficult to sterilize. Also sterilization is more time consuming and expensive when compared to sanitizing. In practice, sanitizing is very effective in eliminating most contaminants that stand in the way of clean beer.

Cleaning Supplies

Before brewing equipment can be sanitized, all the soil must be removed from the surface. There are a few strategies you can use to eliminate stuck-on brewing debris and achieve a spotless clean. For lightly soiled equipment, chemical cleaning agents do a relatively quick and thorough job. More heavily soiled brewing equipment benefits from a combination of mechanical and chemical cleaning.

Mechanical Cleaning and Its Tools

Mechanical cleaning essentially means using tools and elbow grease to remove debris from brewing equipment before using cleaning agents. Because excess debris can reduce the effectiveness of cleaning agents, it's best to first use mechanical methods to remove loose brewing debris, then eliminate the harder to remove, stuck-on debris with chemical cleaning agents.

At the heart of mechanical cleaning are cleaning tools. There are many cleaning tools available for the homebrewer, more than can be covered comprehensively here. Instead, I'll cover the two cleaning tools I think are must-haves for both beginner and advanced brewers: the jet washer and brushes.

Jet washer As its name implies, the jet washer is a converging tube that attaches to a faucet and sprays pressurized water at a high velocity, dislodging stuck-on brewing debris. This is especially useful for removing krausen, trub, and hop matter in carboys and blasting off yeast sediment in bottles and kegs. The advantage of jet washing versus scrubbing is that it prevents scratching of the soft surfaces of plastics. In addition to removing debris, I also use the jet washer to rinse carboys, kegs, and bottles after using a cleaning agent.

Brushes Although the jet washer works very well, sometimes hardened stuck-on debris, usually thick and crusted krausen or dried yeast sediment in glass bottles, is difficult to remove by water pressure alone and further scrubbing is required. Brushes do this well. Brushes come in many shapes and sizes, the smallest for tubing and kegging parts and the largest for carboys. I typically view brushes as a last resort to cleaning surfaces. If you clean your brewing equipment while debris is still moist, jet washers and cleaning agents will remove all brewing debris without the need for brushes and the elbow grease.

> **BREWING TIP**
>
> Clean plastics gently. Unlike glass or metal, plastics scratch and crack easily. When scratches occur, they can harbor unwanted contaminants such as wild yeast or bacteria from future cleaning cycles, ruining a nice piece of brewing equipment and potentially a batch of homebrew. Use soft sponges or towels when mechanically removing debris on plastic. Also, avoid using very hot water, which can cause warping and eventually cracking.

Chemical Cleaning and Its Agents

Chemical cleaning is achieved by soaking brewing vessels and equipment in an active agent diluted with water to remove brewing debris. A close analogy here is soaking very dirty dishes in soap in lieu of scrubbing. Like dishes, greater dilution strengths are needed for more heavily soiled items. A variety of cleaning agents are available to the homebrewing community. When used properly, these cleaning agents are very effective, safe, and often environmentally friendly. The following is a list of recommended cleaning agents and how to use them.

Percarbonates and powdered oxygen cleaners Often used for laundering, percarbonates and powdered oxygen cleaners are also a great way to clean brewing vessels and equipment. This cleaning agent is essentially a stable form of baking soda (sodium bicarbonate) and hydrogen peroxide, both very effective cleaning agents outside of the brewing world. Percarbonates are by far my favorite brewing cleaning agent as they are very friendly to a wide range of brewing materials and very effective at cleaning all sorts of brewing debris. Powdered Brewery Wash (PBW) produced by Five Star Chemicals is my go-to cleaning agent; however, generic powder oxygen cleaners are also very good.

To clean brewing equipment with an oxygen-based cleaner, use approximately 1 tablespoon for every gallon of water. Alternatively, PBW recommends ¾ ounce per gallon for lightly soiled vessels and stronger dilutions for more heavily soiled equipment. In general, check the manufacturer's recommended dilution for the desired cleaning application. Once the dilution is mixed, let the brewing vessel or object soak for 30 minutes and then fully rinse to remove any residual agent.

 BREWING MYTH

Myth: Powdered oxygen cleaners clean and sanitize at the same time.

Beware of any advertisements suggesting a one-step process. In order to appropriately clean and sanitize using powdered oxygen cleaners, two separate solutions are required. A cleaning solution is prepared to remove any stuck-on materials and brewing debris. After cleaning, this solution should be discarded and the brewing vessel or object rinsed thoroughly. Then, prepare a second solution solely to sanitize.

Detergents Essentially dish soap, detergents are another effective method for cleaning brewing equipment, although they come with some minor drawbacks. To use, simply add a few drops of liquid soap per gallon of water and allow the brewing object or vessel to soak for 30 minutes to remove brewing debris. However, because they are designed to clean heavily soiled items, such as a casserole pan with baked-on food, dish soaps also tend to leave behind thin films of residue, which can be potentially disruptive to the brewing process. If you use a detergent for cleaning, choose an unscented version without too many additives and rinse thoroughly to fully remove residual cleaning agent.

Bleach Bleach is my least favorite cleaning agent, although it can be very effective when used properly. For budget-strapped homebrewers, or when homebrewing supplies are limited, bleach is a sure-fire way to remove brewing debris. For most plastic and glass brewing equipment, a cleaning dilution of 3 to 4 tablespoons of bleach per gallon of water works well. Like detergents, make sure to thoroughly rinse after cleaning to remove any residual bleach.

There are many drawbacks to cleaning with bleach, but most occur with improper use. Bleach can easily burn skin and stain clothing, so wear gloves and take precautions. Also, be sure to use unfragranced bleach. When properly diluted and applied with care, bleach can be used on all brewing materials; however, when implemented improperly it can be very corrosive to commonly used brewing metals, such as stainless steel, copper, brass, and aluminum. If you are not confident using bleach with metals, I would avoid it as it may activate corrosive reactions and cause surface pitting.

Sanitization Supplies

After cleaning, sanitization is the next step in the process. However, unlike cleaning, which uses a combination of mechanical and chemical methods to remove brewing debris, sanitation purely relies on chemical means to eliminate residual contaminants at the surface.

There are several types of sanitizing agents for brewing purposes, each working in a unique way. Essentially all sanitizers reduce microorganism contaminates through prolonged contact with an active chemical diluted in water. Typically, all surfaces need full contact with a sanitizing agent for a minimum exposure time to effectively remove contaminates. The following are some of the most commonly used products for sanitization.

Star San This is a commercially available sanitizer manufactured by Five Star Chemicals. It uses a blend of acids to sanitize surfaces. One of the best things about Star San is that it doesn't require rinsing after use, which lowers the chance for reintroducing unwanted wild yeast and bacteria through the rinse water. Additionally, any residual Star San can actually benefit fermentation, as it contains phosphorus, a yeast nutrient. Star San foams excessively when mixing and pouring, but the foam is not a cause for concern. In fact, the foaming aids sanitization by increasing surface contact. Since it is a no-rinse, nutritionally additive, reusable sanitizer, Star San is my preferred sanitizing agent throughout the brewing process. To use, add 1 ounce of Star San for every 5 gallons of water and leave in full contact with the brewing object or vessel for at least 30 seconds, although 2 minutes is preferred.

> **BREWING TIP**
>
> If you're looking to save a few bucks while brewing, consider reusing Star San. As a sanitizing agent, it can be reused multiple times as long as appropriate cleaning methods are observed. Star San actively sanitizes with a pH below 3. To test, use pH strips or a tabletop pH meter. Do not reuse Star San when the pH rises above 3, if the Star San solution comes in contact with an unclean surface and becomes dirty, or has a cloudy appearance.

Powdered oxygen cleaners These can be used for sanitization as well as cleaning. Manufactured by several companies, powdered oxygen cleaners use sodium percarbonates to sanitize surfaces. Sanitizing dilutions are generally weaker in strength than cleaning dilutions, typically 1 tablespoon per gallon of water. At these dilutions, no rinsing is required, but if you feel compelled, rinse with sterile water to avoid reintroducing contaminates through the rinse water. Although effective as a sanitizing agent, I only use powdered oxygen cleaners to clean dirty brewing equipment and stick with Star San to do the sanitizing. To use, add 1 tablespoon of powdered oxygen cleaner for every 1 gallon of water and leave in full contact with the brewing object or vessel for at least 2 minutes.

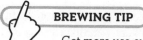

Get more use out of powdered oxygen cleaners! Unlike Star San, powdered oxygen cleaners cannot be reused as a sanitizer. However, after a sanitizing cycle, the powdered oxygen cleaner solution is still effective as a cleaning agent. Consider saving the remaining solution for cleaning dirty brewing equipment.

Iodophor An iodine-based sanitizing agent, Iodophor is often used as an alternative to Star San since it does not foam, which is useful when sanitizing long tubing and kegging equipment. Its major drawback is its propensity to stain light-colored plastics with a brownish color. Don't worry; this staining is purely cosmetic and won't harm the brewing equipment effectiveness or introduce any off-flavors. Like Star San and powdered oxygen cleaners, Iodophor at the recommended dilution does not need to be rinsed. To use, add 1 ounce of Iodophor for every 5 gallons of water and leave in full contact with the brewing object or vessel for at least 2 minutes.

Bleach Bleach is an effective agent for sanitization, although among my least favorite. As with cleaning, use only unscented bleach and be sure to use proper skin protection when handling. Although it is not necessary to rinse when used at the proper dilution, residual amount of chlorides may result in off-flavors, typically a harsh phenolic character. For this reason, I recommend rinsing with sterile water to avoid bleach-based off-flavors without reintroducing potential contaminants. Also, avoid using bleach with metal brewing equipment such as stainless steel, copper, or aluminum materials due to its corrosive nature and propensity for surface pitting. To use as a sanitizer, add 1 tablespoon of bleach for every 1 gallon of water and leave in full contact with the brewing object or vessel for at least 2 minutes.

General Cleaning and Sanitizing Procedure

With the cleaning and sanitizing process explored, it's now time to combine this knowledge to clean and sanitize your brewing equipment. Prior to the end of the boil, brewing items only need to be cleaned, not sanitized, as the boil will sanitize the wort from contamination. However, post-boil, it's important to remember that both cleaning and sanitization are necessary for the remainder of the brewing process. What needs to be sanitized? The simple answer is anything and everything that comes into direct contact with the wort and beer.

From start to finish, the cleaning and sanitizing process follows a 10-step procedure. For cleaning only, follow steps 1 to 5. When cleaning and sanitizing lightly-soiled pieces, steps 2 and 3 can be skipped. For heavily soiled items, steps 2 and 3 are recommended. See the cleaning and sanitizing agents section for detailed instruction on using specific cleaning tools and cleaning and sanitizing agents.

On brew day, common items for sanitization include fermentors, airlocks, tubing, and racking canes. When packaging, common items for sanitization include buckets, spigots, tubing, and bottles or kegs. When sanitizing buckets or fermentors, I fill the vessel to the brim with sanitizing solution, whereas with miscellaneous brewing objects like racking canes and tubing, I like to keep a bucket with all of my brewing gear sanitized, readied for any step in the brewing process.

General 10-Step Cleaning Procedure

1. Rinse off any loose brewing debris, such as spent grain, dried beer or wort, krausen, trub, and yeast.

2. Remove stuck-on brewing debris using mechanical methods, typically jet washing or soft scrubbing with brushes.

3. Rinse again to wash away mechanically removed debris.

4. Soak in a cleaning solution made at an appropriate dilution to ensure the remaining brewing debris is removed.

5. Discard used cleaning agent.

6. Thoroughly rinse with water to remove residual cleaning agent.

7. Protect clean vessel or equipment from reintroduced debris, and prepare sanitizing solution.

8. Use sanitizing solution made at the appropriate dilution to reduce any possible remaining contaminants.

9. Discard sanitizing agent. Air dry or rinse with sterile water if any residual sanitizer-based off-flavors are possible.

10. Lastly, protect freshly sanitized vessel or equipment from reintroduced contaminants.

The Least You Need to Know

- Keeping brewing equipment clean and sanitized are critical steps practiced throughout the brewing process.

- Contaminants such as bacteria and wild yeast can ruin a batch of beer.

- Several effective cleaning and sanitizing agents are available to homebrewers to avoid unwanted contamination.

CHAPTER 10

Brewing Measurement and Recordkeeping

Brewing measurement and recordkeeping are important aspects of the brewing process. Although it is not strictly necessary to measure and record every step of your brewing process, the best homebrewers perform a multitude of brewing measurements and keep detailed records for each beer they brew. In this chapter, you learn what measurements you need to take, how to take them, and how to record them for later reference.

Why Are Measurements and Recordkeeping Important?

In homebrewing, taking measurements involves testing various properties of your wort and beer to ensure the desired end result: great tasting homebrew. Recording your measurements is the next part, so you can track these properties in your process over time. Homebrewing can be done without measurement, but it will result in a great deal of variability from brew to brew, and you may end up with an undesirable product. Another way of saying it is this: you can make good beer without brewing measurement and recordkeeping; however, you can't make world-class beer without it.

There are four motivating factors for brewing measurement and recordkeeping: quality, consistency, replication, and process improvement.

Quality

Nobody wants to drink poor quality beer, at least not among the craft beer community, right? As a homebrewer, you have the power to create high-quality beers at home. Quality is driven through a number of brewing factors like ingredient freshness, source water, and sanitization, but also through brewing measurement and recordkeeping. Using these tools, you can ensure you hit the right temperature and pH targets, which greatly affect the overall beer quality, and achieve at the very least your personal quality standards.

Consistency

Consistency, consistency, consistency! Motivational business quotes aside, consistency is always the goal of the master brewer. At the homebrewing level, consistency does not necessarily imply the ability to exactly replicate a beer batch after batch, but rather brewing at the same level of quality and character batch after batch. Because consistency is directly related to quality and replication, it should be no surprise that brewing measurement and recordkeeping is key in achieving this goal.

Replication

The kick-yourself-in-the-butt moment. I've met several brewers who have "junk drawer" brew sessions, where they use up leftover brewing ingredients nearing expiration instead of throwing them away. In these sessions, they'll throw a random assortment of ingredients together, not really measuring or recording anything, because they expect the end result to be passable. However, unexpectedly, the beer turns out great, worthy of a rebrew. A few measurements and a simple record would have prevented this moment, but instead, this information is gone forever. Sad stories aside, replication is just that, being able to make a great beer again without guess work. Keeping a simple recipe is a start, but recording more detailed brewing information is better.

Process Improvement

Last, but not least, process improvement is only really possible with detailed measurement and recordkeeping. When you get unexpected results from a homebrew, you'll want to figure out what happened in order better understand and possibly prevent reoccurrence during future brew sessions. Once the problem is correctly identified through tasting evaluation, the answer almost certainly lies within your brewing process and having a good record can accelerate the search for a solution.

Brewing Measurement Devices

The thorough brewer utilizes a variety of measuring tools to keep wort and beer attributes within their desired ranges and to provide technical feedback throughout the brewing process. Some of the basic attributes measured in homebrewing are temperature, weight, volume, specific gravity, and acidity. This section covers the tools needed to make these measurements and explains why they're important.

Several simple measurement devices are used by the brewer, even at the beginner level, including thermometers, hydrometers, and pH test strips.

Measuring Specific Gravity: Hydrometers and Refractometers

The measurement specific gravity is an informative metric used throughout the brewing process. Generally speaking, specific gravity (SG) is a ratio of the density of a substance compared to the density of a reference substance. In brewing, the measured substance is wort and beer while the reference substance is nearly always pure water.

Specific gravity, which is often loosely called simply "gravity," determines a number of key brewing parameters. Typically, specific gravity is used to measure the ABV of a fermented beer, although it is also often employed for several other aspects of the brewing process. In all-grain brewing, specific gravity is key to determining the end point of the sparge process. During wort production, specific gravity is often measured to determine the gravities prior to the boil, a key metric in isomerization. During fermentation, maintaining stable final gravity readings over a few days suggests a complete fermentation. Lastly, the difference between the wort gravity before pitching, defined as starting gravity, and the beer gravity after fermentation, defined as final gravity, is the recommended method for determining the degree of attenuation and its associated ABV.

The measure of specific gravity utilizes a number of scales to represent its ratio. The most intuitive is the specific gravity scale, which expresses changes in density by decimal number. This scale is calibrated to pure water, which has a reading of 1.000 on the scale. Sugar water solutions, like wort and beer, have a higher density than water and thus a decimal greater than 1. For example, a common wort gravity is 1.050, and from this scale, means it has 5 percent more density than water. Instead of quoting the decimal number or percentage, brewers often use the points terminology, like bond and stock traders. From the gravity reading, the last three digits of gravity are referred to as points. In the previous example, 1.050 would also be called 50 gravity points.

Scales other than the specific gravity scale are used in brewing, particularly the Plato (°P) scale. These scales are actually a relative measure of weight rather than density. Brewers commonly use Plato and specific gravity scales interchangeably, and as a close estimate, Plato is approximately 4 times less than specific gravity points. For example, 12°P is approximately equal to 48 gravity points, or 1.048 on the specific gravity scale.

In the brewing process, specific gravity is measured using either a hydrometer or a refractometer. A hydrometer is a tubular weighted glass device with a long thin stem that measures wort and beer gravity through buoyancy. The hydrometer floats with its thin glass stem sticking above the test sample. The glass stem has calibrated markings on it that correspond to a range of gravities. The greater the density, the higher the hydrometer floats, corresponding to a greater specific gravity reading on its stem.

To measure the gravity of a sample, pour the sample into a tall, narrow vessel and then insert the hydrometer. Once this is set up, you can take a reading. For most hydrometers, you ignore the meniscus, the upward bend curvature due to surface tension between the sidewalls and wort or beer sample. Instead, align your eye with the bottom of the curvature. Find the closest marking to this level and record in your brewing log.

To obtain accurate measurements with a hydrometer, you have to follow a few guidelines. Your test jar must be large enough to hold a 4- to 6-ounce sample of wort or beer without the hydrometer touching the sides or bottom. Also, make sure to record the sample temperature, as the density of wort changes dramatically with temperature. Most hydrometers are calibrated for samples at 59°F. If your sample is significantly warmer or colder than 59°F, there are online calculators you can use to correct your reading (for example, davesdreaded.com/homebrew-calculator).

This hydrometer reading is 48 gravity points.

Refractometers are another tool to measure specific gravity. Instead of measuring density, refractometers use a light source and prism to measure the refraction of light in the liquid. Sugar water solutions, like wort, have a higher index of refraction than pure water. When viewed through the eye piece of refractometer, the relative degree of light bending appears on a scale calibrated to specific gravity. The greater level of sugar in solution provides a greater degree of bending, and thus corresponding to a higher reading on the calibrated scale. Refractometers commonly come in scales calibrated to specific gravity, Plato, and/or Brix.

Unlike hydrometers, the main benefit of refractometers is that you only need a few drops of a sample to get a reading, as opposed to the 4- to 6-ounce sample needed with hydrometers. Also, refractometers are less sensitive to the temperature of the sample. However, unlike hydrometers, refractometers are only accurate for wort and not beer, since it contains alcohol, which introduces error as it adds an uncalibrated index of refraction. Luckily, there are free online calculators available that can be used to correct for alcohol in hydrometer readings (see seanterrill/2012/01/06/refractometer-calculator).

In terms of resolution, hydrometers and refractometers are about the same, with readings near 0.0005 on the specific gravity scale or 0.2°P. The main difference is cost and convenience, where refractometers are a bit more expensive, but often worth it in convenience. This is especially true for all-grain brewers taking pre-boil gravities during lautering; with a refractometer, only a few drops a necessary for a quick, simple, and accurate reading. Using a hydrometer, the brewer must remove and cool a 4- to 6-ounce wort sample, which is cumbersome on a brew day. However, most brewers utilize both hydrometers and refractometers in gravity measurement as both are accurate and have advantages during various parts of the brewing process.

Measuring Ingredients: Scales

It should be no surprise that scales are used to measure the weights of brewing ingredients called for in beer recipes. However, the range of weights used in brewing varies widely, from tens of pounds for malted grains to fractions of an ounce for hops, spices, and water additions. Thus, for the precision homebrewer, a range of scales are necessary to accurately measure brewing ingredients and record recipes.

There are main two tradeoffs in brewing scales: maximum capacity and resolution. Scales with a high maximum capacity are able to handle greater amounts of weight, while scales with high resolution are able to record smaller amounts. In general, scales with high maximum capacity have low resolution, and vice versa. Because of this, you may need to use more than one scale for weight measurement.

Scales used for homebrewing can be categorized into two types: analog and digital. The analog scales are the same type commonly seen in the produce section of your grocery store and measure ingredients using a calibrated spring-and-lever system. Analog scales can handle large amounts of weight and they are also very affordable compared to digital scales. The downside to analog scales is that their resolution is typically lower, so while they're great for measuring pounds of base malt and malt extract, they're typically not able to record amounts smaller than an ounce.

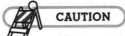 **CAUTION**

Do not exceed the maximum weight or mass capacity specified by the scale manufacturer. Weighting elements are highly sensitive, and pushing a scale beyond its capacity limit will require recalibration or possibly cause damage beyond repair. To avoid this, slowly add ingredients to the scale. If close to maximum capacity, break up weight additions into multiple sets to safely measure without causing scale damage.

Digital scales are the next level up in weight accuracy, and measure ingredients through load cells, which convert voltage changes in a strained circuit into a calibrated weight measurement. The upside to digital scales is that they are incredibly precise, with resolutions down to fractions of a gram. Also, they have a "tare" function, meaning you can easily subtract out the weight of a bowl or bag holding an ingredient. The downside to digital scales is the cost; high-precision models can be on the expensive side compared to analog scales.

Kitchen-grade digital scales are a good option for homebrewers as they offer the necessary maximum capacity, generally up to 11 pounds with resolution down to 1 gram, which is good for most brewing ingredient weights except for the extremely low weight items like water additions, spices, herbs, and small hop additions. For these items, a high-precision scale should be used. These scales typically have capacities ranging from 100 to 500 grams and resolution in the 0.01 to 0.1 gram range.

Brewing Scale Summary

Type	Max Capacity	Resolution	Use in Brewing
Analog	5–55 pounds	0.5-2 ounces	base malts, malt extract
Digital	5–55 pounds	1 gram	base malts, malt extract, specialty malts, hops
Digital	100–500 grams	0.01–0.1 gram	water additions, spices, herbs, small hop additions

Brewing Volumes

Unlike other measurements in the brewing process, brewing volumes are not as strict when it comes to method and degree of accuracy. Essentially, when brewing a batch of beer, you want to determine how are close you are to the desired batch volume. Luckily for the homebrewer, there are a few relatively easy methods to determine wort and beer volumes without having to use a highly calibrated device.

On the brew day, a simple plastic pitcher with marked volumes works well for adding water to kettles and hot liquor tanks. Measuring out 3 to 6 gallons of water for a 5-gallon batch can be done fairly quickly with a half-gallon pitcher. However, even this method is at a slight inconvenience for many brewers. An even easier method is to create a measuring tool calibrated to your brew kettle using a wooden dowel.

To do this, insert a wooden dowel in your empty brew kettle and hold it so it stands straight up. Using a calibrated pitcher, add water to the kettle in half-gallon increments. With each addition, mark the height that the water reaches on the dowel. Once you have the dowel marked, cut notches over the marks for permanence.

For future brew sessions, water pitchers are no longer necessary to measure out volume, provided you're using the same brew kettle that you used when creating your calibrated dowel. In addition, you can easily estimate boil volumes by simply placing the dowel into the kettle and seeing where the level hits the markings. Boil volume measurement is less accurate, since the boiling action and slight wort expansion at boil temperatures causes some uncertainty; however, the overall estimate shouldn't be too far off.

A similar strategy can be employed to mark volume levels on glass or plastic fermentors. In this case, you add water to the fermentor using a calibrated pitcher and mark the level on the side of the fermentor with a permanent marker (for glass fermenters, you may need to write on a piece of masking tape). Many brewers only mark off the 5-gallon level, which works well for 5-gallon batches; however, marking gallon, half-gallon, and even quarter-gallon increments would be better.

 BREWING TIP

If you've purchased a brew bucket with preprinted volume measures on the side, double check the measurements to make sure they are accurate. Preprinted volume measures are a nice gesture, but often are not well-calibrated. Simply add water in measured intervals (half gallon, gallon, etc.) to confirm or adjust these markings. That way, you'll have a reliable volume scale for future use.

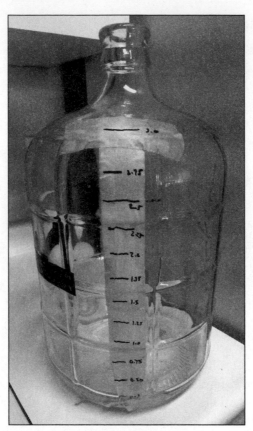

A small 3-gallon carboy used for cider making, calibrated and marked for every quarter gallon.

Keeping Track of Date and Time

Keeping track of date and time is key in the brewing process, and unsurprisingly is the easiest measurement to make. More importantly, durations, scaling from minutes to weeks, are a good metric for performance in the brewing process. Fortunately for most brewers, a simple timer and calendar is all you need to take these measurements.

On the brew day, timing is everything, especially during wort production. You may have one or more boil additions that need to be added during the last 15 minutes, and the timing of these can affect the quality and character of the finished beer. For this, all you need is a simple watch, but a timer would be better.

Looking at the big picture, from start to finish, the brewing process for a standard beer takes about three weeks, and keeping track of the days and hours can at the very least alleviate any confusion of where you are within the process. More productively, fermentation tracked day by day is a good gauge of performance, and will help you troubleshoot any problems like stuck fermentation and yeast health.

Measuring Temperature

If you only pay attention to one measurement in the brewing process, it should be temperature. Temperature is a fundamental brewing parameter that is monitored almost continuously throughout the brewing process. On brew day, temperature is key to a good specialty malt steep for extract brewers and is crucial for the all-grain brewer performing a mash. After the boil, the brewer needs to cool the wort to pitching temperature, and during fermentation, temperature needs to be monitored at the very least, but ideally controlled.

There are three common types of thermometers used in brewing: dial, glass bulb, and digital. If you've picked up a homebrew starter kit, it likely has a glass bulb thermometer in it. For the extract brewer, a glass bulb thermometer is a good starter version, as it's inexpensive with resolution near 1°F, which is sufficient for most measurement needs. That being said, they have a few downsides. They are fragile, somewhat difficult to read (especially over a steaming kettle), slow to adjust to temperature changes, and they cannot be calibrated if they fall out of adjustment. Although glass bulb thermometers are accurate enough for all-grain brewing, many brewers upgrade to a dial or digital thermometer for a higher degree of speed, accuracy, and durability.

CAUTION

Avoid glass bulb mercury thermometers. Although they have a high degree of accuracy and are very reliable, mercury-based thermometers are not recommended for food-based applications, like brewing.

Dial thermometers are a relatively inexpensive alternative to glass bulb thermometers. They consist of a metal probe that sticks into a substance (in our case wort/beer) and a clocklike dial that displays the measured temperature. They are available in handheld versions and as brew kettle fixtures, which are permanently attached to the kettle. Dial thermometers measure temperatures quickly, usually within 15 to 20 seconds, and can be recalibrated using a set screw, much like winding a mechanical wristwatch. However, there are a few drawbacks, mainly resolution within 1°F and often poor quality dials, which get stuck and require gentle tapping to ensure an accurate dial reading.

Due to the downsides of both dial and glass bulb thermometers, many brewers move toward digital thermometers, not only for wort production, but also for controlled fermentation. Like dial thermometers, digital thermometers have a metal probe for insertion; however, the temperature reading is shown on a digital display. Since the temperature reading is electronic, it can be fed directly to a computer, allowing logic to control things such as burner power or chamber temperature without the brewer's involvement. For more information on digital temperature control, check out Chapter 20.

Digital thermometers are capable of gauging temperature within 2 to 5 seconds, have resolution near 0.1°F, and can be easily recalibrated at a press of a button. The downside to digital thermometers is that they can be on the pricey side, with many computer-controlled models running in the hundreds of dollars. However, many high-quality handheld versions run around the same cost as dial thermometer in price.

Summary of Brewing Thermometers

Type	Resolution	Speed
Glass bulb	within 0.5–1°F	1–2 minutes
Dial	within 0.5–2°F	15–20 seconds
Digital	within 0.1–1°F	2–5 seconds

Measuring Acidity: pH Meters and Test Strips

Acidity in wort and beer is often a major factor for the advanced homebrewer, especially when controlling mash chemistry and monitoring fermentation. In order to hit target pH levels, the brewer must measure mash, wort, and beer acidity. For the homebrewer, pH measurement devices come in two forms: pH test strips and electronic pH meters.

The simplest way to measure pH is by using test strips, small pieces of paper with a chemically treated surface that reacts to the pH of a tested solution. Once dipped and removed, the reaction type causes the paper to change color, which corresponds to a pH range shown on a colored key. Test strips are an attractive option for the homebrewer as they are fairly inexpensive and do not require active calibration before use; however, there are a few downsides. Primarily, they typically offer less resolution, ranging from 0.1 to 0.2 pH; a higher resolution is preferred for brewing. Also, the color is often difficult to read and compare against the color key, adding to inaccuracy.

If you want to give pH test strips a try in your brewing, make sure to use the recommended soak and drying times for accurate results; it's a common misconception that test strips are instantly read. Also, find test strips within beer's pH range, between 4 and 6 pH works best. If possible, use custom beer pH test strips. These are usually a bit more expensive than generic kinds, but lend a higher degree of resolution and accuracy as its tailored for wort/beer conditions. Additionally, make sure you test the pH when your sample is at the temperature recommended by the pH strip manufacturer. (This is usually around room temperature.) Lastly, make sure the strips are new, as older pH strips lose their accuracy over time.

Many of the difficulties associated with pH test strips motivate brewers to use electronic means to test mash, wort, and beer pH. Although a hassle at times, pH meters offer a high degree of accuracy for measuring acidity. Electronic pH meters are essentially volt meters, and measure the difference in electric potential associated with the pH of a solution. Meters commonly come in three types—pen, handheld, and bench top—but all essentially work using the same principle. Many feature temperature corrected readings, a plus for brewers who want to measure mash pH at temperature. Pen and handheld versions are useful for convenience, ease of use, and affordability; however, they are typically less accurate and have less stable calibrations. Bench-top models are the cream of the crop, offering the highest degree of accuracy, and unlike their name suggests, can still be held in hand, just a little on the large side. Bench-top models are also expensive, sometimes $100 or more, so you certainly require a bit of investment for its high degree of accuracy.

The main hassle with pH meters is the constant need for recalibration. The probe that is placed in the solution for measurement is highly sensitive, and must be recalibrated before every use to yield accurate results. When done using, the sensitive probe must also be stored in a buffer solution. Also, the pH meter probes have a limited lifetime, and usually last between one to three years. This is by far the biggest drawback to using electronic pH meters.

Overall, pH meters offer a high degree of accuracy, with the major downsides of constant calibration, cost, and maintenance. When selecting a meter, make sure it has accuracy and resolution within 0.1 pH, but after going through the tedium of calibration, 0.01 pH would be better. With proper care, your pH meter will give you accurate measurements for several years. If you are an occasional mini-mash brewer, I would stick with pH test strips due to their low cost and ease of use. However, if you plan to extensively brew using all-grain, then a solid bench-top pH meter is highly recommended, and well worth the accuracy for dialing in your mash chemistry.

Brewing pH Device Summary

Type	Range	Resolution
Beer test strips	3–7 pH	within 0.1–0.4 pH
Handheld meter	0–14 pH	within 0.1 pH
Bench-top meter	0–14 pH	within 0.01–0.1 pH

Brewing Recordkeeping

One of the hallmarks of great breweries are their decades—or even centuries—of old brewing logs. For example, Fuller's Brewery, famous for London Pride Special Bitter and ESB, has brewing logs dating back to the nineteenth century. Like Fuller's, brewing logs for the homebrewer are all about recording brewing information throughout the process, like durations, observations, and brewing measurements for later reference.

BREWER'S LOG

DATE _____   BEER
NAME _____   BATCH
SIZE _____

MALT

TYPE	AMOUNT	COLOR	YIELD

HOPS

TYPE	AA	AMOUNT	TIME	IBU

OTHER ADDITIONS

TYPE	AMOUNT	TIME

BREWER'S NOTES

WATER PROFILE

$CaCO_3$	Ca	Mg	Na	Cl	SO_4	OTHER WATER TREATMENT

WORT PRODUCTION

Pre-boil Volume _____   Pre-boil Gravity _____

Boil Duration _____   Expected IBU _____

Post-boil Volume _____   Original Gravity _____

YEAST AND FERMENTATION

Type _____   Number of Cells _____   Pitching Temperature _____

Primary Fermentation Temperature _____   Duration _____

Secondary Fermentation Temperature _____   Duration _____

Final Gravity _____   Percent Attentuation _____   ABV _____

PACKAGING

Number of Bottles / Volume in Keg _____   Priming / CO_2 Volumes _____

A brewer's log doesn't have to be fancy; a simple piece of paper and a pen or pencil will do the trick. A step up would be to keep a notebook, binder, or folder to organize your brewing records. More technologically savvy brewers can utilize cloud-based recipe storage, allowing easy access to your brewing information anywhere you go. No matter what method you chose, it's important that you use it and infuse as much detail as you can. A poor record is of little use, but an overly detailed entry can do no harm. The preceding sample brewing log template can be used as a starting point for recording your brewing data. You can also download and print this log at idiotsguides.com/homebrewing.

If you are new to brewing, you may not be sure what to record. The following is a list of brewing parameters that may be useful to record during the process. At a minimum, note the date of the brew day and a short recipe including grist, hops additions, and pitched yeast strain. This is a good starting place and gives you a point of reference for future reference.

Recipe: grist along with weight, yield, color contribution, and maltster; hops, including packaging data, alpha acid content, and type (whole, plug, pellet, extract); other ingredients sugars, etc.

Wort production: steeping malt temperatures, water profile, boil duration, evaporation rate, pre-boil volume, post-boil volume, time to chill

Pitching: yeast strain type, racked volume, pitching temperature, pitch rate, aeration parameters (technique, concentration), original gravity

Fermentation: time to high krausen, time to krausen fall, fermentation temperature profile, primary fermentation duration

Conditioning and packaging: attenuation, packaging volume, priming conditions, condition duration, final gravity

Evaluation: appearance, smell/aroma, taste/flavor, mouthfeel/body, overall impression, feedback for next brew session or recipe modification

All-grain brewing (optional): mash water profile, mash technique, mash temperature profile, mash thickness, lauter/sparge volumes, sparge water profile, mash pH, efficiency

The Least You Need to Know

- Brewing measurement and recordkeeping can elevate the overall quality of your homebrew and refine your process.
- Several brewing measurement parameters are key, such as temperature, gravity, and acidity, and can be measured using a wide array of devices.
- Keeping a brewer's log is straightforward and can be done in an organized fashion using the worksheet in this chapter.

The Brewing Process

There are three major steps to making beer: constructing the wort, fermentation, and packaging. This part covers each of these steps in detail, expanding upon the important factors and considerations of each step, and in particular, focusing on strategies for pushing your brewing process from good to great.

Making Wort

Making wort is arguably the most fun part of the brewing process aside from drinking your hard-earned homebrew. On the brew day, the extract brewer makes flavorful and fermentable wort through a series of steps, chiefly steeping specialty malts, mixing malt extract with water and bringing it to a boil, adding hops and other ingredients throughout the boil, and chilling it down. This chapter walks you through the process of constructing wort with malt extract, and details the wort boiling and chilling process used by both extract and all-grain brewers.

Before diving into the process, you may be wondering, "How do I make wort from base malts as opposed to malt extract?" When brewing with base malts, the all-grain brewer constructs the wort using a mash, which is not covered in this chapter, but fully detailed in Part 6 of this book. Except for the first few pages, the majority of this chapter is applicable to both extract and all-grain brewing, especially the boiling and chilling stages.

In This Chapter

- How to construct wort using malt extract and specialty malts
- Bringing wort to a boil and adding hops
- Why chilling wort is important and how to do it quickly

Constructing Pre-Boil Wort with Malt Extract

When constructing wort, the extract brewer has two main ingredients to work with: malt extract, both liquid and dry, and specialty malts, both crystal and roasted varieties. These malt types are discussed at length in Chapter 3. This section focuses on how to integrate these ingredients to make wort. It also addresses some optional but useful ingredient addition considerations to enhance malt and hop flavor in wort before a boil is achieved.

Working with Malt Extract

Adding malt extract to brewing water is as simple as opening a can, jug, or bag and dumping it in a brew kettle full of water. However, like most things in brewing, there are some finer points to consider. When adding malt extract to water, hot water is better than cold, as the malt will dissolve more quickly and will not create a sticky mess inside the kettle. How warm? Well, it depends on the malt extract type. When using DME, you want the water to be warm, but not too hot. Aim for the temperature you would use to wash dishes. If the water is too hot, DME will lump up in small balls that are hard to break up and annoyingly persist throughout the boil. Conversely, when using LME, it's best to add it to very hot, near-boiling water. LME is very dense, like molasses, and takes time to dissolve. In this case, hot water means faster integration.

However, for both DME and LME, there is one major thing to watch out for on brew day, and that's making sure the burner power is off before adding malt extract. Due to its high density relative to water, DME, and especially LME, falls straight to the bottom of the kettle. A burner on full blast, whether stove top or propane, will likely burn the extract and cause burnt wort flavors that are undesirable in your homebrew.

Steeping Specialty Malts

As detailed in Chapter 3, specialty malts are added to infuse color, flavor, and mouthfeel to many beer styles. In a 5-gallon batch, specialty malts may be added in quantities ranging from ¼ pound to 2 pounds. Since these malts are already converted, they don't require a mash to get the goodness out, and instead they are steeped like tea.

Specialty malts yield the best results when steeped in hot water (150°F–170°F) for 30 minutes. Similar to tea, there is an optimal water-to-specialty-malt ratio to maximize extraction without yielding tanninlike off-flavors. For the best performing steep, use 1 gallon of brewing water per pound of crushed specialty malt. Large steeps can be done right in your brew kettle. For smaller additions, on the order of a quarter pound, the water in your brew kettle may be too shallow, so a saucepan or large glass liquid measuring cup can be used instead. Lastly, if using the kettle, be sure to steep before adding malt extract, as it can reduce extraction.

Optimizing Brewing Water

As mentioned in Chapter 6, minerals in brewing water greatly affect malt and hop flavor expression in beer. In particular, chloride softens flavors and accentuates malt, while sulfates sharpen flavors and express hops. In low to medium concentrations, the relative ratio between the two ions, known in brewing as the chloride-to-sulfate ratio, is the most important metric for its expressive contributions in beer. While water chemistry and mineral additions are mostly a concern of the all-grain brewer, flavor additions are independent of the mash, and can be utilized by both the extract and all-grain brewer to fine-tune malt or hops character.

The chloride-to-sulfate ratio is the relative concentration between the chloride and sulfate ions in brewing water. This ratio can be adjusted, depending on whether a particular recipe is meant to be malt-forward, hop-forward, or balanced. In practice, brewing water must have an excess of one ion over the other to sway the water profile beyond balanced.

Typically, brewers tailoring brewing water use a chloride-to-sulfate ratio of 2:1 for malt-forward expression and a chloride-to-sulfate ratio of 1:2 for hop-forward expression, with balanced ratios falling roughly in the 1:1 range. As previously mentioned, the absolute ion concentrations have little effect when kept in the low to average brewing concentrations. This is convenient, as the brewer has to do very little to modify source water in order to achieve the desired effect. As long as your source water has reasonably low levels of sulfate and chloride concentrations, all you have to do to achieve a desired ratio is add measured amounts of either calcium chloride (to boost chloride ion concentration) or gypsum (to boost sulfate levels). With some practice, you can experiment to see how far to push the chloride-to-sulfate ratio to maximize effect. Many brewers report successful results when pushing ratios as high as 6:1 for malt-forward styles and as high as 1:9 for hop-forward styles, like IPAs. Starting out, it's good to stick with 1:2 and 2:1 ratios and work your way up as needed, as higher ratios risk mineral off-flavors.

To yield a specific chloride-to-sulfate ratio, you'll need to do a bit of calculation based on your source water chemistry in order to correctly estimate the amount of brewing minerals needed. The calculation isn't hard, just a bit of math. Say your water report reveals your tap water has 70 ppm chloride and 50 ppm sulfate concentrations, and you are trying to make a hoppy IPA with a sulfate-forward profile at a chloride-to-sulfate ratio of 1:2 to enhanced hop character. To yield this ratio, you'll need to increase sulfate concentration to 140 ppm, two times the chloride concentration of your unmodified brewing water. However, since you already have 50 ppm, you'll only need to add 90 ppm to achieve this concentration. To increase sulfates using gypsum, 1 gram will yield 147 ppm of sulfate in 1 gallon of pure water. Since only 90 ppm is needed, only 0.61 grams of gypsum are needed per gallon of brewing water. Thus, in a 5-gallon batch, a total of 3.05 grams of gypsum is needed. When measuring out by teaspoon, gypsum yields 4 grams per level teaspoon, meaning that you'll only need to add approximately ¾ teaspoon to hit the desired chloride-to-sulfate ratio of 1:2 in your 5-gallon batch.

Following that logic, you should be able to calculate the water additions needed to achieve any ratio based on your unmodified brewing water and brewing mineral additions. If you'd rather not perform hand calculations, there are several online brewing water calculators that can do the math for you, such as brewersfriend.com/water-chemistry. However, it's good practice to understand where this magic math comes from. Lastly, for more information on the types of brewing minerals, concentrations in brewing water, and grams per level teaspoon, check out Chapter 6.

Going forward, be aware that the chloride-to-sulfate ratio is an adjustment tool, not the source of malt or hop character in beer. When the malt or hops are not at the level desired, you're better off modifying the recipe by changing the malt and hops rather than steepening the ratio or increasing ion concentrations. Also, make sure the ion concentrations are within the recommended brewing ranges; exceeding these can result in harsh off-flavors. If your source water has a restrictively high chloride or sulfate concentration, it's best to dilute your source water with pure water to achieve an appropriate ratio rather increasing hardness. Lastly, if you are unsure or in doubt over water additions, it's best to under modify than over. Like seasoning, you can always add more, but you can't take out what you've added.

First Wort Hopping

First wort hopping is a technique derived from the German brewing tradition where hops are infused in the wort before the boil to preserve flavor and aroma while also yielding a smooth bitterness. The first wort hop infusion typically takes place over an hour during the wort runoff in a mash, but can be replicated by the extract brewer by simply steeping the first wort addition in hot wort for approximately an hour before boiling the wort. The standard first wort recipe is variable, but commonly suggests replacing approximately 30 percent of your late additions with the first wort addition and using a lower alpha acid variety. Even though the hops are present in the wort throughout the boil, many brewers report a smoother bitterness, equivalent to a 20-minute addition, leaving a majority of the hop compounds for flavor and aroma behind in the final beer.

Although many homebrewers and craft brewers utilize this technique, often with great results, first wort hopping is not a universally accepted practice and its effectiveness is still hotly debated. First wort hopping has been widely studied by the craft and homebrewing communities and tasting panel results are mixed at best. Recent IBU studies suggest isomerization equivalent to a bittering addition occurs; however, the jury is still out over the flavor and aroma contributions and whether it results in a smoother bitterness. While I do not practice first wort hopping in my brewing, it's not something I view unfavorably. It's up to you to decide whether first wort hopping can work for you and your brewing process.

Boiling Wort

Once the wort is constructed, either through extract or all-grain techniques, the next step in the process is bringing the wort to a boil. When a boil is achieved, the wort goes through several biochemical reactions with multifaceted brewing purposes, including hop isomerization, sanitization, and protein precipitation.

Wort Sanitization

One of the primary roles of the boil is wort sanitization. Boiling wort for at least 1 hour eliminates most living microorganisms that cause contamination. The sanitization achieved by the boil is the reason brewing equipment does not require a sanitization cycle before use. Also, boil sanitization can work double duty, sanitizing other brewing equipment for post-boil, like wort chillers. It's worth mentioning that not all microorganisms are eliminated through the boil. *Clostridium botulinum*, a bacteria responsible for the toxin that causes botulism, can survive the boil and remain in your wort. However, this bacteria is slow to produce the toxin and inhibited by acidic environments below a pH of 5.5. Luckily for brewers, fermented beer is at least 10 times more acidic, typically having a pH between 3.9 and 4.4, meaning that yeast-fermented beer is quite safe to drink.

Watching for the Hot Break

Once a boil is reached, a large foamy cap forms on the surface of the wort. This is known as the *hot break*. At boil temperatures, the proteins and tannins in wort begin to clump up, producing this foamy cap, which can grow with vigor, much like a boiling pot of pasta. After a few minutes of boiling, the foamy head will die down as the hot break sufficiently binds up and falls out of suspension, appearing as a brownish clumps in the boiling wort.

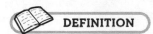 **DEFINITION**

> **Hot break** is the point during the beginning of the boil when the proteins and tannins that form in the wort coagulate and precipitate out of suspension. During the hot break, the wort will become foamy, then eventually the foam will clump up and fall to the bottom of the kettle. The foam can rise quickly during the hot break, so watch for boilovers.

If there's one red-alert stage in the brewing process, this is it. That's because it can get out of hand quickly, growing to the proportions of a B-movie monster and spilling over the sides of your brew kettle, known as a boilover. If you need to fight this foamy beast, there are a few tricks you can use. For small rises, you can spritz water from a spray bottle on the foam surface, which breaks the surface tension and keeps the rise at bay. However, more aggressive foaming requires more active methods, with the best course of action being quick stirring while keeping the burner power off. This will bring the hot break down to a manageable size. Turning the power back on may produce another hot break, especially in its early stages, so this may need to be done in intervals until a boil can be achieved without a hot break foaming.

> **BREWING TIP**
>
> Consider using FermCap-S, an antifoaming agent, for keeping a hot break at bay. Brewers suggest using 3 drops per 5-gallon batch to reduce the chance of a boilover.

As a preventative measure, make sure your brew kettle has at least 1 gallon of headspace for rising wort and hot break accommodation. Also, make sure to keep a watchful eye on the brew kettle when the boil is near. It may seem like a watched pot never boils, but it will. Remember, an unattended brew kettle will boil and boil over.

Just before the boil, many of the hot break proteins start clumping, forming a floating brown sludge at the top of the kettle.

Boil Size: Partial vs. Full Boils

When starting out with extract brewing, many brewers use a partial boil to make wort. Partial boiling refers to a reduced boil volume, not boil duration. For a 5-gallon batch, a partial boil starts around 3 gallons in total volume (2½ gallons of brewing water plus the malt extract, which adds about ½ gallon of volume). Post boil, the boiled wort is added to the fermentor and then topped off with plain water to yield 5-gallons of wort.

A 5-gallon batch full boil for extract and all-grain brewers requires at least 5 to 6 gallons of brewing water, depending on evaporation rate. A partial boil is not typical in an all-grain brewing, as the collected wort generally exceeds 5 gallons. Once the boil is complete, the remaining wort is transferred to a fermentor, and when done properly, yields 5 gallons without needing to top off with water.

For the extract brewer, the partial boil is engineered to be a sort of gateway boil. Due to the lower volume, it doesn't require an 8-gallon brew kettle, the hot wort can be chilled quickly through an ice bath, it's possible to achieve a boil on most kitchen stovetops, and there's less weight to haul around.

The tradeoff for the ease and convenience of the partial boil is potentially compromised wort character. The concentrated boil increases the gravity of the wort, which results in greater darkening and browning through increased Maillard reactions. This isn't much of a problem for dark-colored beers like stouts and porters, but it can be problematic on a cosmetic level for beer styles like blonde ales and wheat beers, rendering them orange or copper in appearance instead of straw yellow or gold. The increased boil gravity also reduces hop isomerization, so more hops are needed to achieve the same bitterness levels. Lastly, topping off with water that is not sterilized adds a risk of contamination. For these reasons, most extract brewers move on to full boils for more desirable wort characteristics.

There is one trick you can use to reduce many of the partial-boil drawbacks. Since malt extract is pre-boiled, it doesn't require a full 60-minute boil. Thus, the partial-boil brewer can add half the malt extract up front, mimicking the full-boil wort concentration, and precede as normal until the 15-minute remaining mark, when the other half of the malt extract is added for sanitization. Using this method avoids the high concentration of sugars during boiling and reduces drawbacks such as poor hop isomerization and wort darkening. While I would encourage most partial-boil brewers to look into full-boil batches, especially if all-grain brewing is anticipated in the future, utilizing the late-boil addition trick can yield high-quality results.

Condensing the Wort

As the wort is boiled, evaporation reduces kettle volume over time, condensing the wort. This is a welcomed development for the full-boil brewer, since the kettle volume must be reduced to achieve the desired fermentor volume. However, the brewer needs to tailor the evaporation rate so that there isn't too much left behind in the kettle or too little in the fermentor. Evaporation rate is typically expressed as a percentage of wort lost in 1 hour of boiling. It is determined by several factors, especially burner power, boil rate, kettle geometry, and external factors like relative humidity and whether you boil indoors or outdoors. In lieu of making calculations or estimations, your boil rate can be empirically determined in practice on brew day. Simply measure the pre-boil and post-boil volumes over a 60-minute boil. At the homebrewing level, the evaporation rate is best kept between 8 and 16 percent per hour, which works out to roughly ½ gallon to 1 gallon of wort volume per hour for a 5-gallon batch.

An evaporation rate outside of the recommended range may result in minor off-flavors. For all-grain brewers in particular, slow rates may yield increased levels of dimethyl sulfide (DMS), which causes a creamed-corn off-flavor. Evaporating too quickly can result in elevated melanoidin formation and increased Milliard reactions, causing wort browning. Fast rates are also counterproductive to late hop addition, as these high boil rates are capable of blowing off more volatile hop compound in the boil. If you suspect your evaporation rate is outside the target range, the remedy is as simple as adjusting the burner power to yield the desire rate.

For the partial-boil brewer, dialing in evaporation rate is less important since the fermentor is topped off later. Still, many of the off-flavor effects apply to the partial boil and are generally worth considering for overall wort quality. As a rule of thumb, a mild boil, near an elevated simmer, is sufficient for hop isomerization and sanitization.

Bringing the Bitterness

As discussed in Chapter 4, hops provide the bittering in beer through the isomerization of alpha acids in wort. While there are several ways to yield hop isomerization, it is primarily achieved through the boil. The brewer can control bittering through several variables, namely boil duration, alpha acid content, and boil gravity. Hops boiled for longer durations will have greater bitterness than hops boiled for shorter durations. For example, in a 5-gallon batch of 1.055 wort, 1 ounce of 10 percent alpha acid hops will generate 32 IBUs when boiled for 60 minutes, but will only generate 16 IBUs when boiled for 15 minutes. Also, hops with higher alpha acid content will produce greater bitterness than lower alpha acid hops. For example, in a 5-gallon batch of 1.055 wort, 1 ounce of 10 percent alpha acid hops will generate 32 IBUs when boiled for 60 minutes, while 1 ounce of 5 percent alpha acid hops will generate 16 IBUs when boiled for the same amount of time. And finally, hops boiled in higher gravity wort will generate less bitterness than hops boiled in lower gravity wort. For example, 1 ounce of 10 percent alpha acid hops boiled for 60 minutes in 1.055 wort will generate 32 IBUs, while the same hops boiled in 1.040 wort will generate 38 IBUs when boiled for the same amount of time.

Like most trends, limits exist when pushed to the extremes. Bitterness by alpha acid content is limited by solubility, which means that after 60 minutes, further boiling will only achieve a marginal increase in bitterness. For example, extending the boil duration from 60 to 90 minutes only changes the IBU level from 32 to 35, less than a 10 percent increase. Thus, if more bittering is desired, you are better off adding more bittering hops than increasing the boil duration, as longer boiling can also lend harsher bittering. Also, the concentration of isomerized alpha acids appears to saturate around 100 to 120 IBUs. This bitterness saturation is generally not a problem, as most beers do not require these bittering levels, and further expression of bitterness for intensely hop-forward beer styles like IPAs can be modified through low finishing gravity and sulfate-forward water profiles.

On a practical level, most brewers achieve bitterness through a bittering addition, typically added at the beginning of a 60-minute boil. High to ultra-high alpha acid hop varieties are best for bittering additions, as a little will go a long way. Also, high alpha acid bittering typically yields a cleaner, more neutral bitterness, has a low cost per IBU, and leaves less hop sludge in the kettle post-boil.

Low alpha acid hops are primarily used for their flavor and aroma qualities, and while they can be used for bittering, it is not recommended. To do so requires a substantial quantity of hops, usually 2 to 3 ounces per 5-gallons to yield standard bittering levels. These high quantities may lend an unpleasant vegetal or tanninlike quality to the beer. Also, the large volume of hops in the kettle will absorb more wort, leaving less to be transferred to the fermentor. Unless you have a reason to use low alpha acid bittering, such as recreating a traditional style, I would stick with your favorite high alpha acid variety for less difficulty in the boil on brew day.

Hop Flavor and Aroma

Flavor and aroma additions in the brewing process truly start at the end of the boil, and are often referred to as *late additions*. While these hop additions still generate bitterness, the reduced time in the boil leaves more of their volatile hop compounds behind in the wort in the form of beta acid and oils. In general, the later the addition to the boil, the fewer hop compounds are volatized through temperature and boil evaporation.

 **DEFINITION**

Late addition is a brewing term that describes any ingredient, but particularly hops, that is added during the last 15 minutes of the boil.

In the brewing process, flavor additions are added with 10 to 30 minutes left in the boil, whereas aroma additions are added much later, with 0 to 10 minutes left in the boil. For bitterness considerations, a 15-minute addition will isomerize approximately 50 percent of the hop's bittering potential, so when using large late hop additions, be sure to account for their bitterness.

Stylistically, late hopping is most common in hop-forward American-style ales, especially IPA styles. However, when designing these recipes, be aware that late boil additions are not solely responsible for the hop character in beer. Both flavor and aroma can be infused into wort post-boil and post-fermentation, so consider these additions merely as one method on the spectrum of hopping techniques.

 BREWING TIP

Try hop bursting! Hop bursting is a technique in which the majority of the bitterness is achieved with less than 15 minutes left in the boil. It requires at least double the hops compared to a standard 60-minute bittering addition to achieve the same level of bitterness, but leaves a large majority of aromatic hop compounds behind, yielding an intensely flavorful yet satisfying bitter beer. Try it in your next pale ale or IPA.

Chilling Wort

After the boil is complete, the wort must be chilled as quickly as possible from boiling temperature down to yeast-pitching temperature, which is below 75°F. This section will cover the importance of rapid cooling and what you can do to speed up the cooling process.

The Importance of Rapid Chilling

Although rapid chilling of wort is not an essential part of the brewing process, brewers are motivated to do so for several reasons, mainly sanitization, haze reduction, and arresting isomerization. The first and main reason for rapid chilling is sanitization. Sweet and sugary wort is a welcoming home for brewer's yeast, but also a nice place for contaminants, like bacteria and wild yeast. Once the wort is below 140°F, it will support most microorganism life, and the more time that passes between the boil and pitching, the more time these unwanted guests have to make the wort their home. Bacteria in particular are fast growers, so the brewer has extra motivation to chill and pitch quickly so that the brewer's yeast has the leg up on contaminants.

The second motivation for fast chilling is to encourage the formation cold break and reduce chill haze. Similar to hot break, cold break is a coagulation of another set of proteins and tannins in wort that fall out of suspension when rapidly chilled. The faster the liquid is chilled, the more pronounced the cold break will be. Although a cold break isn't a brewing requirement, beers without a substantial cold break suffer from a hazy appearance at cold serving temperatures, known as chill haze. Chill haze doesn't affect the flavor of the beer, but it is a cosmetic problem when brilliant clarity is desired. Also, beer with chill haze has been observed to have less shelf stability and increased oxidation, so this may be a concern for aged beer styles.

The third and final reason for fast chilling is the termination of hop isomerization after boiling. Slow chilling allows the wort to stay at elevated temperatures, which means the alpha acids continue to isomerize. This is a problem for recipes with late hop additions for flavor and aroma that are not intended for bittering. Fast chilling effectively arrests isomerization, allowing for more controlled hop bittering and general hopping practices.

Chilling Techniques

Brewers use a variety of methods to cool wort rapidly. For the new brewer, a simple yet effective way is to use an ice bath. This requires a great quantity of ice and water along with a tub or sink large enough to fit the ice bath and the nearly fully submerged brew kettle. Overall, the effectiveness of the ice bath depends on how much ice is added. Ideally, the ice bath should be made mostly of ice, with additional ice added as the original ice melts.

A 20-gallon plastic tote is large enough to hold an ice bath and an 8-gallon kettle.

When using an ice bath, there are some best practices to achieve fast chilling. In general, the greater amount of ice, the better chilling effect. Also, make sure the water line of the ice bath is high enough to make good contact with the majority of the kettle area, but not so high that it exceeds the wort level in the kettle. In addition, take care when adding the kettle to the ice bath, and remember that it will displace water, so a mostly filled tub will likely overflow. If you're working with a large batch or a small tub, more than one ice bath may be needed to chill the wort down to pitching temperatures. In my brewing, cooling wort to the ale pitching temperature of around 68°F is not difficult to achieve with one large ice bath; however, reaching lager pitching temperatures of around 50°F requires a second ice bath.

Overall, ice baths can be an effective means of chilling wort and achieving good cold breaks without risk of contamination. The upside of ice baths is that they don't require any additional equipment. The downside is that they are typically the slowest chilling method, due to low surface contact, which limits heat transfer between the hot wort and cool ice water. As such, chilling time often exceeds 30 minutes, depending on batch size. For the beginning extract brewer using partial boils, ice baths are typical and quite effective. However, once you progress to all-grain full boils, alternative chilling methods are recommended.

As you become more serious about brewing, you may want to move beyond the ice bath and onto the cooling devices known as wort chillers. Wort chillers at the homebrewing level fall into three categories: immersion, counterflow, and plate chillers.

Immersion chillers are the next step up from the ice bath, and work by running cold water through coiled metal piping, which is submerged in the wort. Immersion chillers are typically made from copper and are added to the brew kettle during the boil, usually during the last 15 minutes to sanitize. After the boil is finished, the immersion chiller is connected to a faucet, allowing cold water to flow through the coiled tubing. The heat from the hot wort is transferred to the cold water in the tubing, cooling the wort. Immersion chillers work quickly, often taking as little as 10 minutes to reach ale pitching temperatures.

When selecting an immersion chiller, make sure its diameter and height can fit within your brew kettle. They are often sold by the precoiled tubing length and diameter, and generally the price increases with the amount of tubing. There is a direct tradeoff between cost and chilling time; the largest lengths and diameters are most expensive, but they are also the most efficient due to their increased surface area contact with wort. Lastly, to avoid brew day disasters, make sure you're able to connect an immersion chiller to your faucet, and do a test run to check for leaks, especially between the plastic tubing and metal coil attachment.

Even a small immersion chiller can make a world of difference. I opted for a
stainless steel version to avoid corrosion.

BREWING TIP

Keep your wort chiller clean! Even though you don't have to worry about sanitization, using a dirty chiller can lend a whole range of off-flavors. This is especially important with copper, which, when improperly stored, can develop black, green, or blue deposits that should not enter your wort. To clean a wort chiller, soak it in a vinegar solution until the deposits are removed and rinse well with water.

At the most advanced level of wort chiller technology are counterflow and plate chillers, which produce the fastest chilling times by moving both hot wort and cold water past highly conductive metal, usually copper. Because both the wort and water are moving, surface area contact is maximized, allowing for a great amount of heat transfer between these two liquids. It's no surprise that professional brewers utilize these chillers to cool barrels of wort in their brewing process.

While quick chilling is the biggest benefit to counterflow and plate chillers, they do have a few drawbacks at the homebrew scale that make them less appealing to the homebrewer. Both require purchasing quite a bit of additional equipment in order to operate properly, which can become expensive. Also, since wort is flowing through these chillers, they require more thoughtful cleaning and sanitization prior to use. Finally, many brewers find that for smaller, homebrew-size batches, there is not a pronounced difference in chilling time between these more advanced chillers and standard immersion chillers. Thus, for the new brewer working with extract or the all-grain brewer looking to keep things inexpensive, a solid immersion chiller is probably the best way to get fast chilling. However, for a serious all-grain brewer looking to achieve the fastest chilling, especially for 10-gallon batches or larger, the benefits of a counterflow or plate chiller may be worth the expense and operation drawbacks.

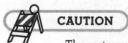

CAUTION

The water exiting the immersion chiller can be very hot, so use caution. Remember, the heat from the wort is exchanged with the water, which in the early stages of chilling will be near boiling temperature. Thus, make sure the exit tube is fixed to a draining source and wear any necessary skin protection to avoid burns.

Finally, if you live in a hot climate or you're brewing during the summer, your tap water may run on the warm side, making it difficult or impossible to achieve the appropriate yeast pitching temperatures without extra cooling assistance. To solve this problem, many brewers utilize a prechiller, which is essentially an immersion chiller, but instead of adding it to boiling wort, it is submerged in a bucket of ice water. That way, your source water flows from the tap to the prechiller, which cools it down to near freezing temperatures before it enters the wort chiller (either immersion or counterflow).

Post-Boil Hop Additions

It should come as no surprise to learn that hop-heads leave no moment in the brewing process unutilized, seeing every step as an opportunity to add more hops. Wort chilling is one of them. When infusing hop flavor and aroma, the post-boil time is especially useful, since boil evaporation is no longer pushing off volatile hop compounds, allowing them to infuse into wort. To add hops during wort chilling, brewers chiefly use two methods, the hop stand and the whirlpool.

The hop stand can be thought of as a large-scale hop steeping in hot wort. Brewers utilize a wide range of temperatures to perform a hop stand. Some use hop stands just off the boil, at approximately 210°F, essentially a long-duration, 0-minute addition. At these elevated temperatures, some hop isomerization occurs, around 15 percent, as well as a very good hop oil extraction. Alternatively, some brewers employ a cooler hop stand at 160°F to 170°F. At these cooler temperatures, hop isomerization is limited but there is still good extraction of hop oils. In either case, both preserve delicate hop compounds from boil evaporation, while any degree of isomerization can be adjusted via wort temperature.

Hop stands can add as much hops as desired, generally between 1 and 4 ounces per 5-gallon batch. Also, once the hops are added, their steeping duration in hot wort can range from 10 to 60 minutes, with many brewers using 15 to 30 minutes for typical hop stands. After steeping is complete, you can follow standard chilling procedures to cool wort to pitching temperatures.

The Least You Need to Know

- Extract wort production begins by adding specialty malts and malt extract to water. Extract malts are stirred into warm or hot water, while specialty malts are steeped like tea.
- Once malt has been added, the wort is brought to a boil. At this point, it's important to watch for the "hot break" when wort develops a thick, foamy head.
- During the boil, hops and other ingredients are added for bitterness, flavor, and aroma.
- After the boil, the wort must be chilled as quickly as possible using an ice bath or special devices called wort chillers.

Fermentation and Conditioning

"Brewers make wort, yeast makes beer" is a common saying in the brewing world used to emphasize the importance of yeast and its fermentation in the production of beer. While it is up to the yeast to transform flavorful wort into delicious beer, the brewer has considerable control over the direction of fermentation, which makes a significant difference on the overall quality of the finished beer. In this chapter, you'll learn the basics of the fermentation process, from pitching to conditioning, and what you'll need to achieve well-controlled, high-performing fermentation in your homebrew.

Note that the recommendations in this section apply to average-strength ales. While much of the information also applies to lagers and high-gravity beers, some additional or alternative techniques may be necessary. For more information on these fermentation techniques, check out Chapter 20.

In This Chapter

- The four phases of yeast fermentation

- The most important fermentation variables and how to control them

- Techniques for conditioning beer and secondary fermentation

The Phases of Fermentation

The core of yeast fermentation is the process of converting sugar, primarily from malt, into alcohol and carbon dioxide. As simple as this may sound, the process of yeast fermentation is quite complex, going through several phases in the production of alcohol in beer. Qualitatively, the average yeast cell will go through four stages during fermentation: pitching, lag, growth, and stationary. Strictly speaking, it's important to recognize that these stages are for conceptual purposes only; yeast cell growth and fermentation involve complex metabolic processes that are beyond the scope of this text. However, use these fermentation phases as a stepping stone to gaining a deeper understanding of yeast's role in the fermentation process.

The Pitching Phase

The pregame show to the main event, pitching is when the brewer adds yeast to the wort, at which time fermentation officially begins, and the wort is now called beer. A sort of zeroth phase, the pitching phase is a transitional period in the fermentation process where the brewer hands over the controls and puts the yeast in the driver's seat.

Before pitching, it's up to the brewer to create optimal conditions for fermentation. Once adjusted and pitched, the brewer is at the point of no return, and the yeast is now in control. The brewer acts more as a navigator in the fermentation journey, capable of making small corrections in temperature, aeration, and nutrition as needed. However, it's important to recognize that this journey is one way with no going back, so it's up to the brewer to make sure it's set off under the best conditions.

 BREWING TIP

Avoid long delays between wort chilling and pitching. Even though the wort is racking into a sanitized fermentor, there are still unwanted microorganisms moving in and making it their home. This is especially true of bacteria, which grows rapidly in wort—much faster than yeast. Simply stated, pitch early and avoid contamination.

The Lag Phase

With the yeast pitched, the lag phase (also known as the adaptive phase) begins, during which the yeast becomes acclimated to wort and prepares for growth and reproduction. During the lag phase, oxygen and wort nutrients are important. Immediately after pitching, the yeast cells start to scavenge dissolved oxygen, which they convert into sterols, the key ingredient in building robust, permeable cell walls. In addition, yeast absorbs nutrients, like phosphorous, potassium, sodium, and zinc, all of which are needed to produce its necessary enzymes for growth.

Why focus of building walls? Well, several reasons. Yeast reproduces asexually through a process of budding, which, when viewed through a microscope, resembles twisting off a balloon, as when making balloon animals. The yeast cell must be robust enough to survive this process several times. Secondly, cell wall permeability allows sugars and other nutrients to flow into the cell, while simultaneously prohibiting the transport of other compounds, contributing to overall cell health.

From the brewer's perspective, the lag phase looks like nothing is happening. After a few hours, the pitched beer appears much as it did as wort. However, rest assured that the yeast is quite active, making preparations for the later fermentation phases. The duration of the lag phase, known as lag time, can range from a couple of hours to just over a day and is highly dependent on pitch rate (the number of cells pitched into the wort) and temperature, where two general trends emerge. Both higher pitch rates and warmer temperatures result in a shorter lag phase. Under typical ale yeast conditions, the lag phase lasts between 3 and 15 hours, sometimes as long as 24 hours, all of which are acceptable.

After 24 hours, you should see signs that fermentation is beginning, including bubbling in the airlock and the formation of krausen. However, if no signs of fermentation are observed after two days, the pitched yeast are very likely insufficient, either unhealthy or not in high enough quantities, and adding more yeast is necessary.

The Growth Phase

After a short lag phase, the growth phase (also known as the log or exponential phase) emerges in full swing, where asexual reproduction and sugar consumption begins. Early in the growth phase, yeast cell growth is exponential, with cells doubling several times over the course of the phase. Also, the yeast starts consuming the simplest sugars, like glucose and fructose, which are readily digestible, before moving on to more complex sugars, like maltose and maltotriose. Also, throughout these processes, the yeast produces several fermentation by-products. The major (and obvious) by-products are alcohol and carbon dioxide, but yeast may also produce minor by-products, notably ester, phenols, and fusel alcohols.

This is a dynamic phase of fermentation that most brewers look forward to watching. The growth phase is marked by the appearance of a foamy, creamy head on the surface of the beer known as the krausen. This naturally forming cap is among the first signs that the lag phase is nearing an end and the growth phase has begun. A bubbling airlock provides further confirmation. During the height of fermentation, the krausen grows quite large, sometimes exceeding the volume capacity of the fermentor and requiring a blow-off tube in support. At its largest state, the krausen is called "high krausen." This generally represents the peak of the growth process to the brewer.

Total duration of the growth phase depends on a number of fermentation variables, with temperature as a key separator. Warm-fermented ales typically ferment in 1 to 2 days, while lagers and cold-fermented ales may take 4 days.

The Stationary Phase

The stationary phase (also known as the conditioning phase) is the last phase in the fermentation process, when the yeast growth plateaus, several fermentation by-products are re-absorbed, and flocculation and sedimentation occur. Due to the lack of oxygen, nutrients, and other factors like elevated levels of alcohol, yeast growth rates begin to decrease. Also, the large majority of simple sugars are metabolized and the active yeast cells work on the more complex sugars maltose and maltotriose.

Toward the end of the stationary phase, the yeast begins to absorb other fermentation by-products, such as diacetyl and acetaldehyde, which are considered off-flavors in beer and are unwanted even at very low levels. In the stationary phase, yeast will "clean up" these by-products through reabsorption before going into dormancy. However, not all by-products can be reabsorbed, notably most fusel alcohols, esters, and phenols, which remain in the final beer. Thus, these levels are best managed through the fermentation variables during the growth phase to keep them at desired levels.

The foamy, creamy mound on top of the fermenting beer is the krausen.

From the brewer's perspective, the stationary phase marks a visible slowing of fermentation. The once-high krausen of the growth phase begins to subside and disappear, known as a "fallen krausen." Also, the yeast cells will begin to clump up, or flocculate, and fall out of suspension, settling at the bottom of the fermentor. Once the majority of flocculation occurs, the yeast forms a thick, compacted sedimentation layer known as the yeast cake, and the beer is relatively clear.

The duration of the stationary phase is less rigorously defined than the phases that precede it. It can last from 3 to 10 days, depending on fermentation conditions. Ultimately, the end of fermentation is confirmed by taking consecutive gravity readings to ensure final gravity is reached. Typically, once a terminal gravity is reached, the brewer will wait at least 1 to 2 days to allow the yeast time to clean up any undesirable by-products. Longer conditioning times pushing 2 to 3 weeks may be desirable to encourage flocculation either through cold conditioning, yeast finings, or by gravity itself.

Fermentation Variables and Techniques

While yeast is responsible for turning wort into beer, the brewer has considerable say on how the fermentation process plays out. The brewer is the navigator in the journey of fermentation, capable of setting up and tweaking fermentation variables like aeration, temperature, and pitch rate, which make the difference between great and poor fermentation. To put it another way, there's no point in making delicious wort if the fermentation is poor quality or uncontrolled, resulting in a less-than-desirable beer. This section covers the important variables in the fermentation process that can be actively controlled by the brewer and provides guidance on how to achieve a high-performing fermentation to transform your sweet wort into great homebrew.

Fermentation Temperature Profiles

The most important variable during fermentation is temperature. While other variables like pitch rate and aeration contribute to overall improvement, wort and beer temperatures are deeply connected to just about every aspect of fermentation.

Ultimately, the right fermentation temperature is highly dependent on the yeast strain and the desired fermentation profile. The common goal when selecting a fermentation temperature is to achieve a balanced fermentation, warm enough to maintain active and healthy fermentation but cool enough to limit undesirable flavor formation. In general, fermenting on the cooler side will result in a cleaner fermentation flavor profile and slightly less attenuation, whereas a slightly warmer fermentation will result in greater ester and phenol expression and greater attenuation. Depending on the recipe, the brewer decides which side of the fermentation temperature range is best for achieving the desired character.

If you go beyond the recommended temperature range, you may lose the sweet spot and enter into temperature-dependent fermentation defects. A bit on the low side of temperature may result in sluggish fermentation and a bit on the high side may result in a slightly more aggressive ester/phenolic profile, both of which may be undesirable. Pushing it further, significantly past the low side will cause the fermentation to stall and force yeast into dormancy, while past the high side will produce unpalatable compounds like fusel alcohols and harsh solventlike characters in beer. Thus, the motivation is great for the brewer to identify a good temperature for fermentation and keep it there throughout fermentation.

Many ales ferment around room temperature, between 66°F and 70°F, which may not seem too difficult to maintain. However, even simple ales require a bit of temperature consideration and often some degree of temperature control. At the very least, you need to hit the right pitching temperature, tailor temperature rise, and avoid large temperature swings.

The core of temperature control issues stem from the fact that fermentation is exothermic, meaning that yeast generates heat, which causes the beer to rise in temperature throughout the fermenting process. The temperature rise, also known as free rise, typically increases 3°F to 5°F over the course of fermentation, sometimes rising by as much as 10°F. While the brewer can use free rise to produce clean and well-attenuated beer, if left unchecked, fermentation starting within a good temperature range can quickly be pushed outside it, resulting in an unbalanced ester/phenol profile and off-flavors.

The first step in controlled fermentation is pitching the yeast at the right temperature. While chilling the wort down, the brewer monitors its temperature along the way, racking and pitching when it reaches an appropriate temperature. For ales, chilling and pitching temperatures vary depending on the yeast strain. At the very least, pitching below 75°F is recommended to avoid fermentation flaws. Better yet would be to chill a few degrees cooler than the desired fermentation temperature to accommodate free rise, which will warm up the beer over the course of 18 to 36 hours.

BREWING TIP

Use an adhesive thermometer to gauge fermentation temperature. Essentially a big sticker, these thermometers are applied to the exterior of the fermentor for a quick and easy way to determine fermentation temperature. Although not highly accurate, I've checked mine against calibrated brewing thermometers and it is usually accurate within a degree.

After pitching, the goal is to maintain temperature stability within the desired fermentation range. For ale fermentation, this means at the very least having a location with a consistent temperature, usually a cool, dry closet, away from light or varying heat sources, such as an oven, refrigerator, or water heater. Alternatively, the brewer can employ the additional temperature control techniques discussed in Chapter 20.

Whatever method you use, temperature stability is critical within the first three days, as most flavor compounds are produced during this time, and even small temperature changes can affect fermentation performance and result in flaws. In general, it's best to avoid temperature swings greater than 10°F over the course of fermentation, as this will cause yeast heat shock and stress. Small swings are acceptable, but the smaller, the better. Most professional brewers and serious homebrewers look to maintain fermentation temperatures within a degree of a target temperature. For the beginning brewer, staying within 2°F to 4°F of the target temperature is a good goal to strive for.

Finally, when possible, it's a good idea to ramp up the temperature by a few degrees toward the end of fermentation, which allows for full attenuation and reabsorption of off-flavor by-products, as well as blow off of undesirable aromatic compounds like sulfur.

Pitching Rate

The pitching rate, or number of viable yeast cells added to the wort, is an important fermentation variable that directly affects lag time, attenuation, and contamination prevention, as well as beer flavor characteristics through ester/phenol production. Both pitching too little (under pitching) and pitching too much (over pitching) can have a negative effect on the beer.

Pitch rate is defined either volumetrically (yeast cells/ml) or by gravity density (yeast cell/ml/°Plato), which adjusts yeast count to both volume and starting gravity for a particular beer. The gold standard for commercial brewers is 1 million cells/ml/°Plato; however, Dr. George Fix, author of *Principles of Brewing Science,* proposed a more nuanced rate depending on whether you are fermenting an ale or lager. He recommends 0.75 million cells/ml/°Plato for ales and 1.5 million cells/ml/°Plato for lagers. These rates primary apply to standard-gravity beers, with high-gravity versions often requiring increased pitch rates beyond these recommendations. For more information on pitching with lagers and high-gravity beer, see Chapter 20.

At this point, you may be wondering how to use this odd pitching rate fraction. Let's look at an example. Say you are making a 5-gallon batch of beer using an ale yeast strain with an average starting gravity of 1.048. You'll need to make some conversions, as a 5-gallon batch of wort is equivalent to 19,000 milliliters in volume and has a starting gravity of 1.048, which is equal to 12°Plato. Under these conditions, the recommended pitching rate for ales is 0.75 million cells/ml/°Plato, and multiplying by both the starting gravity in °Plato and batch volume in milliliters results in the whopping number of 170 billion yeast cells. (0.75 × 19,000 × 12 = 170 billion cells) For most ales of average strength, the 150 to 200 billion cell pitch count for a 5-gallon batch is a good benchmark in lieu of a specific pitch rate calculation.

This poses a small problem when purchasing yeast for your batch of homebrew. Although vials and smack packs of liquid yeast are marketed as "pitchable" quantities, they only have about 100 billion cells at the time manufacturing. This may sound like a lot, but as we have shown, it is not quite enough for most 5-gallon batches of average strength beer. Worse still, yeast cells lose viability over time, which means two months after packaging there may be as little as 65 million cells left, far below recommended pitching rates.

This pitching rate problem can be solved by one of two strategies. The first strategy is to simply buy more liquid yeast to ensure suitable quantities; however, many homebrewers view this as expensive. Alternatively, you can culture up more yeast using a technique known as a yeast starter, essentially making a small starter batch of beer and reusing its yeast for a bigger batch of beer. With this method, you buy only one vial or smack pack of liquid yeast, but instead of adding it directly to the wort, you add it to the starter, and through a small-scale fermentation, generate more yeast cells for your future larger batch of beer. Many homebrewers use a simple 2-liter yeast starter as an affordable method of increasing their yeast cell counts up to 200 billion without having to purchase multiple packages of liquid yeast.

Here's a simple starter recipe that can be used to generate additional yeast cells from a vial or smack pack of liquid yeast. Make your yeast starter 48 hours before you plan to pitch the yeast.

Simple 2-Liter Starter Recipe

Ingredients and Equipment

6 ounces light DME

8 cups water

1 vial or smack pack liquid yeast

2-liter Erlenmeyer flask or half-gallon demijohn, sanitized

Small piece aluminum foil, sanitized

3-quart saucepan with lid

Funnel, sanitized

Directions

1. In a saucepan, heat water over medium heat and bring to a warm temperature.

2. Add light DME to warmed water and stir until dissolved. You now have wort.

3. Bring wort to a boil over high heat, then reduce heat to medium-high and gently boil for 15 minutes.

4. Put lid on saucepan and place in an ice bath until the side of the pot is cool to touch or wort temperature measures 75°F using a sanitized thermometer.

5. Pour wort into sanitized flask or demijohn. A sanitized funnel may be useful in the pouring process.

6. Place sanitized aluminum foil over opening, hold down tightly with your hand, and shake vigorously to aerate.

7. Remove foil and add the yeast to the wort.

8. Cover the opening of the flask or demijohn using sanitized aluminum foil.

In a few hours, signs of fermentation should be apparent, and complete fermentation should take place within 48 hours. Every few hours, give the starter a swirl to aerate, as this will help promote greater yeast cell growth. Once fermentation slows, the starter can be pitched into a 5-gallon batch of wort. If only the yeast and not the fermented starter portion is desired, the yeast starter can be placed in the refrigerator for a few hours, which will force sedimentation of the yeast and the starter solution can be decanted, allowing the brewer to pitch the more condensed yeast slurry.

For many brewers, using liquid yeast and making starters is simply not worth the effort, so they use dry yeast as an alternative. Since dry yeast is more shelf stable, it has greater viability over time. When fresh dry yeast is properly rehydrated, it yields 20 billion cells per gram. Most yeast sachets contain over 10 grams, so you can get 200 billion yeast cells per sachet, which is generally plenty for most ales of standard gravity. Although the dry yeast selection at present is more limited than liquid yeast cultures, dry yeast provides the greatest number of yeast cells per dollar.

Just like when making bread dough, dry brewer's yeast benefits from proofing before pitching. This will yield the highest rehydrated cell count, and thus the highest pitching rate. If you're using dry yeast, plan on rehydrating it about 30 minutes before you want to add it to the wort.

Rehydrating Yeast Recipe

Ingredients and Equipment

1 cup warm water (95-105°F)

1 sachet dry yeast (10-11.5 grams)

2-cup glass liquid measure, sanitized

1-quart saucepan

Thermometer, sanitized

Small piece aluminum foil, sanitized

Directions

1. In a saucepan, bring water to a boil over high heat. Boil for 1 minute. This will sanitize the water prior to rehydration.

2. Remove from heat and cool until water is between 95°F and 105°F.

3. Add cooled water to sanitized liquid measure and confirm water temperature is within the recommended range. Make sure the water does not exceed 105°F, as this can harm the yeast.

4. Sprinkle yeast over the warm water. Loosely cover the measuring cup with sanitized aluminum foil to prevent contamination.

5. Allow the yeast to sit for 15 to 20 minutes. The rehydrated yeast is now called a cream. Once it has cooled to within 15°F of wort temperature, the cream is ready for pitching.

BREWING TIP

Do not make a yeast starter with dry yeast. Although this may seem like a good idea to get even more yeast for your money, yeast starters using dry yeast deplete their energy and nutrient reserves resulting in a zero net benefit. If more dry yeast is required, you are better off buying another sachet of dry yeast.

Finally, be aware that significantly straying from the recommended pitching rate can result in poor fermentation and off-flavor production. Pitching too few yeast cells, known as under pitching, is quite problematic and leads to a whole host of fermentation defects. Under pitching forces yeast to work harder in the growth phase, which causes the yeast to become tired and stressed since fewer yeast cells are required to do more work. This results in increased levels of off-flavors such as diacetyl, fusel alcohol, esters, and sulfur compounds. Under pitching can also cause low attenuation or potentially stuck fermentation. Finally, under pitching increases the risk of contamination. Even if your brewing equipment is cleaned and sanitized, there are still unwanted microorganisms in beer. Adding too few yeast cells means the yeast will take longer to begin growing, which gives the unwanted microorganisms a leg up.

Over pitching is not nearly as problematic as under pitching, but it can also lend off-flavors and undesirable fermentation. Although over pitching is far better than under pitching, it is best to achieve a balance. In general, high pitching rates will have a shorter lag time, cleaner fermentation, and lower attenuation.

Aeration

The only time the brewer actively tries to add oxygen to wort is right before pitching. As you may recall, during the early part of fermentation, yeast utilizes oxygen to build healthy cell walls, key to yeast reproduction in the growth phase; however, by the end of the boil, most of the oxygen has been stripped from the wort, and must be added back by the brewer. There are a variety of techniques that can be used to achieve appropriate oxygen levels and ensure a successful fermentation.

Like many things in brewing, the recommended level of dissolved oxygen varies depending on the beer style, the wort conditions, and yeast strain selected. While specific aeration concentrations are often debated, most brewers agree that oxygen levels between 8 and 15 ppm are needed to achieve adequate performance. Aeration levels between 15 and 26 ppm and multistep aeration may be required for more advanced fermentation in lager and high-gravity brewing, which is discussed in Chapter 20.

At the lower end of the scale, concentrations between 7 and 10 ppm are easily achieved using air. Depending on your altitude, oxygen saturation is based on the relative pressure and composition (approximately 23 percent) of atmosphere air. Those at sea level can achieve close to 10 ppm, whereas brewers in higher elevations will achieve a reduced amount, in the 7 to 8 ppm range.

The most common way for beginning brewers to aerate their wort is fermentor shaking, which forces oxygen into the solution via vigorous shaking. For the bucket or carboy brewer, all this entails is placing a lid or stopper to fully enclose the fermentor and then rocking it back and forth rapidly for some period of time.

How much time? Well, duration of shaking depends on the wort gravity and temperature. Starting out, at least 2 minutes should achieve the recommended dissolved oxygen concentrations. If you are shaking the living daylights out of your fermentor and the wort is an average gravity, 1 to 2 minutes should be plenty. However, less furious shaking, higher gravity, or colder wort would benefit from slightly longer shaking duration, around 5 minutes. Also, avoid shaking for more than 10 minutes, as excessive foaming can be detrimental to head retention and foam stability.

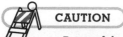 **CAUTION**

Be careful while shaking glass carboys! Before aerating using this technique, make sure the carboy is well-secured on the ground and use gentle back and forth motions to aerate wort. Also, make sure you have plenty of towels on hand in case of any big spills.

In lieu of shaking, wort can be aerated using an aquarium pump and a diffusion stone. With this method, the aquarium pump forces air through a stone with microporous holes, which help dissolve oxygen into wort. Because the source of oxygen is air, the same concentrations will saturate between 7 to 10 ppm no matter how long the pump runs. Why use an aquarium pump instead of shaking? To begin with, it certainly saves you the effort, and shaking may not even be possible if your batch sizes start to exceed 5-gallons. Also, an aquarium pump will always achieve saturation conditions given enough time, whereas vigorous shaking can be more variable. How much time? For standard gravity ales at ale-pitching temperature, brewers report saturation conditions are typically achieved after 10 to 15 minutes of continuous aeration. Starting out, I would recommend using 10 minutes of aquarium pump drive aeration and adjust as seen fit.

Since the diffusion stone and tubing will be in contact with the wort post-boil, these items will need sanitization before use. To sanitize the stone, submerge it in boiling water for 1 to 2 minutes (remove after 2 minutes; longer boiling may harm the stone). Alternatively, the diffusion stone can be sanitized using sanitizing solution, although this may not be as effective. Sanitizing solution is fine to use for the tubing. When sanitizing, make sure to not touch the stone as oils from your hand can plug the small holes. Use sanitized protective gloves or tongs when handling the diffusion stone. Lastly, due to the long duration of the pumping, it's best to include a sterile filter between the pump and the diffusion stone to minimize the incorporation of airborne contaminants into wort during the aeration process.

For those looking to turbo-charge aeration, pure oxygen systems offer fast aeration times and oxygen concentrations above 10 ppm. At the homebrew scale, pure oxygen systems use an oxygen tank fitted with a purpose-use regulator along with the same diffusion stone tubing setup from the aquarium pump. To use, follow the same sanitization procedures for the aquarium pump, diffusion stone, and tubing, although a sterile filter isn't necessary because the high oxygen concentration is not supportive of microorganisms.

Since the source of oxygen is highly concentrated, run times are greatly reduced compared to aquarium pumps. Many brewers report achieving oxygen concentrations between 8 and 10 ppm in as little as 60 seconds. Levels between 10 and 15 ppm can be achieved within 2 minutes, and 15 ppm or greater can be reached in 2 to 5 minutes, depending on wort composition and temperature.

Oxygen concentrations past 26 ppm are not detrimental to fermentation, as the early stages of the fermentation will scrub out excessive oxygen. However, some brewers report that extraordinarily high levels of oxygen can have a negative effect, lending solventlike off-flavors to beer. When starting out with pure oxygen aeration, 1 to 2 minutes is often sufficient to yield concentrations between 10 to 15 ppm in standard gravity wort at ale temperatures.

Nutrients

Yeast nutrients are essential throughout the fermentation process and a lack of nutrients can result in poor or incomplete fermentation. While a discussion of the dozens of nutrients necessary for the fermentation process is beyond the scope of this chapter, there are some key facts to be aware of. All-malt wort, made with either malt extract or base malts, contains the majority of the vital nutrients, minerals, and vitamins necessary for fermentation, such as free amino nitrogen (FAN) and phosphates. However, malt is lacking in some areas, requiring the brewer to add these nutrients through other means. As previously discussed, oxygen is a vital element in cell wall production, and is added to wort through aeration. Calcium and magnesium are important minerals for metabolism and flocculation, and are typically present as hardness in tap water. Brewers using distilled water should add a brewing mineral addition such as gypsum or Epsom salt to add calcium and magnesium in sufficient concentrations for fermentation. If these additions are already being used to tailor mash chemistry, further additions are not necessary for fermentation.

The mineral in which wort is most often deficient is zinc, which is important for cell reproduction and alcohol production. Since malt and brewing water have limited quantities of zinc, the homebrewer has to actively add it into wort prior to fermentation. Although there are a range of methods to do so, the homebrewer typically adds a comprehensive yeast nutrient supplement, also known as a yeast energizer, containing zinc for this purpose. There are many varieties of yeast nutrient supplements available, each one serving a different purpose, so make sure the one you choose contains zinc before adding. Also, make sure to abide by the dosing recommendation of the manufacturer, typically $\frac{1}{2}$ teaspoon for 5 gallons is sufficient. Adding more than the recommended amount is up to the brewer's discretion, but be aware the exceeding the recommended levels can lead to off-flavors and poor fermentation. Yeast nutrients are added to the wort toward the last 15 minutes of the boil to avoid binding and precipitation through trub.

Lastly, wort that contains a high percentage of adjuncts, especially sugars, is nutrient deficient, and it's a good idea to actively compensate for this through yeast nutrient supplements. Simple varieties like diammonium phosphate strictly add back the nutrients phosphate and FAN, which are present in malt wort; however, it is more effective to use a comprehensive supplement containing basic brewing nutrients plus other essential minerals like zinc. As before, make sure to add toward the end of the boil to avoid precipitating out of the wort and to use the recommended dosing.

Conditioning Techniques

After the growth phase is complete, the stationary phase begins, where several processes occur, including flocculation and reabsorption of fermentation by-products that are commonly referred to as conditioning. While the yeast will perform many of these processes naturally over time, the brewer can often accelerate the process using additional conditioning techniques. Also, more involved recipes call for two-step fermentation, which involves secondary fermentation, long-term maturation, or additional hopping through dry hops. This section covers some of the common conditioning techniques used to produce bright, flavorful beer.

Single-Stage vs. Two-Stage Fermentation

Despite what their names suggest, neither single-stage nor two-stage fermentation have to deal with active fermentation, but rather the stationary phase and how to approach it. In a single-stage fermentation, the entire process, including the stationary phase, occurs within a single fermentor, typically referred to as the primary fermentor or primary for short. However, in a two-stage fermentation, the process is split between two fermentors. Here, the fermentation process up to the beginning of the stationary phase occurs within the primary fermentor and then the beer is racked into a second fermentor, known as the secondary, to complete the stationary phase along with any other post-fermentation process.

While a single-stage fermentation is as simple as cleaning and sanitizing a fermentor and following the appropriate fermentation variables, a two-stage fermentation requires a bit more involvement to ensure success. First, the brewer wants to limit oxygen incorporation at all costs to avoid oxidation. Thus, when racking from the primary to the secondary, you'll want to avoid splashy siphon action. Also, you'll want to use a secondary fermentor that is smaller than the primary fermentor in volume to eliminate as much headspace as possible, ideally none. Any leftover headspace will contain oxygen from air, and more headspace means more oxidation. The brewer looking to limit oxygen even further will use a glass or PET carboy as opposed to standard plastic fermentors, as glass and PET plastic have the highest impermeability to oxygen. For short secondary stages, this is likely overkill, but recommended for extended conditioning and aging beer. Finally, sanitization is key, since a racking cane, tubing, and secondary fermentor are all touching the new beer.

The benefit to secondary fermentation is improved beer clarity due to accelerated flocculation and the opportunity to add fermentables like fruit and honey post-fermentation. Also, secondary fermentors are a great venue for dry hopping and other post-fermentation additions like chocolate and chile peppers while also allowing the brewer to save the yeast cake from the primary to be used again at a later date.

For a new brewer, I would recommend bypassing the two-stage fermentation and instead using a relatively long single-stage fermentation. For example, instead of a 1-week primary fermentation and 2-week secondary fermentation, which is often instructed in recipes, I would combine the two and employ a 3-week primary stage. With proper sanitization and temperature control, extended contact with the yeast sediment should not cause trouble and overall result in a cleaner beer without risk of oxidation and contamination.

Once you've gained some experience and are ready for a bit of experimentation, you may find a two-stage fermentation advantageous in your brewing process. Also, be aware that a two-stage fermentations may be recommended for more advanced techniques like lagers, high-gravity beers, and fruit beers, and should be followed accordingly when brewing.

Clarification

When yeast flocculates during the stationary phase, it clumps together and falls out of suspension. As discussed in Chapter 5, some yeast strains are better than others at flocculating and producing clear beer naturally. For example, Wyeast 1968 flocculates incredibly well and doesn't require any additional clarification steps. However, other yeast strains are less good at flocculating, some stubbornly so, like Kölsch yeast strains, which stay in suspension almost no matter what. Thus, the brewer may utilize additional clarification steps in order to achieve clear beer for packaging.

Racking into a secondary fermentor may be useful as the racking process may promote flocculation. In addition to racking, yeast clarifiers, like isinglass and gelatin, and cold temperatures, below 40°F, help to accelerate flocculation. When using a secondary fermentor for clarification, be sure to use two-stage fermentation techniques, using oxygen-impermeable materials like PET plastic or glass with little headspace to avoid oxidation. Also, allow the beer to sit in the primary fermentor for at least 2 to 4 days after fermentation is complete to ensure adequate reabsorption of fermentation by-products to avoid off-flavors.

Secondary Fermentation

A second fermentation is often recommended if you want to add more fermentables, such as whole fruit or sugar, after the primary fermentation is complete. These additions are added after primary fermentation to prevent their aromatic compounds from being scrubbed during a vigorous fermenting.

Although this is technically a two-stage fermentation, this secondary fermentation should be treated more like a second primary fermentation as opposed to a pure stationary phase. Thus, sizable headspace is necessary to allow for a second krausen plus any additional fruit volume. Also, buckets are often preferable to carboys when fruit is used since the small neck of a carboy can get clogged, pressurizing the fermentor and resulting in a big mess.

Unlike primary fermentation, as long as the degree of fermentables is minor, pitching rate and aeration steps are not needed, as the suspended yeast and oxygen incorporation that occurs during racking should be sufficient for a healthy secondary fermentation. Once the secondary fermentation is complete, a tertiary fermentation may be desired to promote clarification or flavor development before packaging. This third fermentation stage should be treated like a stationary phase, avoiding oxidation using the previously described techniques. For more information on brewing with sugar and fruit, check out Chapter 7.

Aging

Several beer styles, especially strong beers, lagers, and sour or wild-yeast beers, benefit from extended aging, anywhere from 3 months to well over a year allows for flavor development and refinement post-fermentation. Aging requires a two-stage fermentation, as prolonged contact with the trub and yeast sediment from the primary fermentation will likely cause off-flavors over an extended period of time. Again, use appropriate two-stage fermentation techniques to avoid oxidative off-flavors in the conditioned beer. Also, while traditional airlocks may be sufficient, they can dry out over time, introducing outside air and causing oxidation or contamination. Instead, consider using one-way silicone bungs, which use a flap to allow post-fermentation gases to exit without reintroducing outside air. Alternatively, aging can be accomplished after packaging in bottles or kegs, accomplishing a similar effect while also introducing carbonation through priming.

Dry Hopping

Dry hopping is the process of adding hops to the beer post-fermentation after the stationary phase. Historically, this was done to help preserve the beer when stored in casks, but dry hops now are added for extra flavor and aroma. Dry hops are particularly useful for adding back hop aromatics into beer as a large portion of the volatile compounds are blown off during vigorous fermentation. Also, dry hop character is slightly different than late hop additions, adding to the spectrum of flavor and aroma to hop-forward beers. Importantly, dry hopping doesn't add to the bitterness of the beer.

There are widely varying opinions on how to implement the best dry hop flavor and aroma. Dry hopping durations can range anywhere from 3 days to many weeks, largely depending on the brewer's preference. Some brewers use short durations of 3 to 5 days and claim longer durations add an unpleasant grassiness to the beer. Other brewers swear by dry hopping sessions of a week or longer. In the end, it's up to you. Just be aware that long duration dry hopping risks leaching harsh tanninlike and vegetal hop compounds, while shorter durations limit the infusion of essential hop oils.

Like duration, opinions vary on whether whole, plug, or pellet hops deliver the best aroma and flavor. Hop purists claim whole hops have the most pleasant flavor, whereas other brewers claim no significant difference. Thus, the dry hopping procedure is ultimately up to you, but a good first start is a 5-day duration using pellet or plug hops. With experience, you'll determine what the best dry hopping methods are for your brewing process.

When to add dry hops? Dry hops are added to any stage after the primary fermentation is complete. In particular, dry hops can be added straight into the primary fermentor or after racking into a secondary fermentor or keg. Any of these options work well with some practice. Some aromas may be removed by yeast in suspension when adding to the primary, but this can be easily remedied by adding more hops. Racking to secondary may have better utilization and sometimes a cleaner flavor, but this also risks oxidation. Kegging with dry hops is another good option, similar to casking; however this risks off-flavors when dry hops sit on the beer for long periods of time. Give all three methods a try and determine which one is best in your brewing process.

> (**BREWING TIP**)
>
> Don't worry about sanitizing dry hops. Even though they are not boiled, hops have antibacterial properties which help protect the beer from contamination. Additionally, since dry hops are added after fermentation, the alcohol and low pH in the beer will also help to protect it against any unwanted guests.

The Least You Need to Know

- There are four stages in the fermentation process: pitching, growth, fermentation, and conditioning.
- While the yeast is responsible for turning wort into beer, the brewer has considerable control over the performance of the fermentation.
- Fermentation variables such as temperature, pitch rate, aeration, and yeast nutrition are key to great fermentation.
- After fermentation, you can use a number of techniques for conditioning beer, including clarification and dry hopping.

Packaging

After fermentation and conditioning is complete, it's time to package your beer! Packaging marks the last major step in the brewing process, when beer is either bottled or put into kegs and carbonated. However, there are several ways to achieve carbonation, and brewers utilize different techniques to make the carbonation just right. This chapter covers what you'll need to bottle and keg your homebrew successfully and how to determine the necessary amount of carbonation to optimize the character and flavors of your hard-won homebrew.

Starting out, it's worth clarifying the purpose and pathways of packaging within the brewing process. Packaging beer, like most beverages, serves two purposes: storage, the process preserving beer for later consumption, and carbonation, a method for delivering and enhancing the texture, flavor, and aroma of beer. To carbonate beer, homebrewers can either naturally carbonate using a small, controlled refermentation known as priming, or artificially carbonate using an external source of carbon dioxide known as forced carbonation. Typically, homebrewers using priming for bottling, known as bottling conditioning, and forced carbonation for kegging; however, either method can be using for bottling and kegging depending on your equipment.

In This Chapter

- Pros and cons of bottling and kegging
- The equipment you need for bottling and kegging your homebrew
- Determining carbonation levels when priming with sugar
- Determining carbonation levels when force carbonating with CO_2

Packaging Equipment

Before you can start packaging your beer, you'll need a bit of extra equipment. Bottling and kegging can be done with just a bare minimum of equipment, but you'll benefit in ease and quality with a few extra devices.

Bottling Equipment

Not much equipment is necessary to bottle your homebrew. As long as you have a racking cane, some tubing, and swing-top style bottles, you can bottle your homebrew without the following equipment. However, many homebrewers look to make the process more flexible, sanitary, and/ or controlled to deliver the best bottle-conditioned homebrew. If you plan to consistently bottle throughout your homebrewing career, then consider obtaining the following items to complete your homebrewery's bottling needs.

Bottles There are two common styles of bottles used for packaging beer: crown-top and swing-top bottles. Crown-top bottles are the style used by most craft breweries; a glass bottle sealed with a cap that you need a bottle opener to remove. For the beginning brewer, crown-top bottles are the least expensive option, costing less than a dollar each when purchased new, or you can simply buy a six-pack of your favorite craft brew and reuse the bottles. When re-using crown-top bottles, make sure to remove any labeling; hot water and a little elbow grease works well. Also, avoid bottles with twist-off caps, such as those used by big macrobreweries. These are incompat- ible with standard crown-top bottling caps and capping mechanisms. Bottles range in size from the standard 12-ounce bottle, also known as a longneck, to 22-ounce bottles, also known as bombers. You will need at least 50 longnecks or 25 bombers to fully package a 5-gallon batch.

Alternatively, swing-top bottles use a spring-compressed rubber gasket to seal in carbonation instead of the standard bottle cap. Swing-top bottles come in all shapes, colors, and sizes, and the number you need for a 5-gallon will depend on the size of the bottles. Many come in the pint size, so you'll need about 38 of these to bottle a 5-gallon batch. To seal, simply place the rubber gasket over the top of the bottle and compress the spring to seal, making sure the rubber gasket is sufficiently touching all edges to achieve a good seal. Over time the rubber gasket will wear and need replacement, so make sure to have some spare gaskets on hand when poor sealing is suspected. Swing-top bottles are more expensive upfront, but many brewers prefer them because they avoid the hassle of surrounding bottle capping.

BREWING TIP

Avoid green and clear colored bottles. Although you can see the color of your beer, they are prone to light staling and defects, causing skunk-like off-flavors. When possible, use brown bottles for best light protection and avoid exposure to light, especially UV light, when conditioning and maturing.

Bottle caps A bottling necessity when using crown-top bottles, bottle caps seal in the carbon dioxide and keep beer fresh. They're available in a range of colors and styles, and I recommend buying in bulk, as you'll get more caps per dollar. Also, when aging beer, I recommend oxygen-absorbing caps, as they capture oxygen in the head space after bottling and any that leaks over time, resulting in less oxidized beer. I buy these exclusively for this reason alone.

Bottle capper Another bottling necessity when using crown-top bottles, cappers are used for crimping the bottle caps onto the bottles. At the homebrew scale, there are two commonly used types, hand-action and bench-top cappers. Hand-action cappers are the entry-level version. These consist of two levers on either side of a bottle cap adapter, which are pushed down to crimp the edges of the cap around the neck of the bottle and form a tight seal. Hand-action cappers range in quality and construction; I recommend spring-actuated versions with magnetic capping regions to hold the bottle cap in place. They are a little more expensive, but they operate smoothly, reduce the chance of improper or partial crimping, and result in fewer broken bottles. I've capped over 40 batches using my red capper (often called an Emily capper) and still use it today.

As an upgrade, consider obtaining a bench-top capper. Much like the hand-action capper, the bench-top capper crimps bottle caps onto crown-top bottles using a spring-load lever mechanism. However, the bench-top cappers have a large supporting structure to reduce pressure on the bottle, and ensure more uniform sealing, resulting in better seals and fewer broken bottles. Also, many homebrewers move toward the bench-top capper due to its very stable capping action. Some bench-top cappers are also capable of corking, which is a very nice addition for those bottling wines, meads, or strong Belgian ales. While bench-top cappers can be much more expensive than hand-action cappers, they are often more reliable, and overall less prone to messes on the bottling day. If you plan to do a lot of bottling, a reliable bench-top capper may be for you.

Bottling wand The bottling wand is a very useful tool used to control the flow of beer from a bottling bucket or racking cane into a bottle of beer. The bottling wand is composed of a hard plastic rod with a spring-loaded tip. When the tip is compressed on the bottom of the bottle, beer flows smoothly into bottles with little turbulence or foaming, limiting oxygen incorporation. When released, the spring-loaded tip seals, stopping the flow of beer without leaking. Budget brewers can forgo the bottling wand and crimp tubing to control the flow of beer into bottles; however, this method can be quite messy, and results in greater oxygen incorporation and foaming. In my opinion, a bottling wand is definitely worth the few extra dollars for a reliable beer flow control on bottling day.

Bottling bucket An intermediate vessel used to temporarily store beer between racking from the fermentor and bottling. The bottling bucket is essentially a plastic bucket fermentor with the addition of a spigot, which allows gravity-fed beer to flow from the bucket into a bottling wand for bottling. Bottling buckets have many advantages over bottling straight from a racking cane. Beer racked off the trub in the fermentor into a bottling bucket allows for more beer and less sediment to enter the bottles. Also, the gravity-fed bottling is more reliable than siphon-action bottling. Lastly, adding priming sugar to the bottling bucket prior to racking ensures even distribution of the priming solution through the racked beer, creating more uniform carbonation.

Bottle tree These plastic structures look like a leafless tree and are used to drip dry and store cleaned and sanitized bottles before bottling. Like the bottles, the bottle tree must also be cleaned and sanitized before use to avoid contamination. Alternatively, the racks of a clean dishwasher can perform the same duty as a bottle tree, and are slightly preferable in my opinion, since the dripping sanitizer flows into the dishwasher rather than a countertop.

Kegging Equipment

After many exhausting bottling sessions, many homebrewers transition from bottling to kegging. This is because kegging offers easier cleanup and faster packaging while also producing several benefits to the beer. With kegging, you have the option of forced carbonation, a technique that uses externally applied carbon dioxide from a pressurized tank to carbonate the beer as opposed to the natural carbonation produced from priming. Forced carbonation significantly shortens conditioning times and greatly benefits quick-maturing styles like American wheat, pale ales, and IPAs, allowing the brewer to enjoy these beers sooner and fresher. Additionally, the brewer can use a regulator to adjust the carbonation level to a specific batch, whereas priming is a one-shot deal.

Not to say that kegging is the best in every situation; many strong ales, especially Belgian beers, benefit from bottle conditioning. There are also many brewers who prefer the character that results from priming. Also, kegging requires a significant investment in equipment, which can be a limiting factor for some. Not only do you need kegs, but also CO_2 equipment, like a tank and regulator, faucets for dispensing homebrew, not to mention a dedicated refrigerator for storage. Kegging can still be done affordably, and many brewers use refurbished kegging supplies; however, it's possible to spend thousands of dollars on a kegging system.

Cornelius kegs The majority of homebrewers use the Cornelius keg (or "corny keg") to package and dispense their beer. Originally used for soda, homebrewers in the United States have repurposed these gems for brewing purposes, partly due to their wide availability, but also because they are the perfect size for a batch of beer, fitting approximately 5 U.S. gallons.

The Cornelius keg is composed of several parts. The keg itself is a long, cylindrical vessel made of stainless steel and fitted with rubber handles and bottoms for easy handling. In the center of the top of the keg is an opening covered by a lid, which is held in place by a hatch clamp, rubber sealing gasket, and the pressure from forced carbonation. This opening is the primary means of racking beer into the keg, as well as cleaning and sanitization. On either side of the lid are the two valve fittings, a carbon dioxide "in" fitting and beer "out" fitting. The valve fittings work via spring-actuated poppets. When depressed, they allow either beer or gas to flow in or out of the keg. When released, the poppet springs back into place and seals the keg. Lastly, attached to the beer "out" fitting is a long piece of tubing called the dip tube, which reaches to the bottom of the keg. When CO_2 gas is applied, its pressure forces beer from the bottom of the keg, up the tube, and out the valve fitting.

Disconnects A disconnect is a small device that forms an interface between the valve fittings and any dispensing faucet or CO_2 tank. Disconnects are placed over the valve fitting and use a small pin to displace the poppet and open the valve. The outside valve fitting contains a gasket that, when the disconnect is seated properly, provides the seal between the disconnect and the fitting to prevent any leaks.

The major divide in Cornelius keg technology originates from the style of valve fittings and disconnects. There are two main types used with Cornelius kegs, the ball-lock and the pin-lock types. The history of the division can be traced back to soda companies, with Coke preferring pin-lock type and Pepsi preferring the ball-lock type. In addition, their Cornelius kegs slightly differed in shape, with the Coke version wide and short and the Pepsi type taller and narrow.

Two Cornelius kegs used in homebrewing. On the left is the pin-lock style keg and on the right is the ball-lock style keg.

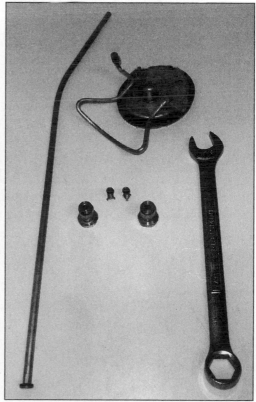

The associated parts of a Cornelius keg including the lid, poppets, fittings, and a dip tube.

The names "ball" and "pin" lock come from the mechanism used to secure the disconnect to the valve fittings. The ball-lock disconnects have steel ball bearings that lock in place when pushed over a ridged wall of the ball-lock style valve fitting. Somewhat differently, the pin-lock disconnects have openings in which small pins on the sidewalls of the pin-lock style valve fitting intersect to lock the disconnect in place. Both types work quite well to dispense beer, but the ball-lock style is generally more popular with homebrewers.

CO_2 tank Resembling a scuba tank, the CO_2 tank is a robust vessel where liquid carbon dioxide is stored for use in dispensing and carbonating beer. Although at atmospheric conditions carbon dioxide is gaseous, when pressurized in a tank, the carbon dioxide remains in liquid form, with the headspace under high pressure gas to maintain the liquid phase. When the gas is used, the headspace drops in pressure, forcing more liquid to convert to gas to maintain the equilibrium, supplying a continuous source of carbon dioxide gas until the stored liquid CO_2 runs out.

When selecting a tank, there are two major factors to consider. First is material construction, either aluminum or steel. Both work quite well; the only difference is certification duration and price. Like brew kettles, aluminum tanks are less expensive than stainless steel varieties. Also, depending on your locality, local laws require recertification through hydrostatic testing, essentially ensuring your tank is a leak-free and of sound structural integrity, every 5 to 10 years. Thus, any material-specific requirements may also factor into your decision, although this is not typical.

The second consideration is storage capacity. Tanks are typically manufactured in 5-pound intervals with most homebrewers starting out with the 5-pound tank. As a rule of thumb, a 5-pound tank will carbonate and dispense 10 to 15 5-gallon batches of beer, which is suitable for most homebrewers. However, extensive brewers may prefer larger 10- to 20-pound tanks simply to avoid having to frequently refill with CO_2.

CO_2 regulator Important for controlling forced carbonation, the CO_2 regulator is connected to the CO_2 tank and applies and maintains a constant CO_2 pressure to the beer. The desired amount of carbonation is measured by psi, or pounds per square inch, where a greater amount of pressure results in greater carbonation levels. Like most brewing measurement devices, when acquiring a regulator, make sure it is of suitable quality and includes a reliable pressure gauge capable over a wide range of pressures, at least 0 to 30 psi. Better yet would be the inclusion of a fill level, much like the gas gauge in a car, so you'll known when you are running low on CO_2. If you want to use several different carbonation levels across multiple kegs, you may be interested in dual or multigauge regulators, which supply dialed-in carbonation through several gauges, all integrated within one unit.

Faucet or tap To dispense your homebrew from a keg, you'll need a faucet. While there are several faucet styles used throughout brewing, most homebrewers use only a few select varieties. The least expensive option is the picnic tap, also known as a cobra tap, which is the black plastic faucet frequently used with kegs at frat parties. Don't be put off by this reputation; picnic taps are an affordable and reliable option to serve beer. When maintained, picnic taps seal well and pour well without foaming. Also, they are great for homebrew gatherings and parties.

The next step up is a metal beer faucet with a characteristic tap handle such as you would see at your local brew pub. Homebrewers will often transition to these faucets simply to add a bit of convenience and style to their kegerator/keezer setup. Beer faucets typically come in either chrome or stainless steel constructions. While the chrome versions are fairly inexpensive, they are prone to sticking, excessive foaming, and degradation over time, causing many brewers to gravitate toward stainless steel constructions over time. Stainless steel faucets require a greater investment up front; however, they typically work more smoothly than chrome versions, with low foam and reduced sticking. Also, stainless steel faucets will last a lifetime when well maintained, so if you plan on staying in the hobby, they are worth the investment. To learn more about serving beer with faucets and kegs, see Chapter 14.

Priming and Carbonation

Often considered the fifth ingredient, carbonation and its intensity greatly impacts the taste and character of a beer on your palate. As such, not all beer has the same level of carbonation, and the level varies significantly by style. This section covers how to estimate the right level of carbonation for your homebrew and how to achieve that level through priming and forced carbonation.

Carbonation Level

Before packaging, it's best to estimate how much carbonation will be needed in a particular beer in order to optimize its character when applied to the palate. Low carbonation can make the body seem heavy and malt sweetness too forward, while decreasing the release of aromatic compounds, like esters and hop oils. Conversely, carbonation that is too high can make the beer seem thin, acidic, and bitter, similar to fizzy pop. Thus, the brewer needs to adjust carbonation levels to find the sweet spot where the beer character in flavor, aroma, and mouthfeel are harmonious and achieve the desired balance.

To gauge the carbonation level, brewers use a measure known as volumes. This unit is the ratio of the volume of dissolved CO_2 in 1 gallon of beer. For example, 2.5 volumes of CO_2, the average carbonation level for most beer, is equivalent to 2.5 gallons of CO_2 dissolved into 1 gallon of beer. By this measure, increasing the volumes corresponds to an increase in carbonation level, and, likewise, a decrease in volumes corresponds to a decrease in carbonation.

Taking into account the effects of carbonation in beer, brewers over time have developed recommended carbonation level ranges for particular styles. Carbonation levels in beer can rane anywhere from 1.0 to 4.5 volumes. Despite the wide range, most ale and lager styles fall within 2.2 and 2.7 volumes, and this is a good place to start if you are unsure on how to gauge carbonation levels in homebrewing.

Beer Styles and Their Typical Carbonation Levels

Style	Carbonation level
British ales	1.0–2.0 volumes
Stout and porter	1.5–2.0 volumes
Imperial ales	1.3–2.3 volumes
American ales	2.3–2.7 volumes
German lagers	2.3–2.8 volumes
American lagers	2.5–3.0 volumes
Belgian ales	2.7–4.5 volumes
Wheat ales	2.7–4.0 volumes

For lighter, more refreshing, crisp beer styles, you may want to push the upper end of the carbonation level, aiming for 2.7 to 3.0 volumes to enhance its quaffable character. For stronger, more sipping beer styles, you may push the lower end of the range, aiming for 1.9 to 2.2 volumes, to help round and smooth intense flavors and characteristics. Starting out, it's best to stay within the general 2.2 to 2.7 volumes range, or use the ranges provided in the following table, and then fine tune it in future batches based on your preference.

Priming

Priming is a traditional carbonation technique that adds carbonation through a secondary fermentation. Instead of letting the carbon dioxide escape through an airlock as in primary fermentation, the carbon dioxide produced during the secondary fermentation is held by a sealed container, forcing it to pressurize. By doing this, part of the carbon dioxide dissolves back into the beer, generating the beer's carbonation. Priming is most commonly used to carbonate beer in bottles, which is known as bottle conditioning. However, this technique is not exclusive to bottles and can be used to carbonate kegs as well.

As previously discussed, brewers don't want any arbitrary amount of carbonation, but instead a specific amount tailored to the beer style. Therefore, it's necessary to precisely control the amount of refermentation in order to achieve the desired level of carbonation. This is especially critical since priming is a one-shot deal, and difficult to fix once fully conditioned.

In order for the secondary fermentation to take place, the yeast left over after primary fermentation must be healthy and viable. For most young ales, the beer retains a small amount of yeast in suspension, typically suitable at the time of bottling, and sufficient to convert the priming addition into carbonation. However, beers using extended aging, lagering, or high alcohol may have very few remaining yeast cells or have unhealthy yeast, both of which are not suitable for priming. Under these conditions, it is advised to add fresh, healthy yeast at the time of priming to yield robust carbonation. A neutral dry ale yeast works well for these purposes, with some yeast manufacturers selling special priming strains for this purpose.

The next step in the priming process is estimating the existing carbonation based on the temperature of your beer at the end of the fermentation process. While the majority of the carbon dioxide generated during fermentation escapes through the airlock, a small portion of it dissolved into the beer. This fermentation-retained carbonation is rather weak, generally less than 1 volume, but needs to be accounted for when estimating the priming addition. Without accounting for this baseline level, you may end up with a higher than desired level of carbonation.

The following table lists the fermentation-retained carbonation based on the average fermentation temperature. The figures should be fairly accurate, as long as large temperature swings and/or significant agitation does not occur. For most ale fermentations, it's safe to assume a baseline carbonation level of 0.8 to 0.9 volumes, which is a good starting point without getting too technical.

Residual Carbonation After Fermentation

Temperature	Residual carbonation
52°F	1.11 volumes
56°F	1.04 volumes
60°F	0.97 volumes
64°F	0.91 volumes
68°F	0.85 volumes
72°F	0.79 volumes
76°F	0.74 volumes
80°F	0.69 volumes

With the temperature-retained carbonation sorted out, it is now time to determine which fermentable to use. The brewer is free to choose whichever type of fermentable to add. For those looking for pure carbonation, simple sugars like corn and cane sugars are best since they are colorless and flavorless and will ferment out completely. However, priming is also an opportunity to add a bit more flavor and color in addition to carbonation. Here, the brewer can prime with a characterful sugar such as honey, agave, or just about any sugar listed in Chapter 7.

BREWING TIP

Traditionally, brewers used fresh wort to prime kegs and bottles, a process called krausening. Today, homebrewers can replicate this technique using DME; however, because it's less fermentable than plain sugar, you'll need to use a bit more to obtain an equivalent level of carbonation.

Since each sugar variety varies in fermentability, the amount needed to carbonate will vary as well. Thus, it's best to estimate the degree of fermentability of the sugar before priming. The following table provides amounts for two of the most common priming sugars, corn sugar and DME.

Basic Priming Amounts for Corn Sugar and DME*

Level	Carbonation	Corn sugar weight	DME weight
Very low	1.6 volumes	2.0 ounces	2.7 ounces
Low	3.1 ounces	3.1 ounces	4.1 ounces
Average	2.4 volumes	4.2 ounces	5.5 ounces
High	2.8 volumes	5.2 ounces	7.0 ounces
Very high	3.2 volumes	6.3 ounces	8.4 ounces

*Assuming a 5-gallon batch at a rest temperature of 68°F.

Lastly, in order to add your priming addition, you'll have to sanitize it, a process known as making a priming solution. While the basic recipe follows, when using corn and cane sugar, you are making simple syrup, and when using DME, a small batch of wort. In particular, when using DME, it's important to abide by wort production rules as specified in Chapter 11, specifically achieving a good hot and cold break, and avoiding the transfer of trub when adding to the bottling bucket. While the priming solution can be made at anytime in the packaging process, I prefer to make the priming solution before racking the beer into a bottling bucket or keg, allowing it to cool to pitching temperatures during the racking process.

Simple Corn Sugar Priming Solution Recipe

Ingredients and Equipment

3 to 5 ounces corn sugar, depending on desired carbonation level

2 cups water

1-quart saucepan

Directions

1. In a saucepan over medium heat, heat water until warm, about 140°F.

2. Add corn sugar to water and stir until dissolved.

3. Increase heat to high and bring solution to a boil. Boil for 1 minute to sanitize.

4. Using an ice bath or cold water, chill the priming solution to pitching temperatures (below 75°F). Cover with a sanitized lid and keep undisturbed until bottling time.

5. Add priming solution to bottling bucket or keg and gently stir with a sanitized spoon to ensure even distribution throughout the beer.

Going forward, here are some helpful priming tips.

- I recommend using an online calculator to calculate the amount and type of priming sugar needed depending on the beer temperature and desired CO_2 volume. The home-brew shop Northern Brew provides a great (and free) calculator at northernbrewer.com/priming-sugar-calculator.

- When estimating priming amounts, it's better to overestimate than underestimate. While extra carbonation can always be released with an aggressive pour and a bit of glass swirling, more carbonation can't be put back in.

- While specialty sugars are a great way to add extra character at bottling time, my go-to priming sugar is corn sugar. It's quick maturing, neutral in character, and easy to make a priming solution without much fuss.

Forced Carbonation

Primarily used in kegging beer, forced carbonation is the process of applying high-pressure carbon dioxide gas to produce carbonation in beer. At these high pressures, carbon dioxide is forced to dissolve into the solution yielding carbonation. The amount of dissolved carbonation is dependent on the level of pressure applied as well as the beer temperature, the two important variables when adjusting the carbonation to a desired level. Since most brewers keep a constant refrigeration temperature, they'll primarily adjust the applied pressure using the CO_2 regulator to obtain the desired amount of carbonation through the forced carbonation method.

The following table gives forced carbonation levels based on temperature and applied pressure. For example, to achieve 2.4 volumes (the typical carbonation level for most ale and lagers), 10 psi of pressure must be applied when refrigerated at 38°F. When a higher level of carbonation is desired, all that is needed is to increase the applied pressure. For example, to achieve 2.8 volumes is desired, 14 psi must be applied when refrigerated at 38°F.

Carbonation Levels Based on Temperature and Applied Pressure

Temperature	Carbonation in volumes				
	1.6	2.0	2.4	2.8	3.2
34°F	1 psi	4 psi	8 psi	12 psi	16 psi
38°F	2 psi	6 psi	10 psi	14 psi	19 psi
42°F	3 psi	8 psi	12 psi	17 psi	21 psi
46°F	5 psi	10 psi	14 psi	19 psi	24 psi
50°F	6 psi	11 psi	16 psi	21 psi	26 psi
54°F	8 psi	13 psi	18 psi	24 psi	29 psi

Although the previously documented carbonation levels will be achieved when applying pressure, the resulting carbonation does not occur immediately, but rather occurs through a slow process of saturation. In fact, it can take over a week to achieve saturation when the constant pressure is applied. Thus, the homebrewer uses a variety of techniques to speed up the forced carbonation process.

One frequently used method is the rocking technique, the process of gently rolling the keg back and forth while CO_2 is connected. The mild agitation of the beer accelerates the saturation process by exposing more beer surface area, and you may be able to achieve the desired carbonation level within a day once allowed to settle. Rolling is done over a matter of minutes, until the sound of dispensing CO_2 is no longer heard. While this method certainly is quick, it is often inaccurate, and known for greatly over carbonating beer when done improperly. Also, the rocking method generates a great deal of foaming inside the keg, which can reduce head retention as a result. Unless you need carbonated beer in a hurry, I wouldn't suggest this method for accelerated forced carbonation.

Another method utilized by the homebrewer is the high-pressure gas technique, which applies a pressure two to three times greater than the desired carbonation level over the first couple of days of carbonation. Due to the very high pressure inside the keg, carbon dioxide gas dissolves more quickly and reaches the desired carbonation levels within a few days rather than a week or more. However, before reaching absurdly elevated levels of carbonation at this high pressure setting, after one or two days the regulator setting is dialed down to the desired carbonation level. Ideally, this adjustment takes place before your beer becomes overcarbonated, allowing the final adjustment to coast to the desire carbonation level. After about three days, you beer will be carbonated at the desired level, ready to serve. Because of the quick and controlled nature of this accelerated method, I exclusively use it for forced carbonation in my brewing.

The Least You Need to Know

- Homebrew is most often packaged in glass bottles or in kegs, both of which have their advantages. While most homebrewers begin with bottling, many transition to kegging due to its ease of use and carbonation control.
- Packaging your homebrew requires a small investment of equipment. Bottling is relatively inexpensive, while kegging requires more expensive equipment.
- Carbonation can be added to beer naturally through priming or externally through forced carbonation.
- Ideal carbonation levels vary depending on the style of beer.

Evaluating Your Homebrew

With your homebrew packaged, it's time to crack one open and give it a whirl. In doing so, it's important to remember that homebrewers drink their beer not only for enjoyment but also to assess their skill and practices. This part will guide you in evaluating your homebrew, starting with choosing the right glassware and applying beer to your palate, and continuing all the way through detecting off-flavors and troubleshooting common homebrew difficulties.

Serving and Tasting

With your beer packaged and carbonated, it's time to have some homebrew! Before serving, it's worth considering how you're going to prepare the beer before enjoyment. This chapter will help you maximize your beer character through serving techniques, and provide the basics of tasting and evaluation.

Serving Beer

While your homebrew can be served any way you like it, there are some general techniques the brewer can utilize to maximize the character of the beer. This section covers some of the basics, such as optimum serving temperature and choosing the right glass, both of which can make a big difference in the overall impression of a beer on your palate.

Serving Temperature

The temperature at which a beer is served and enjoyed has a great effect on how the beer flavor and aroma is expressed on the palate. When served too cold, the tongue is numbed and carbonation isn't released, reducing flavor detection and

In This Chapter

- Choosing the right glass and serving temperature for your homebrew
- How to pour from a bottle and a keg
- Evaluating your homebrew, from appearance to flavor and aroma

limiting volatilization of aromatic compounds, leaving the beer bland. When served too warm, the beer character can become out of balance. Thus, there is a preferred temperature range to serve beer to allow for maximum expression.

What's the right temperature to serve your beer? Overall, the best temperature is dependent on the beer style and character. The following table provides specific temperature ranges, but there are also a few general rules of thumb to keep in mind:

- Light-colored beers are generally served colder than darker-colored beers.

- Stronger beers with high ABVs are typically served at warmer temperatures than low ABV beers.

- Lager styles are usually served at colder temperatures than ale styles.

When following these guidelines, most well-crafted beers should be served between 45°F and 55°F to fully appreciate their character.

Serving temperature	Beer style
35–40°F	American-style lagers
40–45°F	Light-colored German-style ales and lagers, wheat styles
45–50°F	American-style ales, dark-colored German-style ales and lagers
50–55°F	British-style ales; stout styles; porter styles; strong ale and lager styles, like bock and Belgian-style abbey ales
55°F+	Imperial ales and lagers, like barleywine, imperial stout, and doppelbock

BREWING TIP

Let refrigerated beer warm up. Most refrigerators are kept between 38°F and 40°F, so allow your beer to warm up for 5 to 10 minutes in order to reach serving temperatures of 45°F to 50°F before serving.

Using the Right Glass

The glassware in which beer is served can have a significant impact on its character, with differently shaped glasses emphasizing different aspects of the beer on your palate. For example, the character of a beer may come across as expressive and harmonious in one glass while dull or misplaced in another. Thus, it's important to match the right glass to the beer you've brewed.

While many beer styles are associated with a particular glass type, coming in several dozen varieties, there are some general rules when selecting a glass:

- For moderately to highly carbonated beer, use tall, narrow glasses help to channel carbonation and form a persistent head.

- For highly aromatic beers, round, globe-shaped glasses are best to trap volatile aromatic compounds.

- Glasses with stems are a good choice when the beer temperature needs to be maintained to avoid warming from your hand.

- Small glass sizes are best suited for strong beer "sipping" styles, while large glasses are great for quaffable session beer styles.

Based on these rules of thumb, the following are just a few must-have glass styles for any craft beer enthusiast and homebrewer. With these, you'll have something suitable for serving and evaluating most beer styles.

Belgian goblet

Belgian goblet Looking like something from medieval times, the goblet is a bowl-shaped glass that is mounted on a thick stem. The goblet can be held either by the stem to avoid heating the beer with your hand or palmed by holding the bowl to encourage warming by hand. Also, some goblets feature a small amount of inward curvature toward the top, designed to sustain foam and concentrate aroma. Additionally, many come in smaller sizes, perfect for strong ales, especially barleywine and Trappist-style Belgian strong ales. Many breweries produce their own goblets, which are usually emblazoned with their logo and may have other features to enhance the flavor of their beer. In particular, Chimay is known for using laser etching to form nucleation sites at the bottom of the bowl to seed a stream of released carbonation, maintaining a constant head throughout the drinking experience.

snifter

Snifter Similar in shape to the snifters used for fine spirits, the snifter glass is the go-to style for aromatic beers. Like a red wine glass, the snifter glass features a large bowl-shaped vessel with a wide bottom and narrow top. The bowl shape is designed to trap the released volatile aromatic compounds, funneling them toward the nose for evaluation. As such, snifters are a must-have for any intensely aromatic beer styles, such as IPAs, spiced beers, and Belgian strong ales.

pilsner glass

Pilsner glass Varying in shape and size, the pilsner glass is a tall, slender flute-shaped glass used to highlight color, clarity, and carbonation of beer. The narrowness of the glass design channels the carbonation toward the small opening, developing a large, often pillowy head. Many pilsner glasses feature a slight outward taper, which funnels the head into a more compact space with each sip, enhancing head retention throughout the drinking experience. The pilsner glass is obviously a must-have for pilsner-style lagers, but is great for any bright beer that features elevated carbonation levels.

nonic glass

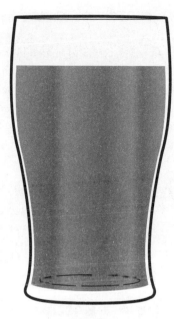

tulip pint

English pub glasses The English pub glass was designed to be easy to fill, easy to hold, and easy to wash and store. There are a few different pub glass styles; my favorites are the nonic glass, which is characterized by a slight bulge on the side of the glass, and the tulip pint, which allows for easy handling while also avoiding hand-induced warming. The English pub glass aren't the most beer expressive, but they are great for enjoying a large volume of low-gravity ale, especially English bitters.

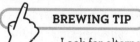

BREWING TIP

Look for alternatives to the shaker pint glass. While synonymous with craft beer in America, the standard pint glass contributes the least toward appearance, flavor, and aroma. While I still like to drink a pint or two out of the shaker style glass on occasion, other glassware will likely produce a better beer character and drinking experience.

Cleaning a Glass

Nothing is worse than making a great homebrew and pouring it into an unclean glass. After giving it a nice pour, the head immediately disappears and you're left was an unappealing, fizzy mess. An unclean glass doesn't necessary mean it wasn't washed either, as unrinsed glasses with residual detergents also can impact beer appearance and character.

To prepare a well-cleaned glass, the first step is washing it using mild detergent. When selecting a beer-friendly detergent, avoid brands using unnecessary additives and fragrances. Also, consider washing glasses by hand, especially with more delicate glassware, where dishwasher cycling may be too harsh. The next step is rinsing, where not only are you washing out any debris but also removing residual detergents. It's best to rinse several times to fully remove any trace of detergent. I typically employ two to three rising cycles to ensure a thorough removal. Once rinsed, you can either serve in the glass immediately or let drip dry. If the beer glass is shelved for a period of time, it's good to do at least one more rinse to remove any collected dust before serving.

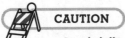 **CAUTION**

Avoid chilling glasses. Not only does the glass make the beer colder and thus less expressive, but they can also pick up funky freezer off-flavors, making the beer overall less enjoyable. If you are drinking outside on a hot summer day, using a glass cozy is a much better method for keep beer at the right serving temperature.

Pouring from a Bottle

With a clean glass in hand, it's ready to pour. Many craft beer drinkers and new brewers approach bottled beer like a delicate flower, pouring it slowly and gently down the side of the glass. While this is an acceptable method, a more aggressive pour is beneficial, as it releases aromatic compounds, produces a solid head, and knocks out extra carbonation, creating a more expressive and characterful beer overall.

A solid pour is a multistep process, and while it may seem pretentious, it's certainly worth the effort. To start, hold your glass at a 40- to 50-degree angle and begin pouring the beer, targeting the middle of the glass. Make sure the flow is at a decent clip; I like to match the flow coming out of my local brew pub's tap as a useful gauge. Once the beer is half poured or the glass half full, bring the glass to a vertical position and continue to pour. Under the same pouring conditions, this should develop a nice head, adding to the overall appearance. Continue to pour like this until the bottle is emptied or the glass is full. If too much head is produced, simply let the head settle and then continue pouring until complete.

Finally, if your beer has been bottle conditioned, it will contain a thin layer of sediment from the bottle conditioning process. You'll want to be mindful not to disturb this sediment while pouring. It's best to maintain a steady hand, avoiding any sloshing within the bottle which can disturb the sediment. Also, the last ounce or so will likely become rich with yeast, so you may want to stop pouring once it gets down to these last drops to avoid adding this sediment to the beer. If a bit gets in, it's not a big deal. The sediment will diminish any perfect clarity, but won't likely affect the flavors.

Pouring from a Keg

To achieve a nice keg pour, the tubing between the faucet and the disconnect must be long enough to provide some resistance to the keg pressure, so the beer pours smoothly. When the beer line is too short, it fails to provide enough pressure resistance, causing the beer to rocket out of the faucet, and foam excessively in the glass.

The ideal amount of line needed is dependent on a number of factors, including tubing length, tubing diameter, faucet height above the keg, and keg pressure, just to name a few. When designing a kegging system, it's worth the time and effort to consider these variables. Using an online calculator, such as calczilla.com/brewing/keg-line-balancing, can make this process easier.

As a general guideline, kegs under typical carbonation (10–14 psi) and temperature (38–42°F), require 5 to 10 feet of $\frac{3}{16}$-inch inner diameter beer line tubing to achieve a good, foam-free pour. Shorter tubing lengths or more highly carbonated beers may require reducing the pressure of the keg headspace, longer beer lines, and/or dispensing with low pressures to achieve suitable results.

As when pouring from a bottle, it's good to pour at a 45° angle with at least a bit of vigor to knock out some carbonation and develop foam. Some kegging systems tend to foam in the first second of pouring, even with a well-designed beer line. To avoid this, simply let this first second of foam fall into a drip tray, and insert the glass under the under the running stream of beer.

Evaluating Your Homebrew

Of course, the only way to determine how well your homebrew turned out is by drinking it! When consuming your homebrew, it's good practice to take careful note of your homebrew's beer character, not only to assess its full quality but also to find areas for improvement in future batches. When evaluating your homebrew, there are four major areas of character to assess: appearance, aroma, flavor, and mouthfeel.

Appearance

Before taking a sip, it's worth giving the beer a look over. While evaluating, you'll want to look for the three main visual characteristics of beer: clarity, color, and foam quality. Clarity is transparency of a beer, which can range from turbid and hazy to brilliantly clear. A good gauge for clarity is how easily an object can be seen through the glass. When looking through a hazy beer, you'll just barely notice a hand or finger, whereas in a brilliantly clear beer, you'll be able to read the small print of newspaper with ease.

Like clarity, color varies widely among beer styles, ranging from straw gold and light copper to deep amber and jet black. To assess color, I find that natural light works best; however, any well-lit room will do well. Also, be sure to take into account the beer clarity, as a hazy beer will sometimes have a lighter color compared to a filtered clear one.

Lastly, brewers look to see a nice head of foam after pouring. When assessing, you'll want to note a number of qualities, such as its texture (whether it's creamy or rocky), color, and how long it lasts after the pour. A long-lasting head, visible down to the final sip, has the quality known as good head retention. In addition, many brewers look for foam clinging to sides of glass as they sip known as *lacing*. Lacing is considered desirable in many beer styles, especially Belgian strong ales and stouts.

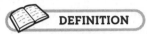 **DEFINITION**

Lacing is residual beer foam that clings to the side of the glass with every sip. Although not required, lacing is a sign of a well-cleaned glass and good fermentation.

Aroma

After assessing the appearance, it is time to give the beer a smell. The aromatic qualities of beer are very diverse, and arguably the widest ranging of all the components of beer character. Those new to aroma assessment may find a steep learning curve, especially when characterizing the more subtle aspects. However, this can be easily remedied by trying and evaluating a multitude of beer styles; it's very much a case where practice makes perfect.

Before evaluation, give the beer a swirl to help free carbonation and release volatile aromatic compounds for assessment. Start out at a distance, give the beer a smell, and work your way closer to the glass. Don't be afraid to really get your nose in the glass. Brewers use a number of sniffing techniques, such as two quick sniffs or one quick sniff and then one long sniff; however, there really isn't any one right way to smell a beer. Also, while smelling, it is good to also be aware of any external aromas that may affect the perception of beer.

For extended evaluation, there a few tips to maximize aromatic quality. After a few sniffs, it's good practice to periodically swirl the glass to refresh the aroma. Also, after a great deal of smelling, it's useful to clear your nose by breathing in some fresh air, in a sense resetting your nose. For highly aromatic beers, it's best to use a bowl-shaped glass, especially the snifter glass, to help trap more volatile aromas, which quickly dissipate after swirling. Lastly, it's good practice to periodically evaluate the aroma as the beer warms. In general, a warmer beer will release more aromatic compounds than a colder one, and as a result may change its overall quality. This is especially true of hoppy beers, which become more intense when warming.

Flavor and Tasting

After smelling, it's time for a taste. However, it would be misguided to say that tasting the beer is an assessment of its flavor, a common misconception of all things tasty. Unlike aroma, tasting is rather limited, with the tongue detecting five major characters: sweet, sour, bitter, salty, and umami. On the other hand, flavor is the effect of both taste and aroma, the combination of which provides a wide range of flavors in beer. While this may be a surprise to some, anyone with a stuffy nose can tell you that food and drink seem to have fewer flavors than at other, less stuffy, times. Thus, when assessing flavors, it's good to remember that both taste and aroma are necessary for a proper evaluation, and that highly flavorful beers may benefit from specialty glassware to emphasize both.

Despite the flavor misconception, a good taste is still key to assessing flavor. To get a good taste, you want to fully coat your mouth and tongue with beer. Avoid taking a small sip and swallowing immediately. Instead, take a moderately sized sip and coat the entirety of your palate, which can be achieved by light swishing, much like mouthwash. Also, taking a slight intake of air while holding the beer in your mouth (kind of like slurping soup) helps to aerate the beer and intensify the flavors. Lastly, when tasting, it's good to note how the flavors evolve over the duration of the sip, chiefly the initial "up-front" flavors, transitional "mid-palate" character, and the finish, where flavors may emerge after the swallow. Highly flavorful beer can have quite a long finish, where many flavors emerge and linger long after the swallow.

For a guide to beer flavors as well as the dreaded off-flavors, check out Chapter 15.

 BREWING MYTH

Myth: The tongue detects sweetness up front, sourness on the sides, and bitterness toward the back.

This myth goes back to the nineteenth century, when tongue maps were used for flavor detection. We now know this to be false; most parts of the tongue detect all tastes equally.

Mouthfeel and Body

Mouthfeel is the evaluation of a beer's fullness and texture, essentially how the beer feels on your palate. Brewers often describe mouthfeel using words like creamy, sharp, coating, astringent, and warm. Similarly, brewers often refer to the degree of fullness in a beer as *body*, using words like watery, airy, thick, rich, and lingering. When assessing mouthfeel, take special note of the physical sensations your mouth and tongue experience throughout the tasting.

To gauge mouthfeel and body, you can practice by utilizing common styles to gauge their own homebrew. An example of a light-bodied beer is an American light lager; anything from your favorite macrobrewery should work, with many approaching a fizzy, watery level in character. At the other end of the spectrum is a heavy-bodied beer, best exemplified by a high-gravity imperial stout, which has a thick, rich, coating mouthfeel that lingers on the palate even after swallowed. Most beer styles fall in the middle, and are considered medium-bodied, such as American pale ale and Munich Helles.

Cleansing Your Palate

After tasting a beer and moving onto other beers, it is best to clear your mouth of previous flavors, known as cleansing your palate. To do this, tasters use several food and beverage items to neutralize the taste buds and prepare for the next beer. Common palate cleansers for beer are simple crackerlike products, such as saltines, pretzels, or oyster crackers. Unsalted varieties are best, as salt can alter your palate. Plain water also helps to remove any remaining food and residual beer character. Make sure the water is filtered to avoid introducing any off-flavors associated with tap water. Some brewers like to use carbonated water as an effective alternative.

When tasting several beers, it's best to start out with the lighter, more subtle beer styles and work your way up toward more intensely flavored ones. For example, you might start out with an English bitter or blonde ale and progress to a pale ale or amber and then finish with the strong stuff, like an imperial IPA or barleywine. This allows your palate to adjust ever so slightly to the more intensely flavored beer. Starting with the stronger beers will flood your palate too soon, making the lighter styles less enjoyable and ultimately tasting quite watered down. This can be rectified with a palate cleaner, but it's best to plan ahead when possible.

When planning a beer tasting, follow these general guidelines.

- Move from lighter-colored beers to darker-colored beers.
- Move from low-ABV, session-style beers to boozy, high-gravity beers.
- If intense hops are present, start with low-IBU beers and move to high-IBU beers and late hop additions.

This strategy is frequently employed by homebrew clubs and beer judges alike when several tastings are evaluated, allowing for maximum palate sensitively over the course of several tastings. Likewise, when combined with palate cleansing, you'll be able to fully experience your future homebrew flights and enjoy every sip of along the way.

The Least You Need to Know

- Temperature can have a significant impact on your perception of a beer's character, and different beer styles benefit from serving at different temperatures.
- Different types of glassware are used to highlight the character of different beer styles. Use the appropriate glass shape for your beer.
- When pouring from a conditioned bottle, use an angled pouring technique and decant the beer off any yeast sediment.
- While drinking, take note of the components of beer character: appearance, aroma, flavor, and mouthfeel.

Beer Flavors

Beer can have many flavors and aromas, often fruity, caramel-y, earthy, herbal, and beyond. However, not all beer flavors are pleasant, and unwanted flavors are referred to as off-flavors by the brewer. This chapter introduces the flavors and aromas of beer and provides guidance on how to infuse or avoid these characters in your brewing process.

Malt Flavor and Aroma

Malts and grains feature a wide range of flavors and aromas ranging from grainy and sweet to roasted and nutty. The following are some of the most common malt flavors and aromas, along with the varieties of malt that best express these characteristics.

In This Chapter

- Common flavor and aroma profiles associated malt and hops
- Flavors and aromas associated with yeast and water
- Common off-flavors and how to prevent them

Caramel

Flavor/aroma descriptors: toffee, light caramel, dark caramel

Style notes: Caramel character can be introduced through caramel malts in nearly all the Lovibond ranges, with slight differences in caramel types depending on the color and maltster. Also, British versions lend more toffee character. Alternatively, caramel character can be added without malts, and utilize wort caramelization, a technique where wort is condensed and slightly caramelized, often utilized to make Scottish ales. For more information on this, check out the Scottish 80/- recipe in Chapter 22.

Malt examples: crystal/caramel malts. For lighter flavors, use in the 10 to 60°L range; for heavier flavors, use in the 60 to 150+°L range.

Smoky

Flavor/aroma descriptors: wood-fired smoke, bonfire, barbecue

Style notes: Smoke character can often be intense as the result of smoking malts over character-ful wood, such as beechwood or cherrywood. In small amounts, black malts lend an impression of smoked character associated with their often charcoal-like flavors.

Malt examples: Rauch malt, oak-smoked wheat malt

Toasted

Flavor/aroma descriptors: light to heavily toasted breads, bread crust

Style notes: Toasted character is a common malt flavor, often present in amber-colored ales and lagers, especially Oktoberfest. It pairs well with most malt flavors, and is also great at rounding out roasted character in stout and porter styles.

Malt examples: Munich malt, Vienna malt, pale chocolate malt

Bready

Flavor/aroma descriptors: pizza dough, fresh baked rolls, milled flour

Style notes: Bready character is a common malt flavor in beer, found in many beer styles, such as American-style wheat beers and English-style bitters. Pairs well with grainy, toasted, and biscuit malt character.

Malt examples: wheat malt, pilsner malt

Roasted

Flavor/aroma descriptors: coffee, chocolate, near-burnt, charcoal

Style notes: Roasted character is essential in stout and porter styles. This flavor changes depending on the level of residual sweetness, with high levels lending a sweetened coffee or milk chocolate character and low levels lending an unsweetened espresso or dark chocolate character. Pairs well with toasted, biscuit, and dried fruit malt character.

Malt examples: roasted barley, chocolate malt, black malt

Nutty

Flavor/aroma descriptors: roasted tree nuts, toasted seeds

Style notes: Nut character in beer can add an extra level of flavor without dominating other characters. Nutty character pairs well with chocolate and coffee flavors in brown ales, stouts, and porters (think Nutella), but also balances hop flavor and aroma in pale ales and IPAs.

Malt examples: biscuit malt, amber malt, Victory malt

Biscuit

Flavor/aroma descriptors: fresh baked biscuits, toasted muffins

Style notes: Biscuit character is a common malt flavor in beer. Great in British-style ales, especially ESBs. Pairs well with nutty, toasted, and roasted malt flavors.

Malt examples: Maris Otter malt, biscuit malt

Grainy

Flavor/aroma descriptors: barley husk, multigrain bread

Style notes: Grainy character is a common malt flavor in beer. A must-have in light German lager styles, but also nice in American-style ales. Pairs well with toasted, biscuit, and bready malt flavors.

Malt examples: pilsner malt, Vienna malt, flaked barley

Dried Fruit

Flavor/aroma descriptors: raisin, currants, figs

Style notes: Dried fruit character can be introduced through either dark-kilned caramel malts or roasted malts, with the type and intensity depending on malt type and amount. For example, Special B malt is known for its fig and plum qualities, while British crystal malts are rich with currant and raisin flavors. Dried fruit character is nice in dark Belgian strong ales, ESBs, and American amber ales.

Malt examples: crystal/caramel malts (80–150°L range), Special B malt

Sweet

Flavor/aroma descriptors: honey, candy-like

Style notes: Sweetness in beer is the result of several brewing variables in addition to malt. Sweetness may be the result of residual sugars leftover after fermentation, or it may be malt-derived from unfermentable sugars like caramels and dextrins common in specialty malts. Sweetness is often an important component to beer, and serves multiple purposes. While it can enhance malt flavor and aroma, it can also provide balance to hop bitterness. Also, sweetness becomes cloying at high levels, so it's best to practice healthy fermentation to achieve good attenuation and add small specialty malt additions to avoid cloying sweetness.

Malt examples: honey malt, crystal/caramel malts (10–30°L range), pilsner malt (when used in large percentages)

Hop Flavor and Aroma

Derived from the essential hop oils, hops feature a wide range of flavors and aromas ranging from earthy and grassy to citrusy and fruity. The following are some of the most common hops flavors and aromas, along with the varieties of hops that best express these characteristics.

Citrus

Flavor/aroma descriptors: lemon, grapefruit, orange, citrus zest

Style notes: Citrus character is a wonderful addition to American-style ales, such as pale ales and IPAs, but it's also great in American brown ale, lending a chocolate-orange character. Pairs well with other fruity varieties.

Hop examples: Cascade, Amarillo, Centennial, Citra

Stone Fruit

Flavor/aroma descriptors: apricot, peach, plum

Style notes: Stone fruit character in hops is becoming more common, and it works well in most beer styles, especially British-style ales and American IPAs. Pairs well with other fruity hops, but also is nice with earthy varieties as well.

Hop examples: Palisade, Rakau, Galena

Floral

Flavor/aroma descriptors: freshly cut flowers, jasmine, perfumelike

Style notes: Floral character is a must-have in many European beer styles. It's wonderful and delicate in German-style pilsners, but also great in English Bitters. Pairs well with herbal varieties.

Hop examples: Ahtanum, Hallertau Mittelfrüh, East Kent Goldings, Sterling

Spicy

Flavor/aroma descriptors: spicy, peppery

Style notes: Spicy hop character is common in many varieties, and is often desirable in German-style lagers. Pairs well with most other hop flavor types, especially herbal and floral varieties.

Hop examples: Liberty, Nugget, Perle, Czech Saaz, First Gold

Earthy

Flavor/aroma descriptors: freshly turned earth, potting soil, tobacco leaves

Style notes: Although potting soil may not sound very tasty, earthy character is desired in beer, and is often featured in British ales such as bitter and porter styles. Pairs well with spicy and herbal varieties.

Hop examples: Fuggle, Tettnang, Spalt, Northern Brewer, East Kent Goldings

Herbal

Flavor/aroma descriptors: fresh herbs

Style notes: One of the main components of the noble hops, herbal character is present in many beer styles, including almost all German- and American-style lagers. Pairs well with spicy and floral varieties.

Hop examples: Strisselpalt, Hersbrucker, Mt. Hood, Czech Saaz

Tropical Fruit

Flavor/aroma descriptors: passion fruit, guava, pineapple, lime oil

Style notes: Tropical fruit character is a great addition to American pale ale and IPA styles. It pairs well with other fruity, citrusy hop varieties.

Hop examples: Citra, Galaxy, Falconer's Flight Hop Blend

Pine and Resin

Flavor/aroma descriptors: evergreen, sap, resin

Style notes: Pine and resin character is often quite rustic and intense. Excellent in American-style IPAs, but also great in California common beer and British ales. Pairs well with earthy, woody hops, as well as citrus varieties.

Hop examples: Simcoe, Northern Brewer, Chinook, Target

Grassy

Flavor/aroma descriptors: fresh cut grass clippings, hay

Style notes: Grassy hop character is derived either through specific hop varieties or the dry hopping technique. Some brewers observe grassy character from hops through extended dry hopping, although this is often debated. Pairs well with herbal and earthy varieties.

Hop examples: Fuggle, Palisade, Tradition, Progress

Woody

Flavor/aroma descriptors: fresh cut wood, cedar, bark

Style notes: Woody hops are another rustic flavor, common in British ale styles. Pairs well with resin-y, earthy hop varieties.

Hop examples: Pride of Ringwood, Challenger, Northdown, Northern Brewer

Musty

Flavor/aroma descriptors: wet leaves, dank, catty, garlic

Style notes: Although it may sound like an off-flavor, musty hop character can be pleasant, particularly in American-style IPAs and double IPAs. Pairs well with resiny, earthy varieties.

Hop examples: Simcoe, CTZ, Summit

Yeast and Water Flavor and Aroma

While yeast and water mostly contribute toward enhancing malt, hop, and overall beer flavor expression, some yeast and water profiles will add flavor and aroma characteristics to beer. Characterful yeast strains produce ester and phenols, which, when pleasant, add fruity and spicy characters to beer, and for some beer styles, this character is the main event. Like yeast, water is more supportive than directly flavorful, but in high mineral contents, water can contribute extra character. The following are the most commonly perceived direct yeast and water characters in beer.

Phenolic

Flavor/aroma descriptors: black pepper, clove, cinnamon

Style notes: Not all yeast strains produce phenolic character, but when pleasant, phenols can lend a spicy character in beer, such as clove or black pepper. Pairs well with balanced fruit esters, commonly banana.

Examples: Saison, Belgian, and German Wheat strains

Estery or Fruity

Flavor/aroma descriptors: ripe banana, pear, tropical fruits, stone fruits, citrus, bubble gum

Style notes: Fruity ester flavors vary widely in character, and may not always be desired. In American-style ales and most lager styles, the fruity flavors of ester are unwanted. However, British and Belgian style ales often feature ester character.

Examples: Most ale strains. Banana and bubble gum are common in German wheat and Belgian strains, while pear and stone fruit character is common in British ale strains.

Minerally

Flavor/aroma descriptors: flinty, mineral water, chalky

Style notes: Mineral character can be found in many beer styles, especially Dortmund Export and British pale ales, owning to the high mineral content of the water in these regions.

Examples: Some yeast strains produce mineral character, especially London ale strains, but mineral flavors are more likely due to high mineral content in the water, especially Burtonized water.

Off-Flavors

Off-flavors are the undesired and unpleasant flavors in beer that are usually the result of a brewing mistake. Common off-flavors include horse blanket, cardboard, and cheese—generally not characteristics you want in your brew. Fortunately, when appropriate brewing techniques are observed, off-flavors are not common.

If you suspect something is off, the following list details the common off-flavors in beer, as well as the likely cause and some preventative measures to eliminate these off-flavors in future brewing. Lastly, if you identity an off-flavor in your homebrew, no worries, you are not alone! I've had of few creep into my homebrew over time, especially with my first few batches of homebrew. Don't let it discourage you; remember, practice makes perfect!

Acetaldehyde

Flavor/aroma descriptors: green apples, freshly-cut squash, cider

Appropriateness: While considered appropriate at very low levels, acetaldehyde should be minimized. This off-flavor occurs most often in American-style lagers, usually when warmed up, and is the culprit of "green beer."

Cause and prevention: Acetaldehyde forms early in the stages of alcohol production, during fermentation. Typically, it's reabsorbed during the lagering and conditioning stages. To prevent acetaldehyde flavors, use appropriate pitching rates, healthy, fresh yeast, and allow for full fermentation and conditioning to take place.

Alcoholic

Flavor/aroma descriptors: hot, burning, unpleasantly spicy

Appropriateness: Alcohol can provide a warming sensation in strong ales and lagers, and is acceptable when pleasant, but never when harsh. Think top-shelf spirits, not cheap tequila.

Cause and prevention: Strong ales and lagers can be harsh when young and will smooth when aged. However, harshness is more common if a strong beer has been poorly fermented. To prevent harsh alcohol flavors, use tailored fermentation for strong beers, with higher pitching rates, controlled fermentation, adequate aeration, and added yeast nutrients. Aging can also create a smoother character, but proper fermentation should be first practiced.

Solvent

Flavor/aroma descriptors: nail polish remover, rubbing alcohol

Appropriateness: Never

Cause and prevention: Similar to alcoholic character, solvent character is likely due to high fermentation temperatures and poor fermentation. High oxygen levels during fermentation can also contribute to higher alcohol formation. To prevent solvent character, use proper fermentation techniques and temperature control.

Oxidized

Flavor/aroma descriptors: wet cardboard and newspaper, or soy sauce and sherry in darker beers

Appropriateness: In low levels, oxidized character is appropriate in strong beers, typically in barley wine styles. In high levels, oxidized character is never appropriate.

Cause and prevention: Oxidation is caused by oxygen incorporation post fermentation, typically during packaging. Also, oxygen can permeate through caps and corks over time, causing beer to oxidize. This is generally unavoidable for extensively aged beers. To prevent oxidation, minimize oxygen incorporation when bottling by using oxygen-absorbing bottle caps or flush the keg headspace with CO_2. Also, store beer cold (below 40°F) when not serving and drink fresh beer styles as soon as possible.

Diacetyl

Flavor/aroma descriptors: butter, theater-style popcorn, butterscotch, slickness in mouthfeel

Appropriateness: In low levels, diacetyl is considered appropriate in English-style ales, but in general, it should be minimized.

Cause and prevention: Diacetyl forms in the early stages alcohol production during fermentation. Typically, it's reabsorbed during the later lagering and conditioning stages. To prevent diacetyl flavors, use appropriate pitching rates, healthy, fresh yeast, and allow for full fermentation and conditioning to take place.

Dimethyl Sulfide (DMS)

Flavor/aroma descriptors: canned or creamed corn, cooked celery

Appropriateness: In low levels, DMS is appropriate in German-style lagers, although it should be minimized. In moderate to high levels, it is never appropriate.

Cause and prevention: DMS commonly occurs in low-kilned malt varieties, especially pilsner malts. Short boils or slow chilling can also increase DMS concentrations in wort. Additionally, DMS is sometimes indicative of contamination, although this is less likely. To prevent DMS, use longer boils, 75 to 90 minutes when using all-grain recipes and utilize fast chilling techniques to limit DMS formation. Also, observe proper cleaning and sanitization practices.

Metallic

Flavor/aroma descriptors: blood-like, sucking on a penny

Appropriateness: Never

Cause and prevention: Metallic character can be caused by several factors. Brewing water with a high mineral content can lend a metallic taste, as can metal brewing equipment, notably brewing kettles, mash tuns, and lauter structures, especially after harsh scrubbing or when dissimilar metals are used, like aluminum on stainless steel. To prevent metallic flavors, use filtered RO water if water is suspected. Also, use similar metals throughout your brewing process and a no-scrub cleaning agent, such as PWB, when cleaning.

Astringent or Tannic

Flavor/aroma descriptors: over-steeped tea, red wine-like

Appropriateness: Astringent character is acceptable in low levels or when pleasant, and is common in highly hopped beers. However, astringency is never appropriate in moderate to high levels.

Cause and prevention: Unpleasant astringent or tannic character may be caused by malts that have been oversparged or mashed at high pH levels, both of which can release tannins from the husks. Over hopping can also create a tannic quality in wort. Additionally, black malts, when used in larger percentages, can lend an astringent character. To prevent astringency, keep the mash and sparge pH between 5.0 and 5.4 (mash temperature), and stop the sparge when runnings reach below 1.008. Lastly, if hops are suspected, use high alpha hops or hop extract for bittering.

Acidic or Acetic

Flavor/aroma descriptors: vinegar, lactic, tart, sour

Appropriateness: Acidic or acetic character is appropriate in sour and wild styles, but it should be pleasant and without harsh vinegar notes. However, this character is never appropriate in most ale and lager styles.

Cause and prevention: Acidic or acetic character is likely due to bacterial or wild yeast contamination. To prevent these flavors, observe adequate cleaning and sanitization practices.

Goaty or Barnyard

Flavor/aroma descriptors: horse blanket, shower drain, farm animals

Appropriateness: A goaty or barnyard character is appropriate in some sour/wild styles, and should be pleasant, without harsh vinegar notes. However, this character is never appropriate in most ale and lager styles.

Cause and prevention: Goaty or barnyard character is likely due to *Brettanomyces* contamination. In prevention, observe adequate cleaning and sanitization practices.

Cheesy

Flavor/aroma descriptors: Parmesan cheese, sweaty socks

Appropriateness: Never

Cause and prevention: Cheesy character in beer is due to several causes. Stale or oxidized hops can have a cheesy aroma/flavor. Also, bacterial fermentation with high aeration levels, such as the sour mash technique, can lend a cheeselike character. To prevent this flavor, use fresh hops, stored cold, packed in nitrogen or vacuum-sealed, and smell hops prior to adding to wort. Also, observe adequate cleaning and sanitization practices.

Yeast Bite or Autolysis

Flavor/aroma descriptors: rubber, rancid, meaty

Appropriateness: Never

Cause and prevention: Autolysis character is a result of yeast death. Here, the yeast cell breaks down, essentially spewing its contents into your beer and with it other off-flavors. Yeast death is caused by several factors, including poor fermentation, sitting on the yeast bed for long durations, or contamination from wild yeast or bacteria. To prevent, use adequate fermentation and conditioning techniques and observe proper cleaning and sanitization practices.

Skunky

Flavor/aroma descriptors: skunk or cat musk, stink bombs

Appropriateness: Never

Cause and prevention: When isomerized alpha acids from hops are exposed to UV light, they undergo a chemical change and become the identical chemical compound produced by the backend of a skunk. To prevent skunky beer, avoid exposing it to direct sources of light, especially intense sunlight, and store in dark-colored brown bottles to reduce light transmittance.

Medicinal or Chlorophenolic

Flavor/aroma descriptors: plastic, bandagelike

Appropriateness: In very low levels, plastic-like flavors are a traditional component to German wheat styles, although for the modern palate, this should be avoided. In low to high levels, it is never appropriate.

Cause and prevention: Medicinal or chlorophenolic character in beer can have multiple causes. Wild yeast contamination can produce phenols generating these medicinal characteristics. Another possibility is a cleaning or sanitization agent like bleach or iodophor used at higher concentrations without rinsing. Also, source water high chloramine levels can produce chlorophenolic character. To prevent this off-flavor, use alternative sanitization agents like Star San or thoroughly rinse cleaning agents. If contamination is suspected, observe adequate cleaning and sanitization practices. Lastly, for water related difficulties, use Campden tablets or metabisulfites to remove chloramines in source water.

Estery or Phenolic

Flavor/aroma descriptors: fruity, clovelike, spicy

Appropriateness: In low to moderate levels, ester or phenolic character is appropriate in ale styles when expected; at high or strong levels, it is rarely appropriate. Also, ester or phenolic character is not appropriate in most hybrid and lager styles.

Cause and prevention: Unwanted ester or phenolic character in beer is a result of uncontrolled fermentation. There are many fermentation causes, such as high fermentation temperatures, large temperature swings, low aeration, low pitching rates, or deficient yeast nutrition. Alternatively, excessive ester or phenolic character can be due to contamination from wild yeast when not expected. To prevent this, use controlled fermentation techniques, including adequate pitching rates, appropriate temperatures, and proper aeration. If contamination is suspected, observe adequate cleaning and sanitization practices.

Moldy

Flavor/aroma descriptors: bread mold, mildewlike

Appropriateness: Never

Cause and prevention: Moldy character is likely due to an unintended mold contamination. In prevention, observe adequate cleaning and sanitization practices.

Soapy

Flavor/aroma descriptors: dish soap, detergent

Appropriateness: Never

Cause and prevention: Soapy character can be a result of poorly rinsed equipment containing residual cleaning or sanitizing agent. The floral character from added herbs and spices, such as chamomile and lavender, can also lend a soapy character due to their association with fragranced soap products. To prevent, thoroughly rinse cleaning or sanitizing agents when called for in the instructions.

Vegetal

Flavor/aroma descriptors: overcooked green vegetables, cabbage

Appropriateness: Slight grassiness is appropriate for dry-hopped beers, but vegetal character in medium to high levels is never appropriate.

Cause and prevention: Vegetal character is likely caused by bacterial contamination. To prevent, observe adequate cleaning and sanitization practices.

Sulfur

Flavor/aroma descriptors: sulfur-like, rotten eggs

Appropriateness: In low levels, sulfur character is common in lagers. However, in medium to high levels, it is never appropriate.

Cause and prevention: Sulfur compounds are produced by lager yeast strains and some ale strains when fermented at cold temperatures. To prevent, try using longer conditioning or lagering times to help to dissipate sulfur character. Scrubbing a kegged beer with CO_2 can also help to reduce high levels. Finally, raising the temperature throughout fermentation helps to drive off sulfur compounds.

The Least You Need to Know

- Beer can have a wide spectrum of flavors and aromas from malt, hops, yeast fermentation, and water characters.
- Some flavors and aromas are desired in some beer styles but not in others.
- Off-flavors are undesired flavors in beer, and often occur from brewing and fermentation errors, but can be easily rectified in future batches.

CHAPTER 16

Troubleshooting

Sometimes, the beer you've brewed doesn't come out the way you expected. This doesn't necessarily mean the outcome was bad, but it may not have the flavor or appearance you intended. It's normal for the new brewer to encounter road-blocks like this from time to time. In a real sense, this is the only way to learn and improve your brewing process. The information in this chapter will help you troubleshoot common brewing difficulties and also provide potential solutions and some preventative measures for future batches.

Note that this chapter does not address off-flavors. For troubleshooting off-flavors, check out the off-flavor section in Chapter 15.

In This Chapter

- Common problems related to appearance, taste, fermentation, mash, and packaging
- How to combat contamination in your home brewery
- What to do if you have a contaminated batch

Appearance Problems

My wort or beer came out too dark in color.

Causes: For the extract brewer, the prime suspect is likely a partial boil, which can result in browning, especially in pale beers, due to the increased Maillard reactions from the high-gravity boil. A less likely cause could be old malt extracts, which tend to darken with time. If this is the case, the dark color is the least of your problems as old extracts are also stale, and can cause cardboard or ciderlike off-flavors in your brew. For all brewers, wort darkening could also be a result a too vigorous boil, which also has increased browning through Maillard reaction.

Prevention: For extract brewers, consider using a full boil, especially in light-colored styles. Also, make sure to use fresh extract both for flavor concerns and to achieve a lighter colored wort. If extract is not the culprit, then consider using a lower boil rate to reduce kettle-related browning. Lastly, if none of these are suspected, double check your specialty malt Lovibond rating, especially roasted types which widely vary among maltsters. For example, roasted barley can vary between 300°L and 600°L, resulting in a significant color change even when using small amounts.

My wort or beer came out too light in color.

Causes: This is generally not a problem for most brewers, but can occur for a few reasons. If there is yeast in suspension, the finished beer may appear lighter than the original wort. Also, if specialty malts were steeped, the water may have been too cold or the steep may not have been long enough, resulting in less than expected extraction of both flavor and color, and thus a paler wort and beer.

Prevention: If yeast is suspected, consider using a fining agent like gelatin to clear the beer before packaging. Alternatively, use cold-conditioning and/or rack to a secondary fermentor to encourage flocculation. For steeping malts, make sure to use water between 150°F and 170°F for 30 minutes and let the steeping bag drain accordingly. Lastly, like wort darkening, double check your specialty malt Lovibond rating, especially roasted types, which widely vary among maltsters.

My beer has a persistent hazy or cloudy appearance.

Causes: Persistent haze can occur for a number of reasons. The most common culprit is low-flocculant yeast. Strains like American ale and Kölsch begrudgingly stay in suspension for several weeks to months before falling clear. Other persistent haze contributors are unconverted starches from a mash, creating starch haze in beer. Also, if you used a large dry-hop addition, your beer may have a haze from hop-derived tannins.

Prevention: If yeast or hops are suspected, consider using a fining agent like gelatin to clear the beer before packaging. Alternatively, use cold-conditioning to encourage yeast flocculation and tannin precipitation. For the all-grain brewer, check your wort before lautering using an iodine test to ensure full starch conversion.

The haze in my beer is temporary and goes away when it warms.

Cause: This temporary haze in beer is known as chill haze. During cold break, the chilling phase of wort production, a coagulation of proteins and tannins in wort falls out of suspension when rapidly chilled. When cold break remains in suspension after chilling, it forms chill haze, where the left behind protein and tannin compounds bind at cold temperatures, causing haze, and then unbind as the beer warms up, increasing clarity.

Prevention: Brewers can use a few techniques to eliminate chill haze. The first step is to decrease wort chilling times by using a more rapid chilling method, like an immersion chiller, to produce a more substantial cold break. If this is not enough, try adding a wort clarifier such as Irish moss to the boil, which helps to attract proteins and tannins in wort during the cold break. Also, after fermentation, gelatin is great at reducing chill haze as its strong positive ionic charge attracts the haze-causing particulates and drops them out of the solution quickly. Lastly, using near freezing cold-conditioning can promote further precipitation of chill haze, post-fermentation and even after packaging.

My beer has little foam or lacks head retention.

Causes: Lack of foam or head retention can be due to several factors. The simplest cause is an unclean glass with residual oils or detergents acting as a surfactant, reducing foam and head retention. Another reason could be simply the grain bill had low dextrin and protein content, common components in foam formation. If other fermentation flaws and off-flavors are apparent, the lack of head retention may be due to poor fermentation and the production of protease and fusel alcohols, which destroy head forming compounds.

Prevention: Use clean glassware when serving beer. Also, adding body-focused malts like dextrin malt or protein-rich adjuncts like flaked barley to mash can encourage head retention. The all-grain brewer may also use a higher mash rest to encourage long-chain dextrin formation. Additionally, make sure to use adequate fermentation practices, like temperature control, to avoid negative beer impacts. Lastly, if all else fails, adding a bit more carbonation and an aggressive pour can help generate a larger, foamy head.

Taste Problems

My beer is too bitter.

Causes: This is not typically a problem, as most craft beer drinkers enjoy a bitter beer. Still, if your batch came out too bitter, this is a result of either underestimating the alpha acid content of the hops and their IBU contributions or using a slow chilling method, causing further isomerization of late hop additions post-boil, increasing bitterness.

Prevention: Use late hop additions for hoppy beer styles to preserve hop character without generating strong bitterness. Also, use a rapid chilling method, such as immersion chilling, to quickly slow isomerization post-boil.

My beer is not bitter enough.

Causes: Less than bitter beer is a common problem and can be caused by several factors. The most likely culprit is old hops, which lose bittering value over time. Most hop varieties lose alpha acid content over time, some varieties lose more than 50 percent in as little as six months. Another possibility is yeast strain, as certain varieties, especially wheat strains, have been shown to strip isomerized alpha acids from beer during fermentation, reducing bitterness. Lastly, your beer may have the predicted IBU levels, but suffer from high levels of residual sweetness, whether through specialty malts or a high finishing gravity, reducing the impact of bitterness on your palate.

Prevention: Use fresh hops with greater alpha acid content. For hoppy styles, reduce specialty malts, focus on attenuation, and use hop-friendly yeast, like American ale strains, to bring out the hop character and bitterness. Also, when all else fails, simply add more hops!

My beer is too sweet.

Causes: Unintended sweet beer is usually the result of too much sugar left behind after fermentation, and can be caused by a few reasons. A high final gravity from sluggish fermentation can result in a greater number of fermentable sugars left behind as yeast go into dormancy before completing fermentation, resulting in greater sweetness in beer. Alternatively, a beer with a large amount of caramel/crystal malts leave behind many unfermentable sugars, causing residual, sometimes cloying, sweetness. Lastly, there may be nothing wrong with your malt and fermentation but rather not enough bitterness from hops to balance out the malt character, resulting in forward sweetness.

Prevention: If fermentation is suspected, use adequate practices, especially aeration and pitching rate, to ensure good growth and cell counts to complete fermentation. Also, consider cutting back on the crystal/caramel malts when used in quantities greater than 1 pound in a 5-gallon batch. Lastly, make sure to use fresh and properly stored hops to hit the desired bitterness needed to balance out malt character without making the beer cloyingly sweet.

My beer is not sweet enough.

Causes: Overly dry beer is what happens when there's not enough malt sugar left behind after fermentation. This can happen for a few reasons. If the wort was produced with a low mash rest and/or with a large amount of fermentable sugar, the yeast may have converted the vast majority of sugar into alcohol, leaving little residual sweetness behind. Ultra-dry beer can often be a sign of an unwanted contaminant. In this case, the lack of sweetness is also accompanied by off-flavors.

Prevention: To add sweetness, consider adding a touch of caramel/crystal malts to your grain bill. For a more honeylike sweetness, use lighter crystal varieties. For a more caramel-like quality, add darker crystal varieties, just remember that these will also lend color as well. Alternatively, consider adding lactose, an unfermentable sugar that adds a bit of sweetness while also adding some body and mouthfeel. Also, consider reducing hop bitterness, using a less attenuative yeast strain, and/or reducing carbonation levels, all of which will make the malt character more present, including its sweetness. Lastly, if contamination is suspended, observed adequate cleaning and sanitization practices.

My beer lacks body and mouthfeel.

Causes: Beer lacking in body and mouthfeel can be caused by several reasons, but chiefly is due to a lack of unfermentable sugars, dextrin, and protein, the sum of which contribute to a beer's mouthfeel. Also, a beer with a low final gravity and a high degree of attenuation will often lack mouthfeel due to the low amount of fermentable and unfermentable sugars left in the finished beer. If there are other defects, such as off-flavors or a very high degree of attenuation, the lack of body may be a result of contamination.

Prevention: Adding mouthfeel and body is a matter of adding more unfermentable sugars and protein. This can be achieved with caramel crystal/malts or dextrin malts, which leave unfermentable sugars behind after fermentation, or with adjuncts like flaked barley or flaked rye, which add protein and considerable body to beer. A little goes a long way with these malts and grains, often less than 1 pound in a 5-gallon batch can turn a beer lacking in mouthfeel into a fuller bodied drink. Also, reducing the carbonation level can help, as increased levels reduce body. Additionally, using a less attenuative yeast strain will leave more fermentable sugar behind after fermentation, adding body and some sweetness. If contamination is suspected, observe adequate cleaning and sanitation practices. Lastly, for the all-grain brewer, consider using a high mash rest to create unfermentable longer-chained sugars, which add body to beer.

My beer is too heavy on the palate.

Causes: Beer that is heavy on the palate is a result of too much body and mouthfeel and related to other brewing difficulties such as high finishing gravities or too much sweetness. Beer with a high finishing gravity has a large amount of sugar left behind after fermentation, which increases mouthfeel and body, and often residual sweetness as well. Also, large amounts of specialty malts, like crystal malts and dextrin malt, add unfermentable sugars, which add body and some sweetness. Additionally, adjunct grains like flaked barley and flaked rye contain large amounts of protein, which can add considerable body. In particular, rye is said to have an almost cough-syrup-like mouthfeel when used in large proportions.

Prevention: There are ways to decrease mouthfeel in your homebrew. If specialty malt and/or adjunct choices are suspected, use less; 1 pound in a 5-gallon batch is often plenty to achieve their unique character. In addition, use more attenuative yeast strains to achieve lower final gravities and leave less sugar behind, thus less mouthfeel. Lastly, for the all-grain brewer, consider using a low mash rest to create fewer unfermentable longer-chained sugars, which reduce the body and mouthfeel of the beer.

Fermentation Problems

Fermentation is slow to start.

Causes: A slow starting fermentation is caused by slow working yeast, and is not necessarily a bad thing. For lager fermentations, especially when pitched below 50°F, cold temperatures cause the yeast to work more slowly within the lag and growth phases, delaying any visible signs of fermentation. Also, at these cold temperatures, carbon dioxide is able to dissolve in higher concentrations, inhibiting visible airlock activity until the later stages of fermentation. If room temperature fermentation is used, then a slow start is likely due to a low pitch rate, which forces the yeast to go through an extended lag and growth phase before the bulk of fermentation can begin. When very low pitch rates are used, visible signs of fermentation can take up to three days to appear, and may produce off-flavors and increase risk of contamination.

Prevention: If cold fermentation is used, it's normal for visible signs of fermentation to take up to two days to appear. If fermentation fails to start after three days, then consider pitching more yeast, or warming it up to jump-start fermentation to avoid competing contaminants. At warmer ale temperatures, visible signs of fermentation should occur within 24 hours after pitching. If 36 hours pass without visible signs of fermentation, consider pitching more yeast. A backup sachet of dry yeast is always a good option for either scenario.

Fermentation is stuck.

Causes: A stuck fermentation is the event where the yeast ceases to ferment, resulting in a very high gravity and undesired fermentation by-products. Stuck fermentation does not often happen, but when it does, it is usually due to yeast falling into dormancy before finishing the fermentation process. This can have several causes. Wort deficient in vital yeast nutrients, especially zinc, magnesium, and calcium, can cause of stuck fermentation. Also, poor yeast growth due to insufficient aeration can cause the yeast to become overworked due to low cell densities, and fall into dormancy before a completing fermentation. Other things like large temperature swings, temperature shock, and highly flocculent yeast can further contribute to a stuck fermentation. Lastly, if other defects are apparent, contamination could be the problem, especially when mold is present, inhibiting the growth of yeast and terminating fermentation.

Prevention: The best defense against a stuck fermentation is to ensure good yeast health. This includes monitoring the temperature, fermenting within the recommended temperature ranges, pitching at adequate rates, and aerating to at least 8 ppm. Also, be sure to add yeast nutrients to wort when using a large amount of adjuncts, especially sugars, as these are nutrient deficient. To stay on the safe side, a bit of yeast nutrient in all-malt wort certainly won't hurt when used at the recommended dosage. Lastly, if contamination is suspected, use adequate cleaning and sanitization practices.

My final gravity finished too high.

Causes: A high final gravity can be caused by several factors including fermentation, yeast selection, or low fermentability of wort. Tired or sluggish yeast, either because of cold fermentation, low growth, or low pitch rate, will want to go into dormancy before the majority of fermentable sugars are converted into alcohol, leaving more sugar behind than desired, and resulting in a high final gravity. Yeast strain selection plays a large part in this as well, with low-attenuating yeast naturally leaving more sugar behind after fermentation, and thus a high final gravity. Alternatively, wort composition can increase final gravity, especially in all-grain brewing, as a high mash rest converts starches into unfermentable long-chain dextrin, and increases the final gravity.

Prevention: If fermentation problems are suspected, use appropriate practices, including adequate aeration and pitching rates, to allow for a complete fermentation. Also, look for more highly attenuative yeast strains, especially for recipes requiring a low final gravity. For the extract brewer, use fresh extracts without adding dextrin malts, and for the all-grain brewer, use a lower mash rest to convert starches into simpler sugar, increasing wort fermentability. Also, for the all-grain brewer, double check your thermometer calibration as it may be off and unintentionally mashing at a higher temperature than expected, resulting in a less fermentable wort.

My final gravity finished too low.

Causes: A low final gravity is not as common as a high one, but it can be caused by several factors. Yeast strain selection plays a large role; highly attenuative yeast will chew through more sugars, resulting in a low final gravity. If there are off-flavors in your beer, a low final gravity may be due to contamination, both from bacteria and wild yeast, as they will work on more complex dextrin, resulting in a thin beer. Wort composition also comes into play when a large quantity of simple sugars are present. For the extract brewer, this could be the result of using a large percentage of corn or cane sugar adjuncts in the wort to boost alcohol. For the all-grain brewer, a low temperature mash rest will create simpler sugars that are highly fermentable by yeast, resulting in a low final gravity.

Prevention: If yeast selection is suspected, use a less attenuative yeast strain to leave more sugar behind after fermentation, increasing the final gravity. If contamination is suspected, use adequate cleaning and sanitization practices. For the extract brewer, steeping dextrin malt or adding maltodextrin to the boil will decrease fermentability, increasing final gravity. For the all-grain brewer, use a higher temperature mash rest to convert starch into longer-chain dextrin, decreasing wort fermentability. Also, for the all-grain brewer, double check your thermometer calibration, as it may be off and unintentionally mashing at a lower temperature than expected, resulting in a more fermentable wort.

A film other than the krausen is over the surface of the beer.

Causes: Unfortunately, there is only one thing that causes this, and that is contamination from wild yeast or bacteria. The characteristic thin film is known as a *pellicle*, and it is formed by many contaminants, especially the wild yeast *Brettanomyces* and bacteria *Pediococcus*.

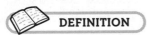 **DEFINITION**

> **Pellicle** is a white, slimy film that forms on top of fermenting beer. It is caused by brewing contaminants, especially wild yeast and bacteria.

Prevention: There is only one way to fight contamination and that's better cleaning and sanitization practices. Sometimes contamination is random or an accident, and in this case, can be chalked up to bad luck. However, when continuous contamination occurs over several batches, this may be a result of a permanently contaminated piece of brewing equipment, which can happen if a scratch in the equipment is harboring bacteria. In this case, it's best to start anew and replace any and all suspected brewing equipment at the source of the contamination. For more information on fighting contamination, check out Chapter 9 and the last section within this chapter.

Packaging Problems

I'm having difficulty starting and/or keeping a siphon.

Causes: A poor performing siphon can turn a perfectly happy bottling/kegging day into a stressful one. A siphon will not work if there is an air leak within the siphoning system, if there is not enough height separating the two vessels, or if the flow is restricted due to clogging debris, like hop matter and trub.

Prevention: Check for air leaks by examining the plastic racking cane and tubing for cracks and ensuring a tight seal between the two. Also, use a large height differential to achieve moderate siphon flow. Lastly, clear any debris at the entrance of the racking cane.

My bottle-conditioned beer is flat.

Causes: Undercarbonated or flat bottle-conditioned beer is usually a sign of a problematic refermentation in the bottle and can be caused by several factors. Primarily, undercarbonated conditioning is a result of sluggish yeast. Either the yeast was tired from the primary fermentation, the yeast cell quantity was too low due to extended aging, or the fermentation environment was too cold to engage fermentation, all of which can result in little to no carbonation. Undercarbonation can also be the result of an insufficient priming addition. Lastly, undercarbonation due to a partial or comprised cap seal allowing the priming carbonation to escape is possible, but less likely.

Prevention: When batch priming, you may require additional healthy yeast for sufficient carbonation, especially for cold conditioned beer, highly flocculant yeast, and/or high-gravity beers. Also, make sure the bottle conditioning occurs in a warm environment, ideally between 60°F to 70°F. Lastly, if the cap seal is suspected, consider purchasing new bottle caps, as the old ones may be defective, and make sure your bottle capping device is working properly.

My kegged beer is flat.

Causes: Undercarbonated or flat beer when kegged is usually a sign of a leaking seal. Alternatively, if you primed your keg for carbonation, you may have slow yeast or not enough priming sugar.

Prevention: Check your keg seals by coating them with soapy water. If there's air escaping, a soapy bubbling will form, indicating that these leaky seals may require regreasing, reseating, or replacement. When batch priming, you may require additional yeast or sugar for sufficient carbonation, especially for cold-conditioned beer, highly flocculant yeast, and/or high-gravity beers.

My bottle-conditioned beer is overcarbonated.

Causes: Overcarbonated beer is the result of excessive refermentation in bottle, and can be caused by several reasons. The most likely cause is incomplete primary fermentation prior to bottling, which results in greater than expected carbonation on top of the added priming sugar. Another reason is contamination; if either wild yeast or bacteria are introduced during bottling, they will consume residual sugars and cause overcarbonation. Contamination-based overcarbonation is very excessive, often explosive, and can be confirmed by tasting the beer, which will likely have off-flavors and a ring around the neck of the bottle. Lastly, too much priming sugar added at bottling can result in overcarbonation.

Prevention: Allow for primary fermentation to complete before bottling. Take consecutive gravity readings as a good way to ensure that the final gravity is steady and complete. Also, observe adequate cleaning and sanitization practices to avoid contamination.

There is excessive sediment in bottle.

Causes: Excessive sedimentation is the result of suspended beer particulate that had not cleared prior to bottling. This sediment is usually yeast, but may be hop debris from dry hops.

Prevention: To reduce sediment, consider using extended conditioning to allow the yeast to naturally flocculate out of suspension before packaging. Also, for stubborn yeast, a fining agent like isinglass can be added to clear the beer before packaging. Additionally, use cold-conditioning to encourage yeast flocculation prior to bottling.

Mash Problems

I stuck my lauter/sparge.

Causes: Possibly the most annoying problem in all-grain brewing is the stuck sparge, where the grain and malt seizes up and prevents the delicious wort from being lautered out. Even with a proper false bottom or manifold, stuck sparge can occur and is caused by a couple of factors. The most common contribution to a stuck sparge is high-protein adjuncts like oatmeal, flaked barley, and flaked rye, which can become quite sticky when used in large percentages. In addition, a finely ground malt that does not leave barley hulls intact can further exacerbate the problem, as the hulls provide a natural filter when rinsing and clarifying wort from the mash.

Prevention: Several mash techniques can help unstick a mash on brew day and prevent one from happening in future brew sessions. When using high protein adjunct, buy yourself some insurance with the addition of rice hulls, which help to break up any gummy messes, allowing for runoff. However, make sure not to add more than 10 percent by weight of grist to avoid off-flavors. Also, you may want to utilize a few mash steps such as a protein rest to help reduce larger proteins into smaller ones. If the problem still persists, consider using a courser grind. While you may lose a few extract efficiency points, at least you won't have a stuck sparge and the extract difference can be make up by adding more malt. Lastly, if these steps do not alleviate your difficulties, consider using the brew-in-a-bag system. While your wort may be a bit cloudier, at least you'll get a good runoff and may even see an efficiency boost.

After collecting the wort, my extract efficiency was very low.

Causes: On the homebrewing scale, extract efficiencies between 70 and 75 percent are normal, with some brewers achieving well above 80 percent. If your extract efficiency is lower than these ranges, especially below 60 percent when a lauter/sparge technique is used, this may be a sign of a fundamental mash/sparge problem, of which there are several causes. A mash pH outside the optimal range of 5.1 to 5.5 (measured at mash temperature) can cause reduced conversion efficiency, resulting in less extraction and often poor taste. A poor lauter can also contribute to low extraction, as a fast runoff or channeling with the grain bed may leave a great deal of sugars behind. Lastly, a very course grind can limit starch exposure to active enzymes, reducing extract efficiency.

Prevention: After dough-in, check the acidity of the mash to ensure it is within the recommended pH range. If not, use brewing mineral additions to adjust the mash pH accordingly. Also, after the mash duration has elapsed, use an iodine test to determine if saccrification is complete. If the mash remains unconverted, consider using a longer mash rest or adding high enzymatic malts, like six-row, to achieve full conversion. Also, when using a traditional mash/lauter system, use a slower runoff to avoid channeling, allowing a greater amount of sugar to be rinsed from the mash. Additionally, use a mash-out temperature rest in the lauter process, as this will lower the viscosity of the wort and make for a higher extract while rinsing. Lastly, for future mashes, using a finer grind may help boost efficiency, although within reason; you don't want to trade efficiency for a stuck sparge.

Finding the Culprit

Finding the source of contamination can often be tricky. In some cases, contamination is completely random, an unfortunate case of bad luck where a hardy airborne contaminant lands in your cooled wort or beer and overpowers your yeast. However, more often than not, the source of contamination is a piece of unclean brewing equipment that touched and inoculated your beer. In this case, it's time to find this piece and eradicate the contaminant to avoid this in future batches.

Examine your equipment and look for any stuck-on soil that may have harbored contamination. Closely examine plastic equipment in particular for cracks or general signs of wear and tear, as small scratches can protect contamination from cleaning agents. Additionally, double check any equipment that has nooks and crannies, such as the spigot on a bottling bucket. In many cases, equipment with scratches or stubborn soil may be worth replacing when a thorough cleansing can't be guaranteed.

If neither a scratch nor soil is the culprit, then consider trying alterative cleaning and sanitizing agents. The contamination you are experiencing could be quite hardy and resistant to the active ingredients in your current agents. Also, double check any expiration dates on your agents, as old agents are less effective than fresh ones.

Saving a Contaminated Batch

Once contamination is detected, the first thing is to do is give it a taste and assess how bad the damage is. In particular, try to determine what kind of contamination it is, whether bacteria or wild yeast, based on the off-flavor character. If the character is pleasant, then consider going forward with the beer as-is. While the batch of beer will not turn out as intended, at the very least you'll a nice funky/sour beer to enjoy.

More likely than not, the contamination character will not be desirable. If it's subtle off-flavor, you may be able to cover it up. Slight off-flavors in general can be covered up by a strong flavor addition, such as dry hops, fruit, and spices. While this is not an ideal situation, these defects will likely be masked, at least enough to create an enjoyable beer to drink and improve upon in the future.

Another possibility is to try blending the contaminated batch with another beer. When the contamination character is somewhat pleasant, blending with another homebrewed batch can provide additional character and balance, potentially creating an all-around interesting, yet pleasantly funky creation.

The last and final option is to simply dump the batch. As horrible as this might feel, sometimes you can't rectify the severe and ill-tasting funk. In this case, it's best to cut your losses and move onto greener, beer-friendly pastures.

The Least You to Know

- Common homebrewing problems can be due to a range of factors, from yeast and fermentation to wort composition.
- Once a problem is identified, there may be a way to fix it or prevent it from occurring in future batches.
- Contamination is never wanted, but there are several ways to find the source and possibly fix the batch.

Becoming a Brewmaster

With the basics under your belt, you're ready to move on to advanced brewing. This part puts you on the pathway to becoming a brewmaster, detailing the science behind the mash and lauter process and the practical techniques used in all-grain brewing. You'll also be introduced to many of the advanced fermentation topics, notably lager and high-gravity fermentation, in order to build your expertise and help you become a grade-A yeast wrangler.

Making a Mash

After a number of extract batches, many brewers take the leap into all-grain brewing. Some start small with a mini mash, while others take a big dive into all-grain. To help you jump into the wonderful world of brewing with malt, this chapter covers the basics of mash chemistry and the key variables that surround it. We'll also take a look at common mash strategies utilized by the homebrewer when performing a mash.

Going All-Grain

The time has come. Extract was great, but you're ready for something more. For many brewers, this comes in the form of all-grain brewing, where the fermentable sugars in wort are created from raw malted grains. Put it another way, all-grain brewing is the last puzzle piece of the brewing process; when you use all malted grain, you can finally say your beer is fully made from scratch.

In This Chapter

- The basics of the mash and all-grain brewing
- Managing important mash variables, like temperature and pH
- Common mash rests and mashing strategies

An Overview of All-Grain Brewing

Until now, we've primarily discussed using malt extract as the fermentable sugar in the brewing process. In all-grain brewing, you no longer use preconverted malt extract and instead convert the starches in base malt into fermentable sugar. Because of this, all-grain brewing requires a bit more knowledge and equipment, but it is no more difficult than extract brewing.

The all-grain brewing process can be viewed as an addendum to your hard-won experience in extract brewing, essentially adding two additional steps to the brewing process: mashing and lautering. To make a mash, the brewer adds crushed malt to hot water, and by adjusting its temperature, can control the enzymatic processes that convert malt starch into sugar. Lautering is the second part, composed of three often optional steps. The first step of lautering is the mash-out, where the mash is raised in temperature to stop mash enzymatic activity. The second step is recirculation, the process of draining wort from the mash by creating a natural filter bed from the hulls in the mash to produce clean, clear wort. And the final lautering step is the sparge, where the remaining wort sugar left behind in the mash is collected through rinsing with hot water.

Other than these steps, it's the same brewing process as extract brewing. However, making a well-performing mash and lauter requires a bit of focus and attention to detail. As with any advanced brewing technique, there is more room to express creativity and quality, as well as an equally large opportunity to mess things up.

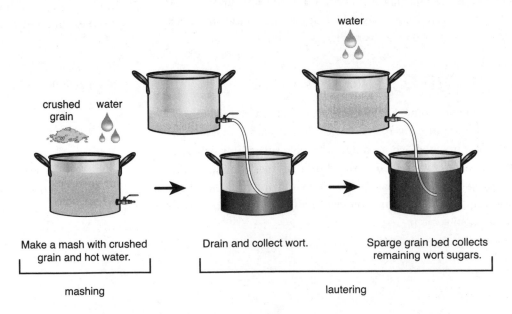

All-grain brewing adds two additional parts to the brewing process: mashing and lautering.

Starting Small with a Mini Mash

In addition to all-grain brewing, there is an intermediary technique that uses both malt extract and malted grains called a mini mash. In the mini mash, or partial mash, a small mash is made to accompany an extract-focused batch. A mini mash typically consists of 2 to 3 pounds of malted grains that are placed in a medium-sized grain bag and steeped much like a specialty malt steep; however, in addition to extracting color and flavor, you are also converting the malted grain starches into sugar. After the mini mash is complete, the rest of the fermentables, which are made up of malt extracts, are added to the brew kettle.

Why use both extract malts and a mash? Several reasons. Mini mashing is a great technique for the new brewer looking to pursue mashing, but at a small scale with little investment. It's also useful for the extract brewer looking to add a characterful malt that must be mashed, like the darkly kilned base malt varieties of Vienna and aromatic malts. Also, mini mashing is very useful for the all-grain brewer who has a small mash tun, which limits the production all-grain versions of big beers that require a great deal of malted grain to mash. In this case, malt extract can make up the difference, essentially performing an amped up version of the mini mash. If you're interested in moving to all-grain brewing, but currently brewing with extract, give mini mashing a try! To do so, check out the all-grain brewing instruction as detailed in Chapter 19.

The Science Behind the Mash

To the casual observer, the mash looks like a thick mixture of crushed malt within hot water. However, a mash isn't merely a large batch of runny grains, but rather the platform for biochemical reactions. At the heart of these brewing-related reactions are enzymes, the source of the conversion from complex malt starches and proteins into simpler forms, like maltose, dextrin, and amino acids.

What Are Enzymes?

Enzymes are formally defined as macromolecular biological catalysts. Biological macromolecules, while sounding complex, are simply very large molecules of biological origin, examples of which are commonly listed on nutritional tables, like proteins, carbohydrates, sugars, and fats (lipids). Catalysts, on the other hand, are chemicals that increase the rate of reaction by reducing the energy needed. As a result, reactions with catalysts occur very fast, millions of times faster than without catalysts. In terms of the mash, this means the brewer is able to convert complex macromolecules such as starch and protein into simpler forms in a matter of minutes rather than years, and that's a good thing, since I usually need a beer sooner than later.

The source of enzymes in the mash is the malted barley itself. As you recall from Chapter 3, during the malting process, the barley kernals produce enzymes to convert starch from the endosperm into sugar. However, before doing so, the enzymatic process is arrested through kilning, preserving the enzymes in the aleurone layer. As a result, the malting process generates a number of enzymes that serve differing functions in the mash.

By now, you've seen in several chapters that the purpose of the mash is to convert complex starches into sugars through a process called saccrification, and while this is the primary function of the mash, enzymes play another important role by converting complex proteins into more simple forms. As such, the enzymatic activity in the mash is separated into two categories by their function. When enzymes break down starches into more simple forms, the process is referred to as *diastatic*. When enzymes break down proteins into more simple forms, the process is referred to as *proteolytic*.

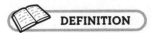

DEFINITION

Diastatic enzymes break down complex starches into sugars.

Proteolytic enzymes break down complex proteins into more simple forms, such as amino acids.

Like most chemical reactions, neither diastatic nor proteolytic enzymatic reactions will occur if the surrounding conditions aren't right. To activate enzymes in the mash, the brewer must adjust two key parameters, the mash temperature and mash pH. If the temperature or pH ranges are off, the enzymes will perform poorly, and when pushed far enough, will degrade or deactivate. As complicated as that sounds, it isn't, as the active ranges for both mash temperature and mash pH are quite large and easy to hit with a bit of measurement and adjustment.

Saccrification and Diastatic Enzymes

To understand diastatic enzymes, you must first understand a bit about starch and saccrification. Starch is a polysaccharide made up of bonded glucose molecules and comes in two forms, a linear form called amylose and a branched form called amylopectin. To speak more plainly, instead of thinking about molecules, imagine starch as a linked chain where the individual chained links are the bonded glucose molecules. In this analogy, amylose would be represented as one long linked chain, and amylopectin would be a multichained structure with single linear chains randomly linked together forming a sort of tree branch.

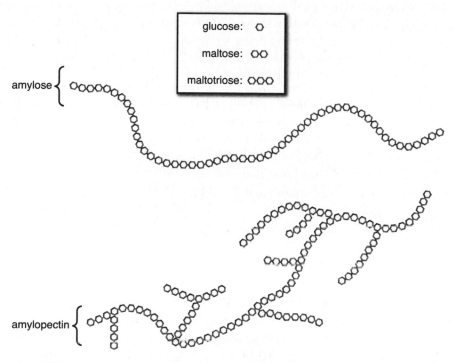

Two different forms of starch, amylose (top) and amylopectin (bottom), are broken up into more basic forms, glucose, maltose, and maltotriose.

Starch is very complex and cannot be easily metabolized by brewer's yeast, but the yeast can consume the starch in links and small chain pieces. In this analogy, the yeast can consume three forms of the starch molecule: *glucose*, represented as a single chain link; maltose, represented as a double-chained link; and, for lager yeast only, maltotriose, represented as three chained links. More complicated chain-linked pieces are unfermentable dextrins, which are too complicated for brewer's yeast to consume.

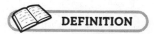 **DEFINITION**

> **Glucose** is a simple carbohydrate and a ubiquitous energy source in all of biology. In brewing, glucose is also referred to as dextrose, the basis of corn sugar.

Turning starch into its more fermentable pieces requires the process of saccrification. However, before saccrification can take place, starch must first go through gelatinization, the process of breaking down intermolecular bonds by the application of water and heat. When starch is added to water, it starts out as a starch granule. In cold water alone, starch is insoluble; however, the application of heat helps open the granule up, allowing water to creep in and expand the granule to 30 times its original size. As a result, the expanded starch granule exposes amylopectin and leaches amylose into the surrounding water.

With the starch links exposed, saccrification can occur, at the core of which are the diastatic enzymes. While malt contains several diastatic enzymes, all having some degree of function within the mash, saccrification primarily relies on two workhorses, alpha amylase and beta amylase. Continuing the chain analogy, alpha and beta amylase can be thought as chain-link cutters, working to break up the complex linkages of starch into smaller, more fermentable parts.

Beta amylase is the true workhorse of saccrification, the primary diastatic enzyme responsible for the creation of maltose in wort. However, beta amylase can't just cut anywhere within the starch molecules, but instead can only snip at its ends, more like a pruner than a chain-link cutter. While active, beta amylase is able to break the second linkage of two glucose molecules at the free end of a starch molecule and as a result, releases a single maltose molecule. After its release, the starch chain has a new free end, from which the same beta amylase enzyme can cut free another maltose molecule, essentially working its way up the starch chain until it is deactivated or denatured.

This pruning approach to saccrification works well for amylose, as beta amylase is easily able to dice up a single continuous chain of glucose molecules by working at both of its free ends to produce maltose. However, when working on amylopectin, beta amylase has a more difficult situation, since the weblike structure of this starch limits the ability of beta amylase to break it down. This is an even bigger problem when you consider that amylopectin can form nearly 80 percent of the starch content in the mash.

Not to worry though, as beta amylase's partner in crime is the mighty alpha amylase. Unlike beta amylase, alpha amylase is more like a battle axe than a pruner, able to break a starch chain anywhere instead of only at its ends. More importantly, alpha amylase breaks the linkages of the branching sites in amylopectin, and as a consequence, converts one amylopectin chain into several chains of amylose, which the beta amylase is free to prune.

Protein Conversion and Proteolytic Enzymes

Proteolytic enzymes break down large insoluble proteins from malt in much the same fashion as diastatic enzymes cleave complex starches. However, unlike starches, which need to be converted into sugars for fermentation, large insoluble proteins do not necessarily need to be broken down. Even still, in large enough quantities, these insoluble proteins can wreak havoc in the wort and mash, primarily by forming a protein haze in the final beer and causing difficultly when lautering wort, known as a stuck sparge or stuck mash. To prevent this, the brewer can utilize two proteolytic enzymes to break down protein masses, protease and peptidase.

Using the previous chain link analogy, protease and peptidase work similarity to alpha and beta amylase in saccrification. Protease is comparable in the cutting action of alpha amylase, breaking large insoluble proteins into smaller ones called peptides, essentially a short chain of amino acids. The protease action alone is responsible for producing more soluble proteins in wort, resulting in protein haze reduction as well as decreased viscosity of the mash. The extra peptides can be worked on by peptidase with a comparable action to beta amylase, nibbling at the free ends of peptides to produce amino acids. Peptidase action in wort delivers extra *amino acids* into wort, which brewers call free amino nitrogen or FAN for short, a vital nitrogen-based yeast nutrient critical in fermentation.

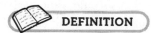 **DEFINITION**

> **Amino acids** are the building blocks of proteins and essentially for life, including humans and the ever-important brewer's yeast.

Mash Variables

The alpha and beta amylase and protease and peptidase form a one-two combo punch in saccrification and proteolytic activity in the mash. However, enzymatic activity doesn't happen for free, but rather requires dialed-in mash variables like time, temperature, and pH to achieve optimal results.

Temperature and Mash Rests

Temperature and mash durations have the largest impact on modifying enzymatic processes. Not only are these variables necessary for achieving processes like saccrification, they also determine the degree to which enzymatic conversions occur. The brewer uses mash temperature steps for specific durations known as *mash rests* to ensure sufficient enzymatic activity and to tailor enzymatic reactions.

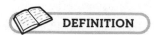 **DEFINITION**

> **Mash rests** are mash steps at a particular temperature and duration to achieve a specific enzymatic process, such as saccrification.

While this section lists the multitude of mash steps used by brewers, most do not apply to standard beer styles. In particular, most brewers utilize a single saccrification rest for the mash and that's it. However, more advanced all-grain recipes or specific mash considerations, one or more of these listed mash rests may be recommended depending on the style and recipe. For more information on how to integrate these mash steps into your all-grain brewing process, see the Constructing a Mash section at the end of this chapter.

Dough-in rest: The dough-in rest is not a fundamental mash rest, but rather a term used by brewers to state the temperature at which the crushed malt grist and mash water are mixed together to form the mash. Dough-in can happen at almost any temperature, and typically occurs between 150°F and 160°F for single infusion mashing. Dough-in above 170°F is not advised as you risk deactivation of enzymes and unconverted starch in the mash. Some brewers employ a dough-in rest between 95°F and 113°F for 20 minutes, which has been shown to help distribute enzymes throughout the mash and improve yield by a few gravity points. At the homebrewing level, the low temperature dough-in rest is not frequently used and mostly unnecessary, but worth mentioning as a potential tool to aid homebrewers who are experiencing low mash efficiencies.

Acid rest: Before brewing water chemistry was well understood, brewers would often perform a low-temperature acid rest to push the mash into its preferred pH range prior to any enzymatic rests. By holding the mash between 86°F and 126°F just after dough-in, phytase enzymes in the mash become active and break down organic phosphates in the mash, creating a weak acid in return, and resulting in a lower mash pH. The trouble with the acid rest is that it takes several hours to successfully perform and is largely unnecessary for the modern brewer, since brewing mineral adjustments achieve the same pH correction without the hours-long wait. Replace any acid rest called for in a recipe with a time-efficient pH adjustment as detailed in Chapter 6.

Beta-glucanase rest: Beta-glucans are nonstarch polysaccharides that do not seem to serve any purpose in the brewing process except to gum up the mash. Luckily, the malt enzyme beta-glucanase can help break up these beta-glucans to produce a less sticky mash for the lautering process. To achieve this, brewers employ a short 20-minute beta-glucanase rest at 95°F to 113°F to reduce mashes with a high degree of beta-glucans. Fortunately, modern malts using a high degree modification do not require a beta-glucanase rest. However, recipes that call for undermodified malts or a substantial amount (greater than 20 percent) of unmalted adjuncts, like flaked oats and flaked barley, may benefit from a short beta-glucanase rest to "de-gum" the mash and improve lauterability.

Protein rest: Today, modern malts are made with a high degree of modification. As a result, proteolytic activity and protein reduction by the brewer are mostly not needed and are instead assumed by the maltster, allowing the brewer to purely focus on saccrification in the mash. However, under certain conditions, like when using undermodified malts or large portions of unmalted adjuncts, proteolytic steps are quite useful. They can improve clarity and head retention while also decreasing the viscosity of the wort, improving lautering and preventing stuck mashes. Thus, on occasion, brewers will engage in a proteolytic process known as a protein rest to improve the mash and/or wort through protein reduction.

Proteolytic activity of both protease and peptidase occur over a wide range of temperatures in the mash, from 113°F to 152°F, overlapping with other enzymatic processes like beta-glucanase and saccrification. Despite this wide range, most brewers utilize a protein rest between 113°F and 131°F for 15 to 30 minutes. Brewers using undermodified malts may favor the upper part of the range, around 131°F, simply to achieve a shorter rise to saccrification. However, brewers using a great deal of unmalted adjuncts may want to employ the lower end of the range, around 113°F, and employ a simultaneous beta-glucanase and protein rest, both of which can significantly reduce the wort viscosity to improve the lautering process.

BREWING TIP

Avoid a long protein rest! Pushing a protein rest beyond 30 minutes is not often advised, as prolonged proteolytic activity can produce a significant reduction of wort proteins resulting in low body and poor head retention.

Saccrification rest: The main event of the mash is saccrification, the conversion of starch to sugar, which is produced through diastatic activity between alpha and beta amylase and achieved by the brewer through a saccrification rest. Like other mash rests, diastatic activity occurs over a wide range of temperatures from 140°F to 167°F; however, unlike these rests, the brewer is highly selective about the temperature used to achieve saccrification. Not only is mash temperature important in producing starch to sugar conversion, but also in changing wort fermentability, the degree to which body and attenuation are tailored. As a result, mashing-produced wort is highly customizable and sensitive to mash temperature, with the change of one or two degrees making a considerable difference in fermentability.

At the heart of fermentability in wort is the relative activity between alpha and beta amylase in the mash. Alpha amylase is a fairly robust enzyme, working quite happily between 140°F and 158°F; however, its cousin, beta amylase is more sensitive to mash temperature, and is primarily active at lower saccrification temperatures between 140°F and 150°F. At the lower end of its range, beta amylase is quite happy, actively chomping away at amylose, producing a great deal of highly fermentable maltose molecules along the way. However, once pushed beyond 150°F, beta amylase deactivates fairly quickly, reducing its population by over 75 percent in as little as 30 minutes. Since it is responsible for the majority of saccrification, once beta amylase kicks out, it leaves behind unfermentable long-chained dextrin in the wort. Thus, beta amylase that slowly deactivates will be able to convert the majority of dextrin into maltose while beta amylase that quickly deactivates will leave a great deal of dextrin behind. As a result, changing the saccrification temperature affects the relative activity of beta amylase in the mash, and consequently the degree of fermentability and dextrin concentration in wort.

From this behavior, the brewer can take away some very practical information when selecting a mash temperature to produce wort. Low mash rests between 140°F and 149°F favor beta amylase activity, producing wort with higher fermentability and lower dextrin content, and thus wort with relatively lower body and capable of a greater degree of attenuation. Conversely, high mash rests between 150°F and 158°F are favorable to alpha amylase activity and less favorable to beta amylase activity, producing wort with lower fermentability and higher dextrin content, and thus wort with relatively greater body and capable of a lesser degree of attenuation. With this in mind, most beer styles require an average amount of fermentability and a medium body. For this reason, brewers use the "sweet spot" for saccrification rest, utilizing mash rests between 150°F and 154°F, which result in the "middle-of-the-road" wort character with medium body and average fermentability.

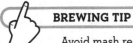

BREWING TIP

Avoid mash rest below 140°F. Although beta amylase is still active between 130°F and 140°F, gelatinization of starch kernels does not occur below 140°F, and they are inaccessible to the active amylase enzymes, inhibiting the saccrification process.

In addition to saccrification temperatures, the brewer must also rest the mash for a given duration to allow for full saccrification. Although the majority of the starch conversion occurs within the first 30 minutes of the mash, greater fermentability can be achieved by extending the mash rest beyond 30 minutes. Thus, typical mash rests last 60 minutes to achieve a reasonably complete saccrification. Mash rests beyond 60 minutes are also common among lower temperature mash rests. Since a low-temperature mash rest is seeking a highly fermentable wort, extending the mash rest to 90 minutes gives sufficient time for beta amylase to covert starch and dextrin to maltose.

Mash pH

While mash rests have a great impact on the type and level of enzymatic activity in the mash, no activity is possible without first achieving an adequate mash pH. Although enzymatic processes have a wide range of pH where sufficient activity occurs, the harmonious range where all enzymatic processes occur at a strong level of performance is fairly narrow. Also, the motivation is high for dialing in mash pH, not only to avoid a poor performing mash but also to create a balanced beer character. The goal of the brewer is to predict and adjust mash chemistry to hit the mash pH "sweet spot" in achieving optimal enzymatic processes and highly flavorful beer.

First things first, what is the optimal mash pH? The "sweet spot" for mash pH is often quoted as 5.2, but where does this number come from? The mash "sweet spot" is derived from the overlapping active pH ranges of the diastatic enzymes alpha and beta amylase. Alpha amylase is enzymatically active over a pH of 4.5 to 5.5 (measured at mash temperature) whereas beta amylase is enzymatically active over a pH of 5.2 to 5.8 (measured at mash temperature). Being within one these ranges will produce some diastatic response in the mash; however, to achieve the one-two combo punch of alpha and beta amylase requires using a pH that overlaps both their active ranges. Based on this, the optimal range for mash pH is between 5.1 and 5.5 (measured at mash temperature) or 5.4 and 5.8 (measured at room temperature). Additionally, proteolytic enzymes have a broad active pH range, working well between 5.0 to 5.5 (measured at mash temperature). Thus, the recommended mash pH range of 5.1 to 5.5 for saccrification also produces well-performing proteolytic activity, and therefore an all-encompassing pH range for a high-performing mash.

With the preferred mash pH range indentified, the role of the all-grain brewer is to confirm and adjust mash condition to achieve this range. While there are several variables, like grind quality and mash thickness that contribute to mash pH, you can easily understand the behavior of mash pH through the balance between malt acidity and residual alkalinity. As you can recall from Chapter 3, malt is a result of kilning and other specialty malt processing such as stewing and roasting after the malting. As such, these malts will go through additional reactions including Maillard reactions, which cause the malt to darken in color and also become more acidic. Thus, base malts, especially the lightly kilned varieties, have significantly less acidity than darker, more kilned base malts and specialty malts. The acidity contributions of malt must be managed and often counteracted to maintain the desired mash pH range of around 5.2.

The counterpoint to malt acidity is alkalinity, the ability for mash water to neutralize malt acids. As you recall from Chapter 6, the key brewing metric for alkalinity is residual alkalinity, a comparative measurement of alkalinity based on a reference mash system using brewing water made entirely from distilled water. Based on this system, residual alkalinity can be either positive or negative depending on whether your mash has more or less alkalinity than the distilled mash system. Thus, brewing water with positive residual alkalinity results in a reference mash with a greater quantity of remaining carbonates and higher pH, whereas brewing water with negative residual alkalinity results in a reference mash with a lesser quantity of remaining carbonates and a lower pH.

Now, what does this mean for the mash pH? Good question! Combining both factors together, the goal of the all-grain brewer is to tailor (and often predict) mash water chemistry with an adequate level of residual alkalinity to facilitate or counteract the acidity of the mash as determined by the range of malt acidity. Putting it more plainly, a mash comprised of lightly kilned malts requires mash water with negative residual alkalinity since the grist has a small component acidity without much power to counteract substantial brewing water carbonates. If the same lightly kilned grist were to use a mash water with a positive residual alkalinity, its respective mash acidity would not be able to counter the brewing water carbonates, forcing the mash pH to rise, likely outside the recommended pH ranges, and producing a poor performing mash.

Conversely, a mash comprised of darkly kilned malts requires a mash water with positive residual alkalinity, since the grist has a large component acidity that must be countered by brewing water carbonates. If the same darkly-color grist were to use a mash water with a negative alkalinity, its strong mash acidity would drive down the mash pH, potentially outside the recommended ranges, also producing a poor-performing mash.

This leads to a final question: how do you estimate and adjust the mash water chemistry to best suit the mash and achieve the recommend pH range? This is a good question that doesn't have a simple answer. Predicting mash pH based on grist, mash color, and source water chemistry is quite the complicated business on which entire books have been written. For detailed theory and step-by-step calculations for predicting mash pH based on the most recent research, I recommend the book *Water: A Comprehensive Guide for Brewers* by John Palmer and Colin Kaminski. This text should provide a strong foundation in water modification, mash pH prediction, and the calculations that go along with it.

Taking this for what it's worth, the primary value of mash pH prediction is to facilitate a starting point, essentially a good guess, before making a mash. However, even with a well-treated theory, ultimately, the only way to dial-in, adjust, and confirm your mash pH is through its measurement via a pH meter. Based on the initial guess, further adjustments are made through brewing minerals and acids, the water modification tools as discussed in Chapters 6 and 19.

In addition to pH modification, it's important to remember that the mash serves two purposes: pH adjustment and flavor enhancement. When formulating pH adjustments, it's also worth considering any flavor contribution from sulfates and chlorides in the mash. To do both may require a bit of extra work, especially when trying to achieve a specific sulfate-to-chloride ratio. In many cases, it can be difficult to achieve both the recommended mash pH and water mineral profile based on the chemistry of your source water. To achieve both, you have two options. The first option is to simply add flavor mineral additions to the boil rather than the mash. The second option is to start from a clean slate using reverse-osmosis (RO) or distilled water base. Personally, I prefer the second option as my water in Austin is great for mash color down to around 8 SRM. Below this, it's easier for me to adjust RO water and build up a suitable water profile with both the recommended mash pH and my desired water flavor enhancements.

 BREWING TIP

Don't overdo it! You can easily overthink water modification and worry too much about concepts like residual alkalinity, malt acidity, etc. Unless your source water is completely rubbish, you likely won't require much (if any) adjustments to make a well-performing mash. The key variable behind mash water chemistry is not alkalinity or hardness, but mash pH, and if you're within the recommended ranges, you are good to go.

Mash Thickness

While mash temperature and pH have the largest impact on the mash processes, *mash thickness*, the ratio of mash water to malt grist ratio, has additional effects on mash performance. Mash thickness is often quoted as a decimal number in the units of quarts per pound, meaning quarts of mash water for every pound of dry grist. Using mash thickness is often the starting point in building a mash, determining how much mash water is necessary for a particular recipe's grain bill. For example, let's say your recipe calls for a total of 12 pounds of grain and you typically use a mash thickness of 1.5 quarts/pound. Using this mash thickness ratio, you'll need 18 quarts or 4.5 gallons of brewing water to make your mash.

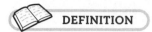 **DEFINITION**

> **Mash thickness** is the ratio of water and ground malt used in the mash. It has a small degree of impact on mash performance.

Selecting the mash thickness for your all-grain brewing depends on several brewing parameters, chiefly your desired wort fermentability and mash system capacity. Mash thicknesses of 1 quart/pound and below are considered very thick, while thicknesses of 2 quarts/pound and above are seen as a very thin. Thick mashes greatly benefit from its oatmeal-like density, as the thin part of the mash is dense with enzymes, resulting in faster saccrification and more effective protcolytic activity. Also, thick mashes are more robust in buffering against changes in pH and temperature, resulting in better protected mash enzymes, specifically the sensitive beta amylase.

The drawback to thick mashes is lower fermentability. Due to the high density, the wort sugars are concentrated, and this high gravity inhibits amylase activity, resulting in a less fermentable wort. As you might expect, thin mashes, with their souplike appearance, have the opposite effects of thick mashes. Although slower to saccrification and more susceptible to changes in temperature and pH due to lower buffering, thin mashes produce a more fermentable wort, since lower gravity wort is less of an inhibitor to enzymatic activity.

Based on the pros and cons of both thick and thin mashes, most brewers utilize an intermediate mash thickness, ranging between 1.25 and 1.75 quarts/pound, which is seen as the "sweet spot," balancing high-density enzymatic buffering and a speedy conversion, while producing a wort of typical fermentability. Starting out, I would recommend a mash thickness of 1.5 quarts/pound and play around with mash thickness once pH, water chemistry, and temperature are dialed in. Also, it's important to remember that while the mash thickness has a minor effect on the mash, the total amount of brewing water calculated from mash thickness is a critical variable in the mashing process, as it helps derive the amount of any brewing water modifiers in predicting your mash pH.

While most brewers utilize an intermediate mash thickness, at times a thick or thin mash may be desirable for other nonenzymatic reasons. Mash systems are often limited by their holding capacity, especially when brewing high-gravity beers like imperial stouts and barleywines. By selecting a thicker mash, the brewer can fit more grains per quart of water, achieving a higher gravity wort in the process. Any low fermentability difficulties can be counteracted by adding a simple sugar addition, like corn or cane sugar, to the boil to make up for any unproduced by the thick mash.

On the other hand, very thin mashes are often utilized by homebrewers to speed up the brew day. A very thin mash process will often include all of the sparge water within the all-grain brewing process, a technique known as no-sparge brewing. Using this technique speeds up the brew day by eliminating any sparge process. Also, homebrewers report good fermentability using the no-sparge technique, and any mouthfeel deficiencies can be easily counteracted using dextrin malt, maltodextrin powder, or a protein-rich adjunct to improve body and mouthfeel.

Constructing the Mash

With the basics of mash science and its variables behind us, it's time to implement this knowledge through practical mashing techniques. When making a mash, there are a range of methods from the basic yet effective single infusion to the ever involved triple decoction, each unique in tailoring fermentability and yielding characterful malt expression in the final beer. This section covers the commonly used profiles and process for constructing the mash.

Single-Infusion Mash

The simplest mash profile is the single-infusion mash, where a single mash temperature is used to achieve the entire saccrification. To do so, the brewer heats mash water, adds crushed malt, and lets the mash rest at a single temperature until saccrification is complete. While this may seem too simple and easy, single infusion mashing is commonly utilized by both homebrewers and commercial brewers alike due to its very effective saccrification and applicability to most beer styles.

Since the single-infusion mash utilizes one rest temperature, it's critical that you choose a mash temperature to achieve the desired balance between fermentability and dextrin-based body. For beer recipes requiring a great deal of attenuation and/or low mouthfeel, a low temperature rest between 140°F and 150°F favors beta amylase activity, resulting in wort with higher fermentable and lower body. On the other hand, for a beer recipe requiring a heavier body or less fermentability, a high temperature rest between 155°F and 158°F will favor alpha amylase activity, resulting in wort with less fermentability and more body. Most beer styles require fermentability and body somewhere in the middle of these opposing mash rests. Thus, for the brewer looking to achieve a medium body and typical fermentability, a mash temperature between 150°F to 154°F is frequently used.

Making a single-infusion mash is as simple as heating mash water, adding crushed malt, and stirring. However, the critical step in the single-infusion process is heating the mash water to hotter than the infusion temperature, which is known as the *strike temperature.* The purpose for heating strike water hotter than the infusion rest temperature is to account for heat losses when the malts are added, with the goal to achieve an equilibrium temperature between the malts and the strike water temperature.

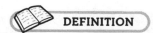 **DEFINITION**

Strike temperature is the temperature of the mash water prior to adding crushed malt. Typically, the strike temperature is approximately 10°F higher than the mash rest temperature to account for heat losses.

The difference between the strike temperature and infusion rest temperature depends on a number of variables, chiefly the temperature of your malt and mash tun before strike water is added. If your mash tun is the same temperature of your strike water, then you'll only need to compensate for the grain temperature, which is generally 7°F to 12°F at the homebrew scale.

 BREWING TIP

Keep ice cubes nearby in case your infusion is too hot. A half a dozen ice cubes in a hot mash can cool it down a few degrees with stirring. This will make sure you don't deactivate your enzymes and will correct to your target mash temperature.

Single-Infusion Mash Procedure

1. Crush malt and heat mash water to strike temperature roughly 10°F above the desired saccrification temperature. The necessary temperature differential may be more or less depending on your mash system.

2. Dough-in, stir, and correct for any temperature differences.

3. While maintaining a constant temperature, let the mash rest for 60 minutes to allow for complete saccrification.

4. Once complete, move on to the lauter process as necessary.

Step Mash

The next level up from single infusion is the step mash, also known as step-infusion mash, where multiple mash temperature rests are used to achieve saccrification and other enzymatic process, like protein reduction through a protein rest. Although modern malts feature a high degree of modification and largely do not require the step mash technique, brewers utilizing undermodified malts or large portions of unmalted adjuncts can greatly benefit from tiered mash rests.

The central strategy of the step mash is to progressively increase the mash temperature, starting from the lowest planned mash rest and rising to highest mash rest. The reason for this temperature profile is enzyme protection. By starting out at a low temperature, you protect sensitive enzymes like beta amylase from denaturing before it can be later utilized. That way, all enzymatic processes can occur, producing a well-performing step mash.

While step mash temperature strategy holds for most all-grain systems, implementing each temperature rise is dependent on your mash equipment. Based on frequently employed mash systems at the homebrewing scale, there are two main approaches to achieve each temperature rise depending on your mash tun design. Homebrewers employing cooler tuns for mash and lautering can utilize hot water infusions at around 190°F to 200°F in temperature to increase the mash temperature between each step. While calculations can be helpful in estimating the total amount of hot water is necessary, I find it easier and more reliable to heat roughly a gallon of water to 200°F, and then stir in 1 quart of hot water at a time, and checking the mash temperature after each addition until the next rest temperature is achieved. While these hot water infusions are a bit tricky to nail down and require a bit of trial and error to sufficiently dial-in, many homebrewers report great results with practice. Also, keep in mind that each successive hot water infusion decreases mash thickness, so if this is important in your brewing process, consider doughing-in at a greater mash thickness to account for successive mash dilutions and to maintain an adequate range of mash thickness over the course of the mash.

Other the other hand, kettle tuns are much easier for temperature adjustment, since the application of heat through an electric or gas burner generates the temperature rise for each step. Under the application of heat, all the brewer needs to do is stir the mash to avoid scorching and monitor the mash temperature. Once the temperature step is achieved, all that's necessary is to allow the mash to rest, maintain its temperature, and prepare for any additional steps. Optionally, kettle tuns can employ the hot water infusion process as detailed for cooler tuns, but I find the increased accuracy and overall less work of the burner-applied temperature rise to be an easier process. Also, the mash is not diluted by hot water infusions, a constant mash thickness is maintained throughout the step mash, eliminating any variation concerns while performing. For more information on mash equipment check out Chapter 18.

While step mashes allow you to mix and match any number of mash temperature rests, brewers commonly utilize two step mash rest profiles: the protein rest step mash and the alpha/beta saccrification step mash. Starting out, the protein rest step mash is designed to maximize the proteolytic benefits of the protein rest. Implementation of this step mash can be thought of as simply adding a short protein rest to your typical single-infusion mash schedule.

Protein Rest Step Mash Procedure

1. Crush malt and heat mash water to strike temperature, roughly 10°F above the desired protein rest temperature. The necessary temperature differential may be more or less depending on your mash system.

2. Dough-in, stir, and correct for any temperature differences.

3. While maintaining a constant temperature, let the mash rest for 20 minutes to allow for sufficient proteolytic activity.

4. Once complete, increase mash temperature to desired saccrification temperature. While heating, stir thoroughly and avoid scorching.

5. Once temperature is adjusted, let the mash rest for 60 minutes.

6. After saccrification is complete, move on to the lauter process as necessary.

While similar in procedure, the alpha/beta saccrification step mash is a bit more subtle in motivation. Instead of performing a single infusion where the activity between alpha and beta amylase is averaged based on the rest temperature used, the brewer can utilize separate mash rests to optimize each of their performances within the mash. Essentially, the alpha/beta saccrification step mash can be thought as splitting your single infusion into two separate saccrification steps, a low-temperature mash rest to favor beta amylase and a high-temperature mash rest to favor alpha amylase. Using this procedure, brewers report improved mash performance, including wort with more fermentability and improved mash efficiency. To implement in your brewing, use the simple alpha beta saccrification step mash procedure detailed as follows.

Alpha/Beta Saccrification Step Mash Procedure

1. Crush malt and heat mash water to strike temperature of 155°F to 159°F (roughly 10°F above the desired beta amylase rest temperature of 145°F–149°F). The necessary temperature differential may be more or less depending on your mash system.

2. Dough-in, stir, and correct for any temperature differences.

3. While maintaining a constant temperature, let the mash rest for 30 minutes to allow for beta amylase activity.

4. Once complete, increase mash temperature to alpha amylase rest temperature of 158°F. While heating, stir thoroughly and avoid scorching.

5. Once temperature is adjusted, let the mash rest for 30 minutes.

6. After saccrification is complete, move on to the lauter process as necessary.

Decoction Mash

To best describe decoction mashing first requires a bit of explanation and then some historical context. Decoction mashing can be thought as a form a step mashing. However, instead of increasing each temperature step via hot water infusion or burner heating, the temperature rise is accomplished by removing some of the thick part of the mash (essentially hydrated crushed malt), boiling it, and adding it back to the main mash until the desired rest temperature is achieved. The pulling of the thick mash from the main mash is defined as a decoction, and the type of decoction mashing you employ is determined by how many decoctions you pull. For example, pulling one decoction is called a single decoction, and is employed either to achieve saccrification or mash-out. Likewise, double and triple decoctions are performed when multiple temperature rests are required. Other than heating via thick mash, a decoction mash follows the general procedure outlined in the step mash section.

Now, some historical context. Decoction mashing is a historical form of mashing used in the German tradition of brewing. Before highly modified brewing malts were available, the previously detailed methods of mashing delivered poor extract and efficiency. Boiling thick mash and systemically reintroducing it to the main mash resulted in great extract while also producing beer with rich colors and flavors. Today, high modification of malt and a wide range of specialty malts eliminate the need to boil mash, and thus decoction mashing is rarely used in commercial brewing. However, as brewing enthusiasts, homebrewers keep this tradition alive by recreating traditional German brewing practices.

 BREWING MYTH

Myth: A triple decoction is maltier than single decoction.

While decoction mashing is known for its enhanced malt character, the number of decoctions is not indicative of maltiness, but rather the boil duration of each decoction. Thus, a short-boiled triple decoction will have the same malt enhancement as a long-boiled single decoction.

Cereal Mash

As you recall, before malt can be accessed by enzymes in the mash, its starches must be gelatinized. Luckily for modern brewers using highly modified barley and wheat malts, gelatinization occurs quickly within the saccrification temperature range, and thus separate steps are not required. However, for unmalted adjuncts like corn and rice, gelatinization occurs at a higher temperature beyond optimal saccrification range. Also, the gelatinization of raw cereal grains can take quite a long time, and is not practical at the typical timescales of a modern mash. To achieve an accessible and complete gelatinization of cereal grains within a short period of time, the brewer can make a secondary mash prior to the main mash for these purposes, and its process is the cereal mash.

While simply boiling cereal grains would achieve full gelatinization, most brewers employ a cute trick to make the process easier. By including a small portion on malted barley in the cereal mash and holding a short alpha amylase rest, its enzymatic activity will break up some of the starch into sugars prior to boiling. Thus, when a boil is achieved and full gelatinization occurs, the cereal mash doesn't seize up like overboiled oatmeal at breakfast and instead remains liquid, allowing for an easier integration with the main mash.

Lastly, if the cereal grain you seek is available in a flaked form (as most are), you do not have to perform a cereal mash since flaked adjuncts are pregelatinized and therefore can be added straight into the main mash. Furthermore, I would recommend seeking fresh, high-quality flaked adjuncts simply to avoid performing a cereal mash and adding an extra hour or so to the brew day. However, for the brewer looking to increase their brewing skills or incorporate locally sourced unmalted cereal grain, the following procedure details step-by-step instructions for achieving gelatinization through a cereal mash.

Cereal Mash Procedure

1. Crush the unmalted grain. This step may be a bit difficult since unmalted grains are much harder than malted grains, so more robust crushing technology (also known as a hammer) can be used if your grain mill is not up for the task.

2. Dough-in crushed cereal grains along with 4 ounces crushed malted barley per pound of cereal grain. Keep the mash thickness thin, between 2 to 3 quarts/pound to help prevent scorching of the cereal mash while boiling.

3. Slowly increase cereal mash temperature for an alpha saccrification rest between 155°F and 158°F. Stir the mash frequently to avoid scorching.

4. Once saccrification temperature is reached, hold the cereal mash at this temperature for 15 minutes for partial saccrification.

5. Once rested, slowly increase mash temperature until a boil is achieved. As before, stir constantly to avoid scorching.

6. Once a boil is achieved, continue boiling the cereal mash for 15 minutes. Your mash is now thoroughly gelatinized.

7. After the boil is finished, add your cereal mash to the main mash. Similar to decoction mashing, the cereal mash can be treated as a heat source to achieve the saccrification rest temperature in the main mash. Alternatively, you can simply wait until the cereal mash reaches the mash saccrification temperature before adding to the main mash. Either way, make sure to take into account any temperature increase of a hot cereal mash to avoid pushing the main mash outside the recommended temperature range.

8. With the cereal grain gelatinized and integrated into the main mash, proceed as directed by the main mash procedures for full saccrification.

The Least You Need to Know

- All-grain brewing uses a mash to convert malt starches into sugar and the lauter process to separate the wort from the grain.
- Enzymes are responsible for converting starches and proteins into simpler forms in the mash.
- Temperature and pH are key to a well-performing mash and are best controlled when measured and adjusted for appropriately.
- There are several mash strategies that can be used to modify enzymatic action depending on your recipe.

CHAPTER 18

Collecting the Wort

While making a mash is often thought as the center point of the all-grain brewing process, an equally key component is the separation and collection of the wort from the mash, known as lautering. To accomplish this, the brewer uses special mash equipment to filter the wort from the mash, known as recirculation, and rinses any remaining wort from the grain bed, known as sparging. In this chapter, we'll cover the basics on separating wort from the mash through the lauter process.

Mash/Lauter Equipment

Mash/lauter equipment serves the dual purpose of holding and insulating the mash while also filtering, separating, and rinsing the wort from the mash. This section covers the primary mash/lauter equipment used in all-grain brewing at the homebrew level. There are two commonly used systems, the traditional mash/lauter setup, including the mash/lauter tun, and the basic, yet effective brew-in-a-bag (BIAB) grain bag system.

In This Chapter

- The mash and lauter equipment you need to start your first all-grain batch
- The basics of the lauter process
- How to calculate your mash efficiency

Traditional Mash/Lauter Tun

Starting out, the traditional form of mash/lauter equipment is the mash/lauter tun (MLT). At its core, the MLT serves two purposes: maintaining mash temperature and separating the wort from the main mash. In support of the mashing process, the MLT is the vessel that holds the mash and maintains its temperature. Then, in support of the lautering process, the MLT houses the lautering structure, a series of devices that facilitate the filtration and separation of the wort from a settled grain bed. To achieve these two primary mash/lauter tasks, the homebrewer can choose from a wide range of differing MLT designs and equipment based on their brewing process and preference.

As previously stated, the primary mashing function of the MLT is to adjust and maintain mash temperatures. To accomplish this task, the homebrewer can utilize one of two different types of mash equipment: the cooler tun or the kettle tun. Cooler tuns are constructed from insulated cooler technology, typically rectangular "picnic" coolers or cylindrical "beverage" coolers. While originally designed to keep things cool, their insulating properties work both ways, and they do a good job of keeping mash hot. In fact, a well-constructed cooler tun can hold a mash within 1°F to 2°F over the course of an hour. Also, cooler tuns are often considered an entry-level MLT as they can easily be constructed at home or affordably purchased preconstructed from your local homebrew shop.

While the cooler tuns are great at holding mash temperature, a heat source cannot be directly applied to the cooler tun system. In order to heat the mash, the brewer must use hot water infusions, which makes involved mashing procedures like step mashes more complicated. For this reason, the cooler tun is best for single-infusion mashing.

Cooler tuns are constructed from either a picnic or beverage cooler (shown) and typically employ a false bottom for lautering.

An alternative to the cooler tun is the kettle tun, which is a retrofitted brew kettle. Since a brew kettle is at the core of the design, you can refer to the brew kettle section in Chapter 8 when home-building or purchasing your own kettle tun. While brew kettles are not as insulated as cooler tuns, the kettle tun is designed for direct temperature adjustment using burner-applied heating. This means you can adjust the temperature of the mash without hot water infusions, making the kettle tun a great candidate for more complex mashing procedures, like step and decoction mashing.

BREWING TIP

If your MLT is prone to heat loss, wrap it in heavy sheets, foam pads, and/or sleeping bags to provide additional insulation.

Kettle tuns are made from retrofitted brew kettles. This one is small enough to adjust mash temperature on my stovetop.

The second task of the mash/lauter tun is supporting the lauter process, the separation and removal of wort from the grain. To do this, the mash/lauter tun employs a lautering structure, which accomplishes three items: assists in filtering the wort from the grain, drawing wort from the bottom of the tun, and controlling the flow of wort through an externally fitted valve.

The first two lauter structure items are accomplished through integrated tubing and filtration aids, of which there are several types. The first type is a lauter manifold, essentially a series of rigid tubing, usually made of PVC plastic or copper, with small drilled holes, which runs along the bottom of the tun and exits through an externally fitted valve. The second type is a false bottom, a metal mesh and tubing platform that creates a small region below the mash to draw wort using a dip tube (much like a keg), which exits the tun through an externally fitted valve. Last but not least is a steel-braided hose, which separates grains from wort using interwoven metal braids. Its tubular shape funnels the wort to an externally-fitted valve.

Any of these lauter structures work well in tuns; however, some work better with certain styles of tuns. False bottoms designs are typically cylindrical and thus directly benefit cylindrical cooler and kettle tuns. If constructing yourself, make sure the false bottom is well-fitted to the diameter of the tun; improper fitting can reduce lauter performance. Lauter manifolds can be applied to any mash/lauter system, but are typically utilized in rectangular cooler tuns. If constructing yourself, make sure the manifold has appropriately sized holes and has enough bottom coverage to efficiently collect wort from all bottom tun areas. Lastly, the braided hose is often considered a one-size-fits-all solution, and can be easily integrated in any cooler or kettle tun. If constructing yourself, make sure it has sufficient length to collect wort from all areas of the tun bottom. For more information on constructing an MLT at home, check out the wide array brewing resources in Appendix A.

 BREWING MYTH

Myth: The lauter structure filters the mash.

The mash and grain bed itself performs the filtration step. The lauter structure is designed to aid in the filtration process and chiefly to collect the wort from the draining mash.

The final lauter component in the mash/lauter tun design is an external valve, used to control the rate at which the wort drains during the lautering process. Starting out, the valve type can be just about anything that is able to start and stop the flow of wort. Entry-level systems use a tube clamp, which pinches the draining tubes to stop the flow, and when removed, starts the flow. This type can work well, especially for *batch sparging*, a rinsing method using hot water infusions; however, brewers often require a greater deal of flow control during the lauter process.

For this, ball valves are the next step up. They work by turning a lever, like a kitchen faucet, and allow a great range of flow from a slow trickle to a heavy stream. Ball-valve-controlled wort flow is optional for batch sparge brewers but almost essential for *continuous sparge* brewing, since this sparge method requires an equilibrium between in-flowing sparge water and out-flowing wort to continuously rinse wort sugars while draining. Also, while custom-made kettle tuns often have a welded ball valve in place, both home-built kettle and cooler tun designs can easily integrate a ball valve using a weldless kit.

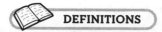 **DEFINITIONS**

Batch sparge is a rinsing technique using large volumes of hot water to dissolve and collect wort sugars from a previously drained mash.

Continuous sparge is a rinsing technique in which a continuous flow of hot water is added and maintained throughout the initial draining process to collect wort sugars.

Sparge Equipment

In addition to mash/lauter equipment, the all-grain brewer also needs an extra kit to aid in the sparge process. The primary equipment addition is an extra vessel referred to as the hot liquor tank (HLT), used to heat and deliver sparge water to the main mash. The HLT can simply be a second brew kettle, perhaps a smaller brew kettle, to hold and heat sparge water to its desired temperature. Like a brew kettle, the size of your HLT depends on your sparge process. HLTs for the continuous sparge are large, often the same size as a full-boil kettle, since a 5 gallon batch of beer may require up to 6 gallons of hot sparge water. On the other hand, a smaller HLT can work well for the batch sparge process, since batch sparge can be split up into multiple infusions.

In addition, although an unmodified brew kettle can be used as an HLT, many brewers find the addition of a ball valve makes easier work of the sparge process. If you intend to employ a gravity-fed continuous sparge, then I would recommend the addition of a ball valve to control the flow of hot water into the mash tun. A simple hose clamp will work fine, but the robustness and precision of a ball valve will make for an easier brew day. If you intend to batch sparge, no modifications to the standard brew kettle setup is required, although a ball valve can be useful when gravity feeding multiple hot water infusions.

Lastly, you may require extra sparge equipment depending on your brewing process and preferences. Although the all-grain brewing process only requires one nice and powerful burner, having more than one can make the brew day a bit easier if space and cost permits. Many brewers utilize multiple burners to heat the MLT, HLT, and brew kettle separately. Also, for the continuous sparge brewer, consider investing in a sparge arm. This is a device used to sprinkle hot water across the mash surface, ensuring a uniform distribution, avoiding disruption of the grain bed, and preventing sparge defects from occurring. Sparge arms come in many shapes and sizes. Make sure you choose one that fits the opening of your mash tun and has the necessary height adjustment mechanisms to dial-in the sprinkling action across the mash.

Brew in a Bag (BIAB)

Invented by Australian homebrewers, "brew in a bag," or BIAB for short, does away with traditional mash equipment and rethinks how the lautering process can be achieved on the homebrew scale. Instead of removing the wort from the grain, BIAB turns the tables and removes the grain from the wort using a large food-grade grain bag. At the commercial scale, the BIAB method for lautering is impractical; however, at the homebrew scale, wort/grain separation is easily achieved with two hands.

To set up BIAB, all the brewer needs to do is add a grain bag filled with crushed malts to the brew kettle.

While BIAB includes each step of the mash process, it differs in approach to the traditional lauter process. BIAB often employs a technique known as no-sparge brewing, where both the mash and sparge water volumes used in a traditional mash/lauter system are combined to form the entire mash volume. While more on no-sparge brewing is detailed in the sparge section of this chapter, there are a few procedural and equipment considerations when engaging in BIAB brewing.

The primary equipment addition for BIAB is the grain bag. For a 5-gallon batch, typical BIAB grain bags are on the scale of 30×30 inches, although the more important dimension is that it should be able to hold the entire volume of hydrated crush malt and suitably fit within your brew kettle. Also, make sure your grain bag is well made, as it needs to hold anywhere from 20 to 30 pounds of soaked malt and grain while draining. Finally, if you intend to do 5-gallon batches using the BIAB technique, a 15-gallon brew kettle is often recommended instead of the standard 8-gallon version, as the no-sparge technique includes 8+ gallons of water and malt and grain, and when combined can easily exceed 10+ gallons for standard gravity ales.

To set up for BIAB, all you need to do is fill your BIAB grain bag with crushed malt and add it to your brew kettle. Once set up, The BIAB process proceeds as any normal mash would as specified by the recipe, albeit with a very thin mash. Then, when the mash is complete, the bag is removed from the brew kettle and allowed to drip dry. In the BIAB system, the combination of the fine-mesh grain bag and suspended grain bed act as the filtration structure, producing mostly clear wort. Importantly, since the brew kettle is also effectively the mash tun, when the grain bag is removed, what's left behind is the wort, ready for the boil without any additional transferring or racking processes.

The obvious upside to BIAB is that it requires little monetary investment to start all-grain brewing; only a few dollars are needed to obtain a grain bag and that's it. Of course, if you intend to make 5-gallon batches, a new full-boil kettle will also be needed. In addition to low equipment needs, the BIAB process is significantly faster than the traditional 1- to 2-hour lauter process with full sparge. That being said, there are a few downsides, primarily, BIAB produces cloudier wort than traditional lauter, but is it typically a nonissue at the homebrew scale. Also, bigger beers (1.060+ OG) may be more difficult to structurally contain and drain using a single grain bag, although this can be remedied using reiterative mashing or double bagging. While you will ultimately be the judge on the effectiveness of BIAB in your brewing, it's definitely worth a try and a great gateway process into all-grain brewing.

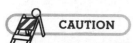 **CAUTION**

Beware of the ripped grain bag. Make sure to double check the seams of your grain bag before mashing-in. Also, don't overload your grain bag with malt. It will gain considerable weight while soaking, increasing the chance of a bag failure. Lastly, keep a spare bag on hand in case a seam becomes loose.

Separating the Wort: Lautering

After saccrification is complete, the wort is ready to be separated from the grain material in the mash. At the surface, the lautering process may seem a daunting task; however, traditional brewing techniques have illuminated a very straightforward path comprised of three steps: performing an enzyme deactivating mash-out rest, recirculating wort via grain bed filtration, and rinsing the mash through sparge. This section covers the common practices for lautering the mash, including the mash-out rest and recirculation to successfully separate and collect the sweet wort from the mash. The third part of the lautering process, sparging, is detailed in the next section, since brewers use varying methods in rinsing a mash.

Mash-Out

After all mash steps are completed but before any draining begins, many brewers complete the mashing process by arresting any further enzymatic activity through the mash-out rest. By elevating the mash temperature to between 165°F and 172°F, any remaining active enzymes are denatured, terminating enzymatic processes, and fixing the fermentability of the wort. Also, the mash-out rest is seen as the transition from mashing process to the lauter process, using the elevated mash temperature to allow for easier separation of the wort from the mash by decreasing the wort viscosity.

Most brewers use a mash-out rest at 170°F for 10 minutes to ensure full deactivation of enzymes. Pushing beyond 172°F is generally not recommended, as both temperature and pH changes in the mash encourage tannin extraction, lending an astringent, over-steeped tea off-flavor in the final beer. Also, elevated mash-out temperatures can extract remaining starch from the granules, causing starch haze. Lastly, mash-out is a great place to add any late addition specialty malts to the mash, like roasted malt and dark crystal malts, that were previously omitted from the main mash for pH reasons.

Recirculation

After mash-out, the wort is separated from the grain potion of the mash via draining. However, simply draining the wort straight into the brew kettle isn't the most effective means of lautering, as the raw wort is full of particulates, such as small bits of grain hull and coagulated protein, which are undesirable in the boil. Thus, prior to draining into the brew kettle, the wort goes through the process of recirculation (also known as the *vorlauf*), where the mash particulates are removed via filtration.

In modern times, filtration, whether for water or coffee, can be achieved through a number of technologies and techniques. Despite this, brewers rely on a traditional yet incredibly effective method for wort filtration: creating a natural filter from the bed of grain hulls in the mash. To do so requires the process of recirculation, where a small portion of the wort is drained and added back to the main mash.

 BREWING TIP

Use rice hulls before lautering to improve filtration performance, especially when sticky malt and unmalted adjuncts like wheat and oats compose a significant portion of the grain bill. Add 2 to 5 percent rice hulls by weight to the mash to achieve the desired results.

To start the recirculation, the brewer begins by opening the mash/lauter tun valve connected to the lauter structure, which is seated at the bottom of the tun. Generally, the valve isn't fully opened, but rather cracked just enough for the wort to flow. The wort is collected and drained into a large secondary container, typically a beer pitcher, large glass liquid measure, or a clear growler. You'll notice that the initial wort runoff is pretty turbid and cloudy, full of small grain particulates; however, once 1 to 2 quarts are collected, the wort should start to run clear and free from particulates. Once this occurs, the wort is ready to be collected into the brew kettle and readied for the sparging process. The turbid and particle-filled wort initially collected in the large secondary container can be added back to the main mash for filtration, taking special care to add it slowly and gently as to avoid disturbing the grain bed.

While successive recirculation will produce a visibly clearer wort, don't get caught up in trying to produce crystal clear wort. Effective recirculation will produce wort with a slight haze in appearance (think apple cider, not apple juice) and only needs to have the grain particulates removed before entering the brew kettle. Its remaining haze will be eliminated through the hot and cold break in the boil process.

Rinsing the Grain: Sparging

Once recirculation is achieved, the sparge process begins. Like many processes in brewing, there is more than one way to sparge the mash, each yielding differing benefits depending on the degree of rinse needed and your brewing preferences. This section covers the commonly used techniques: batch sparge, continuous sparge, and no-sparge processes.

Sparge Water Considerations

Before jumping into specific sparge techniques, there are some general sparge water properties to consider. All sparge techniques share the same water considerations, which greatly impact their performance. Hot water infusions are best performed when the mash reaches 168°F to 172°F to decrease wort viscosity, but should not exceed 172°F to avoid tannin extraction. While mash pH isn't as critical a concern, well-rinsed grains do start to lose their buffering capacity as wort is diluted and removed. Thus, when using sparge water with high alkalinity or over-rinsing, the mash pH can rise above 5.8 (at mash temperature), at which point it will begin to extract tannins and produce off-flavors.

Sparge-related pH is often overstated as a big concern, but in practice, as long as you are using clean brewing water without high levels of hardness or alkalinity, you are likely fine. Before going out of your way to modify sparge water, simply check your rinsed wort using a calibrated pH meter or test strips to see if your runoff is within an appropriate pH range. If you notice you are close to the edge of the range then you may require additional sparge water modification.

There are two basic methods for modifying sparge water. The easiest solution is to simply use filtered, distilled, or RO water as your sparge water. Since the sparge water chemistry isn't necessary in the rinsing process, its average pH of 7 should keep the mash within the desired range without taxing its buffering capacity.

Alternatively, the method many commercial brewers use is called acidification of sparge water, in which small doses of food-grade acid are applied to lower the sparge water pH to between 5.5 and 6.0. By doing so, when rinsing, the sparge water acidity prevents the mash for rising above its own pH value, even if the mash loses its buffering capacity. To implement this technique, many homebrewers use online calculators to estimate the necessary amount acid adjustment; however, it's best performed using small additions of acid, stirring to integrate, and confirming the pH reduction using a calibrated pH meter or test strip. In reality, this process isn't really necessary on the homebrew scale, as pH rises are easily prevented by not over-rinsing the mash. However, its basic principle may be in your interest when using your tap water as the source of sparge water. Lastly, if tap water is your sparge water source, remember to remove any associated chloramines to avoid phenolic off-flavors in your final beer.

Sparge Volume Considerations

Regardless of which sparge process you use, you need to figure out how much sparge water is needed. Because the grain portion of the mash absorbs a large portion of its original mash water, the combination of both mash and sparge water must exceed the desired pre-boil kettle volume in order to achieve it.

The first metric for estimating sparge water is the mash water absorption. As a rule of thumb, many brewers assume mash water losses around 0.125 gallons per pound of malt. For example, if your recipe uses 10 pounds of malt, you'll likely lose around 1.25 gallons (or 5 quarts) of mash water due to grain absorption. Then, based on your mash thickness, you can determine the total amount of water you'll expect to collect from the mash itself. For example, if this same recipe uses a mash thickness of 1.5 quarts/pound, from the original 15 quarts of water added to the mash, you would only expect to extract and collect about 10 quarts into the kettle due to grain absorption.

Based on mash losses, you can estimate how much sparge water is needed to achieve your desired the pre-boil volume. As discussed in Chapter 11, pre-boil volume is closely determined by your estimated evaporation rate. As most homebrewers average around 1 gallon/hour evaporate rate, this implies you'll require at least 1 gallon more in pre-boil kettle volume to achieve your desired batch size at the end of the boil. For example, a standard 5-gallon batch will often require 6 gallons in the brew kettle prior to the boil. Assuming the mash loss from the previous recipe example, since you need 6 gallons (24 quarts) in the brew kettle but expect to lose 5 quarts to the mash, this implies you'll need approximately 14 quarts (or 3.5 gallons) in sparge water to achieve this pre-boil volume.

While these calculations work well for most standard gravity beers, for beer at the extremes (low-gravity and high-gravity beers) sparge volume may require a bit more consideration. Low-gravity beers start out with a small grain bill, so a large sparge volume to make up kettle volume is not suggested since this may over-rinse the grain, producing tannin off-flavors. Instead, sparge until the rinse water has a gravity between 1.008 and 1.012, and pH rises above 5.8 (at mash temperature). If your kettle volume is less than your desired pre-boil volume, simply top of the kettle off with clean water to achieve it. Similarly, on the high-gravity side, you may require a great deal of sparge water to extract the as-calculated amount of sugars, and thus collecting a great deal of water beyond your pre-boil volume requirements. To avoid this, many brewers will assume a lower batch efficiency, leaving more sugars behind in the mash in order to achieve an appropriate pre-boil volume in the kettle.

Batch Sparge

Once these sparge water considerations are addressed, you can apply them to the many sparge techniques. The first method for sparging mash is called the batch sparge, the process of rinsing wort sugars from a previously drained mash by repetitively infusing and draining large volumes of hot water. After the initial mash recirculation, the batch sparge process begins by draining the wort from the mash and collecting it in a brew kettle. In batch sparge, the initial wort runoff is termed first *runnings*, and unsurprisingly will have the darkest color and highest gravity compared to its subsequent batch sparges.

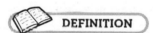 **DEFINITION**

Runnings is the brewing term for wort runoff during the recirculation, draining, and sparge processes. Since batch sparge has multiple runnings based on each sparge addition, each running is labeled according to order in occurrence (first runnings, second runnings, etc).

Once the first runnings are collected, the first batch sparge addition begins and starts the lautering process. First, batch sparge water is heated. Batch sparge water additions are best heated so that the combined temperature of the hot water infusion and the mash is near 170°F. Then, the batch water addition is added to the mash tun and stirred to integrate. While doing so, spot check the mash with a thermometer and make sure this combined batch sparge temperature is at or below 170°F to avoid tannin extraction. Once fully integrated, the now rinsed wort can be drained from the main mash. However, since the grain bed was disturbed, it will require a second recirculation in order for the wort to run clear and free from grain particulates. After a second recirculation is complete, the wort can be drained into the brew kettle, now termed the second running, combining with first running to form the pre-boil wort.

Interestingly, batch sparge can be done multiple times, with each batch sparge infusing, rinsing, and draining wort sugars in the process. If more than one batch sparge is used, then their runnings would be coined accordingly (third running, fourth running, etc.). In fact, multiple runnings may be necessary for those with small mash tuns who are unable to infuse the total sparge volume addition as estimated in one sitting. However, as discussed previously, make sure to avoid over rinsing, and keep the pH of each batch sparge running above 1.012.

Continuous or Fly Sparge

The second method for sparging mash is called the continuous sparge, or fly sparge, a process of constantly infusing hot water into the mash while draining (hence the name continuous). Unlike batch sparge, where there are multiple runnings, continuous sparge engages in one long rinsing process, which in itself forms one large running. The continuous sparge begins by running the hot wort into the brew kettle after recirculation. Once the wort level drops to approximately 1 inch above the grain bed, the brewer slowly adds hot sparge water to the mash. Here, an equilibrium between the entering sparge water and exiting wort is desired, with the goal of maintaining the this 1 inch of wort buffer above the grain bed. Starting out, it's good to keep the runoff slow by barely opening the externally-fitted valve, partly because it makes it easier to achieve these equilibrium conditions and partly because brewers report better wort extraction using a slower sparge rate.

In addition to flow condition, how the sparge water is added to the mash during the continuous sparge is key to the success of this method. Sparge water must be added slowly, ensuring that the sparge water additions are not dumped such that it disturbs the grain bed. Homebrewers doing continuous sparge by hand can use a glass liquid measure and carefully distribute water through a colander, so that the small holes generate a light sprinkling action. Alternatively, brewers can utilize a sparge arm, which generates the sprinkling action, so you can focus on other things in the brew day. Also, the continuous sparge water only needs to be heated to 170°F, as its constant addition to the mash will maintain this temperature.

As an inch of wort is maintained throughout the process, the sparge water additions continue until the pre-boil volume is collected or until the runnings drop below a specific gravity of 1.012. To judge the latter, a refractometer can make easy work, essentially spot checking the runoff to ensure it is above 1.012. For standard and high-gravity ales, it is unlikely to reach 1.012 before reaching your pre-boil volume; however, is likely in smaller mashes for low-gravity beers. In this case, I recommend keeping a close eye on the runnings to avoid over-rinsing. Also, if your runoff gravity is prematurely low, this may be a sign that the grain bed is not set properly or has formed too many large channels. If this is the case, stop the sparge process, stir the mash to break up the grain bed, recalculate to clear the wort, and start anew.

No-Sparge

The last sparge technique is no-sparge, the process of lautering and draining the mash without any rinsing steps. This may sound a bit odd; however, homebrewers report several advantages in doing so. Chiefly, no-sparge brewing quickens the brew day by eliminating the sparge steps, which typically add 1 to 2 hours to the brew day. Also, brewers report increased wort quality including a softer, richer malt character and a deeper color in the final beer. For these reasons, the no-sparge technique may be worth considering, at least on occasion, in your brewing process.

No-sparge brewing is easy to do, but requires a few considerations to yield a well-performing process. Since the mash runnings are the sole contribution of fermentables, the brewer can use one of two no-sparge techniques to produce the kettle wort volume. The first no-sparge strategy is to simply combine the traditional mash and sparge water additions into one large main mash containing the full volume of water used in the entire brewing process. As a result, this creates a very thin mash thickness, usually about 4 quarts/pound.

A thin mash thickness may make traditional all-grain brewers cringe due to possible mash defects including low body and poor efficiency. However, most full-volume no-sparge brewers report little to no negative effects using thin mashes, and argue that body and efficiency are more a function of temperature, pH, and malt crush quality than mash thickness. Lastly, when using a full-volume no-sparge mash, the mash vessel must be significantly larger than usual. For BIAB which frequently uses this no-sparge technique, a large 15-gallon brew kettle is needed. Likewise, for the traditional mash/lauter system, you'll need a large mash tun capable of holding at least 12 gallons or more of mash.

The second no-sparge strategy is simply making a mash using traditional methods along with standard mash thicknesses and skipping the sparge process. Since the mash is not rinsed, you leave a considerable amount of wort sugars behind and end with a significantly lower efficiency. In order to make up for these losses, you'll have to add extra malt when designing your recipe to achieve your expected original gravity. Brewers report adding about 33 percent more malt than typically needed when performing the traditional mash/lauter brewing method. Also, you may consider using a thinner mash, around 2 quarts/pound, to yield a bit more sugar in the runoff.

After the mash, the no-sparge process follows the basic mash-out and recirculation techniques. A mash-out is recommended since it will reduce wort viscosity and help drain as much wort sugar as possible. After mash-out, simply *vorlauf* and drain the mash as normal when using a mash/lauter tun or grain bag removal via BIAB techniques. Then top off the wort with the clean water to make up the volume as needed for your boil process. For the second no-sparge strategy, this can be as much as 4 to 5 gallons when producing a full-volume boil.

Be aware that your efficiency estimates for your first few no-sparge batches will likely be off, but after some trial and error, you should be able to make more accurate estimates. Lastly, while no-sparge brewing doesn't have to be the primary technique in your brewing process, give it a try for your next English bitter or mild and see if it produces a richer, more colorful beer. At the very least, it will make for a quicker brew day.

Brewing Efficiency

Once the mash and lauter are complete, the brewer will often confirm how much sugar was converted and collected through the measurement and calculation of all-grain brewing efficiency. Not only is efficiency a useful metric in determining your mash and lauter performance, but also a key brewing parameter for scaling all-grain recipes to fit your brewing process.

Calculating Efficiency

As mentioned in the Chapter 3, base malt and specialty malt have maximum yields. For example, two-row malt typically contributes a maximum yield of 37 ppg, meaning if all of the starches were converted to sugar and extracted from the mash, 37 ppg would be its maximum gravity contribution to the wort. In practice, both homebrewers and commercial brewers find it difficult and unnecessary to extract absolutely all of the starches and sugars from malt, and usually end up with an extraction that is close to, but not at, the maximum yield. The difference between the actual extraction and the maximum yield is called *brewing efficiency*.

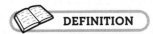 **DEFINITION**

Brewing efficiency is the percentage of total extract generated from your all-grain process based on the maximum possible yield the malt can produce. Typically, homebrewing efficiencies range from 65 to 80 percent.

Some brewers would argue that there isn't one type of all-grain brewing efficiency but rather several, measuring the effectiveness of the mash, lauter/sparge, boil, and post-boil transfer. Although they are technically correct, starting out, it is simple and effective to measure efficiency by looking at how much sugar was converted, extracted, lautered, sparged, and condensed from the start of the mash, throughout lauter/sparge process, to the end of the boil. This measure of efficiency is sort of a "junk drawer" metric, as it doesn't tell you what parts of the your all-grain brewing process are at a high or low efficiency; however, it is a useful metric for tracking consistency from batch to batch and is important for scaling all-grain recipes to fit your brewing system.

To calculate brewing efficiency based on the maximum gravity points of a grain bill and your post-boil gravity, you first need to calculate the maximum amount of gravity points possible from a grain bill by multiplying the weight of a malt by its maximum yield in units of ppg. For example, let's say you're brewing a 6-gallon all-grain batch of German pilsner with a grain bill composed of 10 pounds of Pilsner malt. Assuming its maximum yield is 37 ppg, 10 pounds of malt would contribute a maximum of 370 gravity points of potential sugar. If multiple malts are used, then this calculation would be performed for each malt and the resulting calculations would be added for a total maximum gravity. Interestingly, dividing the total maximum gravity points by its intended batch size in volume yields the maximum possible original gravity after post-boil. Revisiting the previous example, dividing 370 gravity points by 6 gallons yields 61.5 gravity points, or 1.0615 specific gravity.

The second step in the brewing efficiency calculation is measuring your post-boil wort gravity using either a hydrometer or refractometer. If no other fermentables are added to the wort, then this post-boil gravity would also be your original gravity. Once measured, you'll also have to measure how much wort volume is present in the brew kettle. Then with both measurements taken, you can calculate the total amount of gravity extracted from the original grain bill by multiplying your measured post-boil gravity by the kettle volume. Continuing the previous example, after when you mashed, lautered, sparged, and boiled, let's say you measure a post-boil original gravity of 1.047 or 47 gravity points. Confirming the post-boil kettle volume as 6 gallons, the total extract is calculated as 47×6 = 282 gravity points. Not bad.

Now, the last part, completing the efficiency calculation! Taking the previous two calculations, the brewing efficiency is calculated simply by dividing the as-measured total extract by the maximum extract possible from the grain bill. To finish the example, the measured gravity is 282 points and the maximum possible is 370 gravity points. In dividing these, you find 282 ÷ 370 = 0.762, or about 76.2 percent brewing efficiency. As expected, the maximum level of extract was not quite achieved, but 76 percent is quite good. You can modify this example to produce a brewing efficiency calculation any all-grain recipe.

Typical Brewing Efficiency

At the homebrew scale, the absolute number behind efficiency is generally not critical, but rather it's consistency from batch to batch. My all-grain brewing process routinely produces efficiencies near 85 percent, which on its own is not bad, but more importantly it is so consistent that I don't bother to check pre-boil gravities anymore. That being said, typical efficiency at the homebrew scale ranges from 65 to 80 percent, and anywhere in that range is considered good. Efficiency ranging in the 80 to 90 percent range is impressive but also requires diligent pH gravity analysis to avoid over-extraction. Likewise, efficiencies below 65 percent are acceptable and common in no-sparge brewing. However, if your efficiency is significantly below 60 percent and you've completed a full sparge, this may be a sign of a mash or sparge-related problem, like incomplete conversion or grain bed channeling.

Grind Quality

The one mash variable not yet discussed that significantly contributes to brewing efficiency is malt grind quality, or the degree of coarseness in the ground malt prior to mashing. Interestingly, grind quality is brewer-tailored variable for brewing efficiency, with finer crushes yielding a higher efficiency than coarser grinds. The efficiency boost behind fine grinds is due to the further release of starch granules. Since more starch is exposed, more is gelatinized, allowing greater access to diastatic enzymes in saccrification and resulting in greater efficiency. However, like all good things, there is always a drawback, and in this case it is lautering impairment. While a very fine crush improves efficiency, it also shreds the malt hulls, which are key to the recirculation process. Since the hulls are responsible for forming the natural filter, a very fine crush can lead to a poor performing lauter, or worse, a stuck mash.

Brewers looking for an efficiency boost via a fine crush can consider the following options. Rice hulls, essentially the protective covering for the rice cereal grains, are great when lautering problems occur due to a fine crush or sticky unmalted grains like flaked oatmeal. To use, add between 2 and 5 percent by weight before lautering to improve wort flow and filtration without adding color or flavor to the mash. Alternatively, high-precision roller mills are known to produce a high grind quality, in many cases crushing the malt endosperm without considerable damage to the barley hull. In either case, make sure to use sufficient lautering controls when using fine crushes in your brewing.

The Least You Need to Know

- Traditional all-grain brewing requires equipment like the mash/lauter tun and hot liquor tank, but new brewers can get started without the equipment investment by using large grain bags and the brew-in-a-bag method.

- Lautering is the process of draining and filtering the wort from the mash and is comprised of three core steps: mash-out, recirculation, and sparge.

- Sparging is often optional but frequently utilized process to rinse remaining wort sugars from the mash using hot water.

- Mash efficiency is the percentage of the malt starch converted into fermentable sugars. It is a good baseline for mash performance and recipe adjustment.

Brewing Your First All-Grain Beer

Now that you know the basics of all-grain brewing, it's time to put your knowledge into practice with your first all-grain brewing. This chapter will guide you through the all-grain brewing, from dough-in to sparge and everything in between.

Before You Begin

This chapter is organized as a supplement to the extract brewing instructions. Thus, for a quick guide to fermentation, chilling, and/or packaging, check out Chapter 2. Also, this chapter assumes that your first batch is a 5-gallon batch. For the small-batch brewer wanting a scaled down approach, cutting everything by a constant proportion is a good place to start, although some small adjustments may be necessary depending on the recipe.

At this point, if you are not sure what recipe to start with, consider purchasing a prebuilt recipe kit from your local homebrew shop. These usually contain a recipe with all the necessary ingredients, so you don't have you worry about formulating one from scratch. Also, stick with something simple and straightforward, like an American-style ale.

In This Chapter

- Prebrewing checklists for all-grain brewing
- Step-by-step guides to the mash and lauter process
- How to fight a stuck sparge and other all-grain brewing tips

If you want to start out using a recipe and buy the ingredients separately, check out the all-grain recipes in Chapter 22. Again, I recommend starting out with entry-level recipes and highly recommend the following:

The Nazz, a session-style American IPA recipe, designed and brewed by Chip Walton and Drew Beechum, intended as a sessionable clone of the famous Pliny the Elder Double IPA by Vinnie Cilurzo of Russian River Brewing Company.

Boat Bitter, an English-style bitter recipe, designed and brewed by Michael Dawson, producing a great session ale with low ABV, yet full of English character.

Steamin' Wife Lager, a California common recipe designed and brewed by Don Osborn, featuring Northern Brewer hops and the wonderful Wyeast 2112 California Lager yeast strain.

All-Grain Brewing Prep

Before the all-grain brewing begins, there are a few extra things to organize and check in addition to the standard brewing checklists. It's best to do this at least a day in advance, in case any last-minute brewing items are needed. For new and advanced homebrewers alike, it is useful to look through the following brewing checklists in prevention of any brewing disasters. Remember, a planned and organized brewing is a peaceful and fun brewing.

Brewing Supplies Checklist

Note to the brewer: if any ingredients are missing or unavailable, and there is not enough time to pick them up, check out the ingredients substitution list at idiotsguides.com/homebrewing to make the closest possible match in your beer recipe.

Additional All-Grain Ingredients

- ❑ Malt: base malt, specialty malts, and malt extract for mini-mash brewers
- ❑ Water: clean source water, RO water, brewing modifiers (mineral, salts, acids), sparge water
- ❑ Other ingredients: wort clarifiers, foam control, yeast nutrients, etc. depending on the recipe goals.

Additional All-Grain Supplies

- ❑ Mash/boil equipment: mash/lauter equipment (mash tun, hot liquor tank, grain bag), full boil kettle, mash paddle, two or more containers for recirculation
- ❑ Measurement tools: hydrometer with thief and test tube, refractometer for pre-boil gravity readings, digital thermometer, calibrated pH meter or test strips, paper and pen for brewing log.
- ❑ Chilling supplies: ice, wort chiller, etc.

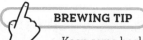

BREWING TIP

Keep some back up six-row malt on hand. Old malt or a mash mistake can result in deactivated enzymes and incomplete mash. A pound or two of six-row malt with its high enzymatic properties can help jump-start a mash and save your brewing.

Other Pre-Brewing Considerations

Make sure your malt is crushed prior to dough-in. If you do not have a grain mill, your local homebrew shop will likely do it for you for a small fee. Also, when possible, freshly mill your malt as close to the brewing as possible. As you recall, the outer hull of the malt protects the starches and sugars from the air, preventing staling. Premilled grain can work well when it's protected from air; however, milling it on the brewing will allow for the freshest malt to enter the mash and avoid any off-flavor flavors or enzyme reduction due to prolonged air exposure.

If you have a malt pantry, consider bagging but not grinding the malt for your recipe the night before. This eliminates some of the stress on the brewing day, such as measuring out the malt weights. Also, this gives you a heads up in case you are missing a malt ingredient for your recipe, giving you plenty of time to obtain it from your local homebrew shop.

If you are planning considerable water adjustments, you may want to do some predictive mash pH calculations based on your brewing water and grain bill so that you only need to measure pH in confirmation rather than successive measurements in readjustment. Brewing software and/or online applications are the easiest way to do bulk water chemistry calculations. Many are free, quite accurate, and reliable. Of them, I recommend John Palmer's Brewing Water Spreadsheet, which is free on his website at howtobrew.com. For more information on water modification using brewing minerals, see Chapter 6.

If this is your first time making an all-grain brew and your brewing water is good to taste, it's best to dial-in the rest of the all-grain brewing process rather than fiddling with water. If your tap water has high alkalinity or is very high in other mineral concentrations, consider using a filtered, spring, or RO water source and build a simple mineral profile such as adding 1 teaspoon of either calcium chloride or calcium sulfate to your mash.

Also, make sure to pick up any source water that isn't tap water as required by the recipe and your brewing process. I typically require at least 5-gallons of RO water for most of my recipes, and this is something I pick up the day before my brewing.

Lastly, if you are using a pH meter, you'll likely need to calibrate it prior to using it in the mash. Most electronic meters are calibrated using known pH solutions; however, this step is best done closer to dough-in rather than the night before, as pH meters are known for losing their calibration quickly. Likewise, if you have a digital thermometer, it's best to check its calibration before using. A good quality digital thermometer doesn't lose calibration very easily, but if it appears off, use the manufacturer's recommendations for recalibration. For more information on pH measurement devices, check out Chapter 10.

Let's Mash

With the brewing preparations in order, it's time for the main event: your first mash! Building a mash is as simple as heating water, adding crushed malt, stirring, checking its temperature, and letting it rest. This covers the mashing process, pointing out the key steps and common missteps along the way. For the most part, the brewer's role is setting up the mash and then sitting back and having a homebrew while the enzymes do their work.

Step 1: Heat Mash Water

The first step in constructing a mash is heating the mash water to strike temperature. Here, strike water is heated beyond the initial mash rest temperature by 7°F to 12°F to account for heat losses when the crushed malt is added to the mash/lauter tun. The degree to which strike water is heated above the initial infusion temperature largely depends on your brewing conditions. Starting out, it's best to underestimate the strike temperature. It's easier to heat the mash up than cool it down. Also, underestimation doesn't endanger the temperature-sensitive beta amylase, but significant overestimation can cause degradation or even deactivation. Lastly, once the strike water is heated, it's now ready for transfer. This is typically only necessary for a cooler tun system, as kettle tuns are designed to heat strike water without the need of a hot liquor tank.

In my kettle tun, I've heated 2.5 gallons of mash water to 160°F, ready for dough-in.

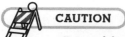

CAUTION

Be careful when transferring hot water! Although the water is not at boiling temperatures, you can still give yourself a nasty burn. Use pot holders and keep your arms covered to avoid burns and a bad start to the brewing.

Strike Water Procedure

1. Calculate the amount of mash water needed based on your preferred mash thickness For example, if your recipe called for 10 pounds of malt, using a common mash thickness of 1.5 quarts/pound, the amount of mash water required is 15 quarts or 3.75 gallons.

2. In a brew kettle, heat mash water to strike temperature, roughly 7°F to 12°F above the desired initial mash rest temperature.

3. If you are using a cooler tun, you'll have to transfer the strike water into the cooler tun. Before doing so, consider preheating the cooler tun with hot water. If you are using a kettle tun, no further action is required.

Step 2: Dough-In

When the strike water is heated and transferred, the mash is ready for dough-in, the process of adding crushed malt and any water modifiers to the mash water. Add any water adjustments, like brewing mineral additions, acids, etc., before adding the malt. The exception is chalk, which is best added to the mash for solubility reasons.

Once the mash water is suitability modified, it's time to add the crushed malt. While it's perfectly fine to dump the entire grist into the mash/lauter tun, many brewers prefer stirring in a few pounds at a time to inhibit the formation of *dough balls*. When stirring, it's advised to turn off any burner heat to avoid scorching. Also, I find it best to stir from the bottom up to provide a more even temperature distribution, as soaked malt tends to sink to the bottom. Lastly, once the malt is fully integrated, make sure there are no dough balls. If any are detected, simply slide it to the edge of the mash tun, smash with your big spoon or mash paddle, and stir its dry content into the mash.

DEFINITION

Dough balls are dry pockets of crushed grain in the mash, much like the small balls of flour in pancake batter. However, mash dough balls are not small and can often reach the size of softballs when the dough-in is done too rapidly.

Dough-In Procedure

1. Crush malt to your desired grind coarseness.

2. Add any water modifiers to mash water and stir to dissolve.

3. Dough-in, stirring in the malt in small doses to avoid dough balls.

4. Once the malt is completely added, give a few more stirs to fully integrate and double-check for dough balls.

With the mash added, I'm ready for saccrification rest.

Step 3: Measure the Mash Temperature and pH

Once dough-in is complete, it's time to check the mash temperature and pH. Begin by checking the mash temperature. If it's only off by a degree, you are better off leaving it alone, since this difference is not likely to change much in the final beer. However, if the temperature difference is greater than 1°F, you can adjust the mash temperature using several methods.

To heat things up, cooler tun brewers can add small, 1-quart hot water infusions (190°F–200°F) until the desired mash temperature is reached. Kettle tun brewers can simply use burner power to increase mash temperate, making sure to use constant stirring to avoid scorching. To cool things down, rapid stirring can help reduce small differences, although large temperature differences are best reduced via ice cube additions, making sure to thoroughly stir and spot check before adding more ice to avoid excessive cooling.

Measuring and Adjusting Mash Temperature Procedure

1. Insert a thermometer into thoroughly mixed mash and check the mash temperature to see if it's in range. Check several mash positions, as the initial dough-in can still be variable.

2. If the mash is on the cold side, increase mash temperature to desired initial rest temperature through hot water infusion or burner power, making sure to stir well while doing so.

4. If on the hot side, stir aggressively to release heat or add a few ice cubes to lower mash temperature.

5. Recheck the temperature and continue adjustment until desired temperature is reached.

Once temperature is measured and adjusted, it's now time to measure mash pH. For many homebrewers, this is an optional step; however, at some time in your homebrewer career, it's worth confirming your mash pH for quality purposes. To measure pH, spoon out a small sample of mash and rapidly cool to room temperature. If you have a pH meter with ATC, this is not necessary. Once cooled, measure the mash pH. More likely than not, the mash pH will be between 5.4 and 5.8 at room temperature, and if so, you are good to go for optimal enzymatic processes. However, if you are off, consider adjusting the main mash with some brewing mineral additions. Add roughly a ¼ teaspoon at a time, using calcium sulfate or calcium chloride to decrease pH or sodium bicarbonate or chalk to increase pH. Once adjusted, repeat the measurement to confirm.

Measuring and Adjusting Mash pH Procedure

1. With a thoroughly mixed mash, remove a small wort sample and rapidly cool to room temperature. If you have an ATC pH meter, you can skip chilling step and instead measure at mash temperatures.

2. Using a test strip or calibrated pH meter probe, measure pH following the manufacturer's recommended procedure.

3. If the pH is between 5.4 and 5.8 at room temperature or 5.1 and 5.5 at mash temperature, you are good to go for all mash enzymatic processes. However, if you are outside this range, the mash may require a bit of adjustment.

4. If mash pH is low, add ¼ teaspoon sodium bicarbonate or chalk to help to neutralize acids and bring the pH up to the recommended range.

5. If mash pH is high, add ¼ teaspoon calcium chloride or calcium sulfate to help lower the pH a few points. More significant pH lowering can be achieved with a lactic or phosphoric acid addition, but remember this is strong stuff and only adjust with a milliliter per addition before checking.

6. Once readjusted, mix well and remeasure to confirm proper adjustment.

Step 4: Mash Rest

Once measured and adjusted, the mash can finally be left alone and allowed to rest for the recipe-specified duration. How long you rest your mash is determined by your mash profile. Most homebrewers starting out with all-grain brewing use a single-infusion rest, in which the mash rests at a single saccrification temperature (148°F–158°F) for 60 to 90 minutes. For more information and instruction on mash profiles like single infusion, see Chapter 17.

While the mash is resting, there are a number of things the brewer can do to improve the mash and all-grain brewing. While it's perfectly fine to let the mash rest untouched for its recommended duration, consider stirring the mash every 15 minutes or so to help eliminate temperature gradients and distribute enzymes throughout the mash. Also, when stirring, it's worth checking the mash temperature. If a temperature drop greater than 2°F is observed, this may require adjustment midrest using the preceding temperature adjustment techniques. Lastly, make sure to prepare and heat any brewing water needed for future mash/lauter processes. This includes steps like mash-out and sparge, which may require 3 to 6 gallons of hot water in total.

Step 5: Check for Conversion

When the mash rests are complete, it's just about time for the lauter/sparge process to begin. However, before doing so, many new brewers like to check that saccrification was successful using two methods in verification. A quick, first-pass check is a simple visual inspection. Either by looking at the top part of the mash or by drawing off a sample of wort, note the transparency of the wort. If it looks clear, this is indicative of sugars, since the once insoluble starches are now soluble sugar and dextrin, and as a result the once cloudy mash is now clear wort in appearance. However, if the wort looks very milky, this may be a sign of incomplete saccrification, since insoluble starches remains in the mash water, creating the opaque appearance.

If the visual inspection is inconclusive, you can apply a more direct measurement of conversion through an iodine test. Here, a small sample of the wort (approximately 15 milliliters) is drawn from the mash and a drop of iodine is added. If the iodine droplet remains brown in color, this implies sugar and dextrin are present and that saccrification was complete. However, if the iodine turns purple, blue, or black, this is a sign of starches present, implying an incomplete saccrification.

If incomplete conversion is suspected from either of these tests, the brewer has two options to complete saccrification. The first option is to mash for a longer time, 20 to 30 minutes before retesting the wort. Alternatively, you can jump-start enzyme activity by adding a couple of pounds of six-row malt or enzyme concentrate to the mash and rest for another 30 to 45 minutes.

Let's Lauter

After the mash is complete, it's time to drain the wort. This requires three steps: setting a grain bed for filtration, draining the wort, and sparging the grains, the sum of which is the called the lauter process.

Step 1: Mash-Out Rest

To start the lauter process, many brewers perform a mash-out rest. As discussed in Chapter 18, the mash-out helps decrease wort viscosity as well as fixing fermentability by enzyme deactivation. To do this, the brewer must increase the mash temperature to between 168°F and 172°F and rest for 10 minutes. For the cooler tun brewer, using a small hot water infusion is the best pathway to achieve this temperature increase. For the kettle tun brewer, increasing the mash via a burner is best, making sure to stir constantly to avoid scorching. In either case, check the mash temperature frequently to avoid overshooting 172°F, past which can lead to starch-haze and tanninlike off-flavors in the final beer.

Step 2: Recirculation

Most lauter processes call for a recirculation step, where the wort is filtered through the bed of grain hulls in the mash, allowing for clear wort to enter the brew kettle during the draining and/or sparge process. Remember that the wort clarity doesn't need to be crystal clear before running into the brew kettle, it just needs to be free from large grain particulates. A slight haze is still considered to be an effective recirculation.

After mash out, I've drained a portion of the mash into this 2-quart growler.
I can tell from the clarity one recirculation is all that's needed.

Recirculation Procedure

1. Once mash is complete, perform a mash-out rest by increasing the mash temperature to 170°F and resting for 10 minutes.

2. Position a clean, 1- to 2-quart container below the valve on the mash/lauter tun, and open the valve just enough to start the wort with a slow flow.

3. Continue collecting wort until your container is full.

4. If the wort remains cloudy by the end of the first collection, swap with a new container and gently pour the first container back into the mash without disturbing the grain bed.

5. Continue this process until the wort begins to run clear.

Step 3: Sparge

Once recirculation is complete, it's time for the sparge, or rinsing the grain. As detailed in Chapter 18, there are several sparge techniques, each using different strategies to rinse wort sugar from the mash. While each method differs, all sparge techniques share the same basic water and volume considerations. When sparging, make sure to keep mash temperature at or below 170°F and mash pH at or below 5.8 (at mash temperature) to avoid tannin extraction. Also, avoid sparging below a gravity of 1.008 to 1.012, as this is considered over-rinsing and strongly indicative of pH rise above 5.8. Additionally, while sparge volumes can be estimated using mash parameters, as a quick rule of thumb, you'll need to heat approximately 1 to 1.5 times your mash water addition to yield the necessary pre-boil kettle volume (6–7.5 gallons) for 5-gallon batches.

Batch Sparge Procedure

1. Once the recirculation sets the grain bed, continue to leave the valve open at its current position and allow the wort from the mash tun to drain completely into the brew kettle.

2. Once the first runnings are drained, add a large volume of hot water to the mash and stir to integrate.

3. Check mash temperature, make sure it's at or below 170°F, and correct as necessary.

4. After stirring, perform a second recirculation to set the grain bed, and once clear, drain the second runnings into the brew kettle.

5. Repeat the batch sparge process until the pre-boil volume is collected or until batch sparge gravity is below 1.012.

Continuous Sparge Procedure

1. Once the recirculation sets the grain bed, drain the wort from mash until an inch of wort remains above the grain bed.

2. Then, using a liquid glass measure and colander or a sparge arm, slowly trickle water over the grain bed, maintaining the 1 inch wort buffer.

3. Continue the continuous sparge until the pre-boil volume is collected or until the sparge gravity is below 1.012.

No-Sparge Procedure

1. If you are using a traditional mash/lauter tun, perform a single recirculation, and once the grain bed is set, completely drain the wort from the mash tun into the brew kettle.

2. If you are using a BIAB system, simply pull the bag from the brew kettle and allow it to drip drain.

3. (Optional BIAB step) Some brewers will speed up the process by squeezing the grain bag. If you do this, wear thermal protective gloves to avoid burns and avoid aggressive wringing, which can promote tannin extraction.

The Dreaded Stuck Sparge

If the wort runoff appears very slow or nonexistent while there is still plenty of wort in the mash tun, then you likely have a stuck sparge. Even among the best brewers, this happens from time to time, and when it does, it's never a good feeling. No worries, with a few simple steps, you can get back to your brewing, and with luck, avoid further mash-related drama. For the reasons behind and preventative measures against stuck sparging, see Chapter 16.

How to Fight Stuck Sparge

1. Close the lauter valve to separate the draining hose from the lautering structure.

2. With a big spoon or mash paddle, stir the mash, breaking up the previously set grain bed.

3. When possible, check the lautering structure to make sure it's still correctly assembled and functioning properly.

4. (Optional) Add rice hulls to mash tun at 2 to 5 percent by weight to improve lautering and grain bed formation.

5. Once stirred, begin a new recirculation to set a new grain bed and continue as normal.

6. (Optional) If the mash is on the thick side, add a small hot water infusion to bring the mash back up to 170°F. This will help loosen it up and improve runoff.

Other All-Grain Brewing Considerations

After the mash and lauter processes are complete, the remainder of brewing closely follows the brewing process already covered in Chapter 2 and Part 4 of this book. For further instruction, check out these respective chapters. However, there are a few items that are unique to the all-grain brewing process, which are covered here.

Pre-Boil Gravity and Volumes

After collecting the wort, you are ready for the boil, essentially beginning as you would on an extract brewing. However, before starting the boil, it's best to check your pre-boil volume and gravity to ensure the boil characteristics match those called for in the recipe. First, check the pre-boil kettle volume. If it is too low, you can top off the kettle with clean water to achieve the desired pre-boil volume. Likewise, if you've collected too much wort, simply boiling longer should condense the wort to the expected post-boil volume. However, make sure to the add the bittering addition at the appropriate time called for in the recipe as hops can become harshly bitter when boiled for longer than 60 minute.

Next, check your pre-boil gravity. Based on your pre-boil volume and expected evaporation rate, you should be able to determine what the post-boil gravity will be by simple scaling. Based on the scaled gravity, check to see if it closely matches the recipe. If it's considerably low, you may consider adding DME to boost the gravity. Likewise, if your scaled post-boil gravity is considerably high, then consider diluting your wort with water to achieve the correct boil gravity.

Mash Hops

For the all-grain brewer, mash hopping is a technique used to infuse hop character via the mash. Of all of the potential hopping stages, this is the earliest available stage in the brewing process to add hops. The general idea of mash hopping stems from first wort hopping, where hop compounds are infused into the wort through the mash with the goal of preserving them from isomerization in the boil and leaving a robust hop flavor and aroma in the final beer with reduced bitterness.

Brewers report widely varying evidence on the effectiveness of mash hops, but in general, it seems that when an adequate quantity of hops is used in the mash, hop compounds do infuse into the wort and carry through the boil; however, a substantial amount is isomerized into bitterness and overall hop utilization is quite poor. In my opinion, you are better off using the mash hop addition as a first wort hop, late, or dry hop addition, solely for the sake of utilization and consistency. However, if you feel compelled to give it a whirl, at the very least, it will make the brewing smell nice and hoppy.

DMS Mitigation

One feature of all-grain brewing that may be new to the extract brewer is potential mitigation of dimethyl sulfide (DMS). As mentioned in Chapter 15, DMS is partly a by-product of mashing and can lend a creamed-corn character that is considered an off-flavor in most beer styles. The all-grain brewer can do a number of things in the boil process to reduce levels of DMS in the final beer. The first is to increase the boil duration from 60 to 90 minutes. DMS is reported to have a half-life of 40 minutes, which means it can be reduced by nearly 80 percent in a 90-minute boil. Also, due to its volatile nature, a good evaporation rate is also said to help achieve reduced levels, although the boil doesn't need to be leaping out of the brew kettle, just an elevated simmer works well. Lastly, quick chilling can help to prevent reformation, as DMS levels can increase by 30 percent for every hour the wort is above 140°F.

On the homebrewing level, brewers have mixed experiences. Some notice a big difference in boil duration changes whereas others, less so. So, instead of a verdict, I give some practical advice. For most beer styles using two-row malts, an extended boil beyond 60 minutes is often not necessary. However, when using very lightly-kilned base malts, especially German pilsner malts, increasing the boil duration is suggested since these malts have high levels of DMS precursors which can convert into DMS post-mashing. Lastly, performing a simple brewing experiment will ultimately determine whether an extended boil is necessary in your brewing process.

Hot and Cold Break

The hot and cold breaks are features of the boil in extract brewing, but in all-grain brewing, these effects are much greater. Since the hot and cold breaks were partially achieved in the malt extract production process, the hot and cold break while brewing with malt extract is actually minimized. Now that you've made your own extract through the all-grain brewing process, you should expect to see a greater quantity of both hot and cold break.

At the beginning of the boil, expect to see more hot break action, including a larger foamy head at the top of the boiling kettle than before. Also, since a good cold break requires quick chilling, you may need to chill the wort more quickly than you did in your extract brewing process. This can be further exacerbated since all-grain brewing requires a full boil and your previous extract chilling technique was optimized around partial-boil batches. Thus, consider upgrading to a more efficient chilling device like an immersion or plate chiller to achieve a good cold break while also quickly chilling a full-boil batch.

The Least You Need to Know

- All-grain brewing requires a few extra preparations, including crushing the malt and planning any water adjustments.
- On brew day, the all-grain brewer heats the mash and sparge water, makes adjustments to water chemistry, constructs the mash by adding crushed malt to hot water, and drains the wort through the lautering process.
- All-grain brewing requires more measurement, including pH, temperature, volume, and gravity, to ensure a successful batch.

Advanced Fermentation

If you want to make crisp, clean, and refreshing lager styles or big and boozy high-gravity beers, the fermentation stage will require a bit of skill and consideration to achieve great results. This chapter covers what you need to know for these more advanced fermentation techniques.

Temperature Control

As you may recall from Chapter 12, temperature is a critical variable in producing clean fermentation. To keep the temperature within recommended ranges, brewers employ a number of strategies. For many brewers, passive methods, like brewing with the seasons, work just fine, especially for those new to brewing. However, many brewers eventually transition to more active control methods in order to produce the whole range of beer styles, often with a high degree of precision.

In This Chapter

- Active and passive fermentation temperature control methods
- Lager and high-gravity fermentation techniques
- How to harvest and reuse yeast for future batches

Passive vs. Active Control

In homebrewing, there are two main forms of temperature control, passive and active, and starting out, it's worthwhile to clarify what each entails within the brewing process. In passive control, the temperature of fermentation is largely monitored and adjusted by the brewer using items like ice and heating pads. In active control, the temperature of fermentation is largely monitored and adjusted by a temperature sensor with programmable logic using more robust means, such as refrigeration. In general, passive methods require more work from the brewer to maintain a temperature range, while active methods are mostly automated and require little work from the brewer. However, passive methods are considerably less expensive than active methods, and as a result, are often the preferred application for new brewers or those brewing on a budget. Finally, it's important to be aware that experienced homebrewers do not necessarily exclusively use one or the other, but can utilize both methods as needed to achieve the highest performing fermentation.

Passive Control Methods

Many beginner brewers and those brewing on a budget can take advantage of the technique known as "brewing with the seasons," a strategy where the brewer selects a yeast strain to fit the ambient temperatures and conditions. For example, a 55°F winter basement is a great time to ferment a lager or hybrid style, while a 75°F summer living room is perfect for many Belgian ales and saison styles. This method delivers the least amount of control, but it also doesn't require any additional equipment. If you use this approach, make sure to pitch on the cool side, allowing for a rise of 3°F to 5°F above your surrounding temperature to avoid overshooting the temperature. Also, make sure to use a fermentation area away from light and one that maintains a consistent temperature without significant swings throughout the day.

While brewing with the seasons can be effective, ambient conditions are not always suitable for fermentation. Also, when exploring new styles and brewing techniques, limited house temperatures can be restrictive. The next layer of control is the addition of heating or cooling equipment to adjust fermentation temperature within desired ranges. Most of these passive methods rely on fairly affordable equipment, and may even be things you already have on hand.

To keep fermenting beer cool, homebrewers utilize a number of techniques. Ice-cooled baths are a popular technique in the summertime months. Here, the fermentor is placed in a large tub or swamp cooler that is filled with water and ice. Due to its large thermal mass, ice-cooled baths are less sensitive to swings in air temperature, and the melting ice acts like a buffer to slow the rise in temperature.

Another handy cooling technique is evaporative cooling. To use this method, wrap your fermentor in a wet towel or T-shirt and set it in front of a table fan. The degree of cooling achieved by this technique depends on the relative humidity of your air, but under typical conditions it drops the fermentation temperature by 5°F and up to 10°F or more in drier climates. To keep the towel wet without constantly resoaking, many brewers place the fermentor in a water-filled shallow tub or oil pan, which enables the towel to wick up more water when it begins to dry out.

Evaporative cooling employs a wet towel or T-shirt and a fan to reduce fermentation temperature.

There are also a number of techniques to keep fermentation warm. The easiest method to implement is wrapping the fermentor in insulating foam pads or heavy blankets. This captures the heat produced in the fermentation process and prevents it from escaping, increasing fermentation temperature. Alternatively, the brewer can use the same water cooler technique discussed previously, but instead of using ice for cooling, an aquarium water heater and a bit of circulation can be used to increase water temperature. This method for water heating is actually partially active, because most aquarium water heaters have a thermostat that can be used to regulate the water temperature.

Finally, direct heating pads and resistive heating belts can be wrapped around the fermentor to increase fermentation temperature. When using direct heating, make sure to apply power gradually, especially when using on glass carboys. Any rapid thermal changes can cause shattering, which is not good for you and your beer.

Active Control Methods

For many homebrewers, passive methods are not sufficient for their fermentation, either due to restrictive ambient conditions or because their fermentation requires a high degree of precision unobtainable through passive adjustment methods. In these situations, brewers can use digitally-controlled temperature monitoring as well as more robust forms of temperature adjustment to achieve the full range of fermentation temperature, from 32°F to 90°F or beyond, with precision within a degree or two.

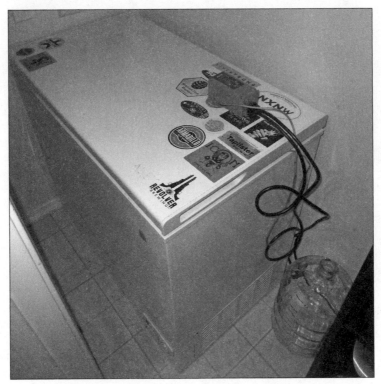

My fermentation chamber consists of a converted chest freezer and a Johnston-brand temperature controller.

At the core of active temperature control is the thermometer-assisted programmable controller. Essentially a mini computer, a temperature controller uses brewer-specified logic to monitor fermentation and electrical powered heat/cooling devices to adjust its temperature. Once the brewer sets a desired temperature range, the controller will monitor fermentation through a thermometer, typically a thermocouple, and send this data back to the controller for assessment. If the temperature is within the desired range, the controller will do nothing, and let fermentation continue uninterrupted. However, if the temperature is outside the desired range, the controller will activate and apply a heating or cooling element to redirect the fermentation back within the desired range.

In order to set up a temperature controller, the brewer must obtain sufficient electrically powered heating and cooling devices to appropriately adjust fermentation and mount a thermometer to accurately read its temperature. For heating, homebrewers typically rely on resistive heating belts, and for cooling, typically construct insulated fermentation chambers with integrated refrigerating elements for cooling. Also, thermometer mounting can be achieved through several means, with the easiest strategy simply mounting the temperature sensor on the side of the fermentor. If you're considering active temperature control, I suggest branching beyond the scope of this chapter, and explore the brewing resources listed in Appendix A.

Lager Fermentation Techniques

As you may recall from Chapter 5, lager brewing is markedly different from standard ale brewing, and uses cold fermentation to produce clear, clean, and crisp lager styles. However, there is more to lager brewing than simply cold fermentation, and it often requires a bit more care and consideration to achieve lager beer with great results.

Pitch Rate Considerations

One of the biggest differences between ale and lager fermentation, other than temperature, is pitch rate. As you recall in Chapter 12, the recommended pitch rate for standard ale fermentation falls around 0.75 million cells/ml/°P. However, due to its cold fermentation temperatures, lager yeast grows and ferments considerably, thus requiring more cells to achieve healthy fermentation. Most brewers recommend doubling the pitch rate to 1.5 million cells/ml/°P to achieve adequate lager fermentation. At this rate, brewers report a faster time to active fermentation and lower levels of ester production and fermentation by-products. Also, using these rates, a single smack pack or vial is inadequate for a 5-gallon batch, so you'll need to purchase additional yeast or make a yeast starter to achieve recommended pitch rates for lagers.

Interestingly, there is an alternative to elevated lager pitch rates, which is commonly referred to as warm pitching. Here, lager yeast is pitched at ale temperatures (65°F–75°F) and at the standard ale pitch rate. Since the lager yeast is warm, its growth is more rapid, and thus does not require the elevated pitching rate necessary at cold temperatures. However, before the lager yeast can produce undesirable esters and fermentation by-products, the fermenting beer is slowly cooled to its recommended lager temperature range within the first 8 to 12 hours after pitching.

Unsurprisingly, this method produces slightly more esters than cold pitching methods; however, when well executed in conjunction with adequate aeration, pitch rate, and temperature control, brewers report excellent results. Also, warm pitching is known for having elevated levels of fermentation by-products, so it is highly recommended to utilize a diacetyl rest after the fermentation phase is complete. Overall, for the lager purists, I'd recommend the cold pitch method for the cleanest possible lager fermentation. However, for new homebrewers who lack robust wort chilling techniques or for those looking for a quicker lager turnaround, the warm pitch method can produce incredibly good results.

Aeration Considerations

Aeration techniques for lagers mostly parallel standard ale methods; however, dissolving oxygen into cold wort will require extra effort in order to achieve recommended levels. Interestingly, while cold wort is capable of higher levels of dissolved oxygen due to increased solubility, the rate at which oxygen dissolves into cold wort is much slower than warmer wort. For this reason, you'll likely need to increase the duration of aeration based on your experience with warmer wort. For example, fermentor shaking in warm wort achieves oxygen saturation within 1 to 2 minutes. Therefore, it will likely require between 2 to 4 minutes of similar shaking to achieve the same level of saturation in cold wort. The same principle applies to other aeration methods, like pump-driven aeration and pure oxygen sources, although the latter is significantly less time consuming, requiring as little as 60 to 90 seconds of pure oxygen application to achieve adequate levels in cold wort.

In addition to cold wort effects, lager fermentation typically requires higher oxygen levels than ale fermentation. Along with increased lager pitch rates, aeration levels scale accordingly to support growth processes. While the recommended range of aeration for ale fermentation is 7 to 15 ppm, suggested lager aeration levels fall closer to the upper end, between 12 and 15 ppm. In fact, some fermentation experts suggest even greater levels, as much as 26 ppm for cold-fermented lagers. The only aeration method capable of achieving these high levels of aeration is forced aeration using a pure oxygen source.

Lastly, it's worth mentioning that many homebrewers achieve great lager fermentation even with lower levels of dissolved oxygen (7 to 10 ppm), which are easily achieved through fermentor shaking or aquarium pump aeration methods. In my experience, both low and high levels of aeration will produce great lagers; however, I find my lagers that have been aerated using a pure oxygen source at a higher aeration level achieve a greater degree of attenuation and are consistently better in quality than those made at lower levels. Going forward, you'll have to be the judge of effectiveness of aeration methods in your lager brewing process.

Packaging

Lager packaging strategies largely depend on the type of packaging employed. When packaging in kegs, the process is basically the same as for other beers. In fact, racking to the keg for the lager stage does double duty, with the keg serving as the lagering vessel for the lagering phase as well as allowing for carbonation to occur either by forced or natural means. Once the lagering phase is complete, any yeast sediment can be drawn off the bottom of the keg through the dip tube.

However, when packaging in bottles, the process requires a bit more consideration and allows for two lagering strategies. The first strategy follows the typical method of lagering in a secondary fermentor and then bottle conditioning afterward. This strategy creates the highest degree of clarity and lowest amount of sedimentation in the bottle; however, it will likely be yeast deficient.

To avoid this, make sure to add fresh yeast at bottling time to ensure the priming addition will produce carbonation.

The second option is to bottle condition first and then employ the lagering phase within the bottle. This strategy doesn't require the addition of fresh yeast because freshly fermented beer has sufficient yeast in suspension for conditioning and may also allow for reduced oxidation defects. When using this method, make sure to allow the beer to condition for 1 to 2 weeks at room temperature to produce carbonation before starting the lagering process. While this strategy eliminates the need for fresh yeast addition at bottling time, lagering in the bottle may produce a greater amount of sedimentation, which can cause cosmetic flaws when pouring the beer.

High-Gravity Fermentation Techniques

While yeast remains active and fairly stress-free throughout the fermentation of standard gravity ales and lagers, yeast is often pushed to its limits in high-gravity beers, and can produce incomplete fermentation and harsh off flavors. This is not just an issue for big beers like barleywine and imperial stout; any beer that exceeds 1.065 in original gravity is likely to require some degree of high-gravity consideration to achieve healthy fermentation. This section covers the techniques surrounding high-gravity brewing and how to adjust these variables to achieve clean and well-attenuated fermentation in your favorite big beer styles.

Yeast Strain Selection

As you recall from Chapter 5, different yeast varieties have widely varying levels of alcohol tolerance during fermentation. For example, Wyeast 1968 London ESB is known for its low-to-medium alcohol tolerance, slowing considerably past 9 percent ABV, while other yeast strains like Wyeast 3787 Trappist High Gravity are perfectly happy above 12 percent ABV. While these figures are relative and can often be increased by suitably tailoring other fermentation variables like temperature, aeration, and wort composition, it's important to take alcohol tolerance into account when designing and fermenting high-gravity beers, especially when exceeding 8 percent ABV. Thus, when starting out on your first big beer, I would recommend selecting a yeast strain that is fairly clean in character and highly alcohol tolerant to avoid any alcohol intolerance effects in your first high-gravity fermentation.

Pitch Rate Considerations

Like other advanced fermentation techniques, big beers require more yeast for healthy fermentation. For ales and warm-pitched lagers, the standard pitch rate of 0.75 million cells/ml/°P is increased according to the starting gravity of the wort. For ales and warm-pitched lagers between 1.065 and 1.083, an elevated pitch rate of 1.0 to 1.1 million cells/ml/°P is recommended, while higher-gravity ales and warm-pitched lagers above 1.083 may require further increasing the pitch rate to 1.4 to 1.5 million cells/ml/°P. Likewise, the same strategy follows for cold-pitch lagers. Above 1.065, cold-pitch lagers may require increasing the pitch rate to 2.0 million cells/ml/°P, and above 1.083 even further depending on recipe.

Aeration and Nutrient Considerations

Aeration and nutrient considerations are arguably the most critical factors in clean and well-attenuated high-gravity fermentation. Big beers require more yeast, which in turn requires more oxygen and nutrients for growth. Inadequate levels of aeration and nutrients produce sluggish or even arrested fermentation and the production of undesirable fermentation by-products. You can prevent these problems by designing a wort with adequate nutrient levels and suitably aerating the wort prior to pitching.

While standard aeration levels of 7 to 10 ppm may be sufficient in high-gravity fermentation, higher oxygen concentrations (10–15 ppm) are often recommended. It's not possible to achieve these levels through fermentor shaking or aquarium pump-driven aeration, so using a pure oxygen source with a diffusion stone is recommended.

When aerating, standard aeration durations to achieve 10 to 15 ppm will likely apply; however, be aware that high-gravity wort has lower oxygen solubility than standard-gravity wort and may require adjustment in aeration procedures to achieve these same concentrations. Also, when wort gravity exceeds 1.083, brewers recommend a second dose of oxygen during active fermentation. Ideally, this dose occurs after one full cell division during the growth phase of fermentation, approximately 12 hours after pitching. Recommended dose rate is between 7 and 12 ppm, equivalent to 1 to 2 minutes of pure oxygen.

While nutrients levels are generally not a concern with all-malt wort in standard gravity fermentation, wort gravity past 1.083 requires additional yeast nutrients to guarantee sufficient nutrient conditions during fermentation. Most brewers recommend adding yeast nutrients and the amount of yeast nutrients needed varies depending on the manufacturer, but are typically in the range of ½ to 1 teaspoon per 5 gallons of high-gravity wort.

Fermentation Temperature

High-gravity fermentation temperatures closely follow standard gravity ales and lagers. When fermenting, make sure to pitch at the appropriate temperature and control fermentation temperatures within the recommended range. Toward the tail end of fermentation, when the alcohol content starts to increase, it's recommended to raise the fermentation temperature for both high-gravity ales and lagers as this keeps the yeast suitably active to complete fermentation and reabsorb by-products before falling into dormancy. While a few degrees is highly suggested, many fermentation experts suggest significantly increasing temperature to 77°F for ales and 68°F for lagers within 48 to 72 hours after pitching. When adequate pitching rates and aeration are used, the scale of this temperature increase may be unnecessary at the homebrew scale, but it's definitely worth consideration for high-gravity beers like Belgian strong ales and double IPAs, where a high degree of attenuation is required.

Aging and Conditioning

Many high-gravity beers benefit from extended aging and conditioning. This will improve and refine flavor, allow yeast and brewing matter to fall out of suspension, improve clarity through chill haze precipitation (when cold conditioning is used), and continue the reabsorption and reduction of fermentation by-products. Also, aging is often the time when other brewing additions, like wood, are added for further flavor development.

For relatively fresh high-gravity styles, like double IPA, extended aging isn't suggested as these beer styles, even though big, are meant to be served fresh. With high-quality fermentation, beers like double IPAs should not have any harsh alcohol character requiring aging to mellow. However, big and boozy styles like barleywine and imperial stout benefit from a 1- to 3-month aging period to mellow flavors, and may even require extended aging of 1 to 3 years or more before peak flavors emerge.

BREWING TIP

Use breathable silicone bungs when aging beers. Sanitizer-filled airlocks work great for primary fermentation but often dry out over time, which can cause accidental airborne contamination. Just make sure the silicone which have a one-way flap to allow fermentation gases to escape.

Packaging

The recommendations for packaging high-gravity beers are very similar to those for packaging lagers. When kegging a high-gravity beer, no extra effort is needed beyond typical practices. Additionally, the keg can act as a secondary fermentor, doing double duty by simultaneously aging the beer and producing carbonation. When bottling, you will likely need to add fresh yeast to high-gravity beers, whether you are bottling from a secondary fermentor or immediately after primary fermentation. This is because the yeast from high-gravity beers is often in poor health by the end of primary fermentation and will need reinforcement to achieve carbonation.

Harvesting Yeast

After fermentation is complete, a large amount of yeast settles to the bottom of the fermentor. This is commonly referred to as the *yeast cake*. This yeast isn't dead, but rather dormant, ready to fight the good fight on another day. After racking a beer from a fermentor, you may think,

It would be such as waste to simply dump this down the drain. I wonder if I can reuse this yeast for a future batch? The short answer is, yes, yeast can be harvested and reused. However, some yeast and fermentations are better suited for reuse than others.

> **DEFINITION**
>
> **Yeast cake** is the flocculated, settled, and often compact mass of yeast at the bottom of the fermentor after fermentation is complete.

Simple Harvesting Process

The yeast harvest starts out like most things in brewing: cleaning and sanitization. On racking day, in addition to your typical brewing equipment, you'll need to sanitize a few extra items, including a small funnel (4–6 inches in diameter) and a storage container (or containers). While advanced yeast wranglers use Erlenmeyer flasks, most yeast harvesters use simple glass mason jars for yeast storage. Clean these items using standard sanitizing agents, or boil to sterilize if long-term storage is a consideration.

The next step in harvesting is making a homogenous mixture of yeast and beer known as a *yeast slurry*. Prior to harvesting, while racking, keep about an inch or so of beer on top of the yeast cake to protect the top surface from air. Then, using a gentle swirling motion, mix the yeast cake and remaining beer into a slurry. This can often be more difficult than expected as many yeast strains become very compact and adhere tightly to the bottom of the fermentor.

> **DEFINITION**
>
> **Yeast slurry** is the mixture of fermented beer and yeast cake often produced to save yeast after fermentation.

Once suitably mixed, the last step in the harvesting process is to carefully pour the slurry into the prepared storage container(s). Before doing so, you'll need to sanitize the lip of the fermentor to avoid contamination from its outer surface. This can be done with sanitizing spray or, for glass carboys only, use a stick lighter to flame sanitize. Once sanitized, the thick slurry can be poured into containers, using a funnel as necessary. When filling, make sure to leave about 10 percent headspace to minimize air exposure while also to allowing room for residual fermentation gases to enter when displaced. Once filled, move the containers to the refrigerator and use the slurry within 2 weeks.

Simple Yeast Harvest Procedure

Equipment

Funnel (4- to 6-inch diameter), sanitized

1 (32-ounce) mason jar with lid, sanitized

Spray sanitizer

Stick lighter (optional)

Instructions

1. Rack beer off the yeast cake, leaving behind 1 inch of beer on top of the yeast cake.

2. Using a gentle swirling motion, mix the yeast cake into a thick homogenous mixture. You now have a yeast slurry.

3. If using a glass carboy, flame sterilize the lip with a stick lighter. Alternatively, spray sanitizer on the lip and neck of the carboy or lip of the plastic bucket to eliminate any surface contaminates.

4. Carefully pour the yeast slurry into sanitized mason jars. Use a sanitized funnel for easier transferring.

5. Seal mason jars using sanitized lids and store in the refrigerator.

6. Use the yeast slurry within 2 weeks.

Harvested yeast can be stored in a mason jar.

Yeast Rinsing

While this simple harvesting technique is adequate for saving yeast, many homebrewers take further steps for yeast refinement through techniques called *yeast rinsing*. Essentially, before the yeast is harvested from the fermentor, it's mixed with a large addition of sterile water and allowed to stratify, leaving the pure yeast mixture on top, ready to be transferred off other unwanted brewing matter like trub, hop particulates, and dead yeast cells. To try yeast rinsing, the previously discussed harvesting procedure continues as follows.

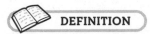

> **DEFINITION**
>
> **Yeast rinsing** is the process of removing unwanted brewing matter, such as trub and hop debris, from a harvested yeast slurry through decanting.

In a large sanitized container, combine harvested yeast slurry and sterilized water at a ratio of 1 part slurry to 4 parts sterilized water. To sterilize water, bring to a boil and then cool to room temperature before mixing with slurry. Gently swirl to create a homogenous mixture and then allow it to settle.

After about 10 minutes, the mixture will begin to stratify into three components: a thin bottom layer containing unwanted brewing matter (often brown in color), a thick middle layer containing the desired yeast and water (usually creamy white in color), and a thin top layer containing light yeast cells, protein, and water.

Once settled, the yeast can be harvested via decanting. First remove the top layer, then carefully pour off the creamy middle layer into a new sanitized container, and lastly dump the rest of the unwanted brewing matter. Compared to the original harvest, the rinsed yeast should look considerably purer and whiter in color; however, using only one rinse will still likely contain unwanted brewing matter. Because of this, many brewers will often perform two or more yeast rinses to produce a very clean yeast cake. This is fine; just remember that each time the yeast is exposed to air and new containers, the risk of contamination increases. Also, multiple rinses will remove more pitchable yeast, so if only a few ounces of yeast are preserved, consider making a yeast starter to ensure suitable numbers at pitching.

Harvesting Recommendations

Once you've harvested your yeast, there are some best practices to consider. Unlike lab-grade yeast, where viability decreases as little as 15 percent over 1 month, harvested yeast has a considerably shorter lifetime, with viability dropping below 50 percent over 1 month. For this reason, it is commonly recommended to reuse yeast within 2 weeks after harvest for best results. Also, due to a number of factors, many brewers suggest using a higher pitching rate than normal with harvested cultures. If longer storage beyond 2 weeks is desired, a suitable pitch rate can be easily achieved using a yeast starter to increase cell count prior to pitching.

On the topic of pitch rate, the cell count of harvested yeast is often difficult to determine, complicating how much yeast slurry should be pitched into the next beer. At the homebrew scale, slurry cell count is at best a good guess based on density without using a microscope and slide counting, as is typically done on the commercial scale.

In lieu of this, Wyeast Laboratories has provided a great guide to estimating cell count based on cell slurry density. As a rule of thumb, assuming low amount of trub and high viability, a slurry composed of 40 percent yeast solids has a cell density of approximately 1 billion cells per milliliter. For example, if 200 billion cells are needed for a 5-gallon batch of standard gravity ale, you would need to pitch 200 milliliters (about 7 ounces) of yeast slurry containing 40 percent yeast solids to achieve this pitch rate. While not foolproof, this estimation works well in my brewing when using a fresh slurry along with adequate fermentation temperature and aeration. For more information on yeast cell estimate and other great fermentation advice, check out the Wyeast Laboratories website at wyeastlab.com.

While most standard-gravity ales and lagers are good candidates for harvesting yeast, there are some situations when it is not recommended to reuse yeast for future fermentations. Skip a yeast harvest if …

- It comes from high-gravity fermentation, generally original gravities above 1.065.
- It comes from poor fermentation, including long lag phases, poor or uncharacteristic flocculation, and unexpectedly high final gravities.
- It comes from beer with excessive or unexpected off-flavors, such as diacetyl, phenols, esters, or fusel alcohols.
- The yeast smells uncharacteristically foul.
- Proper cleaning and sanitization practices were not observed.
- It comes from a batch with long conditioning and aging.
- It comes from a beer above 45 IBUs.

Based on these recommendations, many brewers will plan batches to maximize the number of yeast harvests, known as generations. The key strategy here is to start the first generation of yeast with a small beer that has low gravity, low ABV, and low IBU levels, and then design future batches that step up the gravity and/or bitterness accordingly until the one of the batches exceeds one of the recommendations, at which point harvesting is not suggested. A good example of this strategy would be starting out with an American-style wheat beer, harvesting its yeast and pitching the second generation into a American pale ale, harvesting its yeast one last time and pitching the third generation into an American-style IPA, at which point the gravity, ABV, and hop levels will likely be high enough to warrant discontinuing a fourth generation pitch and obtaining fresh yeast for future batches.

As a rule of thumb, many yeast manufacturers do not recommend more than three generations to be used on the homebrew scale to avoid poor fermentation and possible contamination. However, many homebrewers report good results with generations exceeding three deep. Personally, I don't use for more than two generations, simply because I like to try different yeast strains. If more than three generations is desirable in your brewing, make sure to use the highest level of cleaning and sanitization in your brewing process.

This section on yeast harvesting barely scratches the surface. Homebrewers and commercial brewers alike use a whole host of methods and techniques for harvesting and handling yeast that are not covered here, including microscope-based cell counting, making yeast bank reserves on wort auger slants, and culturing yeast from bottled beers. For more information on yeast harvesting and handling techniques, I recommend reading *Yeast: The Practical Guide to Beer Fermentation* by Chris White and Jamil Zainasheff.

The Least You Need to Know

- While ambient conditions are suitable for fermentation, many brewers progress to more advanced temperature control methods, such as digital temperature controllers.
- Lagers and high-gravity beers ferment similarly to standard ales, but require greater consideration of variables like temperature, pitch rate, and aeration to achieve a strong and healthy fermentation.
- Reusing yeast can be a thrifty way to a save a bit of time and money for future batches; however, it's important to make sure your yeast is suitable for harvesting.

Beer Recipes

Now that you have the know-how, you're probably eager to experiment with a variety of beer styles. This part will walk you through the basics of reading a beer recipe and provides some pointers on making recipe adjustments based on your brewing system, ingredients, and process. Best of all, there are 60 great beer recipes, ranging from beginner to advanced, with tips and guidance on how to best brew each recipe.

Brewing with Recipes

Brewers share their homebrews through recipes, much like those found in a cookbook. However, beer recipes are structured differently from those used in the kitchen, often detailing every ingredient and how it is constructed within the brewing process. This chapter will walk you through the process of breaking down a beer recipe and will help you modify existing recipes to fit your brewing needs.

How to Read a Beer Recipe

Reading beer recipes is a straightforward process. Beer recipes are designed to easily communicate the ingredients and processes necessary to replicate, as best as possible, a specific beer at home. There are two types of beer recipes, which parallel the major dividing line in the hobby: extract and all-grain recipes. For the most part, these recipes share common items, like hops schedule and fermentation, but they have minor differences in how the wort is prepared.

In This Chapter

- How to read the extract and all-grain recipes presented in this book
- How to convert a recipe from extract to all-grain and vice-versa
- How to adjust a recipe to fit your brewing process

Extract Recipes

In general, beer recipes are broken down into two parts: the beer ingredients and brewing process. The ingredients are further broken down into five parts: malt and fermentables, hops, yeast, other ingredients, and sometimes a water profile. The brewing process, in which these ingredients come together, is typically broken down into fermentation, conditioning, and packaging.

Most new brewers begin with extract recipes, so let's look at a typical extract recipe for the Texas Brown, an American-style brown ale with rich caramel/roasty malt character and citrusy, fruity hops. Here's the complete recipe. Each part of the recipe is explained in detail in the following sections.

Texas Brown

Brewing Stats

BREWING LEVEL:	Easy
BOIL DURATION:	60 minutes
OG:	1.052
FG:	1.013
ATTENUATION:	75%
IBU:	36
ABV:	5.1%
COLOR:	21 SRM

Fermentables

6 lb.	Light LME	37 ppg	2°L	70%
1.25 lb.	Crystal 40L	34 ppg	40°L	14%
1 lb.	Wheat DME	44 ppg	3°L	11%
8 oz.	Chocolate Malt	30 ppg	475°L	5%

Hops

1 oz.	Amarillo	60 min.	Boil	9% AA
1 oz.	Amarillo	10 min.	Boil	9% AA
1 oz.	Amarillo	0 min.	Boil	9% AA

Other Additions

1 tsp.	Irish Moss	15 min.	Boil
0.5 tsp.	Yeast Nutrient	10 min.	Boil

Fermentation

Yeast: Safale US-05

Pitch 200 billion cells, equivalent to 10 grams rehydrated dry yeast. Ferment at 68°F.

Packaging

Carbonate to 2.4 volumes or prime with 4 ounces corn sugar.

Brewing Stats

Beer recipes begin with brewing stats, the key metrics for the recipe. These include original gravity (OG), final gravity (FG), attenuation, IBU level, ABV, and estimated color. In the sample recipe, the Texas Brown calls for an OG of 1.052, an FG of 1.013, an attenuation of 75 percent, and ABV of 5.1 percent. Based on the hop schedule and malt colors, the recipe should yield 36 IBUS and a medium brown color around 21 SRM.

The brewing stats also include the recommended boil duration and provide a suggested difficulty level. Typically, extract ales are considered easy; recipes that require one advanced brewing technique like lagering, mashing, or high-gravity brewing, garner an intermediate level, and any recipe requiring two or more advanced brewing techniques are designated as advanced.

Fermentables

The next part of the recipe is the malt and fermentables section, commonly referred to as the grain bill. This section is arguably the most complicated part of the recipe, but it's still quite easy to understand. You will usually see this section presented as a table, with a row for each fermentable and columns logging the anticipated metrics. Of the five columns shown here, the first two left columns are the most important to follow, those being the amount of fermentable to be added by weight and the type, style, or brand of fermentable to be used in the recipe.

Next are the third and fourth columns, which list the maximum anticipated yield and the color of the fermentables. While this information is less important than the first two columns, brewers looking to precisely replicate a recipe may take it into account to achieve the predicted color, original gravity, and IBU level as stated in the brewing stat section.

The last column is the relative percentage of each fermentable by weight. These percentages are calculated based on the total weight of the combined fermentable, and many brewers will report the grain bill by percentage rather than weight as this allows for easier scaling and adjustment, as we'll see later on.

In addition to sourcing fermentables by weight, type, color, and yield, the extract brewer must be able to determine which fermentables need to be added to the boil and which need to be steeped. Common fermentables to be added to the boil are LME, DME, and sugar additions like corn sugar, candi syrup, etc., while all specialty malts of the crystal and roasted varieties must be infused via the steeping process. In the sample recipe, there are two malt extract additions, Light LME and Wheat DME, as seen in rows one and three, respectively, and two specialty malt additions, Crystal 40L and Chocolate Malt, as seen in rows two and four, respectively.

For ease of reading, each row is sorted by weight, from greatest to least, with the top row the primary fermentable and the bottom row a minor fermentable contribution. Typically, the topmost rows contain malt extracts and the bottommost rows contain small specialty malt additions. However, as seen in the example, some recipes call for larger specialty malt additions, in this case Crystal 40L, and smaller extract and sugar additions, in this case Wheat DME. For more information on these ingredients and how to make them into wort, check out Chapters 2, 3, and 11.

Hops

The third part of a recipe is the hop section, commonly referred to as the hop schedule. Much like the grain bill, the hop schedule is organized in tabular form with the recipe's hop additions individually listed by row and each column logging the anticipated metrics for each hop addition. However, unlike the grain bill, each column is important for creating the hop profile for a given recipe. The first two columns list the hop variety and how much is needed by weight. The third and fourth columns are the hop addition times and where to add them.

Most hop additions are added to the boil and represented by the term "Boil." Also, most boil additions are added between 0 and 60 minutes, with a 60-minute addition added at the very beginning of the boil and a 0-minute addition added at the very end of the boil. The example recipe has three hop additions of Amarillo hops rated at 9 percent alpha acids (AA), which are to be added to the boil in 1-ounce quantities at the 60-, 10-, and 0-minute marks. Other additions are first wort hop, mash hop, and dry hop and each are listed as such. For dry hop additions, the recommend infusion period is usually quoted in days.

The last column is the assumed alpha acid content of the hop variety in calculating the IBU level in the recipe. As you may recall from Chapter 4, the alpha acid content of a hop variety can vary depending on harvest year and age. You can expect the quoted alpha acid content to be close to the actual alpha acid content of your purchased hops, but it likely will not be exact. If you want to adjust your hop additions to hit the calculated IBU level for the recipe, follow the adjustment instructions in the last section of this chapter.

Other Additions

The fourth part of the recipe is the "Other Additions" section, which acts as a junk drawer for miscellaneous ingredient additions. Common ingredients listed here are wort clarifiers, like Irish moss and yeast nutrients, as well as flavoring ingredients like coffee, chocolate, fruit and spices. Like the hop schedule, this section is tabulated by weight, type, where to add, and at what time. In the sample recipe, both an Irish moss and yeast nutrient addition are called to be added at the 15-minute and 10-minute mark, respectively.

Note that the recipes in this book do not include a water section. Since water is highly dependent on your source water, it is difficult to suggest what mineral additions are needed to enhance the flavor and/or fermentation of a particular recipe. If a flavor enhancement is suggested, these additions are labeled as optional in the "Other Additions" section. If you are not confident on your source water brewing chemistry, it's best to withhold this addition.

Fermentation and Packaging

Finally, the last parts of the recipe cover yeast, fermentation, and packaging. The fermentation section lists the recommended yeast strain and fermentation profile based on temperature and pitch rate. Since fermentation has the largest impact on the character of a recipe, it's worth identifying any possible adjustments to the recipe, like grain bill and attenuation, when switching yeast strains. Also, fermentation temperatures and pitch rates are more suggestions than rules, and are based on typical ranges that brewers report to successfully make the style, although like yeast strains, adjustments to temperature and pitch rate may be necessary depending on your preference and brewing process.

Lastly, the packaging section contains the recommended carbonation level and an estimated priming addition to attain it. If using forced carbonation, check the pressure versus temperature carbonation chart in Chapter 13 to achieve the recommended level. When priming, the recommended addition may change based on the factors specified in Chapter 13, like beer temperature, volume. It's worth adjusting the priming addition as needed to avoid under- or over-carbonation.

All-Grain and Mini-Mash Recipes

Reading an all-grain recipe is virtually the same as reading an extract recipe, but there are a few differences due to the difference in brewing technique. In the fermentables section, you'll notice that base malts are listed instead of malt extracts. Also, while the extract brewer needs to identify and separate out any specialty malts from the extract and sugar additions, the all-grain brewer can mash the entire grain bill except for any listed simple sugars.

In addition to the base malt swap, an all-grain recipe also includes mash instructions. In this book, you'll find these instructions inserted between the other ingredient and fermentation sections. Here, you'll find the recommended mash technique along with any temperature and rest duration steps. The all-grain recipes in this book all utilize the single-infusion technique, but feel free to modify the rest temperature or change the mashing technique to enhance or change the character of the beer recipe. In doing so, keep in mind that alterative mash techniques may change the degree of fermentability of the wort and thus require recipe adjustment to hit the key brewing stats as detailed in the recipe.

Lastly, most all-grain recipes specify the assumed efficiency when calculating the target original gravity. All of the recipes in this book assume an all-grain efficiency of 75 percent, a typical efficiency for most homebrewers. If you experience higher or lower efficiencies based on your brewing system and practice, the grain bill can be increased or decreased accordingly to hit the key brewing stats at the beginning of the recipe. To do so, check out the recipe adjustments section at the end of this chapter.

Converting Between Extract and All-Grain

Often when searching for brewing recipes, you find a great recipe that's not designed for your current brewing technique. Instead of looking for a different recipe, you can convert it to match your brewing process and achieve as true a match to the original recipe as possible.

Extract to All-Grain

Converting an extract recipe to all-grain is a fairly simple process, as base malts are the source of malt extract in the first place. The most important step in the extract-to-all-grain conversion process is estimating how much base malt by weight is necessary to match the original gravity called for in the recipe. Since malt extract is a condensed form of wort, the amount of base malt needed is proportionally more by weight that the malt extract by weight as specified in a recipe. Thus, two main factors contribute to the extract-to-all-grain conversion: your expected mash efficiency and the difference in maximum yield between the base malt and malt extract varieties.

Converting a recipe from LME to base malt is the simplest conversion. The typical yield of most LME brands is around 37 ppg, which also happens to be the typical maximum yield of lightly-kilned base malts. Thus, the amount of base malt necessary by weight to convert a recipe from LME can be found by simply multiplying by the inverse of your all-grain efficiency. Homebrewers typically average around 75 percent all-grain efficiency. Thus, the proportional increase in base malt by weight is 1 ÷ 0.75, or 33 percent more base malt by weight than the LME by weight, as stated in the recipe. For example, if an extract recipe calls for 6 pounds of LME, you would increase that amount by 33 percent, which means you would need 8 pounds of base malt to yield the same original gravity as called for in the recipe.

A similar calculation can be used to convert recipes using DME to base malt. However, an extra step is needed since the yield of DME is more concentrated than LME, yielding on average 44 ppg instead of 37 ppg, and thus requiring more base malt to make up the difference. For example, using the previously quoted yield for DME and base malt varieties, its yield difference is 44 ppg/37 ppg, equivalent to 19 percent more base malt by weight than DME by weight. When you include the previously determined difference in mash efficiency, the resulting total conversion is 58 percent more base malt by weight than DME by weight. This is not surprising considering that DME is more concentrated than LME and thus requires proportionally more base malt to yield the equivalent original gravity quoted in a recipe.

In lieu of these approximate conversion factors, a general conversion can be made using the following formula. This formula can be very useful when dealing with nonstandard malt extracts, base malt with variable maximum yields, or widely differing mash efficiencies.

1 pound malt extract =
yield of malt extract in ppg ÷
(maximum yield of base malt in ppg × mash efficiency percent in decimal form)

BREWING TIP

While actual conversion rates depend on your specific mash efficiency and the proportional difference in yield between extract and base malt varieties, you can use the following conversion rates as a general rule of thumb, assuming 75 percent efficiency.

1 pound LME = 1.33 pounds base malt

1 pound DME = 1.58 pounds base malt

Lastly, here are some additional tips when converting a recipe from extract to all-grain. Specialty malts do not require a conversion step, largely because the steeping process and mash process result in roughly the same efficiency, around 75 percent. Also, it's important to remember than malt extracts often contain multiple base malt varieties and sometimes even specialty malts. Common examples are Wheat DME and Munich LME, which for mashing purposes contain a substantial amount of pilsner malt. Thus, in order to perform the conversion, you'll need to both identify the extract composition by percentage and proportionally divide the as-calculated total base malt by weight among the individual base malt varieties based on this composition.

For example, the Oktoberfest recipe in this book calls for 9 pounds Munich LME, which is a 50/50 blend of Munich and pilsner malts. To convert to all-grain, you much first determine the total amount of base malt needed (12 pounds) and then apply the proportions of the original Munich LME. In this case, you need equal parts Munich malt and pilsner malt (6 pounds of each) to form the equivalent all-grain recipe.

All-Grain to Extract

Converting an all-grain recipe for extract brewing methods, while achievable, may require a bit more effort. The core of the conversion difficulty is that many brewing malts and grains are not available in extract form, so some creativity and skill are necessary to yield good substitutions. Base malts like two-row, Munich, and pilsner malts are commonly available; however, be aware that some maltsters use blends, such as in Munich and wheat malt extracts, so their individual percentages must take into account each malt component in order to achieve the ratios as called for in a recipe. Also, any specialty malt of the crystal and roasted varieties in the recipe can be integrated via steeped in hot water to infuse their color, flavor, and character into extract recipes.

The best-case scenario for all-grain to extract conversion is a recipe solely utilizing base malts with readily available extract equivalents and only specialty malts that require steeping. Under these conditions, the all-grain to extract conversion is the reverse of the extract to all-grain conversion previously discussed.

1 pound base malt =
(maximum yield of base malt in ppg × mash efficiency in decimal form) ÷
yield of malt extract in ppg

For example, an all-grain recipe that calls for 10 pounds of two-row base malt and 1 pound of Crystal 60L will require a substitute 7.5 pounds of light LME or 6.3 pounds of light DME, assuming the all-grain recipe is scaled to 75 percent efficiency. The remaining pound of Crystal 60L can then be directly steeped since it is a specialty malt.

If you want to convert an all-grain recipe for extract brewing and the base malts are not available in extract form, you have few options for achieving the closest possible conversion. Recipes that contain adjuncts like flaked barley, flaked wheat, and flaked rice have extract-friendly substitutes that can be found in the online ingredients substitution list at idiotsguides.com/homebrewing. When making replacements, make sure to adjust for any fermentability differences following the general outline applied to the extract-to-base-malt conversion previously discussed.

On the other hand, darkly-kilned base malts and aromatic malts are not extract-friendly and are more difficult to replace. If you need to make this conversion, you have two options. The first is to simply omit these malts completely and replace them with the best available malt extract, typically Munich LME, and adjust for any color differences with small additions of roasted specialty malts. When omitting at small percentages, this will work okay; however, at larger percentages, this may be undesirable.

Alternatively, I recommend a second option, which is to perform a mini mash. Here, the portion of irreplaceable darkly-kilned base malt is mashed with a lightly-kilned base malt variety, like two-row or pilsner malt, together converting their starches into sugar while also yielding their color, flavor, and character. When doing so, follow the all-grain brewing procedures as specified in Chapters 17 and 19 for best results.

Lastly, while all-grain recipes by nature utilize a full boil in making wort, extract brewers have the option to use either partial or full boil in their brewing process. To achieve the closest match, the extract brewer should employ a full boil; however partial-boil brewers can utilize the late malt addition technique as detailed in Chapter 11 to yield a close result.

Recipe Adjustments

Since ingredients vary across maltster and harvest as well as brewing process from brewer to brewer, it's not always easy to replicate recipes exactly. As such, most brewing recipes require some degree of adjustment prior to brew day to achieve a close match.

Bitterness

Adjusting the bitterness level is one of the most common recipe modifications for both extract and all-grain brewers. Bitterness adjustment isn't about making a recipe more or less bitter based on your taste preferences, but rather adjusting the hop amounts by weight to accurately reflect the as-specified bitterness level in a recipe. Due to variations in harvest year, age, storage conditions, etc., the hops you purchase from your local homebrew shop will almost certainly not have the exact alpha acid content assumed in the recipe and thus, if you are seeking to match the level of bitterness as specified, you'll have to make bittering adjustments to accurately reflect the recipe.

In order to adjust the bittering, you must first estimate how much bittering potential has been lost. Hops stored in airtight, vacuum-sealed packaging at freezer temperatures can retain 80 to 90 percent of its original alpha acid content for over a year. However, hops stored outside of these conditions will have a more significant alpha acid loss. For example, hops stored at room temperature in an airtight, vacuum-sealed package can lose over half its bittering potential in a year. Thus, consider the age and storage conditions of your hops and include any significant alpha acid losses in hop schedule adjustment.

Based on your estimated alpha acid content, the second step is to adjust the hop amount by weight, based on the hop schedule. If your estimated alpha acid content is within 10 percent of the specified amounts in the hop schedule, then your best course of action is to move forward without any major adjustment.

However, if your alpha acids content is significantly different from alpha acid content as called for in the hop schedule, then you may consider adjusting to maintain bitterness levels for the recipe. A simple approach is to simply scale up or down the hop amounts by weight based on any the alpha acid difference.

> your hop addition by weight =
> hop addition in recipe by weight × (hop AA content in recipe ÷ your hop AA content)

For example, a recipe calls for adding a bittering addition using 1 ounce of hops with an alpha acid content of 5 percent. However, your hops are estimated to have 4 percent AA, a difference of 1 percent AA from what is specified in the hop schedule. To adjust, simply increase your additions by the alpha acid differences to maintain the IBU level. Using the prior example, this will require adding more hops, equivalent to 1.25 ounces of your 4 perecent AA hops, to maintain the same bittering level.

Attenuation

Another brewing metric that often requires adjustment is attenuation. In order to accurately replicate a recipe, the brewer must achieve the same degree of attenuation as called for in the recipe, not only to produce a beer with the same final gravity and ABV, but more importantly, to strike the right balance of flavors and character in the final beer. Based on your brewing practices, you may have noticed whether you typically underattenuate or overattenuate after fermentation is complete. From these observations, you can predicatively adjust a recipe to achieve the desired degree of attenuation without significantly changing its overall character.

If you typically underattenuate, one quick fix is to substitute the yeast with a more attenuative strain that will be able to chew through more sugar before falling into dormancy. If you do this, it's best to choose a yeast strain within the same category, for example substituting an English yeast strain for another English one, to maintain general fermentation character.

Alternatively, you can keep the yeast strain fixed and instead replace a portion of the malt-based fermentables with a simple sugar, like corn sugar. Since it's comprised entirely of glucose, it will nearly completely ferment out and produce a more highly attenuative beer. When substituting sugar for fermentables, make sure to adjust for yield differences to maintain the original gravity of the recipe. Lastly, if you are an all-grain brewer, you can increase fermentability by using a lower mash rest temperature than the mash rest called for in the recipe.

The adjustments for overattenuation are the opposite of the recommendations for underattenuation. If a recipe calls for simple sugar additions, one quick fix is to reduce or eliminate the called for amount and substitute with a malt-based fermentable, making sure to account for any yield differences. Additionally, substituting the yeast with a less attenuative strain is also a good option, with the best substitutions maintaining the same yeast category. Finally, if you are an all-grain brewer, you may employ a higher mash rest temperature than called for in the recipe.

Color

Color is a relatively minor factor, but adjustment may be necessary when the expected color of a recipe doesn't suit the color preference of the brewer. Before adjusting the color of your recipe, take note of the particular maltster producing for your malt, as its color can vary widely based on their processes. This is especially true for roasted barley.

When slight color adjustments are called for, specialty malts, especially de-bittered roasted varieties, can be useful to darken wort. While the particular amount is up to the brewer's preference, as little as 2 ounces of de-bittered black malt in a 5-gallon batch is enough to change the color of beer by 5 SRM without adding significant flavors. When adjusting color, make sure you verify the color and/or maltster for your malt, and adjust wort color accordingly.

Brewing Efficiency

One of the most important recipe adjustments for the all-grain brewer is brewing efficiency. All-grain recipes are formulated assuming some baseline efficiency, which affects nearly all of the brewing stats, such as original and final gravity, IBU levels, attenuation, etc., as well as a recipe's flavor, balance, and overall character. Thus, one of the main responsibilities of the all-grain brewer is to tailor the grain bill to achieve an equivalent extract as called for in the recipe based on your typical brewing efficiency.

The primary technique to adjust a recipe for efficiency is achieved by simple scaling factor. Let's take a look at these two methods using a simple brewing example. Suppose you're brewing an American pale ale with 1.046 OG. The recipe calls for 9 pounds of two-row malt and 1 pound of Crystal 40L, assuming on a brewing efficiency of 75 percent. However, your brewing efficiency is typically 65 percent; thus, if you brew this recipe as-is, you'll end up with a significantly lower gravity than expected.

To modify this recipe, you must calculate the scaling factor needed to match your efficiency. In doing so, divide the recipe specified efficiency by your expected brewing efficiency.

recipe efficiency ÷ your efficiency =
0.75 ÷ 0.65 =
1.15

The result of 1.15 tells you that about 15 percent more malt is needed to achieve the original gravity from the recipe.

Next, you will need to multiply this scale factor to each amount of malt to calculate the necessary adjustments by weight. From the example recipe:

amount of two-row malt in recipe × scaling factor =
9 pounds × 1.15 =
10.35 pounds of two-row malt adjusted to your efficiency

amount of Crystal 40L malt in recipe × scaling factor =
1 pound × 1.15 =
1.15 pounds of Crystal 40L adjusted to your efficiency

From the example, this scale factor produces an increase of two-row malt from 9 to 10.35 pounds and an increase of Crystal 40L from 1 to 1.15 pounds.

Interestingly, if you divide each of these adjustments by the adjusted weight of the total grain bill, you'll find that the relative percentages are the same between the original unadjusted recipe and your adjusted recipe, maintaining the recipe original character. As a final note, while the example here demonstrates recipe adjustment to accommodate a lower mash efficiency, the same formula and methods can be used to adjust a recipe to accommodate a higher mash efficiency. The only difference is that the scaling factor will be less than one.

The Least You Need to Know

- Much like recipes in a cookbook, beer recipes consist of an ingredients list and brewing process instruction.

- Beer recipes can be converted between extract and all-grain brewing techniques, although it requires a bit of calculation and other process considerations.

- Most brewers modify recipes to suit their ingredients and brewing process, such as hop alpha acid and all-grain efficiency adjustments.

Homebrew Recipes

Recipe Assumptions and Brewing Tips

Before getting started, it's good to know some of the assumptions behind recipe formulation. While the typical batch size in homebrewing is the 5-gallon batch, these recipes are scaled to yield 6 gallons because approximately 1 gallon or so of beer is lost over the course of the brewing process. Also, these recipes assume the use of a full boil. Since 6 gallons in the brew kettle is desired post-boil, you'll likely need at least 7 gallons in the brew kettle pre-boil, while this pre-boil volume may differ depending on your typical evaporation rate. Also, the all-grain recipes presented here assume a mash efficiency of 75 percent, thus if your system differs from this assumption, it may require recipe adjustments. To do so, check out Chapter 21 for suggested efficiency adjustments.

In This Chapter

- A variety of extract, all-grain, and hybrid recipes, ranging from basic to intermediate brewing level

- A selection of high-gravity and lager recipes for the advanced brewer

- Guest recipes from pillars of the homebrew community, including Jamil Zainasheff, Michael Tonsmeire, Drew Beechum, and Denny Conn

Extract Ale Recipes

This section includes 25 great extract ale recipes ranging from pale ales and IPAs to porters, saisons, and everything in between.

Summertime Blonde

With its light malt character and balancing bitterness, blonde ale is a quaffable drink and one of the staple lawnmower beers. As a homebrewer, blonde ale is a great style to brew up for friends and family new to craft beer. When modifying the recipe, keep the specialty malt additions low to prevent the beer from becoming too sweet and to maintain its pale color. Also, while the recipe calls for clean American ale yeast, it's also nice with dry English ale strains like Wyeast 1098 British Ale and German ale strains like Wyeast 1007 German Ale.

Brewing Stats

BREWING LEVEL:	Easy
BOIL DURATION:	60 minutes
OG:	1.045
FG:	1.010
ATTENUATION:	78%
IBU:	17
ABV:	4.6%
COLOR:	3 SRM

Fermentables

7 lb.	Light LME	37 ppg	2°L	94%
8 oz.	Crystal 15L	34 ppg	15°L	6%

Hops

1 oz.	Willamette	60 min.	Boil	5% AA
0.5 oz.	Willamette	5 min.	Boil	5% AA

Other Additions

1 tsp.	Irish Moss	15 min.	Boil
0.5 tsp.	Yeast Nutrient	10 min.	Boil

Fermentation

Yeast: Safale US-05

Pitch 170 billion cells, equivalent to 8.5 grams of rehydrated dry yeast. Ferment at 68°F.

Packaging

Carbonate to 2.4 volumes or prime with 4 oz. of corn sugar.

Changing Colors Amber Ale

American amber ale is an interesting style with richer malt and less hop character than American pale ale. A well-brewed example is nice to enjoy when the weather starts to become cooler in September. In my brewing, I avoid the more caramel-heavy interpretations, which I find cloyingly sweet and one-dimensional. Instead, I take a page from German Altbier and brew mine with Munich malts, lending a dark toasted character rather than caramel. As an interesting twist, I like to use all Centennial hops, which folds in a pleasant, light citrus character on top of the rich malt. You could also substitute a more earthy, herbal hop, like Willamette, in this recipe.

Brewing Stats

BREWING LEVEL:	Easy
BOIL DURATION:	60 minutes
OG:	1.054
FG:	1.013
ATTENUATION:	76%
IBU:	34
ABV:	5.4%
COLOR:	11 SRM

Fermentables

5 lb.	Light LME	37 ppg	2°L	55%
3 lb.	Munich LME	37 ppg	8°L	33%
1 lb.	Crystal 60L	34 ppg	60°L	11%
2 oz.	Pale Chocolate	30 ppg	207°L	1%

Hops

1 oz.	Centennial	60 min.	Boil	10% AA
0.5 oz.	Centennial	10 min.	Boil	10% AA
0.5 oz.	Centennial	0 min.	Boil	10% AA

Other Additions

1 tsp.	Irish Moss	15 min.	Boil
0.5 tsp.	Yeast Nutrient	10 min.	Boil

Fermentation

Yeast: Safale US-05

Pitch 200 billion cells, equivalent to 10 grams rehydrated dry yeast. Ferment at 68°F.

Packaging

Carbonate to 2.4 volumes or prime with 4 ounces corn sugar.

West Coast Pale Ale

I'm very fond of hoppy pale ales. Sessionable, complex, and refreshing, I try to keep one on tap at all times. In my brewing, I like to keep my pale ales simple, typically just a few malts and one hop. With 2.5 ounces of late additions, this recipe is hop forward. Citrus-y and grapefruit-y in character, Cascade is a traditional hop from the Pacific Northwest and makes for a great pale ale hop. Alternatively, hop aficionados can substitute Cascade for any new hop variety, being mindful of any alpha acid differences. This pale ale is fermented with the famous West Coast Chico strain, which helps keep it clean and well-attenuated, further accentuating the hop character. Overall, this recipe makes for a light, refreshingly hoppy West-coast style pale ale great for any occasion.

Brewing Stats

BREWING LEVEL:	Easy
BOIL DURATION:	60 minutes
OG:	1.046
FG:	1.010
ATTENUATION:	78%
IBU:	37
ABV:	4.7%
COLOR:	5 SRM

Fermentables

7 lb.	Light LME	37 ppg	2°L	90%
12 oz.	Crystal 40L	34 ppg	40°L	10%

Hops

1.5 oz.	Cascade	60 min.	Boil	6% AA
1.5 oz.	Cascade	10 min.	Boil	6% AA
1 oz.	Cascade	0 min.	Boil	6% AA

Other Additions

1 tsp.	Irish Moss	15 min.	Boil
0.5 tsp.	Yeast Nutrient	10 min.	Boil

Fermentation

Yeast: Safale US-05

Pitch 170 billion cells, equivalent to 8.5 grams rehydrated dry yeast. Ferment at 68°F.

Packaging

Carbonate to 2.4 volumes or prime with 4 ounces corn sugar.

15-Minute American Pale Ale

Guest recipe from James Spencer: James Spencer is the man and voice behind the Basic Brewing Radio and Video podcasts, which have been a great homebrewing resource for over a decade. One of James's specialties is simplifying the brew day, and this recipe doesn't get much simpler. Since malt extract is already refined, it doesn't need a full 60-minute boil to blow off undesirable volatile compounds as it would when brewing all-grain. Also, by utilizing hop bursting, large charges of late hops can achieve the full 40+ IBU bitterness while also preserving the wonderful hoppy flavor and aroma. As a result, this 15-minute recipe produces a great American pale ale, full of hop character, all within an ultra-short brew day. For more information on this particular recipe or great brewing information in general, check out the Basic Brewing podcasts at basicbrewing.com and James's blog posts at beerandwinejournal.com.

Brewing Stats

BREWING LEVEL:	Easy
BOIL DURATION:	15 minutes
OG:	1.048
FG:	1.011
ATTENUATION:	78%
IBU:	43
ABV:	4.9%
COLOR:	8 SRM

Fermentables

6 lb.	Light DME	44 ppg	2°L	85%
1 lb.	Crystal 60L	34 ppg	60°L	14%

Hops

2 oz.	Simcoe	15 min.	Boil	12.0% AA
1 oz.	Simcoe	5 min.	Boil	12.0% AA
1 oz.	Simcoe	0 min.	Boil	12.0% AA

Other Additions

1 tsp.	Irish Moss	15 min.	Boil
0.5 tsp.	Yeast Nutrient	10 min.	Boil

Fermentation

Yeast: Safale US-05

Pitch 180 billion cells, equivalent to 9 grams rehydrated dry yeast. Ferment at 68°F.

Packaging

Carbonate to 2.4 volumes or prime with 4 ounces corn sugar.

Texas Brown

This American brown ale is an homage to its strange history. Originating in California, this overly-hopped English brown style was first given recognition at the Dixie Cup in Texas. Despite its California origins, the AHA first named it a Texas Brown Ale. While subsequent style guidelines have removed this name, many homebrewers still like to refer to the style as a Texas brown. Whatever you like to call it, the American-style brown ale is a fusion of the malty, caramel-y, roasty character of an English-style brown ale with the aggressive hop character from American variety hops. In my brewing, I prefer the citrusy varieties of American hops, especially Amarillo, which lend a chocolate-orange character in the final beer. This one is a great way to start the fall brewing season.

Brewing Stats

BREWING LEVEL:	Easy
BOIL DURATION:	60 minutes
OG:	1.052
FG:	1.013
ATTENUATION:	75%
IBU:	36
ABV:	5.1%
COLOR:	21 SRM

Fermentables

6 lb.	Light LME	37 ppg	2°L	70%
1.25 lb.	Crystal 40L	34 ppg	40°L	14%
1 lb.	Wheat DME	44 ppg	3°L	11%
8 oz.	Chocolate Malt	30 ppg	475°L	5%

Hops

1 oz.	Amarillo	60 min.	Boil	9% AA
1 oz.	Amarillo	10 min.	Boil	9% AA
1 oz.	Amarillo	0 min.	Boil	9% AA

Other Additions

1 tsp.	Irish Moss	15 min.	Boil
0.5 tsp.	Yeast Nutrient	10 min.	Boil

Fermentation

Yeast: Safale US-05

Pitch 200 billion cells, equivalent to 10 grams rehydrated dry yeast. Ferment at 68°F.

Packaging

Carbonate to 2.4 volumes or prime with 4 ounces corn sugar.

West Coast IPA

The immensely popular West Coast IPA is the first style to come to mind when thinking of the craft beer movement. Intensely hoppy, pale in color, and dry on the finish, American IPA makes for a highly flavorful yet dangerously quaffable drink. The key to the style is attenuation, getting the finishing gravity below 3°P. To achieve a great deal of attenuation, IPA brewers utilize a fairly large corn sugar addition, around 10 percent of the fermentables, as it dries the beer out and ferments out completely. When brewing, West Coast IPA goes great with any hops from the Pacific Northwest. My personal favorite is a 50/50 blend of Centennial and Columbus hops, although the Falconer's Flight hop blend by Hop Union is a close second.

Brewing Stats

BREWING LEVEL:	Easy
BOIL DURATION:	60 minutes
OG:	1.059
FG:	1.011
ATTENUATION:	82%
IBU:	69
ABV:	6.3%
COLOR:	5 SRM

Fermentables

8 lb.	Light LME	37 ppg	2°L	85%
1 lb.	Corn Sugar	45 ppg	0°L	10%
8 oz.	Crystal 40L	34 ppg	40°L	5%

Hops

1 oz.	Magnum	60 min.	Boil	14% AA
1 oz.	Columbus	10 min.	Boil	15% AA
1 oz.	Centennial	10 min.	Boil	15% AA
1 oz.	Columbus	0 min.	Boil	15% AA
1 oz.	Centennial	0 min.	Boil	10% AA
1 oz.	Columbus	5 days	Dry Hop	10% AA
1 oz.	Centennial	5 days	Dry Hop	10% AA

Other Additions

0.5 tsp.	Yeast Nutrient	10 min.	Boil
1 tsp.	Irish Moss	15 min.	Boil

Fermentation

Yeast: Safale US-05

Pitch 240 billion cells, equivalent to 12 grams rehydrated dry yeast. Ferment at 67°F.

Packaging

Carbonate to 2.4 volumes or prime with 4 ounces corn sugar.

All-Extract Special Bitter

English special bitter is one of the great session styles, coming in at around 4 percent ABV. The source of its sessionable character is the balance between characterful malts and English variety hops, which produce a fairly light, drinkable beer while still being flavorful and satisfying. This recipe is a ultra-simplified riff on the style that uses all dry malt extract to make quick work of brew day. For this recipe in particular, I especially like the combination of late Fuggle and Willamette hops. When fermented with Wyeast 1028 London Ale, this beer is light and clean with a slight apricot-y/stone fruit character and balancing bitterness. If you are in need of a quick brew day and an easy drinking beer, give this quickie recipe a whirl and make sure to drink it by the imperial pint.

Brewing Stats

BREWING LEVEL:	Easy
BOIL DURATION:	60 minutes
OG:	1.040
FG:	1.010
ATTENUATION:	75%
IBU:	30
ABV:	4%
COLOR:	4 SRM

Fermentables

3 lb.	Light DME	44 ppg	2°L	55%
2.5 lb.	Amber DME	44 ppg	10°L	45%

Hops

1 oz. Willamette	60 min.	Boil	5% AA
1 oz. Fuggle	15 min.	Boil	5% AA
1 oz. Willamette	10 min.	Boil	5% AA
1 oz. Fuggle	0 min.	Boil	5% AA

Other Additions

0.5 tsp.	Yeast Nutrient	10 min.	Boil
1 tsp.	Irish Moss	15 min.	Boil

Fermentation

Yeast: Wyeast 1028 London Ale

Pitch 150 billion cells, equivalent to 1 to 2 fresh smack packs. Ferment between 65°F and 67°F.

Packaging

Carbonate to 1.9 volumes or prime with 2.7 ounces corn sugar.

London-Style ESB

The extra special bitter, or ESB, is the richest, hoppiest version of the bitter beer category. If you are unfamiliar with this style, the ESB is similar to an American pale ale in body and hop character but has comparatively more malt character. Although the listed Light LME works well here, a nice English malt extract like Maris Otter LME could also be used to lend the characteristic biscuit flavors commonly associated with the style. This recipe exclusively uses East Kent Golding, a traditional English ale hop; however, any characterful English hop variety will work well. Finally, this recipe features Wyeast 1968 London ESB strain, famous for its malty, fruity English fermentation character and low attenuation. To help drive down the final gravity, this recipe features an attenuative corn sugar addition. If you plan to switch to another, more attenuative English yeast strain, consider omitting the corn sugar addition and replacing with additional LME.

Brewing Stats

BREWING LEVEL:	Easy
BOIL DURATION:	60 minutes
OG:	1.051
FG:	1.014
ATTENUATION:	72%
IBU:	35
ABV:	4.8%
COLOR:	8 SRM

Fermentables

7 lb.	Light LME	37 ppg	2°L	83%
1 lb.	Crystal 60L	34 ppg	60°L	12%
8 oz.	Corn Sugar	45 ppg	0°L	5%

Hops

2 oz.	East Kent Golding	60 min.	Boil	5% AA
1 oz.	East Kent Golding	10 min.	Boil	5% AA
1 oz.	East Kent Golding	0 min.	Boil	5% AA

Other Additions

0.5 tsp.	Yeast Nutrient	10 min.	Boil
1 tsp.	Irish Moss	15 min.	Boil

Fermentation

Yeast: Wyeast 1968 London ESB Ale

Pitch 200 billion cells, equivalent to 2 fresh smack packs. Ferment between 63°F and 65°F.

Packaging

Carbonate to 1.9 volumes or prime with 2.7 oz. of corn sugar.

Scottish 80/-

Scottish shilling beers (the /- symbol stands for "shilling") are maltier, slightly sweeter versions of English bitters. This recipe employs a traditional technique known as wort caramelization. Here, part of the unhopped wort is condensed to promote caramelization and Maillard reactions, imparting unfermentable sweetness, color, and malt character in the final beer. In all-grain brewing, wort caramelization is typically accomplished by collecting 1 gallon of first runnings and condensing down by 75 percent before adding back to the boil. In extract brewing, this same technique can be mimicked by removing 1 gallon of wort from the brew kettle before hops are added, condensing it by 75 percent and then adding it back to the main boil. While the wort caramelization technique is a bit more effort, I find it gives this style that extra bit of malt character that seems to be missing in other 80/- recipes.

Brewing Stats

BREWING LEVEL:	Intermediate
BOIL DURATION:	120 minutes
OG:	1.050
FG:	1.013
ATTENUATION:	74%
IBU:	18
ABV:	4.9
COLOR:	11 SRM

Fermentables

8 lb.	Light LME	37 ppg	2°L	98%
3 oz.	Roasted Barley	30 ppg	550°L	2%

Hops

1 oz.	East Kent Golding	60 min.	Boil	6% AA

Other Additions

0.5 tsp.	Yeast Nutrient	10 min.	Boil
1 tsp.	Irish Moss	15 min.	Boil

Additional Instruction

Use wort caramelization by condensing 1 gallon of unhopped wort by 75% and add back to main boil once reduced.

Fermentation

Yeast: Wyeast 1728 Scottish Ale

Pitch 260 billion cells, equivalent to 2 to 3 fresh smack packs. Ferment between 55°F and 57°F.

Packaging

Carbonate to 2.1 volumes or prime with 3.2 ounces corn sugar.

 BREWING TIP

Make a 60/-, 70/-, or 90/- version of this recipe by simply scaling up or down the malt extract. As a rough estimate, 1 pound of LME per 10/- should work achieve the desired result.

SMaSH Beer

SMaSH beer, or just SMaSH for short, is an acronym for single malt and single hop, a popular homebrewing style. A SMaSH beer allows the brewer to explore the character of brewing ingredients by exclusively employing only one hop variety, one base malt variety, and one yeast strain. Since the beer recipe is simple, it allows for easy evaluation of individual ingredients. When developing this recipe, I sought to learn the character of a new Bohemian floor-malted pilsner malt, Hersbrucker hops, and the White Labs San Francisco Lager yeast strain. It was a great success, and helped me to learn and evaluate the character of these three brewing ingredients, which in turn helped me to dial-in other recipes, like the California Common Beer and Pilsner recipes in this chapter. When you discover a new hop variety or interesting yeast strain, consider using a SMaSH beer recipe as its first brew.

Brewing Stats

BREWING LEVEL: EASY

BOIL DURATION: 60 MINUTES

OG: 1.043

FG: 1.011

ATTENUATION: 75%

IBU: 17

ABV: 4.2%

COLOR: 2 SRM

Fermentables

7 lb.	Pilsner LME	37 ppg	2°L	100%

Hops

1 oz.	Hersbrucker	60 min.	Boil	4% AA
1 oz.	Hersbrucker	10 min.	Boil	4% AA

Other Additions

1 tsp.	Irish Moss	15 min.	Boil
0.5 tsp.	Yeast Nutrient	10 min.	Boil

Fermentation

Yeast: White Labs WLP810 San Francisco Lager

Pitch 230 billion cells, equivalent to 2 to 3 fresh vials. Ferment between 58°F and 60°F.

Packaging

Carbonate to 2.4 volumes or prime with 4 ounces corn sugar.

Cream Stout

Cream stout, also known as sweet stout and milk stout, is similar to oatmeal stout in character, full of rich, flavorful malt with a coffee/chocolate-like roastiness and hints of dark fruit and caramel. Cream stout draws its name from a special ingredient: lactose, an unfermentable sugar originally derived from the milk of dairy cattle. The lactose is left behind after fermentation, creating a stout with a full body, creamy mouthfeel, and a bit of sweetness. When paired with roasted barley and chocolate malt, the result is a beer character similar to sweetened espresso. When brewing, I find neutral yeasts like American and Dry English Ale, work best. Also, if you keg, consider using a nitrogen system and stout faucet, the combination of which helps to enhance the creaminess of this style.

Brewing Stats

BREWING LEVEL:	Easy
BOIL DURATION:	60 minutes
OG:	1.054
FG:	1.011
ATTENUATION:	72%
IBU:	30
ABV:	5.1%
COLOR:	44 SRM

Fermentables

6 lb.	Light LME	37 ppg	2°L	65%
1 lb.	Crystal 40L	34 ppg	40°L	10%
1 lb.	Roasted Barley	30 ppg	550°L	10%
1 lb.	Lactose	41 ppg	1°L	10%
8 oz.	Chocolate Malt	30 ppg	475°L	5%

Hops

0.75 oz.	Magnum	60 min.	Boil	14% AA

Other Additions

0.5 tsp.	Yeast Nutrient	10 min.	Boil
1 tsp.	Irish Moss	15 min.	Boil

Fermentation

Yeast: Wyeast 1450 Denny's Favorite 50

Pitch 220 billion cells, equivalent to 2 to 3 fresh smack packs. Ferment at 68°F.

Packaging

Carbonate to 2.1 volumes or prime with 3.2 ounces corn sugar.

Robust Porter

Rich, malty, and roasty, Robust Porter is a modern spin on the traditional strong porters from the eighteenth and ninetieth centuries. The grain bill in this recipe closely matches Jamil's from Brewing Classic Styles and is one I've brewed many times. My favorite to use in this recipe is Wyeast 1028 London Ale, which yields a light English ester profile and balances the intense roasted character from the Chocolate and Black Patent Malts. When brewing, avoid replacing any of the roasted malt with roasted barley, the signature specialty malt in stout. Also, this recipe becomes better with age, peaking in flavor between 3 to 5 months, in my experience.

Brewing Stats

BREWING LEVEL:	Easy
BOIL DURATION:	60 minutes
OG:	1.064
FG:	1.016
ATTENUATION:	75%
IBU:	37
ABV:	6.3%
COLOR:	39 SRM

Fermentables

7 lb.	Light LME	37 ppg	2°L	63%
2 lb.	Munich LME	37 ppg	8°L	18%
1 lb.	Crystal 40L	34 ppg	40°L	9%
12 oz.	Chocolate Malt	30 ppg	475°L	6%
8 oz.	Black Patent	30 ppg	550°L	4%

Hops

1 oz.	Magnum	60 min. Boil	14% AA
1 oz.	East Kent Golding	0 min. Boil	5% AA

Other Additions

1 tsp.	Irish Moss	15 min.	Boil
0.5 tsp.	Yeast Nutrient	10 min.	Boil

Fermentation

Yeast: Wyeast 1028 London Ale

Pitch 300 billion cells, equivalent to 3 fresh smack packs. Ferment between 65°F and 68°F.

Packaging

Carbonate to 2.1 volumes or prime with 3.2 ounces corn sugar.

Belgian Blond

While light in color, malt, and hop character, Belgian blond is a highly flavorful Belgian strong ale style that features the pleasant fruit esters and spicy phenols you expect from Belgian yeast strains. If you are unfamiliar with the style, Belgian blond is similar in color and character to Belgian tripel except a bit less malty and a bit lower in ABV. The key to this style is attenuation, and keeping the malt from becoming cloyingly sweet. To strike the key balance, this recipe uses a great deal of cane sugar to achieve a characteristic dry finish. If necessary, further attenuation can be achieved by slowly ramping up the temperature to 72°F toward the end of fermentation. Also, while any of the many Belgian yeast strains will work well, I prefer the fermentation character from Wyeast 3787 Trappist High Gravity in this recipe.

Brewing Stats

BREWING LEVEL:	Easy
BOIL DURATION:	60 minutes
OG:	1.062
FG:	1.010
ATTENUATION:	83%
IBU:	20
ABV:	6.7%
COLOR:	3 SRM

Fermentables

6 lb.	Pilsner LME	37 ppg	2°L	65%
1.5 lb.	Cane Sugar	45 ppg	0°L	15%
1 lb.	Wheat DME	44 ppg	3°L	10%
1 lb.	Munich LME	37 ppg	8°L	10%

Hops

1 oz.	Styrian Golding	60 min.	Boil	5% AA
1 oz.	Styrian Golding	15 min.	Boil	5% AA

Other Additions

1 tsp.	Irish Moss	15 min.	Boil
0.5 tsp.	Yeast Nutrient	10 min.	Boil

Fermentation

Yeast: Wyeast 3787 Trappist High Gravity

Pitch 250 billion cells, equivalent to 2 to 3 fresh smack packs. Ferment between 64°F and 70°F.

Packaging

Carbonate to 2.7 volumes or prime with 5 ounces corn sugar.

Belgian Witbier

Belgian Witbier (Wit) is a popular wheat beer style known for its light golden appearance and delicate balance of flavors. This recipe reflects this great style by keeping things simple. Using just fresh Wheat LME and a touch of Hallertau Mittelfrüh for bittering, the majority of the flavor comes through spice additions and fermentation character. In my Wits, I prefer a 50/50 blend of bitter and sweet dried orange peel, although many brewers report great results using fresh orange zest. Also, when adding coriander, make sure to use freshly ground seed to give the beer a fragrant, lemony punch. Additionally, any Belgian yeast strain will do well in this recipe, although I am partial to Wyeast 3944 Belgian Witbier, which has a nice balance between ester and phenolic compounds. Brew this refreshing and characterful Belgian Wit during the hot summertime months.

Brewing Stats

BREWING LEVEL:	Easy
BOIL DURATION:	60 minutes
OG:	1.049
FG:	1.011
ATTENUATION:	78%
IBU:	12
ABV:	5%
COLOR:	3 SRM

Fermentables

8 lb.	Wheat LME	37 ppg	3°L	100%

Hops

1 oz.	Hallertau Mittelfrüh	60 min.	Boil	4% AA

Other Additions

1 tsp.	Irish Moss	15 min.	Boil
1 oz.	Bitter Orange Peel	10 min.	Boil
0.5 tsp.	Yeast Nutrient	10 min.	Boil
0.5 oz.	Ground Coriander Seed	10 min.	Boil
1 oz.	Sweet Orange Peel	10 min.	Boil

Fermentation

Yeast: Wyeast 3944 Belgian Witbier

Pitch 190 billion cells, equivalent to 2 fresh vials. Ferment between 66°F and 70°F.

Packaging

Carbonate to 3.2 volumes or prime with 6 ounces corn sugar.

German Hefeweizen

German Hefeweizen is the ever-popular wheat beer style that showcases yeasty, bready malt with pleasant banana esters and clove phenolics. The best German Weizens follow a fairly basic recipe but use dialed-in fermentation to achieve a balanced character. Many brewers report a well-balanced fermentation on the lower end of ale fermentation temperatures, in low to mid-60s. Unlike most bottled-conditioned beers, it's traditional to serve a Hefeweizen with its yeast sediment. To do so, swirl the remaining ounce of beer and top off your glass.

Brewing Stats

BREWING LEVEL:	Easy
BOIL DURATION:	60 minutes
OG:	1.043
FG:	1.011
ATTENUATION:	75%
IBU:	16
ABV:	4.2%
COLOR:	3 SRM

Fermentables

7 lb.	Wheat LME	37 ppg	3°L	100%

Hops

1 oz.	Hersbrucker	60 min.	Boil	5% AA

Other Additions

0.5 tsp.	Yeast Nutrient	10 min.	Boil
1 tsp.	Irish Moss	15 min.	Boil

Fermentation

Yeast: Wyeast 3068 Weihenstephan Wheat

Pitch 170 billion cells, equivalent to 1 to 2 fresh smack packs. Ferment between 62°F and 65°F.

Packaging

Carbonate to 3.2 volumes or prime with 6 ounces corn sugar.

Farmhouse IPA

This farmhouse IPA recipe is a cross between the peppery, fruity, pizzazz of a saison and the intense herbal, spicy hop character of an American IPA. Of all the beers I've ever brewed, I've never had a beer evolve as much over time as this one did. Initially, its character was fresh, intensely herbal, and spicy, with a bit of saison fermentation character on the finish. However, after a few weeks, it emerged as a very rustic drink with pronounced saison character balanced by dank, earthy hop character. Then, toward the end of six months, it became very fruity and toasty with a bit of supporting orange-citrus, herbal hop character. While its character was always a bit unexpected, it made for an entertaining drink and was very refreshing during the early summer months. When you're looking for something interesting, give this Farmhouse IPA recipe a whirl; your taste buds certainly will not be bored.

Brewing Stats

BREWING LEVEL:	Easy
BOIL DURATION:	60 minutes
OG:	1.056
FG:	1.004
ATTENUATION:	92%
IBU:	45
ABV:	6.7%
COLOR:	5 SRM

Fermentables

6 lb.	Pilsner LME	37 ppg	2°L	67%
3 lb.	Munich LME	37 ppg	8°L	33%

Hops

1 oz.	Magnum	60 min.	Boil	14% AA
1 oz.	Saaz	10 min.	Boil	4% AA
1 oz.	Saaz	0 min.	Boil	4% AA
2 oz.	Saaz	5 days	Dry Hop	4% AA

Other Additions

0.5 tsp.	Yeast Nutrient	10 min.	Boil
1 tsp.	Irish Moss	15 min.	Boil

Fermentation

Yeast: Wyeast 3711 French Saison

Pitch 220 billion cells, equivalent to 2 to 3 fresh smack packs. Ferment between 68°F and 77°F.

Packaging

Carbonate to 2.7 volumes or prime with 5 ounces corn sugar.

American-Style Wheat Beer

Unlike its fruity and spicy German and Belgian wheat cousins, American wheat beer is clean and neutral, showing off a nice bready, cracker malt along with a low degree of American hop character. To achieve this, brewers utilize clean ale (and sometimes lager) yeast, most often American ale strains like US-05 but also Kölsch and Altbier strains, all of which help emphasize the bready character of this style. While American wheat beers can be quite diverse, my preference is to keep them simple and sessionable, using just enough fresh wheat malt to get to 4 percent ABV. However, for something unique, try adding a bit of late hops like Citra or Centennial to add a citrusy, tropical fruit character in the final beer. Either way, it will be a refreshing addition to your next summer barbecue.

Brewing Stats

BREWING LEVEL:	Easy
BOIL DURATION:	60 minutes
OG:	1.041
FG:	1.009
ATTENUATION:	78%
IBU:	18
ABV:	4.2%
COLOR:	3 SRM

Fermentables

7 lb.	Wheat LME	35 ppg	3°L	100%

Hops

0.5 oz.	Centennial	60 min.	Boil	9% AA

Other Additions

1 tsp.	Irish Moss	15 min.	Boil
0.5 tsp.	Yeast Nutrient	10 min.	Boil

Fermentation

Yeast: Safale US-05

Pitch 160 billion cells, equivalent to 8 grams rehydrated dry yeast. Ferment at 68°F.

Packaging

Carbonate to 2.7 volumes or prime with 5 ounces corn sugar.

Imperial Apricot Wheat

While I don't consider myself a competition brewer, I'll occasionally enter a few of my brews. This is one of my award winners, an imperial version of an apricot wheat beer. This recipe imperializes both the malt and fruit character of a standard fruit wheat beer, using 10 pounds of Wheat LME, 6 pounds of apricot purée, and 4 ounces of apricot extract. The result is a 7 percent ABV strong ale with a big, bready malt flavor and intense apricot/stone fruit character. When brewing, use standard American wheat beer brewing techniques, and after primary fermentation is complete, rack the beer and apricot purée into a secondary to ferment out the sugars from the purée. After secondary fermentation is complete, add the apricot extract and package as desired.

Brewing Stats

BREWING LEVEL:	Intermediate
BOIL DURATION:	60 minutes
OG:	1.062
FG:	1.010
ATTENUATION:	83%
IBU:	19
ABV:	6.7%
COLOR:	4 SRM

Fermentables

10 lb.	Wheat LME	37 ppg	3°L	100%

Hops

0.5 oz.	Magnum	60 min.	Boil	14% AA

Other Additions

0.5 tsp.	Yeast Nutrient	10 min.	Boil
6 lb.	Apricot Purée	14 days	Secondary
4 oz.	Apricot Extract	N/A	Bottle

Fermentation

Yeast: Safale US-05

Pitch 280 billion cells, equivalent to 14 grams rehydrated dry yeast. Ferment at 68°F.

Packaging

Carbonate to 2.7 volumes or prime with 5 ounces corn sugar.

Simcoe Imperial IPA

Intensely hoppy, imperial IPA is the king of the hop bombs, not only for its fierce bitterness but also highly flavorful and aromatic hop character, often featuring the newest and best American hop varieties. The keys to a great double IPA are judicious late hopping and a high degree of attenuation (below 1.010 is best). Any Pacific Northwest hop varieties will do well in a double IPA, but this recipe relies on the mainstay of IPAs, Simcoe hops. This recipe also includes a high proportion of corn sugar to aid in the high degree of attenuation that is critical for striking a balance between the intense hop character and supportive malt structure. Be sure to package and carbonate sooner rather than later; even though this is a big beer, double IPAs are best enjoyed fresh.

Brewing Stats

BREWING LEVEL:	Advanced
BOIL DURATION:	60 minutes
OG:	1.070
FG:	1.008
ATTENUATION:	88%
IBU:	94
ABV:	8.2%
COLOR:	5 SRM

Fermentables

9 lb.	Light LME	37 ppg	2°L	82%
1.5 lb.	Corn Sugar	45 ppg	0°L	14%
8 oz.	Crystal 40L	34 ppg	40°L	4%

Hops

2 oz.	Simcoe	60 min.	Boil	12% AA
1 oz.	Simcoe	15 min.	Boil	12% AA
1 oz.	Simcoe	10 min.	Boil	12% AA
1 oz.	Simcoe	5 min.	Boil	12% AA
1 oz.	Simcoe	0 min.	Boil	12% AA
2 oz.	Simcoe	5 days	Dry Hop	12% AA

Other Additions

1 tsp.	Irish Moss	15 min.	Boil
0.5 tsp.	Yeast Nutrient	10 min.	Boil

Fermentation

Yeast: Safale US-05

Pitch 450 billion cells, equivalent to 23 grams rehydrated dry yeast. Ferment at 68°F.

Packaging

Carbonate to 2.4 volumes or prime with 4 ounces corn sugar.

Saison

The ever popular saison is known for its highly flavorful, fruity, peppery, spicy, and near wildlike yeast character. While this recipe features four different malts, it's merely to provide a canvas for showing off the main event, the saison fermentation character. This recipe works well with any saison yeast strain or saison yeast blend; however, I am personally partial to the fermentation character from Wyeast 3724 Belgian Saison, which I think tends to have a more pronounced peppery quality. If you plan to use this yeast strain, be prepared for a bit of a battle, as it is known for fermentation trouble including sluggish and even stuck fermentation. In fermentation, progressively increase its temperature by 1°F to 2°F per day throughout the active portion of fermentation, ending at 80°F to 90°F to achieve full attenuation. All this being said, your hard work will not go unrewarded, as this yeast produces a wonderfully characterful and complex saison, perfect for warming springtime weather.

Brewing Stats

BREWING LEVEL:	Easy
BOIL DURATION:	60 minutes
OG:	1.057
FG:	1.010
ATTENUATION:	82%
IBU:	29
ABV:	6.1%
COLOR:	3 SRM

Fermentables

6 lb.	Pilsner LME	37 ppg	2°L	67%
1 lb.	Cane Sugar	45 ppg	0°L	11%
1 lb.	Munich LME	37 ppg	8°L	11%
1 lb.	Wheat LME	37 ppg	3°L	11%

Hops

0.75 oz.	Magnum	60 min.	Boil	14% AA

Other Additions

0.5 tsp.	Yeast Nutrient	10 min.	Boil
1 tsp.	Irish Moss	15 min.	Boil

Fermentation

Yeast: Wyeast 3724 Belgian Saison

Pitch 220 billion cells, equivalent to 2 to 3 fresh smack packs. Ferment between 68°F and 80°F+.

Packaging

Carbonate to 3.2 volumes or prime with 6 ounces corn sugar.

My First Stout

This recipe is called "My First Stout" not because it is a beginner stout recipe (although it is a good choice for beginners), but because it is the recipe from my very first homebrewing kit. Reminiscent of a dry Irish stout in style, this stout has a prominent coffee/roasted character from the substantial dose of roasted barley which is complemented by the firm hop character of the Northern Brewer and Fuggle hops, lending a bittersweet chocolate quality. The dry yeast S-04 is quite a characterful strain, and will lend a noticeable fruitiness when fermented warm. The intense flavors of this recipe hide flaws well, making it a solid recipe for beginners. Just reading it reminds me of my very first brew days, and its magic still carries on today in my brewing.

Brewing Stats

BREWING LEVEL:	Easy
BOIL DURATION:	60 minutes
OG:	1.047
FG:	1.012
ATTENUATION:	74%
IBU:	32
ABV:	4.6%
COLOR:	31 SRM

Fermentables

7 lb.	Light LME	37 ppg	2°L	88%
1 lb.	Roasted Barley	30 ppg	500°L	12%

Hops

1 oz.	Northern Brewer	60 min.	Boil	8% AA
1 oz.	Fuggle	15 min.	Boil	5% AA

Other Additions

0.5 tsp.	Yeast Nutrient	10 min.	Boil
1 tsp.	Irish Moss	15 min.	Boil

Fermentation

Yeast: Safale S-04

Pitch 180 billion cells, equivalent to 9 grams rehydrated dry yeast. Ferment between 64°F and 68°F.

Packaging

Carbonate to 2.1 volumes or prime with 3.2 ounces corn sugar.

Belgian Tripel

Belgian tripels feature a deep gold color and soft malt character that allows the spicy phenols and fruity esters to shine. Like a Belgian dubbel, fermentation is key to achieving the desired balance and attenuation. This recipe uses a large addition of cane sugar to maximimize fermentability and achieve a high degree of attenuation. Because of this, you may want to bump up the nutrient addition as simple sugars are nutrient deficient. Also, to aid in attenuation, I suggest slowly ramping up the fermentation temperature roughly 1°F per day until 70°F to 72°F is reached. This will increase yeast activity and help to further dry out the beer. Lastly, this recipe works well with any Trappist yeast strain, although I am very fond of the balanced fermentation character of Wyeast 3787 Trappist High Gravity in this beer style.

Brewing Stats

BREWING LEVEL:	Advanced
BOIL DURATION:	60 minutes
OG:	1.079
FG:	1.012
ATTENUATION:	85%
IBU:	24
ABV:	8.8%
COLOR:	4 SRM

Fermentables

10 lb.	Pilsner LME	37 ppg	2°L	80%
1.5 lb.	Cane Sugar	45 ppg	0°L	12%
1 lb.	Munich LME	37 ppg	8°L	8%

Hops

0.75 oz.	Magnum	60 min.	Boil	14% AA

Other Additions

0.5 tsp.	Yeast Nutrient	10 min.	Boil
1 tsp.	Irish Moss	15 min.	Boil

Fermentation

Yeast: Wyeast 3787 Trappist High Gravity

Pitch 600 billion cells, equivalent to 6 fresh smack packs. Ferment between 65°F and 68°F.

Packaging

Carbonate to 2.4 volumes or prime with 4 ounces corn sugar.

Rye Pale Ale

Citrusy and spicy, this rye pale ale is an interesting twist on the American pale ale style. At one time, rye beers were exclusive to all-grain brewing, as rye requires mashing. However, due to the explosive growth of homebrewing, fresh rye malt extracts are now widely available. While rye LME varies in composition, this recipe assumes 70 percent pale malt, 20 percent rye malt, and 10 percent Crystal 60L blend (other formulations may require some recipe adjustment). When brewing, I like to pair mine with 100 percent Centennial hops, as I find its clean citrus character cuts through the more prominent body and spiciness of the rye character. Also, this recipe uses a 10 percent corn sugar addition to help attenuate the beer and counteract the heavy mouthfeel of rye malt, thus keeping the beer at a medium body. I've brewed this recipe both as all-grain and extract versions, and both were incredibly enjoyable, especially during late spring and early summertime months.

Brewing Stats

BREWING LEVEL:	Easy
BOIL DURATION:	60 minutes
OG:	1.054
FG:	1.012
ATTENUATION:	77%
IBU:	30
ABV:	5.4
COLOR:	7 SRM

Fermentables

6 lb.	Rye LME	37 ppg	9°L	72%
1.5 lb.	Amber DME	44 ppg	10°L	18%
12 oz.	Corn Sugar	45 ppg	0°L	10%

Hops

0.5 oz. Centennial	60 min.	Boil	10% AA
1 oz. Centennial	15 min.	Boil	10% AA
1 oz. Centennial	0 min.	Boil	10% AA

Other Additions

1 tsp.	Irish Moss	15 min.	Boil
0.5 tsp.	Yeast Nutrient	10 min.	Boil

Fermentation

Yeast: Safale US-05

Pitch 210 billion cells, equivalent to 11 grams rehydrated dry yeast. Ferment at 68°F.

Packaging

Carbonate to 2.4 volumes or prime with 4.0 ounces corn sugar.

Nut Brown Ale

Toffee, nutty, and biscuity in quality, English brown ales are unlike their American cousins, featuring round, slightly sweet malt and balanced hop character. This recipe is a tribute to the Northern English brown style and best brewed with English versions of the specialty malts. While this recipe calls for Light LME, using an Maris Otter LME when fresh will enhance the overall biscuity character in this recipe. Also, while this recipe only features bittering hops, a hoppier version can be easily made by adding approximately an ounce East Kent Golding as a late addition, with 5 to 15 minutes left in the boil.

Brewing Stats

BREWING LEVEL:	Easy
BOIL DURATION:	60 minutes
OG:	1.049
FG:	1.013
ATTENUATION:	74%
IBU:	22
ABV:	4.8%
COLOR:	15 SRM

Fermentables

7 lb.	Light LME	37 ppg	2°L	82%
8 oz.	Special Roast	33 ppg	50°L	6%
8 oz.	Crystal 60L	34 ppg	60°L	6%
4 oz.	Biscuit Malt	35 ppg	23°L	3%
4 oz.	Chocolate Malt	30 ppg	425°L	3%

Hops

1.5 oz.	East Kent Golding	60 min.	Boil	5% AA

Other Additions

1 tsp.	Irish Moss	15 min.	Boil
0.5 tsp.	Yeast Nutrient	10 min.	Boil

Fermentation

Yeast: Wyeast 1098 British Ale

Pitch 190 billion cells, equivalent to 2 fresh smack packs. Ferment at 68°F.

Packaging

Carbonate to 2.1 volumes or prime with 3.2 ounces corn sugar.

Dunkelweizen

As its name suggests, Dunkelweizen is a darker, richer German wheat beer, with a character that can be thought of as a cross between a Munich Dunkel and German Hefeweizen. In addition to featuring wheat malt and banana/clove fermentation character, Dunkelweizens typically use a substantial portion of Munich malt, producing a rich malt and amber color. When brewing, follow the basic recipe suggestions in the German Hefeweizen recipe. Also, consider brewing a Dunkelweizen by repitching the yeast from a recent Hefeweizen batch using harvesting and rinsing techniques discussed in Chapter 20.

Brewing Stats

BREWING LEVEL:	Easy
BOIL DURATION:	60 minutes
OG:	1.052
FG:	1.013
ATTENUATION:	75%
IBU:	11
ABV:	5.1%
COLOR:	14 SRM

Fermentables

5 lb.	Wheat LME	37 ppg	3°L	58%
3 lb.	Munich LME	37 ppg	8°L	35%
8 oz.	CaraMunich	34 ppg	50°L	5%
4 oz.	Carafa Special II	30 ppg	418°L	2%

Hops

1 oz.	Hersbrucker	60 min.	Boil	4% AA

Other Additions

0.5 tsp.	Yeast Nutrient	10 min.	Boil
1 tsp.	Irish Moss	15 min.	Boil

Fermentation

Yeast: Wyeast 3068 Weihenstephan Wheat

Pitch 200 billion cells, equivalent to 2 fresh smack packs. Ferment between 62°F and 65°F.

Packaging

Carbonate to 3.2 volumes or prime with 6 ounces corn sugar.

All-Grain Ale Recipes

This section includes 16 world-class all-grain recipes. For the all-grain brewing, there are a few extra assumptions worth consideration. The all-grain recipes presented here assume a mash efficiency of 75 percent and single-infusion mash technique. However, feel free to modify these recipes to use step or decoction mash techniques accordingly.

The Nazz (Session IPA)

Guest recipe by Chip Walton and Drew Beechum: If you don't know Chip Walton, you should. Chip is the man behind the explosively popular web TV show *Chop and Brew*, documenting the culture behind food and fermentation. In episode 3, Chip and friends brew a few beers in honor of 311 Day, including this recipe, a session-style American IPA. Jointly developed with Drew Beechum, this recipe was designed to be a session version of the great Pliny the Elder Double IPA by Vinnie Cilurzo of the Russian River Brewing Company. When you are looking for something light and sessionable yet full of intense American-style hoppiness, give this recipe a whirl.

Brewing Stats

BREWING LEVEL:	Intermediate
BOIL DURATION:	60 minutes
OG:	1.046
FG:	1.012
ATTENUATION:	75%
IBU:	55
ABV:	4.5%
COLOR:	3 SRM

Fermentables

4.75 lb.	Maris Otter Malt	37 ppg	3°L	47 %
4.75 lb.	Two-Row Malt	37 ppg	1°L	47 %
8 oz.	Dextrin Malt	34 ppg	1°L	5 %

Hops

0.88 oz.	Warrior	60 min.	Boil	15.0% AA
0.88 oz.	Columbus	10 min.	Boil	12.0% AA
0.5 oz.	Falconer's Flight	5 min.	Boil	10.0% AA
0.5 oz.	7C's	0 min.	Boil	10.0% AA

Other Additions

1 tsp.	Irish Moss	15 min.	Boil
0.5 tsp.	Yeast Nutrient	10 min.	Boil

All-Grain Instructions

Use a single infusion mash at 152°F for 60 minutes.

Fermentation

Yeast: Wyeast 1056 American Ale

Pitch 200 billion cells, equivalent to 2 fresh smack packs. Ferment at 68°F.

Packaging

Carbonate to 2.4 volumes or prime with 4 ounces corn sugar.

Dry Irish Stout

When most people think of stout, they think of Guinness Draught, the most popular version of the dry Irish stout style. While dry Irish stout is not my favorite stout style, I make sure to make one in the late winter to have on tap for St. Patrick's Day. This recipe is the common starting point for the style, composed of roughly 70 percent pale malt, 20 percent flaked barley, and 10 percent roasted barley. While the roasted barley gives the beer its coffeelike character, the flaked barley is key, lending the sought-after creamy mouthfeel and dense head. As an all-grain recipe, I would recommend using a step mash including a protein rest to handle this large proportion of flaked barley.

Brewing Stats

BREWING LEVEL:	Advanced
BOIL DURATION:	60 minutes
OG:	1.042
FG:	1.011
ATTENUATION:	74%
IBU:	45
ABV:	4.1%
COLOR:	34 SRM

Fermentables

6.5 lb.	Maris Otter Malt	37 ppg	3°L	69%
2 lb.	Flaked Barley	32 ppg	2°L	21%
1 lb.	Roasted Barley	30 ppg	550°L	10%

Hops

1 oz.	Magnum	60 min.	Boil	14% AA

Other Additions

0.5 tsp.	Yeast Nutrient	10 min.	Boil
1 tsp.	Irish Moss	15 min.	Boil

All-Grain Instructions

Use a single infusion mash at 150°F for 60 minutes.

Fermentation

Yeast: Wyeast 1084 Irish Ale

Pitch 160 billion cells, equivalent to 1 to 2 fresh smack packs. Ferment between 65°F and 68°F.

Packaging

Carbonate to 1.9 volumes or prime with 2.7 ounces corn sugar.

Belgian Dubbel

One of the Trappist ales, Belgian dubbel is an amber-brown strong ale with rich malt and complex ester/phenol character. Like all Belgian strong ales, fermentation is key to achieving the balance and attenuation in a well-brewed example. To achieve a high degree of attenuation, this recipe uses both a low temperature mash rest at 148°F and a simple sugar addition to maximize fermentability. While corn or cane sugar will work well, this recipe uses 1 pound of amber Belgian candi syrup, contributing fermentability and lending notes of toffee, vanilla, and toasted bread in the final beer. Lastly, this recipe works well with any Trappist yeast strain, and although I am fond of the fermentation character of Wyeast 1214 Belgian Abbey, Wyeast 3787 is also very nice.

Brewing Stats

BREWING LEVEL:	Advanced
BOIL DURATION:	90 minutes
OG:	1.064
FG:	1.008
ATTENUATION:	87%
IBU:	18
ABV:	7.3%
COLOR:	17 SRM

Fermentables

7.5 lb.	Pilsner Malt	37 ppg	1°L	53%
3 lb.	Munich Malt	35 ppg	7°L	22%
1.5 lb.	Aromatic Malt	35 ppg	33°L	10%
1 lb.	Amber Belgian Candi Syrup	32 ppg	45°L	7%
12 oz.	CaraMunich	34 ppg	50°L	5%
8 oz.	Special B	34 ppg	115°L	3%

Hops

0.5 oz. Magnum 60 min. Boil 14% AA

Other Additions

0.5 tsp.	Yeast Nutrient	10 min.	Boil
1 tsp.	Irish Moss	15 min.	Boil

All-Grain Instructions

Use a single infusion mash at 148°F for 60 minutes.

Fermentation

Yeast: Wyeast 1214 Belgian Abbey

Pitch 350 billion cells, equivalent to 3 to 4 fresh smack packs. Ferment between 64°F and 68°F.

Packaging

Carbonate to 2.4 volumes or prime with 4 ounces corn sugar.

Winter Solstice Winter Warmer

The winter solstice marks the longest night of the year, and even though it occurs in the dead of winter, every day afterward gets a little bit brighter, which makes me cheerful for the coming spring weather. Thus, as a personal tradition, I brew a winter warmer style beer to mark the occasion, and this recipe was one of my favorite iterations. A fusion of brewing traditions, this recipe merges the grain bill from a Belgian dubbel, hops and yeast from American ales, and wort caramelization techniques from Scottish shilling ales, the result of which is a very rich, malty ale with notes of toffee, dark fruit, and toast. At 7.4 percent ABV, this is not a big beer by any strong ale standards, but a large snifter full certainly puts a flush in your cheeks.

Brewing Stats

BREWING LEVEL:	Advanced
BOIL DURATION:	120 minutes
OG:	1.069
FG:	1.012
ATTENUATION:	82%
IBU:	36
ABV:	7.4%
COLOR:	18 SRM

Fermentables

9 lb.	Two-Row Malt	37 ppg	1°L	64%
1.5 lb.	Munich Malt	35 ppg	10°L	10%
1.5 lb.	Corn Sugar	45 ppg	0°L	10%
1 lb.	CaraMunich	34 ppg	50°L	7%
1 lb.	Special B	34 ppg	115°L	7%
4 oz.	Pale Chocolate Malt	30 ppg	207°L	2%

Hops

1 oz.	Magnum	60 min.	Boil	14% AA

Other Additions

0.5 tsp.	Yeast Nutrient	10 min.	Boil
1 tsp.	Irish Moss	15 min.	Boil

All-Grain Instructions

Use a single infusion mash at 148°F for 60 minutes.

Additional Instruction

Condense the 1 gallon of first runnings by 75% (4 cups) and add to the boil. In my brewing process, I notice the 75% reduction mark to corresponding to 216°F on my digital thermometer.

Fermentation

Yeast: Wyeast 1272 American Ale II

Pitch 450 billion cells, equivalent to 4 to 5 fresh smack packs. Ferment between 66°F and 68°F.

Packaging

Carbonate to 2.4 volumes or prime with 4 ounces corn sugar.

Smoked Porter

Porter is one of most versatile beer styles, pairing well with fruit, chocolate, and, in this case, smoke. When done well, smoked porters balance bonfirelike smoke character with rich, malty, roasted character from the base porter style. The grain bill in this recipe closely matches Jamil's from Brewing Classic Styles, and uses 30 percent German Rauch malt, a traditional smoked malt used in German Rauchbier that lends a sweet, moderately intense smoked character to the beer. In brewing, this recipe is all-grain simply because you need to mash the smoked malt in order to incorporate its character; however, this recipe can be converted to extract if a suitably fresh Rauch malt extract can be found. Also, in fermentation, any neutral ale yeast will work, but I prefer Wyeast 1728 Scottish Ale for this recipe.

Brewing Stats

BREWING LEVEL:	Intermediate
BOIL DURATION:	60 minutes
OG:	1.062
FG:	1.018
ATTENUATION:	71%
IBU:	28
ABV:	5.7%
COLOR:	40 SRM

Fermentables

6 lb.	Two-Row Malt	37 ppg	1°L	44%
4 lb.	Rauch Malt	37 ppg	3°L	30%
1 lb.	Munich Malt	35 ppg	10°L	7%
12 oz.	Chocolate Malt	30 ppg	475°L	5%
12 oz.	Crystal 40L	34 ppg	40°L	5%
12 oz.	Crystal 75L	34 ppg	75°L	5%
8 oz.	Black Patent	30 ppg	550°L	4%

Hops

0.75 oz.	Magnum	60 min.	Boil	14% AA

Other Additions

1 tsp.	Irish Moss	15 min.	Boil
0.5 tsp.	Yeast Nutrient	10 min.	Boil

All-Grain Instructions

Use a single infusion mash at 152°F for 60 minutes.

Fermentation

Yeast: Wyeast 1728 Scottish Ale

Pitch 350 billion cells, equivalent to 3 to 4 fresh smack packs. Ferment between 55°F and 65°F.

Packaging

Carbonate to 2.1 volumes or prime with 3.2 ounces corn sugar.

London-Style Brown Porter

Rich, malty, and chocolately, brown porter is a traditional English-style porter with significantly less roasted quality than its robust porter cousin. The key ingredient to this recipe is British Brown Malt, a darkly kilned malt variety known for light roasted, nutty, and slight bitter flavors, which contribute to the slightly roasty, chocolate character in the style. This recipe was the result of my attempt to clone one of my favorite commercial brews, Fuller's London Porter. When served fresh, this recipe comes very close to the real deal, and with age, it becomes nearly indistinguishable. If you are going for a similar clone, make sure to use Wyeast 1968 London ESB, a nearly identical yeast strain to the one used by Fullers.

Brewing Stats

BREWING LEVEL:	Intermediate
BOIL DURATION:	60 minutes
OG:	1.052
FG:	1.012
ATTENUATION:	77%
IBU:	22
ABV:	5.2%
COLOR:	25 SRM

Fermentables

9 lb.	Maris Otter Malt	37 ppg	2°L	80%
1 lb.	British Brown Malt	32 ppg	55°L	8%
1 lb.	Crystal 75L	34 ppg	75°L	8%
8 oz.	Chocolate Malt	30 ppg	475°L	4%

Hops

1.5 oz.	Fuggle	60 min.	Boil	5% AA

Other Additions

1 tsp.	Irish Moss	15 min.	Boil
0.5 tsp.	Yeast Nutrient	10 min.	Boil

All-Grain Instructions

Use a single infusion mash at 150°F for 60 minutes.

Fermentation

Yeast: Wyeast 1968 London ESB Ale

Pitch 200 billion cells, equivalent to 2 fresh smack packs. Ferment between 64°F and 66°F.

Packaging

Carbonate to 2.1 volumes or prime with 3.2 ounces corn sugar.

Saison Ordnaire

Guest recipe by Drew Beechum: Homebrewing legend, prolific writer, and saison aficionado, Drew Beechum is one of my homebrewing heroes. Drew is known for wacky, experimental recipes as well as his "less is more" brewing philosophy he calls "Brewing on the Ones." Following the same brewing principles, this is his simple saison recipe. Since saisons are all about the complex fermentation character, this simple yet elegant recipe keeps its yeast character up front. For more information on Drew's brewing, check out his blog at maltosefalcons.com/blogs/drew-beechum. Also, pick up a copy his latest book, *Experimental Homebrewing* (co-written with Denny Conn).

Brewing Stats

BREWING LEVEL:	Intermediate
BOIL DURATION:	90 minutes
OG:	1.048
FG:	1.008
ATTENUATION:	84%
IBU:	24
ABV:	5.2%
COLOR:	2 SRM

Fermentables

9 lb.	Pilsner	37 ppg	1°L	90 %
0.5 lb.	Flaked Wheat	35 ppg	2°L	5 %
0.5 lb.	Cane Sugar	45 ppg	0°L	5 %

Hops

0.5 oz.	Magnum	60 min.	Boil	14% AA
0.5 oz.	Saphir	10 min.	Boil	4% AA

Other Additions

0.5 tsp.	Yeast Nutrient	10 min.	Boil
1 tsp.	Irish Moss	15 min.	Boil

All-Grain Instructions

Use a single infusion mash at 150°F for 60 minutes.

Fermentation

Yeast: Any Saison yeast strain or yeast blend.

Pitch 180 billion cells, equivalent to 2 fresh smack packs. Pitch between 63°F and 64°F and let fermentation rise to mid-70s.

Packaging

Carbonate to 3.2 volumes or prime with 6 ounces corn sugar.

T-34 (Russian Imperial Stout)

Guest recipe by Chris Colby: All-time great homebrewer and fellow Austin ZEALOTS member, Chris Colby is a pillar of the homebrewing community, known for his work in the *Brew Your Own* magazine, homebrewing experiments on the Basic Brewing podcasts, and more recently, his brewing blog *Beer and Wine Journal.* This is his Russian imperial stout recipe, a rich and robust strong stout with intense roasted malt character and a velvety finish. While imperial stouts require some advanced fermentation techniques, Chris can guide you through the process, detailing the technical and stylistic considerations around the brewing of this recipe in one of the many style series at the *Beer and Wine Journal.* For more information on the T-34 Russian Imperial Stout and overall great brewing information, check Chris's blog posts at beerandwinejournal.com.

Brewing Stats

BREWING LEVEL:	Advanced
BOIL DURATION:	60 minutes
OG:	1.095
FG:	1.021
ATTENUATION:	78%
IBU:	65
ABV:	9.7%
COLOR:	80 SRM

Fermentables

16.5 lb.	Maris Otter Malt	37 ppg	2°L	77%
1.75 lb.	Black Patent	30 ppg	550°L	8%
1.25 lb.	Roasted Barley	30 ppg	500°L	5%
14 oz.	Crystal 90L	34 ppg	90°L	4%
14 oz.	Chocolate Malt	30 ppg	350°L	4%

Hops

2 oz.	Challenger	60 min.	Boil	14% AA
0.75 oz.	Fuggle	15 min.	Boil	5% AA
0.75 oz.	East Kent Golding	10 min.	Boil	5% AA
0.75 oz.	East Kent Golding	0 min.	Boil	5% AA

Other Additions

0.5 tsp.	Yeast Nutrient	10.0 min.	Boil
1 tsp.	Irish Moss	15.0 min.	Boil

All-Grain Instructions

Use a single infusion mash at 150°F for 60 minutes.

Fermentation

Yeast: Safale US-05

Pitch 450 billion cells, equivalent to 23 grams rehydrated dry yeast. Ferment at 68°F.

Packaging

Carbonate to 2.2 volumes or prime with 4.75 ounces corn sugar.

Dewberry's Oatmeal Stout

Guest recipe by Dan and Joelle Dewberry: Fellow Austin ZEALOTS members Dan and Joelle Dewberry are a national award-winning and all-around awesome homebrewing couple from Austin, TX. This is their oatmeal stout recipe, which pushes the limits of the style. Big, bold, and roasty with a creamy finish, this hearty stout is a must-have come wintertime. When brewing, you may want to incorporate a short protein rest to handle the oatmeal addition.

Brewing Stats

BREWING LEVEL:	Advanced
BOIL DURATION:	60 minutes
OG:	1.061
FG:	1.015
ATTENUATION:	75%
IBU:	30
ABV:	6.0%
COLOR:	39 SRM

Fermentables

9 lb.	Maris Otter Malt	37 ppg	3°L	65%
20 oz.	Aromatic Malt	35 ppg	20°L	9%
20 oz.	Flaked Oats	32 ppg	2°L	9%
10 oz.	Roasted Barley	30 ppg	500°L	5%
10 oz.	Chocolate Malt	30 ppg	475°L	5%
10 oz.	Crystal 20L	34 ppg	20°L	5%
5 oz.	Black Patent	30 ppg	525°L	2%

Hops

1 oz.	Challenger	60 min.	Boil	8% AA
0.5 oz.	East Kent Golding	60 min.	Boil	6% AA

Other Additions

1 tsp.	Irish Moss	15 min.	Boil
0.5 tsp.	Yeast Nutrient	10 min.	Boil

All-Grain Instructions

Use a single infusion mash at 152°F for 60 minutes.

Fermentation

Yeast: White Labs WLP007 Dry English Ale

Pitch 250 billion cells, equivalent to 2 to 3 fresh vials. Ferment between 65°F and 68°F.

Packaging

Carbonate to 2.1 volumes or prime with 3.2 ounces corn sugar.

Brass Hat IPA (English-Style IPA)

Guest recipe by Jay Kaffenberger: Jay is one of my good homebrewing buddies and a fellow Austin ZEALOTS member. This recipe is one Jay's favorites, an English IPA featuring biscuity English malts balanced with highly flavorful English hops. Not only is this is a solid recipe, but it's also the winner of the 2012 Flix Brewhouse Pro-Am competition. This recipe is a good example of late hopping coupled with first wort hopping, which Jay highly recommends for this recipe. If you're looking for something English or just taking a break from the ripping hops of American IPAs, give this hoppy, yet well-balanced English IPA recipe a try.

Brewing Stats

BREWING LEVEL:	Intermediate
BOIL DURATION:	60 minutes
OG:	1.064
FG:	1.017
ATTENUATION:	74%
IBU:	52
ABV:	6.2%
COLOR:	11 SRM

Fermentables

11 lb.	Maris Otter Malt	37 ppg	3°L	78%
1 lb.	Biscuit	35 ppg	23°L	7%
1 lb.	Crystal 20L	34 ppg	20°L	7%
12 oz.	Crystal 60L	34 ppg	60°L	5%
4 oz.	Dextrin Malt	34 ppg	1°L	1%

Hops

1 oz.	Magnum	60 min.	First Wort	15% AA
0.5 oz.	East Kent Golding	20 min.	Boil	6% AA
0.5 oz.	Fuggle	15 min.	Boil	5.0% AA
0.5 oz.	Willamette	10 min.	Boil	5% AA
0.5 oz.	East Kent Golding	5 min.	Boil	6% AA
0.5 oz.	Willamette	0 min.	Boil	5% AA
0.5 oz.	Fuggle	0 min.	Boil	5% AA

Other Additions

1 tsp.	Irish Moss	15 min.	Boil
0.5 tsp.	Yeast Nutrient	10 min.	Boil

All-Grain Instructions

Use a single infusion mash at 152°F for 60 minutes.

Fermentation

Yeast: White Labs WLP002 English Ale

Pitch 250 billion cells, equivalent to 2 to 3 fresh vials. Ferment at 67°F.

Packaging

Carbonate to 2.4 volumes or prime with 4 ounces corn sugar.

Denny's Wry Smile (Rye IPA)

Guest recipe by Denny Conn: If there could only be one spokesman for brewing with rye, then homebrewing legend Denny Conn would be it. Among Denny's well-known homebrewing recipes, his rye IPA is arguably the most famous among homebrewers and the gold standard for the rye IPA style. When brewing IPAs, attenuation is key in order to showcase the hop-forward character, and this is especially true for rye IPAs, as rye adds considerable body and mouthfeel to beer. For more information on this recipe and great brewing advice, especially on experimenting with the brewing ingredients and the brewing process, check out Denny's book *Experimental Homebrewing* (co-written with Drew Beechum).

Brewing Stats

BREWING LEVEL: ADVANCED

BOIL DURATION: 75 MINUTES

OG: 1.075

FG: 1.013

ATTENUATION: 82%

IBU: 76

ABV: 8%

COLOR: 10 SRM

Fermentables

11 lb.	Two-Row Malt	37 ppg	1°L	67%
3 lb.	Rye Malt	37 ppg	3°L	18%
1.25 lb.	Crystal 60L	34 ppg	60°L	7%
8 oz.	Dextrin Malt	34 ppg	1°L	3%
8 oz.	Wheat Malt	37 ppg	2°L	3%

Hops

1 oz.	Mount Hood	75 min.	First Wort	5% AA
1.5 oz.	Columbus	60 min.	Boil	16% AA
0.5 oz.	Mount Hood	30 min.	Boil	5% AA
1.5 oz.	Mount Hood	0 min.	Boil	5% AA
1 oz.	Columbus	5 days	Dry Hop	16% AA

Other Additions

1 tsp.	Irish Moss	15 min.	Boil
0.5 tsp.	Yeast Nutrient	10 min.	Boil
1 tsp.	Gypsum (if needed)	60 min.	Boil

All-Grain Instructions

Use a single infusion mash at 153°F for 60 minutes.

Fermentation

Yeast: Wyeast 1450 Denny's Favorite 50

Pitch 375 billion cells, equivalent to 4 fresh smack packs. Ferment between 63°F and 65°F.

Packaging

Carbonate to 2.7 volumes or prime with 5 ounces corn sugar.

Witches Brew Pumpkin Ale

Although it seems like pumpkin-spiced foods become more and more popular each fall, pumpkin beer has been around for a long time and is deeply rooted in American brewing traditions. This pumpkin beer recipe reflects the modern day style and includes pumpkin in the mash and pumpkin pie spices at the finish. You could use canned pumpkin purée in this recipe, but I prefer the character of freshly roasted whole pumpkin. To prepare, remove the seeds from a small pie pumpkin and cut it into 2-inch pieces. Place flesh side down on a baking sheet and roast at 350°F until soft and easily pierced, about 30 to 45 minutes. Remove the skin before adding to the mash. When adding pumpkin to the mash, make sure to use a lautering aid, like rice hulls, as pumpkin is famous for creating stuck sparges.

Brewing Stats

BREWING LEVEL:	Advanced
BOIL DURATION:	60 minutes
OG:	1.051
FG:	1.013
ATTENUATION:	75%
IBU:	20
ABV:	5%
COLOR:	7 SRM

Fermentables

9 lb.	Two-Row Malt	37 ppg	1°L	82%
1 lb.	Munich Malt	35 ppg	10°L	8%
1 lb.	Crystal 40L	34 ppg	40°L	8%
4 oz.	Biscuit	35 ppg	23°L	2%
2 lb.	Roasted Pumpkin	N/A	N/A	N/A

Hops

0.5 oz.	Magnum	60 min.	Boil	14% AA

Other Additions

0.5 tsp.	Yeast Nutrient	10 min.	Boil
1 tsp.	Irish Moss	15 min.	Boil
1.5 tsp.	Pumpkin Pie Spice	5 min.	Boil

All-Grain Instructions

Use a single infusion mash at 152°F for 60 minutes. When using pumpkin, include in the mash with lautering aids.

Fermentation

Yeast: Safale US-05

Pitch 200 billion cells, equivalent to 10 grams rehydrated dry yeast. Ferment at 68°F.

Packaging

Carbonate to 2.4 volumes or prime with 4 ounces corn sugar.

BREWING TIP

You can brew a "pumpkin" ale without the pumpkin. Most people identify pumpkin character through pumpkin spices rather than the pumpkin itself. Save yourself the time and possible frustration by omitting the pumpkin mash and simply add pumpkin spices at the end of the boil.

Boat Bitter (English-Style bitter)

Guest recipe by Michael Dawson: Michael Dawson is a homebrew blogger and the brand manager for Wyeast Laboratories, Inc. He's also a fishing enthusiast, and a few years back, he needed a low-gravity yet flavorful beer to accompany him and his buddies on fishing trips. The aptly named Boat Bitter was thus created, a light and sessionable English-style bitter, full of flavor from floor-malted English malts and English yeast fermentation character. The original recipe calls for the limited edition Wyeast 1026 Cask Ale, but Michael suggests Wyeast 1099 Whitbread Ale as a replacement. For more information on this recipe, check out Mike's blog at thebeerengineblog. com. Also, check out the brew day of this recipe featured on the web TV show *Chop and Brew* at chopandbrew.com.

Brewing Stats

BREWING LEVEL:	Intermediate
BOIL DURATION:	60 minutes
OG:	1.036
FG:	1.008
ATTENUATION:	77%
IBU:	35
ABV:	3.6%
COLOR:	5 SRM

Fermentables

7.63 lb.	Maris Otter Malt	37 ppg	3°L	98%
3 oz.	Dark Crystal 80L	34 ppg	80°L	2%

Hops

1 oz.	First Gold	60 min.	Boil	8% AA
0.63 oz.	First Gold	15 min.	Boil	8% AA
0.38 oz.	First Gold	0 min.	Boil	8% AA

Other Additions

0.5 tsp.	Yeast Nutrient	10 min.	Boil
1 tsp.	Irish Moss	15 min.	Boil

All-Grain Instructions

Use a single infusion mash at 152°F for 60 minutes.

Fermentation

Yeast: Wyeast 1026 Cask Ale or Wyeast 1099 Whitbread Ale

Pitch 150 billion cells, equivalent to 1 to 2 fresh smack packs. Ferment at 68°F.

Packaging

Carbonate to 1.9 volumes or prime with 2.7 ounces corn sugar.

Great Scot Wee Heavy

Strong Scotch ale, commonly referred to as "wee heavy," is the Scottish equivalent of English barleywine. With its rich caramel character and complementary malt sweetness, Great Scot Wee Heavy makes for a great dessert beer and pleasant night cap, especially during the cooler fall and winter months. This recipe closely follows the 80/- recipe, including the wort caramelization technique. Since this is an all-grain recipe, use the first gallon of runnings when performing wort caramelization.

Brewing Stats

BREWING LEVEL:	Advanced
BOIL DURATION:	120 minutes
OG:	1.089
FG:	1.021
ATTENUATION:	76%
IBU:	19
ABV:	8.8%
COLOR:	16 SRM

Fermentables

19 lb.	Golden Promise Malt	37 ppg	3°L	99%
4 oz.	Roasted Barley	30 ppg	550°L	1%

Hops

1.5 oz.	East Kent Golding	60 min.	Boil	6% AA

Other Additions

0.5 tsp.	Yeast Nutrient	10 min.	Boil
1 tsp.	Irish Moss	15 min.	Boil

All-Grain Instruction

Use a single infusion mash at 150°F for 60 minutes.

Additional Instruction

Use wort caramelization by condensing one gallon of unhopped wort by 75% and add back to main boil once reduced.

Fermentation

Yeast: Wyeast 1728 Scottish Ale

Pitch 700 billion cells, equivalent to 7 fresh smack packs. Ferment between 55°F and 57°F.

Packaging

Carbonate to 2.1 volumes or prime with 3.2 ounces corn sugar.

Evil Twin (Red IPA)

Guest recipe by Jamil Zainasheff: This homebrewer truly needs no introduction. Jamil Zainasheff is one of the most decorated competition homebrewers ever. He's also a prolific writer and podcaster, known for his books *Brewing Classic Styles* and *Yeast* as well as The Jamil Show and Brew Strong podcasts on the Brewing Network. More recently, Jamil has transitioned to commercial brewing by founding Heretic Brewing Company in Fairfield, California. This recipe is a Jamil-approved clone of Heretic's flagship beer, Evil Twin, a very bold but balanced red IPA full of rich malt and intense American hops. When brewing, make sure to focus on pitching the right amount of yeast, which helps attenuate the beer enough and results in the great balance of malt and hops. For more information on Jamil's brewing, check out mrmalty.com and hereticbrewing. com. Also, make sure to grab a pint of Heretic beer when on tap at your local brew pub.

Brewing Stats

BREWING LEVEL:	Advanced
BOIL DURATION:	60 minutes
OG:	1.065
FG:	1.013
ATTENUATION:	80%
IBU:	42
ABV:	6.8%
COLOR:	18 SRM

Fermentables

12.25 lb.	Rahr Two-Row Malt	37 ppg	1°L	86%
1.75 lb.	Crystal 75L	34 ppg	75°L	12%
1.5 oz.	Roasted Barley	30 ppg	550°L	1%
1.5 oz.	Carafa Special III	30 ppg	535°L	1%

Hops

1 oz.	Columbus	60 min.	Boil	16% AA
1 oz.	Columbus	0 min.	Boil	16% AA
1 oz.	Citra	0 min.	Boil	14% AA
2.5 oz.	Citra	5 days	Dry Hop	14% AA
1 oz.	Columbus	5 days	Dry Hop	16% AA

Other Additions

0.5 tsp.	Yeast Nutrient	10 min.	Boil
1 tsp.	Irish Moss	15 min.	Boil

All-Grain Instructions

Use a single infusion mash at 154°F for 60 minutes.

Fermentation

Yeast: White Labs WLP001 California Ale

Pitch 250 billion cells, equivalent to 2 to 3 fresh vials. Ferment between 66°F and 68°F.

Packaging

Carbonate to 2.4 volumes or prime with 4 ounces corn sugar.

The Mad Fermentationist's Berliner Weisse

Guest recipe Michael Tonsmeire: Author of the premiere homebrewing blog *The Mad Fermentationist*, Michael Tonsmeire is a sour beer expert, funk specialist, and all-around all-star homebrewer. While sour fermentation is an advanced brewing technique, a great place to start is with his simple Berliner Weisse recipe, a light, tart, lemony sour ale originating from Berlin in Germany. Michael uses the no-boil process, achieved by simply bringing the wort to 210°F to eliminate any bugs from the mash. Also, he recommends the fermentation character produced from the combination of *Saccharomyces*, *Lactobacillus*, and *Brettanomyces*. Lastly, Michael says this is a great recipe for playing with other beer additions like fruit, dry hops, and citrus zest. For more information on this recipe and great sour beer brewing information, check out Michael's blog at TheMadFermentationist.com and his book *American Sour Beers*.

Brewing Stats

BREWING LEVEL:	Advanced
BOIL DURATION:	0 minutes (just bring the wort to 210°F)
OG:	1.032
FG:	1.005
ATTENUATION:	84%
IBU:	7
ABV:	3.6%
COLOR:	2 SRM

Fermentables

4.4 lb.	Wheat Malt	37 ppg	2°L	63%
2.6 lb.	Pilsner Malt	37 ppg	1°L	37%

Hops

0.75 oz.	Saaz	60 min.	Mash Hop	3% AA

Other Additions

0.5 tsp.	Yeast Nutrient	10 min.	Boil
1 tsp.	Irish Moss	15 min.	Boil

All-Grain Instructions

Use a single infusion mash at 152°F for 60 minutes.

Fermentation

Yeast: Safale US-05, WLP672 *Lactobacillus brevis*, and WLP650 *Brettanomyces bruxellensis*

Michael recommends making a 1 liter starter of the *Lactobacillus* and pitching the US-05 and *Brettanomyces* as packaged. Ferment between 65°F and 68°F. Age for 3 to 4 months until gravity is stable.

Packaging

Carbonate to 3.2 volumes or prime with 6 ounces corn sugar.

CAUTION

Avoid shared brewing equipment between sour and nonsour beers! As a rule of thumb, it's best to invest in separate brewing equipment for sour beer brewing to avoid contamination in your nonsour beers.

Extract Hybrid Recipes

This section includes four wonderful extract hybrid recipes, from Kölsch to California common beer.

"Ale"-toberfest

Oktoberfest is a popular style, but the traditional lager yeast requires more temperature control than most new brewers can achieve. Instead of going without, homebrewers have developed a hybrid version of Oktoberfest that has a lagerlike character without the active temperature control. While hybrid ale yeasts like Kölsch and clean ale yeasts like US-05 work well, I'm a big fan of White Lab's San Francisco lager yeast, which produces a clean lager character at ale fermentation temperatures. When possible, give this one as cold a ferment as possible and use a solid pitch rate to minimize production of fruity esters.

Brewing Stats

BREWING LEVEL:	Easy
BOIL DURATION:	60 minutes
OG:	1.051
FG:	1.013
ATTENUATION:	74%
IBU:	20
ABV:	5%
COLOR:	9 SRM

Fermentables

8 lb.	Munich LME	37 ppg	8°L	95%
8 oz.	CaraMunich	34 ppg	50°L	5%

Hops

0.5 oz.	Magnum	60 min.	Boil	14% AA

Other Additions

1 tsp.	Irish Moss	15 min.	Boil
0.5 tsp.	Yeast Nutrient	10 min.	Boil

Fermentation

Yeast: White Labs WLP810 San Francisco Lager

Pitch 270 billion cells, equivalent to 2 to 3 fresh vials. Ferment between 58°F and 60°F.

Packaging

Carbonate to 2.4 volumes or prime with 4 ounces corn sugar.

 BREWING TIP

Try the "Ale-toberfest" pseudo-lager technique with any of your favorite lager styles when cold fermentation temperatures are not possible in your brewing process.

Kölsch

One of my favorite light styles, Kölsch is a German ale originating from Cologne region in Germany. For those who haven't had the style, Kölsch is much like cross between the light, crisp character of a German pilsner and the malt character and color of a Munich Helles, resulting in a malty yet crisp light-colored brew. To brew a great Kölsch, fermentation is key. Using a Kölsch yeast strain is critical, as fermentation character is the defining flavor profile for this light beer. Also, this recipe calls for attenuation near 80 percent, so if you have difficulty with attenuation, I'd suggest replacing some of the malt with corn sugar to help dry things out. Lastly, a relatively cold fermentation will lend a cleaner, more lagerlike character than traditional warm ale fermentation, so do your best to get the temperature down as low as possible; 58°F to 60°F works well in my brewing.

Brewing Stats

BREWING LEVEL:	Easy
BOIL DURATION:	60 minutes
OG:	1.047
FG:	1.009
ATTENUATION:	80%
IBU:	21
ABV:	4.9%
COLOR:	3 SRM

Fermentables

6 lb.	Pilsner LME	37 ppg	2°L	80%
1 lb.	Munich LME	37 ppg	8°L	14%
8 oz.	Corn Sugar	45 ppg	0°L	6%

Hops

0.5 oz.	Magnum	60 min.	Boil	14% AA

Other Additions

1 tsp.	Irish Moss	15 min.	Boil
0.5 tsp.	Yeast Nutrient	10 min.	Boil

Fermentation

Yeast: Wyeast 2565 Kölsch

Pitch 240 billion cells, equivalent to 2 to 3 fresh smack packs. Ferment between 58°F and 60°F.

Packaging

Carbonate to 2.4 volumes or prime with 4 ounces corn sugar.

"Steamy" California Common

Possibly my favorite hybrid style, California common is known for its incredible balance between the slightly toasty, caramel-y malt and the earthy, rustic hop character of Northern Brewer hops, which are signature to the style. Most people are familiar with the California common style through Anchor Brewing's Steam Beer, and this recipe is a close match. When pitching on the cold side, make sure to use adequate pitch rates and aeration to achieve the necessary degree of attenuation. I typically brew this recipe in late summer, as I find its more pronounced malt and rustic hop character to be a perfect fit for the changing of seasons.

Brewing Stats

BREWING LEVEL:	Easy
BOIL DURATION:	60 minutes
OG:	1.052
FG:	1.012
ATTENUATION:	77%
IBU:	35
ABV:	5.2%
COLOR:	11 SRM

Fermentables

7 lb.	Light LME	37 ppg	4°L	82%
12 oz.	Crystal 60L	34 ppg	60°L	9%
10 oz.	Corn Sugar	45 ppg	0°L	7%
3 oz.	Pale Chocolate Malt	30 ppg	207°L	2%

Hops

1.25 oz.	Northern Brewer	60 min.	Boil	7% AA
1.25 oz.	Northern Brewer	10 min.	Boil	7% AA
1.25 oz.	Northern Brewer	0 min.	Boil	7% AA

Other Additions

1 tsp.	Irish Moss	15 min.	Boil
0.5 tsp.	Yeast Nutrient	10 min.	Boil

Fermentation

Yeast: White Labs WLP810 San Francisco Lager

Pitch 270 billion cells, equivalent to 2 to 3 fresh vials. Ferment between 58°F and 60°F.

Packaging

Carbonate to 2.4 volumes or prime with 4 ounces corn sugar.

Altbier

Rich malt paired with noble German hops, Altbier is a flavorful and well-balanced hybrid style originating from the Düsseldorf region in Germany. For those unfamiliar with the style, Altbier can be thought as a cross between a hoppy Oktoberfest and malty American pale ale, essentially a German pale ale. Like Kölsch, Altbier derives its signature character from Altbier yeast strains, which are necessary to achieve the flavor profile and fermentation character associated with the style. Also, while more traditional Altbier recipes utilize Spalt for hopping, I prefer the late hop character from Tettnang, which lends a nice spicy herbal character and pairs well with the grainy, toasted malt profile in this recipe.

Brewing Stats

BREWING LEVEL:	Easy
BOIL DURATION:	60 minutes
OG:	1.047
FG:	1.012
ATTENUATION:	75%
IBU:	46
ABV:	4.6%
COLOR:	11 SRM

Fermentables

7 lb.	Munich LME	37 ppg	8°L	89%
10 oz.	CaraMunich	34 ppg	56°L	7%
4 oz.	Melanoidin	34 ppg	25°L	3%
1 oz.	Carafa Special II	30 ppg	431°L	1%

Hops

0.75 oz.	Magnum	60 min.	Boil	14% AA
1 oz.	Tettnanger	30 min.	Boil	4% AA
1 oz.	Tettnanger	10 min.	Boil	4% AA

Other Additions

1 tsp.	Irish Moss	15 min.	Boil
0.5 tsp.	Yeast Nutrient	10 min.	Boil

Fermentation

Yeast: White Labs WLP036 Düsseldorf Alt

Pitch 240 billion cells, equivalent to 2 to 3 fresh vials. Ferment between 58°F and 60°F.

Packaging

Carbonate to 2.4 volumes or prime with 4 ounces corn sugar.

All-Grain Hybrid Recipes

This section includes three great all-grain hybrid recipes. As before, these all-grain recipes assume a mash efficiency of 75 percent.

'wiser-Guy Cream Ale

Despite its name, cream ales aren't creamy at all, but rather crisp, dry, and clean; more like an American light lager than a cream stout. Like their macrobrew cousins, cream ales have low malt and low hop character, which are achieved through flavorless adjuncts like rice or corn. Because of this, cream ales are often difficult to brew, as small flaws in your brewing process will be more apparent, so take great care in sanitation and fermentation when brewing. A well-brewed cream ale makes for a refreshing lawnmower beer in the summer and is a great way to introduce a macrobrew drinker to the craft beer world.

Brewing Stats

BREWING LEVEL:	Advanced
BOIL DURATION:	60 minutes
OG:	1.042
FG:	1.008
ATTENUATION:	80%
IBU:	12
ABV:	4.4%
COLOR:	1 SRM

Fermentables

5 lb.	Two-Row Malt	37 ppg	1°L	56%
2 lb.	Six-Row Malt	35 ppg	1°L	22%
2 lb.	Flaked Rice	40 ppg	0°L	22%

Hops

1 oz.	Liberty	60 min.	Boil	4% AA

Other Additions

1 tsp.	Irish Moss	15 min.	Boil
0.5 tsp.	Yeast Nutrient	10 min.	Boil

All-Grain Instructions

Use a single infusion mash at 148°F for 60 minutes

Fermentation

Yeast: Safale US-05

Pitch 220 billion cells, equivalent to 11 grams of rehydrated dry yeast. Ferment between 60°F and 64°F.

Packaging

Carbonate to 2.7 volumes or prime with 5 ounces corn sugar.

Steamin' Wife Lager (California Common)

Guest recipe by Don Osborn: Expert and popular homebrewer Don Osborn was one of the first to bring instructional and entertaining homebrewing videos to YouTube and is a frequent guest on the web TV show *Chop and Brew*. He also maintains an extensive online brewing log, which includes recipes and notes dating back to his first homebrew over a decade ago. Within his brewing log is this house recipe, Steamin' Wife Lager, a riff on a California common beer style. While Don changes this recipe up from time to time, this is one of his favorite iterations. Also, Don says this is a great base recipe to explore different hop varieties by using this grain bill to make a single hop beer. For more information on this recipe and all of Don's great homebrewing advice, check out his website donosborn.com and his popular YouTube channel youtube.com/user/donosborn.

Brewing Stats

BREWING LEVEL:	Intermediate
BOIL DURATION:	60 minutes
OG:	1.051
FG:	1.013
ATTENUATION:	75%
IBU:	45
ABV:	5%
COLOR:	5 SRM

Fermentables

10.5 lb.	Two-Row Malt	37 ppg	1°L	96 %
8 oz.	Simpsons Medium Crystal	34 ppg	55°L	4 %

Hops

1.5 oz.	Northern Brewer	60 min.	Boil	8% AA
0.5 oz.	Northern Brewer	30 min.	Boil	8% AA
1 oz.	Cascade	0 min.	Boil	7% AA

Other Additions

0.5 tsp.	Yeast Nutrient	10 min.	Boil
1 tsp.	Irish Moss	15 min.	Boil

All-Grain Instructions

Use a single infusion mash at 153°F for 60 minutes.

Fermentation

Yeast: Wyeast 2112 California Lager

Pitch 260 billion cells, equivalent to 2 to 3 fresh smack packs. Ferment between 58°F and 60°F.

Packaging

Carbonate to 2.4 volumes or prime with 4 ounces corn sugar.

Chris's Smoked Altbier

Guest recipe by Chris Rauschuber: Fellow Austin ZEALOTS member and nationally award-winning homebrewer Chris Rauschuber can brew a solid pint. I'm a big fan of Altbier and smoked beer in general, and Chris's Smoked Altbier recipe is a great twist on the style. When brewing, a cold fermentation will produce a Rauchbier lagerlike character. Also, Kölsch yeast strains have incredibly low flocculation, so longer conditioning times and/or the addition of finings may be necessary to produce bright beer.

Brewing Stats

BREWING LEVEL:	Intermediate
BOIL DURATION:	60 minutes
OG:	1.057
FG:	1.011
ATTENUATION:	80%
IBU:	39
ABV:	5.9%
COLOR:	16 SRM

Fermentables

6.5 lb.	Munich Malt	35 ppg	10°L	51%
5.5 lb.	Rauch Malt	37 ppg	3°L	43%
8 oz.	Caramunich Malt	34 ppg	56°L	3%
3 oz.	Carafa Special II	30 ppg	431°L	1%

Hops

1 oz.	Magnum	60 min.	Boil	14% AA

Other Additions

0.5 tsp.	Yeast Nutrient	10 min.	Boil
1 tsp.	Irish Moss	15 min.	Boil

All-Grain Instructions

Use a single infusion mash at 158°F for 60 minutes.

Fermentation

Yeast: Wyeast 2565 Kölsch

Pitch 292 billion cells, equivalent to 3 fresh smack packs. Ferment between 57°F and 60°F.

Packaging

Carbonate to 2.3 volumes or prime with 3.9 ounces corn sugar.

Extract Lager Recipes

This section includes eight extract lager recipes ranging from Munich Helles to German bock. Before brewing, check out Chapter 20 for more information on lager brewing techniques.

Munich Helles

Malty and slightly sweet with a touch of graininess, a well-brewed Munich Helles is a character-ful yet quaffable drink. The basics behind a good Helles comes down to fresh ingredients and dialed-in fermentation. Because of its low malt and low hops, there is little to hide flaws in fermentation or sanitization. Thus, when brewing, make sure to use cold fermentation, large pitch rates, and adequate aeration to achieve the clean fermentation and balanced attenuation needed for this light, crisp beer style. Brew this one in the late spring and be ready for the hot summertime weather.

Brewing Stats

BREWING LEVEL:	Intermediate
BOIL DURATION:	60 minutes
OG:	1.049
FG:	1.012
ATTENUATION:	76%
IBU:	21
ABV:	4.9%
COLOR:	3 SRM

Fermentables

7 lb.	Pilsner LME	37 ppg	2°L	87%
1 lb.	Munich LME	37 ppg	8°L	13%

Hops

0.5 oz.	Magnum	60 min.	Boil	14% AA

Other Additions

1 tsp.	Irish Moss	15 min.	Boil
0.5 tsp.	Yeast Nutrient	10 min.	Boil

Fermentation

Yeast: White Labs WLP833 German Bock Lager

Pitch 380 billion cells, equivalent to 3 to 4 fresh vials. Ferment between 48°F and 52°F.

Packaging

Carbonate to 2.4 volumes or prime with 4 ounces corn sugar.

German Pilsner

Light, crisp, and nicely hopped, there is nothing like a well-brewed German pilsner. This is also one of best styles to brew at home, since many pilsner imports are degraded due to heat staling and/or skunking from the dreaded green bottle. The key to a well-brewed German pilsner is clean fermentation and attenuation. The cleanest fermentation will result from cold fermentation between 48°F to 52°F using a large pitch of yeast. After the first few days of fermentation are complete, slowly ramping up the temperature will help to further attenuate the beer. This recipe calls for a corn sugar addition, which is not traditional in a German pilsner, but for the extract brewer it helps to dry the beer out and achieve the desired level of attenuation.

Brewing Stats

BREWING LEVEL:	Intermediate
BOIL DURATION:	60 minutes
OG:	1.047
FG:	1.009
ATTENUATION:	80%
IBU:	36
ABV:	4.9%
COLOR:	2 SRM

Fermentables

7 lb.	Pilsner LME	37 ppg	2°L	94%
8 oz.	Corn Sugar	45 ppg	0°L	6%

Hops

0.75 oz.	Magnum	60 min.	Boil	14% AA
1 oz.	Hallertau Mittelfrüh	10 min.	Boil	4% AA
1 oz.	Hallertau Mittelfrüh	0 min.	Boil	4% AA

Other Additions

1 tsp.	Irish Moss	15 min.	Boil
0.5 tsp.	Yeast Nutrient	10 min.	Boil

Fermentation

Yeast: Wyeast 2124 Bohemian Lager

Pitch 370 billion cells, equivalent to 3 to 4 fresh smack packs. Ferment between 48°F and 52°F.

Packaging

Carbonate to 2.4 volumes or prime with 4 ounces corn sugar.

Bohemian Pilsner

Of the pilsner styles, Bohemian pilsner is known for its softer, fuller malt with low yet pleasant spicy hop character. Also, while the German Pilsner seems to work well with any German hop variety, this Bohemian Pilsner really shines with Czech Saaz, lending its characteristic herbal, spicy character you expect in a "Bo pils." This recipe is a bit on the crisper side as I like my pilsners to be; however, feel free to increase the final gravity with a bit of dextrin malt if you like your Bohemian pilsner with a bit more body. Also, water can be critical, even for the extract version, so if your tap water is on the alkaline side, consider replacing with RO water and adding a bit of calcium chloride. When brewing, abide by typical lager fermentation techniques, including cold fermentation and lagering.

Brewing Stats

BREWING LEVEL:	Intermediate
BOIL DURATION:	60 minutes
OG:	1.056
FG:	1.014
ATTENUATION:	74%
IBU:	34
ABV:	5.4%
COLOR:	3 SRM

Fermentables

9.0 lb.	Pilsner LME	37 ppg	2°L	100%

Hops

0.75 oz.	Magnum	60 min.	Boil	14% AA
1 oz.	Saaz	10 min.	Boil	3% AA
1 oz.	Saaz	5 min.	Boil	3% AA
1 oz.	Saaz	0 min.	Boil	3% AA

Other Additions

0.5 tsp.	Yeast Nutrient	10 min.	Boil
1 tsp.	Irish Moss	15 min.	Boil

Fermentation

Yeast: Wyeast 2279 Czech Pils

Pitch 440 billion cells, equivalent to 4 to 5 fresh smack packs. Ferment between 48°F and 52°F.

Packaging

Carbonate to 2.4 volumes or prime with 4 ounces corn sugar.

Helles Bock

My favorite version of the Bock styles, Helles Bock is a strong lager full of rich malt with substantial toasted character and moderate sweetness balanced by smooth bitterness and sometimes a bit of late hops. While Helles Bock can be made entirely with Pilsner malt, I really like mine to have a nice portion of Munich malt, which brings out the rounded, toasted character in the beer. This recipe uses around 25 percent Munich Malt (assuming the Munich LME is a 50/50 blend), and can be altered based on your preferences. However, avoid pushing beyond 40 percent, as this version will likely become more of a traditional Bock than a Helles Bock. Like most lager styles, Helles Bock benefits from a cold fermentation, adequate pitch rate, and lager levels of aeration. Also, like most strong lagers, Helles Bock benefits from an extended lagering period, although in my experience, a well-brewing version can be enjoyed sooner than rather than later.

Brewing Stats

BREWING LEVEL:	Advanced
BOIL DURATION:	60 minutes
OG:	1.068
FG:	1.018
ATTENUATION:	74%
IBU:	27
ABV:	6.6%
COLOR:	7 SRM

Fermentables

6 lb.	Munich LME	37 ppg	$8°L$	55%
5 lb.	Pilsner LME	37 ppg	$2°L$	45%

Hops

0.75 oz.	Magnum	60 min.	Boil	14% AA

Other Additions

0.5 tsp.	Yeast Nutrient	10 min.	Boil
1 tsp.	Irish Moss	15 min.	Boil

Fermentation

Yeast: White Labs WLP833 German Bock Lager

Pitch 600 billion cells, equivalent to 6 fresh vials. Ferment between 48°F and 52°F.

Packaging

Carbonate to 2.4 volumes or prime with 4 ounces corn sugar.

Harvest Season Oktoberfest

Rich and malty with a hint of toast, Oktoberfest is what I crave come the beginning of fall weather. My Oktoberfest recipe had evolved over time, and this is one of my favorite versions. On occasion, I like to brew a bigger Oktoberfest, pushing the OG to 1.057 and FG 1.015, which can be done by adding an extra pound of Munich LME (assuming a 50/50 blend) in this recipe. Also, many brewers prefer hoppier versions than this recipe, so if desired, consider adding an ounce or so of your favorite Noble hop variety late in the boil for extra hop character. When brewing, make sure to use cold fermentation, large pitch rates, and adequate aeration to achieve a clean fermentation and attenuation. Also, while many brewers lager Oktoberfest for a month or more, I've found that well-brewed example can be mature quite quickly in a 2- to 3-week period.

Brewing Stats

BREWING LEVEL:	Intermediate
BOIL DURATION:	60 minutes
OG:	1.051
FG:	1.013
ATTENUATION:	74%
IBU:	20
ABV:	5%
COLOR:	9 SRM

Fermentables

8 lb.	Munich LME	37 ppg	8°L	95%
8 oz.	CaraMunich	34 ppg	50°L	5%

Hops

0.5 oz.	Magnum	60 min.	Boil	14% AA

Other Additions

0.5 tsp.	Yeast Nutrient	10 min.	Boil
1 tsp.	Irish Moss	15 min.	Boil

Fermentation

Yeast: White Labs WLP833 German Bock Lager

Pitch 400 billion cells, equivalent to 4 fresh vials. Ferment between 48°F and 52°F.

Packaging

Carbonate to 2.4 volumes or prime with 4 ounces corn sugar.

Munich Dunkel

Rich and toasty, Munich Dunkel is darker in color and more malt focused than its cousins Munich Helles and Oktoberfest. Like most lager styles, Dunkel benefits from a clean fermentation and appropriate lagering periods. However, when brewing an extract-based Dunkel, the key is sourcing 100 percent Munich malt extract. While the majority of recipes in this book assume Munich LME to be a 50/50 blend of Munich and Pilsner malts (the common blend sold in homebrew shops), this recipe is best brewed with a 100 percent Munich LME. Although often difficult to find, some extract producers, like Weyermann Maltings, make a great 100 percent Munich extract, which will yield the rich, toasted malt character expected in a well-brewed Munich Dunkel. If this extract is not available, 50/50 Munich/Pilsner extract will work okay, but will likely produce more of an Oktoberfest than Dunkel. Instead, consider performing a mini mash using 100 percent Munich malt along with the 50/50 Munich/Pilsner LME for a closer match of the style.

Brewing Stats

BREWING LEVEL:	Intermediate
BOIL DURATION:	60 minutes
OG:	1.050
FG:	1.013
ATTENUATION:	75%
IBU:	21
ABV:	4.9%
COLOR:	14 SRM

Fermentables

8 lb.	Munich LME	37 ppg	11°L	98%
3 oz.	Carafa Special II	30 ppg	418°L	2%

Hops

0.5 oz.	Magnum	60 min.	Boil	14% AA

Other Additions

1 tsp.	Irish Moss	15 min.	Boil
0.5 tsp.	Yeast Nutrient	10 min.	Boil

Fermentation

Yeast: White Labs WLP833 German Bock Lager

Pitch 400 billion cells, equivalent to 4 fresh vials. Ferment between 48°F and 52°F.

Packaging

Carbonate to 2.4 volumes or prime with 4 ounces corn sugar.

Bock

Very rich, slightly sweet, and intensely malty, German Bock can be thought as an amped-up version of an Oktoberfest or Munich Dunkel style. Traditionally, German Bocks come in many grades from standard to the strong Doppelbock and boozy Eisbock. This recipe is a simple yet characterful standard Bock, similar to the Oktoberfest, but with a bit more Munich LME and CaraMunich malts to increase the gravity, color, and sweetness. Like most lager styles, Bocks benefit from a cold fermentation, adequate pitch rate, and lager levels of aeration. However, unlike more sessionable lagers, Bocks greatly improve with extended lagering periods anywhere from 1 to 3 months for standard strength Bocks and up to 6 months for stronger versions. For this recipe, I recommend a 3-month lagering period to yield rich Bock-like character.

Brewing Stats

BREWING LEVEL:	Advanced
BOIL DURATION:	60 minutes
OG:	1.066
FG:	1.017
ATTENUATION:	74%
IBU:	27
ABV:	6.4%
COLOR:	12 SRM

Fermentables

10 lb.	Munich LME	37 ppg	8°L	91%
1 lb.	CaraMunich	34 ppg	50°L	9%

Hops

0.75 oz.	Magnum	60 min.	Boil	14% AA

Other Additions

1 tsp.	Irish Moss	15 min.	Boil
0.5 tsp.	Yeast Nutrient	10 min.	Boil

Fermentation

Yeast: White Labs WLP833 German Bock Lager

Pitch 600 billion cells, equivalent to 6 fresh vials. Ferment between 48°F and 52°F.

Packaging

Carbonate to 2.4 volumes or prime with 4 ounces corn sugar.

Summer Helles

A great alterative to macrobrew light lagers, the Summer Helles is a session version of the famous Munich Helles style. This recipe cuts about 15 percent of the fermentables from the Munich Helles recipe, and when well-brewed, results in a beer a bit lighter in character, but still flavorful and incredibly refreshing at 4.2 percent ABV. I brew this recipe every summer and surprise many of my fellow ZEALOTS on how tasty a light lager can actually be. When brewing, follow the recommendations detailed in the Munich Helles recipe. Also, due to its low ABV level, a short 2- to 3-week lager period is all that's necessary to get this one on tap.

Brewing Stats

BREWING LEVEL:	Intermediate
BOIL DURATION:	60 minutes
OG:	1.043
FG:	1.011
ATTENUATION:	75
IBU:	12
ABV:	4.2
COLOR:	3 SRM

Fermentables

6 lb.	Pilsner LME	37 ppg	2°L	86%
1 lb.	Munich LME	37 ppg	8°L	14%

Hops

1 oz.	Hersbrucker	60 min.	Boil	4% AA

Other additions

1 tsp.	Irish Moss	15 min.	Boil
0.5 tsp.	Yeast Nutrient	10 min.	Boil

Fermentation

Yeast: White Labs WLP833 German Bock Lager

Pitch 340 billion cells, equivalent to 3 to 4 fresh vials. Ferment between 48°F and 52°F.

Packaging

Carbonate to 2.4 volumes or prime with 4 ounces corn sugar.

All-Grain Lager Recipes

This section includes four outstanding all-grain lager recipes. As before, these all-grain recipes assume a mash efficiency of 75 percent. Before brewing, check out Chapter 20 for more information on lager brewing techniques.

Kerry's German Pilsner

Guest recipe by Kerry Martin: Crisp, hoppy, and refreshing, German pilsner is one of my all-time favorite beer styles, and decorated homebrewer Kerry Martin makes one of the best. Nothing gets me more excited than when Kerry brings a 2-liter growler of his latest batch of German pilsner to an Austin ZEALOTS group meeting. Kerry says he changes this recipe up from time to time, but this is one of his favorite iterations. Also, for competition brewers, this recipe is quite the medal winner and made it into the finals of the 2012 Sam Adams LongShot competition. If you're a fan of German pilsners, definitely give this recipe a try.

Brewing Stats

BREWING LEVEL:	Advanced
BOIL DURATION:	90 minutes
OG:	1.047
FG:	1.010
ATTENUATION:	78%
IBU:	38
ABV:	4.8%
COLOR:	2 SRM

Fermentables

9 lb.	Bohemian Pilsner Malt	37 ppg	1°L	88%
1 lb.	Torrified Wheat	37 ppg	2°L	9%
5 oz.	Acidulated Malt	27 ppg	3°L	3%

Hops

2.5 oz.	Hallertau Mittelfrüh	60 min.	Boil	4% AA
1.2 oz.	Saaz	15 min.	Boil	4% AA
1.5 oz.	Saaz	1 min.	Boil	4% AA

Other Additions

0.5 tsp.	Yeast Nutrient	10 min.	Boil
1 tsp.	Irish Moss	15 min.	Boil

All-Grain Instructions

Use a single infusion mash at 148°F for 60 minutes.

Fermentation

Yeast: White Labs WLP830 German Lager

Pitch 350 billion cells, equivalent to 3 to 4 fresh vials. Ferment at 50°F.

Packaging

Carbonate to 2.4 volumes or prime with 4 ounces corn sugar.

A Dark Night in Munich (Munich Dunkel)

Guest recipe by Corey Martin: While the Austin ZEALOTS don't have an official leader, we do unofficially recognize a head honcho, whom we affectionately call "the Primary Fermentor." Corey currently serves as our Primary Fermentor and for good reason: Corey can brew a mean pint. He is most known for this award-winning Munich Dunkel, winner of the 2011 Sam Adams LongShot competition. To make a rich, malty lager for the winter, give this Munich Dunkel recipe a try.

Brewing Stats

BREWING LEVEL:	Advanced
BOIL DURATION:	90 minutes
OG:	1.060
FG:	1.015
ATTENUATION:	75%
IBU:	20
ABV:	5.9%
COLOR:	21 SRM

Fermentables

8 lb.	Munich Malt	35 ppg	6°L	58%
2.25 lb.	Pilsner Malt	37 ppg	1°L	16%
15 oz.	Melanoidin Malt	34 ppg	25°L	6%
15 oz.	Crystal 40L	34 ppg	40°L	6%
9 oz.	Biscuit Malt	35 ppg	23°L	4%
7 oz.	Wheat Malt	37 ppg	2°L	3%
4.5 oz.	Crystal 60L	34 ppg	60°L	2%
3.5 oz.	Carafa Special II	30 ppg	418°L	1%
2 oz.	Chocolate Malt	30 ppg	425°L	1%

Hops

1.5 oz.	Hallertau Mittelfrüh	60 min.	Boil	4% AA
0.5 oz.	Hallertau Mittelfrüh	20 min.	Boil	4.2% AA

Other Additions

1 tsp.	Irish Moss	15 min.	Boil
0.5 tsp.	Yeast Nutrient	10 min.	Boil

All-Grain Instructions

Use a single infusion mash at 150°F for 60 minutes.

Additional Instruction

Pulverize the Carafa Special II and chocolate malt and add them to the mash during the lautering process.

Fermentation

Yeast: Wyeast 2124 Bohemian Lager

Pitch 460 billion cells, equivalent to 4 to 5 fresh smack packs. Ferment at 50°F.

Packaging

Carbonate to 2.4 volumes or prime with 4 ounces corn sugar.

May the Schwarzbier Be with You

Guest recipe from Marshall Schott: Marshall is brains behind the popular homebrewing blog *Brülosophy*. It features a reoccurring segment called "exBEERiment," which challenges many of the homebrewing-scale axioms like trub versus no trub and extract versus all-grain. One of the recipes he uses in performing these homebrewing experiments is this German Schwarzbier, a dark, malty, sessionable German lager with hints of toast and roast. While any German lager strain will work well in this recipe, he recommends a hybrid yeast strain, specifically White Labs WLP029 Kölsch, yielding a lager character without the fuss over lager techniques. For more information on this recipe and Marshall's great blog *Brülosophy*, check out brulosphy.com.

Brewing Stats

BREWING LEVEL:	Intermediate
BOIL DURATION:	60 minutes
OG:	1.052
FG:	1.013
ATTENUATION:	75%
IBU:	28
ABV:	5.2%
COLOR:	26 SRM

Fermentables

8.2 lb.	Pilsner Malt	37 ppg	1°L	71%
2.1 lb.	Munich Malt	35 ppg	10°L	19%
9 oz.	Carafa Special II	30 ppg	418°L	4%
7 oz.	Crystal 60L	34 ppg	60°L	4%
4.5 oz.	Chocolate Malt	30 ppg	375°L	2%

Hops

0.5 oz.	Magnum	60 min.	Boil	14% AA
1.25 oz.	Saaz	15 min.	Boil	4% AA

Other Additions

1 tsp.	Irish Moss	15 min.	Boil
0.5 tsp.	Yeast Nutrient	10 min.	Boil

All-Grain Instructions

Use a single infusion mash at 152°F for 60 minutes.

Fermentation

Yeast: White Labs WLP029 Kölsch

Pitch 270 billion cells, equivalent to 2 to 3 fresh vials. Ferment at 58°F.

Packaging

Carbonate to 2.4 volumes or prime with 4 ounces corn sugar

Mark's Imperial Rauchbier

Guest recipe by Mark Schoppe: Imperial Rauchbier is exactly what it sounds like, an amped-up 10 percent version of a traditional German Rauchbier. The Imperial Rauchbier is not for the tame, and is definitely a challenging recipe that requires advanced brewing techniques such as mashing, lagering, and high-gravity fermentation. This recipe comes from a true brewmaster, Mark Schoppe, winner of the coveted Ninkasi Award from the Nation Homebrewing Conference in 2012. In particular, this recipe has placed in multiple competitions throughout the Lone Star Circuit and medaled at the 2009 National Homebrew Conference. When you're in the mood for a smooth, smoky sensation, give this recipe a try; it will most certainly push your brewing system and skills to the limit.

Brewing Stats

BREWING LEVEL:	Advanced
BOIL DURATION:	120 minutes
OG:	1.100
FG:	1.025
ATTENUATION:	75%
IBU:	61
ABV:	9.8%
COLOR:	12 SRM

Fermentables:

9.9 lb.	Best Rauch Malt		37	3°L	45%
9.9 lb.	Weyermann Rauch Malt		37	3°L	45%
1.1 lb.	Briess Cherrywood Smoked Malt	37	3°L	6%
6.5 oz.	CaraAroma		34	130°L	2%
6.5 oz.	Melanoidin		34	25°L	2%

Hops

2 oz.	Magnum	60 min.	Boil	14% AA
1 oz.	Hallertau Mittelfrüh	15 min.	Boil	4% AA
1 oz.	Hallertau Mittelfrüh	5 min.	Boil	4% AA

Other Additions

0.5 tsp.	Yeast Nutrient	10 min.	Boil
1 tsp.	Irish Moss	15 min.	Boil

All-Grain Instructions

Use a single infusion mash at 150°F for 60 minutes.

Fermentation

Yeast: Any continental lager yeast. Wyeast 2124 Bohemian Lager is a good choice.

Pitch 900 billion cells, equivalent to 9 fresh smack packs. Ferment at 50°F.

Packaging

Carbonate to 2.4 volumes or prime with 4 ounces corn sugar

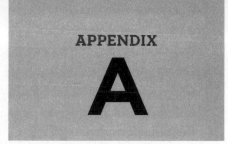

Brewing Resources

This appendix represents a tiny fraction of the many excellent resources for the homebrewer. From books to blogs, this is a list of my personal favorites, which have helped develop my beer and homebrewing education.

Books

Brewing Elements series, published by Brewers Publications

Written by several notable authors, this series is intended to be a practical brewing guide on the technical aspects of each of the primary brewing ingredients: yeast, hops, malt, water. An absolute necessity for the advanced homebrewer and my go-to resource for technical brewing information.

Brewing Classic Styles by Jamil Zainasheff and John J. Palmer

This is a compendium of award-winning recipes mostly culled from Jamil's homebrewing career. It's a great reference for understanding the essence of beer styles and how to design competition-ready recipes.

How to Brew by John J. Palmer

A homebrewing classic, this is a great brewing book that presents technical information in an accessible manner, particularly the information on how to brew with water. It is available for free online at howtobrew.com, but the paperback version is much nicer to read.

Experimental Homebrewing by Drew Beechum and Denny Conn

A fairly recent addition to the homebrewing cannon, this book covers "off-the-wall" brewing ingredients as well as how to execute and evaluate homebrewing-related experiments.

Tasting Beer by Randy Mosher

This is a great introductory text on beer styles that will help you to objectively evaluate beer and develop your palate. It's also a great resource for those training to become a certified beer judge.

The Complete Joy of Homebrewing by Charlie Papazian

The original homebrewing classic, penned by homebrewing legend Charlie Papazian, who is also the president and founder of the Brewers Association. This is another great introductory brewing text from which many homebrewers have learned the wonderful hobby of homebrewing.

American Sour Beers by Michael Tonsmeire

This book explores the wild side of brewing, sour beer, and funk. Great for sour beer techniques and wild brew enthusiasts.

Principles of Brewing Science by George Fix

This is another classic brewing text. While a little on the dated side, it is nonetheless a great technical reference on many aspects of brewing science.

New Brewing Lager Beer by Gregory J. Noonan

Despite its title, this classic brewing text goes far beyond lager brewing and covers both theory and practical techniques for all-grain brewing. Great for the advanced homebrewer and brewers looking to get into more advanced brewing techniques.

Blogs

The Apartment Homebrewer
theapthomebrewer.com

Shameless plug aside, this is my blog. It covers a little bit of everything, but primarily features technical articles on small-batch brewing and advice for homebrewing in apartments or limited spaces. I also post most of my small-batch recipes along with photos and tasting notes.

Don Osborn's Homebrewing Log

donosborn.com

YouTube: *youtube.com/user/donosborn*

Homebrewing celebrity Don Osborn is a frequent guest on homebrewing podcasts and documents many of his homebrewing adventures in video blogs. Don also has great tips for brewing on a budget and brewing with the seasons. Check out his content, especially his recipe logs dating back to 2001, and YouTube channel.

The Mad Fermentationist

themadfermentationist.com

Michael Tonsmeire is a homebrewing celebrity and author of *American Sour Beers.* His blog features all-around great recipes, specializing in sour and wild beers.

The Beer Engine Blog

thebeerengineblog.com

Brand Manager for Wyeast Laboratories and former co-host of *Brewing TV*, Michael Dawson is a master homebrewer. His blog details his adventures in brewing, including many of his great recipes as well as solid advice for homebrewers.

Beer and Wine Journal

beerandwinejournal.com

Written and run by Chris Colby, former editor of the *Brew Your Own* magazine and James Spenser of the Basic Brewing podcasts, the *Beer and Wine Journal* website features the whole spectrum of beer and wine making topics, from brewing science to brewing news. This site also hosts several guest articles from respected brewers. It is always reliable and well researched.

Shut Up About Barclay Perkins

barclayperkins.blogspot.com

Written by Ron Pattinson, author of *The Home Brewer's Guide to Vintage Beer*, this blog explores and recreates historical beer styles. It's also a source for solid brewing information and great for the historical beer enthusiast.

BeerSmith Blog

beersmith.com/blog

Written by Brad Smith, who is known for his handy brewing software, this blog covers a wide range of homebrewing topics, from style profiles with recipes to brewing techniques, as well as a well-represented brewing podcast. An all-around informative resource for the beginner and advanced homebrewer.

Brülosophy
brulosophy.com

Run by homebrewing great, Marshall Schott, Brülosophy provides terrific all-around homebrewing information, primarily focusing on ways to simplify the brewing process. The site features a segment called "exBEERiment," which challenges many of the homebrewing-scale axioms like trub versus no trub and extract versus all-grain.

Podcasts

Basic Brewing Radio and Video
basicbrewing.com

James Spenser has hosted the weekly Basic Brewing Radio podcast and semiregular Basic Brewing Video series for more than a decade. Podcasts usually feature guests and cover a multitude of homebrewing topics, from technical knowledge to homebrewing experiments.

The Brewing Network
thebrewingnetwork.com

Hosted and run by Justin Crossley, the Brewing Network, or the BN for short, hosts several homebrewing and craft brewing podcasts that are both entertaining and informative. The BN also hosts live streams of many brewing events and conferences. My personal favorite is the Jamil Show, hosted by homebrewing legends Jamil Zainasheff and Mike "Tasty" McDole.

Chop and Brew
chopandbrew.com
YouTube: *youtube.com/user/ChopAndBrew*

Chip Walton, the homebrewing videographer known for his work on Northern Brewer's *Brewing TV* and his newest project, *Chop and Brew*. These video podcasts highlight the culture and enthusiasm behind homebrewing and offer the latest insights on brewing ingredients and occasionally good old home cooking.

Organizations

American Homebrewers Association (AHA)
homebrewersassociation.org

The premier homebrewing organization in the United States, the AHA serves a multipurpose role in the homebrewing community. The AHA hosts several homebrewing events, like the popular National Homebrewing Conference (NHC), and is also politically engaged with local, state, and federal legislatures for homebrewing rights. Memberships are fairly inexpensive and come with a pub discount program and complimentary magazine, *Zymurgy*.

Beer Judge Certification Program (BJCP)
bjcp.org

> The BJCP is a nonprofit organization that is central to homebrewing in the United States and abroad. The BJCP has many roles, but is best known for supplying beer style guidelines and training beer judges on a volunteer basis for homebrewing competitions.

Forums

HomeBrewTalk.com Forum
homebrewtalk.com/forum

> One of the largest homebrewing forums. This site also features homebrewing articles and a solid wiki page.

Northern Brewer Forum
forum.northernbrewer.com

> Brewing community associated with the Northern Brewer online homebrew shop.

MoreBeer! Forum
forums.morebeer.com

> Brewing community associated with the MoreBeer! online homebrew shop.

The Brewing Network Forum
thebrewingnetwork.com/forum

> Brewing community associated with the Brewing Network Podcasts.

AHA forum
homebrewersassociation.org/forum

> Brewing community associated with the American Homebrewers Association.

Glossary

AAU See *alpha acid units.*

ABV See *alcohol by volume.*

ABW See *alcohol by weight.*

acetaldehyde A fermentation by-product that can cause a "green apple" off-flavor in beer. It is usually reabsorbed by the yeast during the fermentation cycle in the production of ethanol.

acidity The level of acid in a solution registering below 7 on the pH scale.

acrospire The early stages of the shoot in germinated barley.

actual attenuation The real percentage of sugars in beer after correcting a hydrometer reading due to the uncalibrated lower density of alcohol in solution.

adjunct A fermentable brewing ingredient that is unmalted, usually grains such as rice, corn, and oats, but also other fermentables like sugar and syrups.

aeration The process of dissolving air into solution. In brewing, aeration is used to dissolve oxygen from air into wort for yeast growth during fermentation.

aerobic A system or process utilizing oxygen.

AG See *all-grain brewing.*

AHA American Homebrewers Association

airlock A one-way device added to a fermentor that allows CO_2 to escape without letting outside air to enter, preventing external contamination.

alcohol A by-product created through yeast fermentation. Although technically referring to a chemical group, in brewing, the term "alcohol" is used interchangeably with "ethanol," the primary alcohol produced by yeast fermentation.

alcohol by volume (ABV) The percentage of alcohol volume in a given beverage.

alcohol by weight (ABW) The percentage of the alcohol weight in a given beverage. Typically, alcohol by weight is lower than alcohol by volume in beer.

ale A beer that is made using ale yeast, which is typically fermented at warm temperatures and features complex yeast-derived flavors and aromas.

ale yeast A top-fermenting yeast responsible for ale styles, typically fermented at warmer temperatures, yielding complex malt and hop flavors along with yeast-derived fruity esters and phenols.

aleurone layer The thin layer in barley malt that surrounds the endosperm and contains the enzymes for saccrification.

alkalinity The level of bases in solution registering above 7 on the pH scale.

all-grain (AG) brewing A brewing technique where wort is made entirely from malted grains, requiring a mash to convert their starches into fermentable sugars.

alpha acid A resinous compound in hops that lends bitterness to beer when isomerized in wort through boiling. In hops, alpha acids vary in total percentage, ranging from 2 to 20 percent depending on the strain, and have three main forms: humulone, cohumulone, and adhumulone.

alpha acid units (AAU) A weighted equivalence for estimating hop bitterness in beer through the multiplication of hop weight in ounces by its alpha acid content in percentage. For example, 10 AAUs are equal to 1 ounce of hops at 10 percent alpha acid content.

American pale ale (APA) An American-style ale featuring American-style hops, medium body, neutral yeast character, and pale color.

amino acids The essential building blocks of protein.

amylase A group of enzymes from malt responsible for converting starches into sugars in wort.

anaerobic A system or process without oxygen utilization.

apparent attenuation The hydrometer measured percentage of sugar in beer without correcting for the influence of the lower density alcohol in solution.

aroma hops Hops that are added to wort to infuse flavor and aroma in the finished beer. Additions are typically introduced late in the boil to preserve volatile compounds from boil evaporation. Also called *flavor hops* or *finishing hops*.

attenuation The percent of sugars converted into alcohol and carbon dioxide through yeast fermentation in beer.

autolysis Enzymatic destruction of the yeast cell, known as self-digestion, which lends meaty, rubbery off-flavors to beer.

bacteria Single-celled organisms that are contaminants in most beer styles, lending sour, acetic, or vegetal off-flavors. Also, the primary souring agent in wild beer styles like Berliner Weisse.

barley A cereal grain, which, when malted, constitutes the majority of the fermentable sugar in wort.

base malt The malted grains that make up the majority of fermentables in beer, categorized by their degree of kilning roughly divided between lightly kilned and darkly kilned varieties. In brewing, base malts are mashed to convert their starches into fermentable sugars.

batch sparge A rinsing technique using large volumes of hot water to dissolve and collect wort sugars from a previously drained mash.

beer A fermented beverage made from malted cereal grains and hops.

BIAB See *brew in a bag.*

bittering hops The addition of hops to wort to generate bitterness in the finished beer through isomerization. These are generally added at the beginning of the boil.

BJCP Beer Judge Certification Program

body The physical impression imparted by beer on the palate. Also called *mouthfeel.*

Brettanomyces A type of wild yeast responsible for the funky character in Belgian lambic and American wild styles, often considered "horsey" or "goaty." In other beer styles it is considered a common contaminant and lends undesirable off-flavors.

brewing efficiency The percentage of total extract generated from your all-grain process based on the maximum possible yield the malt can produce.

brew in a bag (BIAB) A mash technique in which the mash is removed via a large grain bag, leaving the resulting wort behind in the brew kettle.

bright beer A finished beer that is transparent in clarity. Also known as clear or brilliant beer.

carbon dioxide (CO_2) A colorless, flavorless gas produced by yeast in fermentation and also used to carbonate beer.

carbonation Dissolved carbon dioxide gas in beer used to tailor mouthfeel and to help release volatile aromatic compounds.

carboy A fermentation vessel made of glass or plastic with a cylindrical shape and a narrow neck opening. Carboys for brewing come in a range of sizes from 2 to 6.5 gallons.

chill haze A hazy appearance in beer that appears at cold temperatures as a result of protein and tannin precipitates.

cold break Coagulated protein and hop matter that precipitates out of wort when rapidly chilled.

conditioning The stage of the brewing process after primary fermentation in which particulates settle and flavors become more refined and mature. This is also that point at which beer can be carbonated through priming, known as bottling or cask conditioning.

contamination The unintended addition of bacteria or wild yeast in a batch of beer, which can cause undesired fermentation and phenolic, acidic, or acetic off-flavors.

continuous sparge A rinsing technique in which a continuous flow of hot water is added and maintained throughout the initial draining process to collect wort sugars.

crystal or caramel malt A specialty malt that has been stewed and kilned, imparting color, residual sweetness, and caramel-like, dark fruit flavors.

decoction mash A multistep mash technique where temperatures are reached by removing the thick portion of the mash, boiling it, and returning it back to the mash tun.

diacetyl A fermentation by-product that is typically reabsorbed by yeast in the production of alcohol. It is commonly associated with buttery and butterscotch-like off-flavors in beer.

diastatic enzymes Enzymes that break down complex starches into sugars.

diastatic power The enzymatic potential of malt to convert starches into sugar.

dimethyl sulfide (DMS) A sulfur compound most commonly occurring from lightly-kilned malt that can cause a creamed corn off-flavor in beer. Performing a 90-minute boil when brewing all-grain beer is said to mitigate its formation.

DME See *dried malt extract.*

DMS See *dimethyl sulfide.*

dried malt extract (DME) A condensed malt sugar in powdered form.

dry hops The addition of hops to beer after fermentation to infuse additional flavor and aroma.

endosperm The starchy center of a cereal grain consisting of carbohydrates, lipids, and protein.

enzymes Protein-based compounds acting as catalysts in biochemical reactions. In brewing, enzymes from malted barley are used in the mash to convert starches into sugars.

esters Higher fermentation by-products lending a complex fruity characteristic to beer, common in ales but generally avoided in lagers.

ethanol/ethyl alcohol A primary alcohol fermentation by-product by yeast in beer. Commonly referred to as alcohol in brewing.

extra special bitter (ESB) The strongest (by ABV) and most flavorful version of the English classification of bitters.

extract brewing A simplified brewing technique where wort is made from malt extracts as opposed to malted grains.

extraction efficiency The percentage of available fermentables present in the kettle wort when it is removed from the mash in the lautering process. Typical efficiency achieves 70 to 85 percent in the homebrewing setting.

FAN Abbreviation for free amino nitrogen, an essential yeast nutrient in the fermentation process.

fermentation The process by which brewer's yeast converts malt sugars into alcohol (ethanol) and carbon dioxide.

fermentor A vessel in which fermentation occurs. Sometimes referred to as a fermentation vessel (FV).

FG See *final gravity*.

final gravity (FG) The specific gravity of beer after fermentation is complete. Also called *terminal gravity*.

finings Substances added to wort or beer to promote clarity through the clumping and precipitation of protein, tannins, and yeast.

first runnings The wort drawn off from the mash before introducing the sparge process. Typically the darkest, most sugar-rich running (if multiple runnings are drawn). Depending on mash method, the first runnings may be the only runnings.

first wort hopping (FWH) A hopping technique where hop additions are added to hot wort prior to the boil. FWH is said to produce a smoother bitterness and leave additional hop flavor and aroma post boil.

flocculation The clumping and precipitation of yeast cells from beer after fermentation. Flocculation varies greatly among different yeast strains.

fusel alcohols A group of alcohols that have a greater molecular weight than ethanol and generate a harsh solventlike off-flavor in beer.

FV See *fermentor*.

FWH See *first wort hopping*.

GABF Great American Beer Festival

germination A phase in the malting process where the acrospire and rootlets grow and erupt from the hull.

grain bed The solid part of the mash that forms a natural filter during the *vorlauf* and recirculation process.

grain bill The list of malt, grains, and sugars in a particular beer recipe. Sometimes also referred to as the *grist*.

gravity The density, specifically weight density, of a solution. In brewing, gravity readings help determine the relative amount of sugars in wort and beer.

grist Milled malt and grain. Also used by brewers to describe the list of malt, grains, and sugars in a particular beer recipe.

hardness The concentration of calcium and magnesium ions in brewing water. Harder water has a higher concentration.

head The foam that forms at the top of a beer when poured.

head retention How well the head is retained after a beer is poured. Head that sticks around throughout the drink is thought to have good head retention.

heat exchanger A thermodynamic device designed to transfer heat from one substance to another. In brewing, heat exchangers are widely used to rapidly chill wort to pitching temperatures.

high gravity Original gravity exceeding 1.060 SG, but typically above 1.075 SG. Additional fermentation considerations like pitch rate and aeration are necessary at these levels.

hops The pinecone-shape flower of the plant *Humulus lupulus*, which grows on climbing vinelike structures and gives beer its characteristic bitterness along with pungent flavor and aroma.

hot break The point during the beginning of the boil when the proteins and tannins that form in the wort coagulate and precipitate out of suspension. During hot break, the wort will become foamy, then eventually the foam will clump up and fall to the bottom of the kettle.

IBU See *International Bittering Units*.

infusion mash A mash technique accomplished by soaking crushed malt in a measured amount of preheated water to achieve the desired rest temperature.

International Bittering Units (IBU) A scale used in brewing to gauge the degree of bitterness in beer. Ranging from 0 to 100+, a higher IBU value represents a beer with more intense bittering.

IPA Abbreviation for India pale ale, a strong ale with intense bitterness and hop flavor and aroma.

isomerization A process of chemically changing one molecule into another without the loss or gain of atoms from the original molecule. In hops, alpha acids are isomerized to form iso-alpha acids, which provide the bitterness in beer.

krausen The yeasty, foamy head that occurs at the surface of beer during fermentation.

lager A type of beer brewed from bottom-fermenting lager yeast, typically fermented at cold temperatures and conditioned through the process of lagering.

lager yeast A bottom-fermenting yeast responsible for lager styles, typically fermented at cold temperatures, yielding low ester formation and refined malt and hops flavors.

lagering The process of conditioning lager-fermented beer at near freezing temperatures over a period of a few weeks to a few months. Although not necessary, lagering helps to refine and soften hop and malt flavors while also promoting beer clarity.

late addition A brewing term that describes any ingredient, but particularly hops, that is added during the last 15 minutes of the boil.

lauter The process of separating and draining wort from the mash.

lauter tun See *mash tun.*

liquid malt extract (LME) Condensed extract of malt sugar in syrup form.

liquor An alternative word for water in brewing, typically referring to heated sparge water in the lauter process.

LME See *liquid malt extract.*

Lovibond scale (°L) A color scale commonly used to judge beer and malt.

lupulin glands Yellow nodes within the hop cone that contain the essential hop resins and oils.

Maillard reaction A browning reaction between sugar and amino acids caused through heating, forming color and toastlike flavors in brewing.

malt A cereal grain or seed that has been steeped, germinated, and kilned. Barley malt is the most common form used in the production of beer.

mash A mixture of cracked malt and grain with hot water used to enzymatically change starch into sugar.

mash thickness The ratio of water and ground malt used in the mash.

mash tun The vessel where the mash is assembled and converted. Also called a *lauter tun.*

mead A fermented beverage primarily made of honey.

melanoidin The flavor compounds produced by Maillard reactions, lending toastlike and caramel-like flavors to beer.

mini mash A brewing technique using both malt extract and mashed base malts to make wort. Also called a *partial mash.*

modification The degree to which protein and starches within the endosperm are broken down during germination.

mouthfeel See *body*.

off-flavor A brewing term describing unpleasant flavor as a result of a brewing flaw or a pleasant flavor inappropriate in a beer style.

OG See *original gravity*.

original gravity (OG) The specific gravity of wort before pitching. Also known as *starting gravity*.

oxidation A chemical reaction between brewing compounds and oxygen that lends cardboard, papery, sherrylike off-flavors in beer.

partial mash See *mini mash*.

pasteurization The process of applying controlled heat over a specified duration to eliminate microorganisms, including yeast and bacteria, that are typically found in food, without the need for boiling.

pellicle A white, slimy film that forms on top of fermenting beer. It is caused by brewing contaminants, especially wild yeast and bacteria.

pH A logarithmic scale of the acidity or alkalinity of a solution.

phenol or phenolic Higher fermentation organic compounds produced by yeast lending unpleasant medicinal off-flavors in beer.

pitch or pitching Term used for adding yeast to wort. The rate at which yeast is added is the pitch rate.

primary fermentor The vessel in which primary, or initial, fermentation takes place.

priming A controlled addition of fermentable sugars to carbonate beer in bottles, kegs, or casks.

proteolytic enzymes Enzymes that break down complex protein into more simple forms, such as amino acids.

rack or racking The process of transferring wort or beer from one vessel to another, typically using siphon action.

RDWHAHB Acronym for "Relax, don't worry, have a homebrew!" This phrase was famously coined by one of the founders of homebrewing in America, Charlie Papazian. It's used to calm the new brewer when part of the brewing process has gone awry.

real ale A traditional British form of packaging and carbonating ale using natural secondary fermentation in cask, known as cask conditioning. Real ale is served using gravity-fed spigots or beer engines.

Reinheitsgebot German beer purity law enacted in 1516 stating that beer may only contain water, malted barley, hops, and yeast.

RO water A more pure form of water that is filtered using reverse osmosis (RO).

roasted malt A specialty malt that has been kilned at very high temperatures, imparting dark color and roasted flavors.

runnings The brewing term for wort runoff during the recirculation, draining, and sparge processes.

Saccharomyces cerevisiae The scientific classification for ale yeast.

Saccharomyces pastorianus The scientific classification for lager yeast.

saccrification The enzymatic conversion of starches into sugars.

sanitize To significantly reduce contamination levels to suitable brewing quantities.

second runnings The lighter, less sugar-rich running resulting from the sparge process.

secondary fermentation The process of racking beer into another fermentation vessel once the primary fermentation is complete. Although not a necessary step in the brewing process, secondary fermentation is commonly used for conditioning, clarification, and aging, or to perform a second fermentation with additional fermentables such as fruit and sugar.

SG See *specific gravity*.

six-row barley A thick-hulled, high-enzymatic, low-yielding barley malt used in brewing, primarily to mash high percentages of unmalted grains, such as corn and rice.

soft water Water that has very low concentrations of calcium and magnesium ions.

sparge The process of rinsing sugars from the mash with hot water.

specialty malts Highly characterful malts that are mashed or steeped to add color, flavor, aroma, and mouthfeel to wort. The main varieties are caramel/crystal and roasted malts.

specific gravity (SG) The weight density of a solution compared against a reference material. In brewing, the specific gravity of wort and beer is measured to determine sugar and alcohol content with respect to pure water.

SRM Standard Reference Measure

starting gravity See *original gravity*.

step mash A mash technique utilizing multiple temperature rests and/or water additions to tailor fermentability in wort.

sterilization The complete removal of all microorganism life forms, usually through high temperature, high pressure, and/or chemical means.

strike temperature The temperature of the mash water prior to adding crushed malt.

stuck sparge The unfortunate event where wort flows slowly or even arrests when draining from the mash tun. Lautering aids such as rice hulls can help mitigate this problem.

table sugar An alternative name for refined cane sugar, which is entirely composed of sucrose.

tannins Polyphenolic compounds present in grain hulls and hops that can cause astringent off-flavors and haze in beer.

terminal gravity See *final gravity.*

trub The compacted sediment found at the bottom of a fermentor that contains coagulated proteins (from the hot break and cold break), tannins, hop matter, and flocculated yeast cells.

volatile compounds Acids, resins, and oils in beer that dissipate quickly through elevated temperature, boil evaporation, and fermentation.

Vorlauf German word for filtering wort through the process of recirculation using a set grain bed from the mash.

wild yeast Any yeast introduced to beer unintended by the brewer, typically resulting in off-flavors and poor fermentation.

wort Malt-based sugar solution, usually containing hops, which is made by the brewer. Once yeast is pitched, the wort is called beer.

wort chiller A brewing device used to rapidly cool wort to pitching temperatures. Wort chillers typically use a cold water source and a highly conductive metal to facilitate heat exchange between the cold water and hot wort.

yeast Single-celled organisms of the *Fungus* kingdom. The genus *Saccharomyces* is solely responsible for beer fermentation, where sugar is converted into alcohol and carbon dioxide.

yeast cake The flocculated, settled, and often compact mass of yeast at the bottom of the fermentor after fermentation is complete.

yeast nutrient A fermentation additive made from a range of elements, mostly free amino nitrogen, which is essential for yeast health and vitality.

yeast rinsing The process of removing unwanted brewing matter, such as trub and hop debris, from a harvested yeast slurry through decanting.

yeast slurry The mixture of fermented beer and yeast cake often produced to save yeast after fermentation.

zymurgy The science of fermentation.

Index

S